THE MANY CAPTIVITIES
OF ESTHER WHEELWRIGHT

THE LEWIS WALPOLE SERIES IN EIGHTEENTH-CENTURY CULTURE AND HISTORY

The Lewis Walpole Series, published by Yale University Press with the aid of the Annie Burr Lewis Fund, is dedicated to the culture and history of the long eighteenth century (from the Glorious Revolution to the accession of Queen Victoria). It welcomes work in a variety of fields, including literature and history, the visual arts, political philosophy, music, legal history, and the history of science. In addition to original scholarly work, the series publishes new editions and translations of writing from the period, as well as reprints of major books that are currently unavailable. Though the majority of books in the series will probably concentrate on Great Britain and the Continent, the range of our geographical interests is as wide as Horace Walpole's.

THE MANY
CAPTIVITIES OF
ESTHER
WHEELWRIGHT

Ann M. Little

Yale
UNIVERSITY PRESS

New Haven & London

Published with assistance from the Annie Burr Lewis Fund.
Published with assistance from the Mary Cady Tew Memorial Fund.

Yale University Press books may be purchased in quantity for
educational, business, or promotional use. For information, please e-mail
sales.press@yale.edu (U.S. office) or sales@yaleup.co.uk (U.K. office).

Set in Baskerville MT type by Integrated Publishing Solutions.
Printed in the United States of America.

Library of Congress Control Number: 2015956884
ISBN 978-0-300-21821-3 (cloth : alk. paper)
A catalogue record for this book is available from the British Library.

This paper meets the requirements of ANSI/NISO Z39.48-1992
(Permanence of Paper).

10 9 8 7 6 5 4 3 2 1

for Alice

CONTENTS

TIMELINE

Wars of the Northeastern Borderlands, 1636–1783

The Pequot War	1636–37
King Philip's War/Metacom's Rebellion	1675–76 (to 1678 in northern New England)
King William's War	1688–97
Queen Anne's War	1702–13
King George's War	1744–48
Seven Years' War/French and Indian War	1756–63
War of the American Revolution	1775–83

A NOTE ON SPELLING AND TERMINOLOGY

With an accent "Québec" refers to the city of Québec only and its immediate environs; the modern Canadian province of Quebec is spelled without an accent, and so in this book refers to all of the Laurentian Valley colonized by the French in the seventeenth and eighteenth centuries.

In order to avoid terms for Native people that are either offensive or alienating to both Canadians and U.S. Americans, I eschew the word "Indian" and the crude translation of the French word *sauvage* as "savage" except when quoting eighteenth-century sources. I also avoid "American Indian," "Native American," "Aboriginal Peoples," "Amerindians," and "First Nations People," because Canadians find the first two phrases exclusionary and most U.S. Americans are unfamiliar with the last three. I try to use the specific language group or nation that a person belongs to—Wabanaki, Mohawk, and so on—when I know it.

Eighteenth-century writers in both French and English were similarly sloppy about ethnic identities among European-descended North Americans, too, calling pretty much everyone who wasn't Native or African American either "French" or "English" to signify broad cultural, religious, and linguistic affiliations. I try to be more precise, using the terms "French Canadian" and "Anglo-American" or "New Englander" to refer to people of European descent who I know were born in North America. I employ the terms "English" and "French" generally to refer to the European imperial states and their colonial governments, although I also use "New England" specifically to refer to Anglo-American government in that region. After the Acts of Union of 1707 uniting the Kingdoms of England and Scotland, I use the term "British."

THE JOHN AND MARY SNELL WHEELWRIGHT FAMILY

Father: John Wheelwright (1664–1745)

Mother: Mary Snell (ca. 1666–1755)   DATE OF MARRIAGE Jan. 28, 1689

1. John, b. Dec. 10, 1689
2. Samuel, b. May 2, 1692
3. Hannah, b. May 1, 1694
4. Esther, b. March 31, 1696
5. Jeremiah, b. March 5, 1698
6. Elizabeth, b. April 16, 1700
7. Mary, b. June 11, 1702
8. Nathaniel, b. June 15, 1704
9. Sarah, b. July 27, 1706

(10. Job, b. Sept. 6, 1708; d. June 1, 1709, aged 8 months)

(11. Lydia, b. Sept. 17, 1710; d. Oct. 6, 1710, aged 3 weeks)

Sources: *Maine Historical Magazine*, vol. 9, January 1894–January 1895 (Bangor: Charles H. Glass, 1895), 76–80; *The Vital Records of Wells, Maine, 1619–1950*, ed. Hope Moody Shelley (Rockport, ME: Picton, 2005), 3–4, 8.

ACKNOWLEDGMENTS

Why do authors usually thank their families last? I want to thank my family first—my husband, Chris, and my daughter, Alice—as they're the people who have lived with this project longer than everyone else. Chris offered financial support for the research for this book when no institution would help, and Alice has unknowingly guided my research in girlhood and adolescence. My mother-in-law, Wendy Moore, also accompanied Alice and me on two trips to Québec and provided child care while I was in the archives. Two Colorado friends and comrades, Nick Syrett and Erin Jordan, listened to me talk about Esther Wheelwright more than anyone, including my family.

Success, they say, has many fathers, but this book has many mothers. I'm pleased to acknowledge their assistance in helping me secure a long-term fellowship at the Huntington Library and in encouraging me along the way: Susan Amussen, Cornelia Hughes Dayton, Linda K. Kerber, and Mary Beth Norton. I can confidently say this book would not exist without their support and encouragement. I would also like to thank my sister in arms of twenty-five years' standing, Sharon Block.

Steve Hindle, the director of research at the Huntington Library, and its long-term fellows of 2014–15 deserve my thanks for their intellectual and social camaraderie, especially Sue Juster, Kathleen Wilson, Julie Park, Susan Barbour, Matt Kadane, Tim Harris, Chris Kyle, Dympna Callaghan, Urvashi Chakravarty, and the former director of research Roy Ritchie. Local early Americanists Catherine Allgor, Peter Mancall, Sharon Salinger, and Terri Snyder were also generous with their time and support for this book. John Demos shared helpful ideas and encouragement. Susan Carlile and Becky Cerling read the entire manuscript and made helpful suggestions for its improvement, and Marie Kelleher and Nancy Caciola were up for almost any kind of fun in Southern California.

I was first introduced to the topic of Catholic history by my colleagues at the University of Dayton, especially Una Cadegan and Father James Heft, S.M., now of the University of Southern California. I did not acknowledge it at the time, but I learned many lessons at their feet. I'm grateful to my friends and colleagues at Colorado State University, especially to Ruth Alexander, Nathan Citino (now of Rice University), Mark Fiege, Fred Knight (now of Morehouse College), Prakash Kumar (now of Penn State University), Diane Margolf, Janet Ore, Jared Orsi, Greg Smoak (now of the University of Utah), and Doug Yarrington. Greeley-based scholars Chris Talbot and Julia Garbus offered crucial support and advice as well. I am a very different historian now than I would have been had I never been invited to join you on the high plains desert, and I'm so very grateful. I would also like to thank Ann Gill, dean of the College of Liberal Arts, and the Professional Development Program for funding several research trips to Québec.

Most of the primary source research for this book was conducted at the Archives of the Ursuline Monastery (les Archives du Monastère des Ursulines de Québec) and at the Ursuline Museum (Musée des Ursulines) in Québec. Many, many thanks to the new generation of young women who are conserving and sharing the documents and objects that keep alive ancien régime Québec, including archivist Marie-Andrée Fortier, document technician Caroline Nadeau, and museum technician Mélanie Pouliot. Special thanks are due to my friend Julie Wheelwright, who published her own version of Esther Wheelwright's life a few years ago, and who shared a 2007 research trip to Québec with me and helped us both get into the archdiocesan records there. Michèle Nelson provided translation assistance for my earliest foray into the French Canadian archives.

Different versions of the main themes and chapters in this book have been presented in various seminars and invited talks. The history seminar at Colorado State University was subjected to early drafts of several chapters, and Susan Sleeper-Smith invited me to talk about the book with both graduate and undergraduate students at Michigan State University in 2010. I presented chapter 2 to the *William and Mary Quarterly*–Early Modern Studies Institute of the University of Southern California workshop at the Huntington Library in 2009, thanks to Peter Mancall and former *WMQ* editor Chris Grasso. Thanks are also due to Karin Wulf and Julie Hardwick for permitting me to share my work at the Centering Families in Atlantic Worlds, 1500–1800, conference sponsored jointly by the Omohundro Institute of Early American History and Culture and the Institute for Historical Studies at the University of Texas in Austin; to Michael Zuckerman for an invitation to talk about the book in an evening seminar hosted by Richard and Mary Maples Dunn for the McNeil Center for Early American Studies at the University of Pennsylvania in Philadelphia; and to Anthony Mora of the University of Michigan's American Culture Department.

I also would like to thank Zara Anishanslan of CUNY–Staten Island for inviting me to present to the Columbia University early American seminar; Susan Amussen for an invitation to the University of California Merced's Center for the Humanities, and Adam Arenson of Manhattan College for inviting me to present at the Huntington Library's Past Tense Seminar. I was also the guest at Colorado State University–Pueblo's second annual Bea Spade Memorial Lecture Series, courtesy of Judy Gaughan.

My readers for Yale University Press, Marla Miller and Sophie White, offered invaluable criticism and very generous advice. Sophie's knowledge of New France and the ways of provincial French noble families helped me correct several silly mistakes. My editor, Chris Rogers; his assistant, Erica Hanson; and Clare Jones at Yale University Press were incredibly encouraging, helpful, and efficient. Dan Heaton's precise copy editing was always intelligent and good-humored.

I'm fortunate enough to be a member of several communities of scholars, one place-based, the others virtual. First, I must thank the Front Range

Early American Consortium, also known as the FREACs, especially Benjamin Irvin and Jenny Pulsipher. Our annual meetings are a sustaining force in my professional and intellectual lives. Thanks to the community of academic bloggers, who have formed an interdisciplinary midcareer support group: Tonya Krouse, Flavia Fescue of Ferule and Fescue (http://feruleandfescue.blogspot.com/), Bardiac (http://bardiac.blogspot.com/), GayProf (http://centerofgravitas.blogspot.com/), Jonathan Rees of More or Less Bunk (http://moreorlessbunk.net/blog/), Janice Liedl (http://jliedl.ca/), Notorious Ph.D., Girl Scholar (http://girlscholar.blogspot.com/), Undine of Not of General Interest (http://notofgeneralinterest.blogspot.com/), Squadratomagico (http://squadratomagico.net/), and the late, great Tenured Radical, also known as Claire Potter of The New School, my Fairy Blogmother. I've met some of you in person and we've become friends—others of you I don't even know your real names, but you've all been so important to me in this midcareer journey.

Finally, I'd like to thank the thousands of readers and commenters at my blog, Historiann (http://historiann.com/) over the past eight years, from whom I have learned so much. I've written about this book at various stages of its development, and you have served as a friendly sounding board for several of my ideas. You have all helped me grow as a scholar and teacher and have made me feel like I have friends wherever I go. (And now I do!)

THE MANY CAPTIVITIES
OF ESTHER WHEELWRIGHT

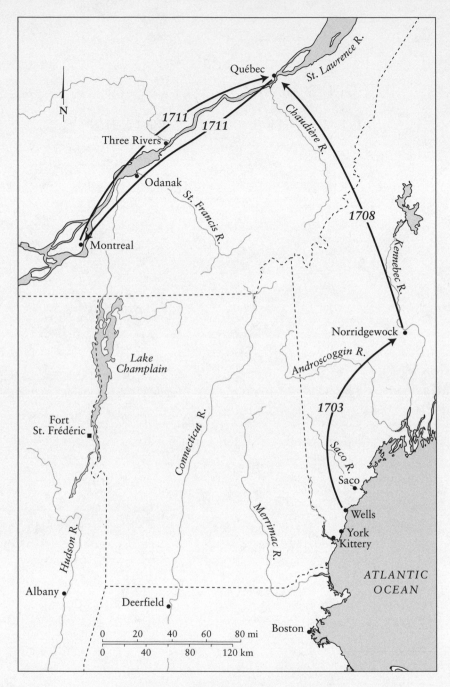

Map of the travels of Esther Wheelwright

INTRODUCTION

The Massachusetts Historical Society, 2015

There she is in the oval seminar room of the Massachusetts Historical Society, captured in a half-length oil portrait painted 250 years earlier. This gallery of New England Protestant fathers, and a few mothers and daughters, in this most storied of New England archival institutions, is a strange place for a Catholic nun. Her pale pink face peers out from a triangle of white wimple, which itself floats in thick layers of black and dark brown oil paint. The face is mostly unlined, but the expression is determined—we might see a forehead wrinkled with care lines if it weren't covered by her cap and band under the wimple and veil. Although it's hard to judge from a portrait, she does not look like a tall woman; her frame seems solid, even a little fleshy in her mid-sixties. Few details are visible outside the wimple and the stern but friendly gaze it frames, except the buckle of the belt around her waist and a glimpse of the aged hands mostly hidden in the sleeves of her robe—a classic tell of the amateur painter, because hands are so incredibly difficult to paint convincingly. The hands that suffered countless pricks of the needle, directed thousands of young students and dozens

of novices, and were folded numberless times in prayer through her long
lifetime were so much harder to render in detail than her face.

My eyes are drawn to the awkwardly pursed lips, a strange expression
that might be further evidence of an amateur artist wielding the brush.
Then again, it's an expression that suggests swallowing a mild frustration,
a face she must have worn frequently as a teacher of young girls and as an
administrator of a convent full of girls and women of all ages. If the eyes
are a little asymmetrical, the features slightly disproportionate to the rest of
the face, the artist was bold and skilled enough to attempt to show us the
subtle play of light on the folds of her gown and wimple. The artist was an
amateur, but she was more than good enough to paint this portrait of Esther Wheelwright, and to make us understand that she was a real person,
not just a type of her era.

Esther Wheelwright was an extraordinary woman, and her portrait is
extraordinary, too. It is evidence of both her exceptional life and her determination that she be known in New England for her accomplishments.
The portrait of Esther Wheelwright is singular in the collections of the
Massachusetts Historical Society for two reasons: first, she undoubtedly
commissioned the portrait herself, which was unusual compared with all of
the portraits of wives and daughters commissioned by husbands and fathers that make up the remainder of the women depicted on these walls.
Second, it was also undoubtedly painted by a woman, probably by a fellow
Ursuline, because the Ursulines were a cloistered women's order, and because the Ursulines of Québec were famous for their artistic skills. How did
she get here amid this collection of prominent Puritans and wealthy merchants, in the company of men she would have disagreed with on nearly
every issue, great or small? And yet, there she is, the pink face floating in
the glowing, white wimple, wearing that determined look.[1]

This book is the story of a little girl and the woman she became as she
grew up—the woman who commissioned and sat for that portrait. But it
is also the story of whole communities of women, and how they lived and
worked, and suffered and thrived in early America. Esther Wheelwright
(1696–1780) lived an exceptional life, one that was quite different from the
life of obscurity she would have lived as an eighteenth-century Anglo-American woman. But for an accident of fate, she probably would have grown

up to marry, bear children, and die like her sisters as a mostly forgotten woman, her name scratched into a few church and court record books, remembered in our day only by the dissolving letters of a porous gravestone in New England. Instead, she lived as a Wabanaki girl, a French Canadian student, and an Ursuline nun in Québec, and became mother superior the year after the British Conquest—the only foreign-born superior in the order's nearly four hundred–year history. By following in her footsteps and observing the worlds around her, we can learn from Esther Wheelwright a great deal about early North America.

Wheelwright family members, genealogists, and historians have delighted in Esther Wheelwright's story of border crossings and connections to three major North American cultures. They have loved to tell of Esther's birth into a family of Anglo-American frontier strivers, her traumatic capture in a Wabanaki raid, her adoption by a Native family, and her eventual embrace of an exclusively religious life among the cloistered Ursuline nuns of Québec. But these different storytellers usually see different morals to her story. For eighteenth-century French Canadian Catholics, her story is that of a providential rescue from English "heresy" and Native "savagery." For nineteenth-century Protestant New Englanders, she represented a curiosity from a world they had lost; her life served to remind them that New England's deforested fields and humming factories had replaced a more violent history that with distance of time they could safely romanticize. And the nineteenth- and twentieth-century Catholic faithful would continue to see her life as one guided by the hand of God.[2]

Since her death, Esther Wheelwright's life has been mostly forgotten by Anglophone historians: she was a Catholic and a woman and a cloistered nun in a historiography that favors Protestant, English-speaking men notable for their westward movement and their enterprising spirit. In other words, the kind of men with whom her portrait now keeps company for the ages at the Massachusetts Historical Society. Her border crossing and multiple languages and identities make her a difficult fit for any kind of nationalist history: she died in 1780, at the moment that some parts of colonial British America became the United States, and nearly a century before the Dominion of Canada was proclaimed. She died in the British-occupied Francophone colony of Québec, a politically ambiguous place that suits her own complicated national identity. Neither English nor French nor

Native or First Nations, her life confuses rather than clarifies most nationalist narratives.

I have my own story to tell about Esther Wheelwright. I hope it's richer and more nuanced than these previous versions of Esther's life, even if it's as didactic. Mine is also a story of the women in her life—the free and unfree women who raised her inside the Anglo-American garrison house in Wells, Maine; the women who catechized her and taught her to work as a Wabanaki girl; the French Canadian and Native girls who were her classmates in the Ursuline school; and the nuns who embraced her as a student and led her to a religious life among them.

In other words, Esther Wheelwright's remarkable life can lead us to see all of the women in colonial America whose leadership, work, and prayer were centrally important to each of their nations. Everywhere she went, across every political, religious, and linguistic border, Esther was surrounded by communities of women. Lest I sound excessively romantic about Esther's life, I should note that these communities were not necessarily loving and supportive—they were riven by status differences and often severely challenged by the disruptions of war. Like most human beings in leadership positions, Esther herself was also sometimes resented and the subject of complaints. Among people who suffered the privations of war and the indignities of occupation, her very presence among them might have rankled as another hungry mouth to feed, and a foreigner sharing intimate spaces with them. Aside from the particularities of her story, these communities were rent by differences and exhausted after decades of near-constant conflict. In Wells, which like the rest of what is now southern Maine was a part of Massachusetts until the nineteenth century, she lived in a busy Anglo-American household that kept several servants, owned African American slaves, and was animated by the growing Wheelwright family. Wells was repeatedly targeted for attack by the Wabanaki. Esther was captured in a 1703 attack on the town. Her adopted Wabanaki community was soon burned out of its village at Norridgewock, and she probably spent her remaining years with them moving among several Catholic mission towns in an effort to avoid destruction at the hands of New England soldiers. Although life inside convent walls in Québec might appear to have been tranquil and secure compared with life in the war-torn Massachusetts northern borderlands, Québec was, throughout the eighteenth century, the object of several attempts by the British to take the city. The city was successfully occupied in 1759 by the British and besieged by U.S. Americans in 1775 upon the outbreak of the war of the American Revolution. Even if Québec had not been taken, Esther's life in the Ursuline monastery was not free from conflict and division. Religious orders have their own strict divisions and status hierarchies. As we'll see, nuns are no angels.

In addition to revealing the important work and lives of women in the colonial North American borderlands, another goal of my book is to demonstrate that there were more compelling similarities in women's lives across these borders than there were differences. In my experience as a historian, looking for continuities in people's experiences is also more interesting than heeding eighteenth-century rhetoric about the vast cultural and religious differences that supposedly separated people from their near neighbors. These continuities suggest that communities of women across the northeastern borderlands—whether they were bound or free, whether they crossed themselves or complained bitterly of "papists," whether they were cloistered nuns or married mothers or widows, whatever language they spoke—had perhaps at least as much in common as they had dividing them.

Esther Wheelwright became by far the most successful and prominent person ever to come from Wells, Maine, and yet most North Americans have never heard of her. (She's almost certainly the only person from Wells, Maine, ever to have her portrait hanging at the Massachusetts Historical Society.) Since her death, she has become an antiquarian curiosity or an object of genealogical interest. My hope is that after you've read a chapter or two, you'll wonder why her life and the lives of the women around her aren't as familiar to you as the stories you've read about the political and military exploits of men.

Why "Many Captivities"?

"Captivity" is a useful concept for understanding the lives of all women in early North America because none of them was free in the sense that North Americans today would recognize: Native women were embedded in kin networks that imposed reciprocal obligations and benefits. Anglo-American women lived most of their lives as *femmes couvertes*, without political or economic liberty as they lived and worked under the legal authority of fathers and husbands. French Canadian women were perhaps the "freest" women in North America from a legal standpoint, because as wives they were empowered as joint owners of the marital estate. However, as wives they also found their reproductive years dominated by pregnancy and nursing the many children in their extraordinarily large families; if they were religious women, most were cloistered inside convent walls. After experiencing life in all three of these communities, Esther Wheelwright chose to spend most of her life inside the cloister as a nun, a fate that may look a great deal like captivity to modern, secular readers. But as William Wordsworth once wrote, there is such a thing as "the weight of too much liberty," and a freedom that can only be found within certain boundaries and borders: *Nuns fret not at their convent's narrow room; / And hermits are contented with their cells; / And students with their pensive citadels.* What makes these boundaries preferable to absolute liberty—whether the rhyme structure for sonnets or the strictures of cloistered religious life—is the fact that they are voluntary fates: *In truth the prison, into which we doom / Ourselves, no prison is.* At the same time, absolute liberty can be almost as deranging as imprisonment.[3]

Because of all of her border crossings and the challenges she faced to ingratiate herself with different captors and new families, Esther Wheelwright experienced not just one captivity among the Wabanaki but instead many captivities. Her life gives us an opportunity to reflect on the relationship between captivity and liberty, between freedom and restraint. What may appear to be a form of captivity might also have been a liberation; what looks like freedom might also have strict boundaries. For example, historians of English and Anglo-American captives have consciously or unconsciously looked upon Native and French Canadian families and communities as foreigners whose unjust attacks destroyed Anglo-American households. Many of us still use language heavy with Christian history reaching back thousands of years, and speak or write of "captivity" as time outside English or Anglo-American Protestant culture. When we write that "captives" of Native or French Canadian people were "redeemed"—that is, restored to Anglo-American Protestant culture—the implication is that they have also been restored to the possibility of spiritual wholeness and eventual salvation. I try to keep a wary distance from this kind of language as much as I can, because all three major North American cultures believed that they offered access to a superior secular as well as spiritual life.

6

Just as New England inhabitants had their understanding of captivity and redemption, the Catholic Wabanaki embraced the opportunity to welcome and eventually convert foreign children and so would have seen "captivity" among them instead as a spiritual liberation. French authorities therefore interpreted Esther Wheelwright's "captivity" among the Wabanaki as a providential redemption because it put her on the path to Catholicism and eventually to her *francisation,* or "Frenchification" as an Ursuline student and novice. But not all captivities in the North American borderlands were created equal, and their differences depended largely on the cultural backgrounds of both the captors and the captives. For example, the hundreds of Anglo-American children and adults who ended up voluntarily in adopted Native and French Canadian households and who freely chose Native and/or French Canadian spouses stand in dramatic contrast to the Native captives who were enslaved by their New England captors. Native northeastern people and the French Canadians in Quebec retained Anglo-American captives by persuasion and integration into their homes and families.[4] They were therefore very successful in retaining war captives after the hostilities ended, while New Englanders were not inclined to offer either French Canadians or Native people space in their homes on anything like equal terms.[5]

Therefore I try to be cognizant of power and volition in all of the different cultures in which Esther Wheelwright lived. Because I researched and wrote this book while raising a baby, toddler, young child, and now a "tween," I considered the possibility that we might see all children as little captives of fortune—they didn't ask to be born, to speak a particular language, or to practice a particular religion. The Wheelwright garrison, like all Anglo-American households, was a space in which captivity and liberty coexisted on a continuum that included everyone; the fact that they were surrounded by garrison walls on a contested frontier highlights the knife's edge of liberty and captivity they lived on. Coming from a family that included a father, a mother, and sons and daughters, Esther would have been aware from the first of the important differences that gender and age created in the Wheelwright household. And growing up in a family that kept enslaved women and men and servants, she might have been aware of the different qualities and kinds of captivities endured every day by people in her household.

Just as we might see her early childhood in New England as the kind of captivity experienced by all young children, so we might see her more literal kidnapping and capture by the Wabanaki at age seven not just as closing doors but opening up new opportunities for her. She was taken in a violent attack on Wells in 1703 in which at least thirty-nine people were killed or captured, a traumatic experience for anyone. The experiences of other Anglo-American captives indicate that her Wabanaki mothers and sisters would have taught her to pray as a Catholic, and to dress, work, eat, and play as a Native girl, things she learned well. Therefore we can't assume that the aftermath of the attack was experienced only as a loss for her. It is both a great grief and a great relief to parents of young children that they are so resilient: we don't like to think of our children surviving and most likely forgetting us at very young ages, but it's also a useful human instinct to convince new families to care for them and to be able to thrive on the care of other parents. Esther Wheelwright must have been an emotionally intelligent and perceptive person in order to survive her ordeal and adjust to her successive cultures and border crossings. In Esther's case, her Wabanaki girlhood was foundational to her chosen vocation as a religious woman in Québec.

When she crossed her final political border from Wabanakia to Québec in 1708, Esther crossed several other borders as well. She was twelve, nearly thirteen, when she was enrolled in the Ursuline convent school as a student in 1709, a small and probably malnourished child on the edge of adolescence. In these fraught years, she developed a strong vocation for religious life, and so committed herself to a cloistered community. Life inside stone walls might seem obviously like a form of captivity from our perspective after so many years as a captive to the fortunes of war. Then again, the Rule, the routine of the Hours, and the formidable solidity of the cloister must have resonated deeply in Esther. Religious women have argued for centuries that the cloister frees them from the responsibilities and cares of secular women and liberates them to devote their lives to work and to prayer. As we will see, the Ursuline convent in Québec in the eighteenth century was far from a fortress; it was in fact knitted into the busy life of a city that was itself walled and fortified, educating its daughters and open even to male visitors, as well as to females, even to foreigners and Protestants, as well as Native students and their parents. At the same time, it freed them to devote their lives in service to God and to their nation in ways that were open only to religious women.

Esther Wheelwright experienced both captivity and liberty throughout her life, and in all of the three cultures in which she lived. Although her border crossing gave her more opportunities than most girls and women in early North America, we might see her life as emblematic of their experiences as well. Free girls and women had different constraints on their lives in different cultures and at different times in their lives, but they also had different opportunities. Esther Wheelwright was among the few who had the challenge of living in three North American cultures, and she was singular in the leadership role she eventually assumed.

The Art of Biography: Seeing the Hole in the Parts

The word "hole" in the subheading above is not a typographical error. You may be familiar with the phrase "seeing the whole in the parts," or "through the parts," but I want to speak here not about *wholes*, but about the significant *holes* in conventional biographies of (mostly male) subjects. The subjects of most biographies in any national history are men. They are also overwhelmingly men who lived in the modern world, and these accounts reflect our contemporary preoccupation with modern history themes: politics, economics, warfare, the nation-state, and so on.[6] These biographies are also invested in a particularly modern kind of subjectivity, that of the heroic individual who bends history to his will. He's a man of singular genius, one whose fortunes aren't made by his family, his community, or the times in which he lived.

American biography, especially early American biography, offers no exception to this rule. Historians of the earliest decades of U.S. history have churned out biographies of the so-called Founding Fathers for audiences whose admiration for these men knows no limits. This vision of biography is literally inescapable: every day as I walk to my office in the Huntington Library to finish writing this book, I must walk the entire length of a larger-than-lifesize, hallway-length display on the life and career of George Washington, the man the exhibit calls "America's greatest leader." It takes thirty of my brisk, purposeful strides to traverse the length of this tribute to Washington. Traditional biographies like these commemorate only some kinds of power and politics, and avoid the rest. The focus of these books is on both personal and national greatness, not the patriarchal, slaveholding world that permitted these privileged white men to rise to the top of their colonial society long before independence from Great Britain was ever imagined. Stories about the sagacity, virtue, and political genius of our "Founding Fathers" sell like hotcakes. Stories that focus on the cruelty and exploitation of the many by the few in colonial North America might receive respectful reviews in academic journals, but they don't move product. Considering the omissions and holes in conventional biographical practice leads us to ask different questions, to look for the stories of unknown people, and to imagine different relationships between our subjects and the world around them.

So why do readers clamor for books about people they've already heard of? Why don't writers or readers look for fresh stories of people they've never heard of before? First, historians' choices have traditionally been restrained by their discipline's obsession with written information, so we must consider the politics of literacy in early America. Because even most free women in North America were taught only to read and not to write until the middle of the eighteenth century, most people, enslaved or free, couldn't generate their own archive, let alone possess the social and cultural capital to ensure its preservation for two or three centuries. It's a lot easier to write about people who wrote endlessly about themselves in journals or diaries, and carried on a voluminous correspondence with friends and col- leagues which was then meticulously preserved. The second reason that biographies of the already well known are more popular has to do with readers' choices. It's better business to write about the rich and famous, because there's already a built-in audience of book buyers for that latest biography of John Adams, George Washington, Andrew Jackson, or Abra- ham Lincoln. It's easier and more fun for middle-class North American readers to identify with rich and powerful individuals rather than the vic- tims of history. Schoolyard bullies know this instinctively: we all want to identify with winners instead of losers.

Therefore, writing about Native protagonists, or enslaved individuals, or people who didn't speak English, or pretty much any nonelite person, not to mention most women in early American history, means methodological and possibly financial risks for American historians and publishers. In recent years, there have been a number of fascinating biographies and microhistories published that have focused on previously obscure individuals or communities, including Native and African American women as well as men.[7] Most of these books employ methods borrowed from American studies, feminist studies, Native American or First Nations studies, material culture, anthropology, archaeology, architecture, art history, and other fields in order to locate and "read" sources that aren't transparent in their meaning, or that aren't even textual sources at all. Public history, with its focus on historic preservation and material culture, has proved to be an especially fruitful subdiscipline for historians who want to—or must—push beyond traditional historical texts in order to tell new stories about early America. Women's historians in particular can learn a great deal from the house museums and material culture that remain—usually preserved, conserved, and passed down by women through female kinship lines. Because they connect us not only to a selected moment in time, but also to previous generations of historians whose work was overlooked or trivialized by professional historians, these objects demand our attention as we are the beneficiaries of centuries of this kind of scholarship.[8]

When it comes to writing the biographies of early American women, recent authors have moved beyond the wives of the "Founding Fathers" to explore the lives of women like Pocahontas, Malintzín, and Betsy Ross, who have mostly survived as cardboard cutouts rather than as real women in historical memory.[9] Some have reconstructed the lives of previously obscure women like midwife Martha Ballard, Anglo-American goodwives Jane Mecom Franklin and Elizabeth Tuttle Edwards, tailor Rebecca Dickinson, American Revolution soldier Deborah Sampson, Moravian preacher Rebecca Protten, the recently canonized Mohawk Saint Catherine Tekakwitha, and the enslaved Sally Hemings and presidential daughter Martha Jefferson Randolph, rival *châtelaines* of Monticello.[10] But most of these biographers still rely heavily on the much more thoroughly documented lives of the men with whom these women were associated.[11]

This book on Esther Wheelwright is enriched immeasurably by this substantial bibliography, but I consciously avoid this trap because it wasn't men who were the most important people in her life. Instead, I found that her life was unintelligible without a focus on the communities of girls and women who surrounded her at every stage of her life, from birth in an

Anglo-American garrison house, to her childhood among the Wabanaki in Maine, to her life as a student and then as a teacher inside the Ursuline convent in Québec. Compared with lives of other fairly obscure nonelite women of the eighteenth century, hers is extremely well documented, mostly because of the Ursulines' literacy and their careful record keeping within their convent. Compared with a so-called Founding Father, whose wealth, literacy, political power, and progeny all helped to ensure his place in the American Pantheon, Esther's existence in scattered eighteenth-century primary sources is hardly a transparent or easily told tale. Therefore I must also tell the stories of the girls and women who loved her, clothed and fed her, educated her, worked and prayed with her, competed with her, and buried her.

Of course, I must pay some attention to the men in her life, as they played crucial roles in transporting Esther across linguistic, religious, and political borders. You as a reader may want to learn more about John Wheelwright, Esther's father, whose name was the same as her famous Antinomian great-grandfather's, or about the brother Jesuits Jacques and Vincent Bigot, or the Marquis de Vaudreuil, governor general of New France, but their stories have been told and continue to be told many times elsewhere, in English and in French. Because of the liberty of movement that most free men enjoyed in early North America, their contributions to Esther's extraordinary life are notable. However, their influence on her was fleeting compared with the influence of the girls and women with whom Esther lived and died.

The fact that my subject became a professed nun, and lived inside a cloister from the age of fifteen until her death at eighty-four, was a large part of my inspiration to look to the communities of women who surrounded her. However, what I discovered in researching this book is that Esther's life among the Ursulines represented not a radical departure from her life in an English colonial outpost or a Wabanaki community, but rather evidence of intriguing continuities that helped explain her choices in adolescence and adulthood. Gender was a crucial organizational category in all three North American cultures in the seventeenth and eighteenth centuries, in Anglo-American, Native, and French Canadian communities and families alike. In all three cultures, one's sex determined one's education, work life, place in the household, and role in religious practice. While there were some important differences in gender ideology across ethnic and cultural borders, men were privileged in all three cultures over women as the bearers of political, military, and spiritual power. These powers expanded and grew by comparison to traditional women's roles and realms of expertise in the contested colonial environment in which Native, French, and English people fought to control North America.

The similarities in male gender ideologies in English and French colonies and Native North America are the most striking, but this book offers several compelling continuities in colonial North American women as well. Some continuities cross time as well as space, and will probably not surprise the reader: for example, in all three cultures, everyday food preparation and early child care were considered women's work, and New England Protestant as well as French Canadian Catholic women feared the perdition they and their children might suffer if they were converted to the religion of their enemies. So, too, status distinctions were important in all three cultures. However, I discovered some similarities that have been overlooked: French Catholic religious women and Wabanaki women both had traditions of sex segregation linked to beliefs about purity and spiritual power. Wabanaki women provided their communities with vital macro- and micronutrients by farming and improving the soil, but so did Anglo-American servants and goodwives who assiduously worked the stony soils of New England. These details, and many others, weave a fascinating web of connections across cultures that reveal an interconnected eighteenth-century northeastern borderlands of North America.

Another feature of this biography is that it concentrates a great deal on Esther's childhood and youth, and then on her old age. We all know—or we think we know—the arc of traditional biographies, in which the convention is to slight both callow youth and the indignities of old age in order to focus on the achievements of vigorous adulthood and middle age. If we were to plot the chapters of most biographies on an x/y axis, they would mostly look like a traditional bell curve, with few chapters at the beginning and at the end, and a great number of chapters in the middle. However, this model doesn't work well for Esther Wheelwright, because for the most part it's her eventful, border-crossing youth and her old age in occupied Québec that are more exciting and better documented than her middle years of maturity, strength, and service to her community. If I were to plot the primary sources I have on an x/y axis, it would look not like a bell but like a very wide and somewhat lopsided letter W: there are a good number of sources on her early childhood, but almost none from ages seven to twelve among the Wabanaki. There is a flurry of sources in her adolescence, very few on her adult years from eighteen to fifty, and then a larger number of sources about her specifically (and even a few letters in her hand) from age fifty to her death at eighty-four.

Although methodologically innovative, this biography is conventional in its chronological organization. I begin with her early childhood, and end with her death. Notable recent biographies have opened with the dramatic deaths of their protagonists, but because Esther Wheelwright lived successively as an Anglo-American child, a Wabanaki child, and then as a French Canadian adolescent and religious woman, she underwent more profound transformations than aging accomplishes on its own.[12] Considering the dramatic changes in the circumstances of her life, I stick to a conventional chronology because each border crossing turns her into a different person who speaks a new language, practices a new religion, wears different clothing, and is embedded within a different family. As for most of us, Esther Wheelwright's life, learning, and new experiences contributed cumulatively to her identity. In the first three chapters, Esther speaks different languages and lives with three distinct families and communities, so accordingly I have named each chapter after the name she probably used at each point in her life to early adolescence: Esther Wheelwright, Mali, and Esther *Anglaise*. As she begins her novitiate and matures in the Ursuline community, she continues to go by different names and to take different leadership roles, so the last four chapter titles signal her growing stature as a religious woman: Sister Marie, Mother Esther, Esther Superior, and Esther Zelatrix.

So why put the name Esther Wheelwright in the title and on the cover of this book, when it seems as though she left it behind at the age of seven? For most of her life, she was officially known by her religious name, Mother Marie-Joseph de l'Enfant Jésus, and neither Esther nor Wheelwright makes an appearance in that string of names. However, as we will see, Ursuline religious names never completely effaced their birth names, and in the status-conscious world of early modern European and North American convents, nuns wanted to remind their peers of the connections and wealth they were born to. Although she did not have a high-status birth family, Esther too came to share these values and adopted this style of personal address, signing her letters with a combination of her birth and her religious names as Sister Esther de l'Enfant Jésus, or even in a letter to her aged mother, Sister Esther Wheelwright de l'Enfant Jésus.

A word of warning: although we can get close to understanding Esther Wheelwright's world and individual experiences, we can't know much about her inner life. Modern biographers are determined to bring their subjects to life and help their readers get inside their subjects' heads, but that's nearly impossible for most North Americans who lived before the Age of Revolutions—before paper got cheaper, before print culture flowered, before literacy became more widespread, and before literate people became writers of letters.[13] There's another reason that Esther must remain a little remote from us as an individual, and that's because she lived in the Ursuline convent for nearly seventy of her eighty-four years. Nuns in the early modern era weren't supposed to distinguish themselves as individuals; their lives were important because of their prayers, their work, and their devotion to God and their communities. Most women in this era led lives that are largely lost to history, but nuns took vows of poverty, chastity, and obedience and were above all supposed to deny their individual desires and interests in the service of God. In my pursuit of Esther Wheelwright, I've learned that she is especially unknowable if we try to see her as a modern biographical subject, as an individual extracted from the communities of girls and women who surrounded her throughout her life. Only in context does her life and work become clear to us, and that context is the busy days, weeks, and years of work, prayer, conflict, and love that bound her to other women.

Esther Wheelwright lived a remarkable life. After a childhood repeatedly disrupted by warfare in the northeastern borderlands, she sought refuge inside the walls of a religious community of women. War followed her nonetheless to Québec, a city that was repeatedly threatened by invasion and occupation through the eighteenth century. She rose to leadership at a critical moment in her community's and her city's history and through her leadership saw the Ursuline convent persist and even expand in spite of Québec's domination by hostile Protestant rulers.

What can we learn by attending to her life and the lives of the women who surrounded her? Everything important to understanding early North America.

CHAPTER ONE

ESTHER WHEELWRIGHT

Palisades and Boundaries

When she awoke most mornings, she was probably first aware of the presence of her older sister Hannah in the trundle bed with her, both of them rolled up in the sheets in the still cool but already muggy dawn. Or perhaps they slept on a simple straw mattress, and folded it up and tucked it in a chest or under a bench after they arose. The coughs, grunts, stretches, yawns, and scratchings of an entire family of nine waking up would have accompanied Esther and Hannah Wheelwright as they made their bed in the room they shared with their parents and other sisters and brothers. Esther would have needed some help getting dressed, even at the age of seven. She would not have been left to wear just a loose shift on hot summer days, but rather she would have been laced into stays by her mother or Hannah, age nine. Men and women, from toddlers to adults, wore knee-length, loose-fitting linen shirts (on women they were called shifts) both to bed and under their daytime clothing. Other garments disciplined little bodies and big bodies alike in daylight.

This discipline began in infancy, and for girls and women, it continued throughout their lives. As a toddler, Esther and all of her siblings would have worn leading-strings, which were short straps sewn onto the shoulders of their gowns or strings secured by a belt that could be held by the mother to steady a toddler just learning to walk. They might also be used to keep the child near, or even to tie her to a bedpost or fencepost to keep her out of harm's way. The stays that enclosed Esther's ribcage and diaphragm might have been made crudely of leather, or more finely crafted of linen stiffened with bone or thin wooden straps. This corsetlike garment was tied snugly over the shift and worn under woolen petticoats, jackets, and gowns, and it was worn by infants and children of both sexes in the early eighteenth century. (Stays were also called a "body," suggesting that one's actual body was fundamentally shaped and molded by one's "body.") Stays were believed to develop good posture in children, and were intended to mold the upper body to become an inverted cone-shaped torso with a flattened back and chest, wider at the shoulders than at the waist, which was the preferred silhouette for women in the seventeenth and eighteenth centuries. Anglo-American girls and women were laced into stays throughout their lives. At the turn of the eighteenth century, another distinctive feature of clothing worn by Euro-American children was that boys and girls alike wore gowns until about age six or seven, when boys would have put aside their stays and gowns to be "breeched," or put into breeches. After that point, with girls forever constrained by stays and boys liberated by their breeches, their clothing was no longer distinctively childlike, just simply smaller versions of the fashions their mothers and fathers wore.[1]

As she dressed that morning, Esther was constricted not just by the stays and petticoat that covered her body. The house she lived in was a garrison, or strong house, surrounded by a palisade fence made of thick logs planted deeply in the ground. It was meant to serve as a fortified shelter for neighbors as well as the Wheelwrights in case of a Native attack on their town. But calling it a garrison makes the Wheelwright home, built originally by Esther's great-grandfather in the 1640s, sound larger and more formidable than it was in 1703.[2] A centrally placed chimney would have heated the two rooms on the main floor, with a sleeping loft or storage space in the half story above.[3] This served as the only indoor living space for at least thirteen people in 1703: Esther, her parents, her six siblings, two indentured servants, and at least two slaves.[4] One room, the hall, would have served as a

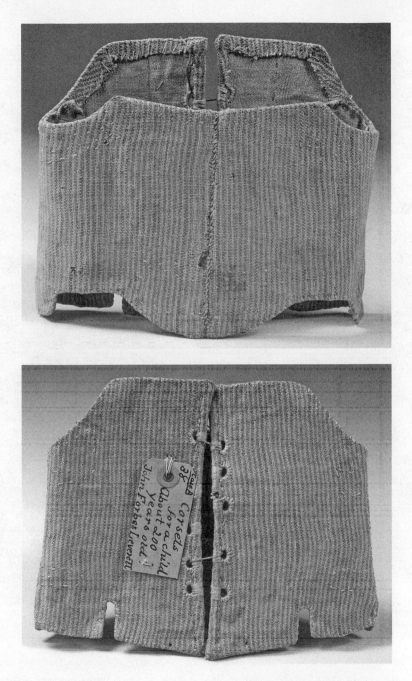

Child's stays, 6.75″ h × 8.75″ w, linen and cardboard, ca. 1760–90, provenance unknown. These tiny stays were used to bind the torso of a toddler or successive toddlers in an Anglo-American family like the Wheelwrights'. Photographs courtesy of the Pocumtuck Valley Memorial Association, Memorial Hall Museum, Deerfield, Massachusetts

Portrait of Alice Mason by an unknown artist, ca. 1670. Silently pointing to an apple she holds before her uterus, Alice Mason suggests that she accepts her destiny to be the dutiful mother of numerous little Christians.
Photograph courtesy of National Park Service, Adams National Historical Park

kitchen and main living space, with perhaps a large table and benches or stools to sit on, and a chest or two for storing linens and kitchen supplies. The other room, called the chamber, was where Esther's parents would have kept their most substantial and only comfortable piece of furniture, a large, four-poster bed with a straw mattress and several pillows and bolsters. It probably was surrounded by thick curtains made of brightly colored wool, or perhaps white wool elaborately embroidered with crewelwork flowers and birds. On cold nights, these curtains could be drawn around the entire bed to conserve heat. The chamber is where the Wheelwrights slept, with the youngest baby or two in the big bed, and older children on trundle beds or mattresses that would be rolled up and stored away so that the family could use the space during the day. Servants and slaves probably bedded down in the hall or in the half-story above on straw mattresses like those the children slept on.[5] The summer of 1703 was the last summer they lived in that house—John Wheelwright tore down that one and built a larger house and garrison that, later in Queen Anne's War, would swell to house seven families and four soldiers, a total of sixty people.[6] Eventually, Esther's parents would have as many as eight children living in these rooms, plus an ever-changing population of bound and enslaved laborers. In both the clothing they wore and in their domestic arrangements, colonial Americans were accustomed to much less bodily liberty and personal space than most modern North Americans.

Work and Life in the Wheelwright Garrison

As Mary Wheelwright, Esther's mother, stoked the fire to prepare breakfast, wood smoke would further permeate the hair, skin, clothing, and all of the personal belongings of the entire family. Because of its pervasiveness, winter and summer, Esther may not have been consciously aware of its acrid yet comforting odor. In colonial America, the smell of wood smoke was the smell of home—whether home was a temporary camp in the woods, a dugout on the banks of a river, a Wabanaki village, a New England wood-framed house, or a stone house in Québec, wood smoke promised light, heat, and cooked food—not to mention human companionship. Esther would not have been permitted the luxury of sleeping in while her mother worked to feed the family—she was probably expected to assist her mother with simple tasks like setting the table for their breakfast, and helping her younger siblings into their clothes (five-year-old Jeremiah, three-year-old Elizabeth, and little Mary, only fourteen months). On most mornings, Mary would probably have given her family a breakfast of small (low-alcohol) beer or hard cider and hasty pudding, a cornmeal mush sweetened perhaps with maple sugar or molasses and enriched with milk and butter. But in the summer, if the air was already too muggy and warm for hot cereal, then the family might have made do with a cold breakfast of cheese, leftover bread, and the remains (if any) of last night's supper. Aside from helping her mother at the table, Esther may also have been responsible for keeping her younger siblings entertained and safely away from the fire.[7] Little girls in colonial America had to learn at a young age to work cooperatively with other girls and women, because all but the most elite of them would work alongside other women for the rest of their lives. The Wheelwright family was a prominent family in Wells, but neither rich nor elite. Although they typically kept servants and even owned slaves, Esther and her sisters were raised to work like their mother.

English and Anglo-American girls and women especially would have been inured to the smell of wood smoke, because so much of the work they did year-round happened indoors or close to the threshold, and usually with the assistance of fire. Fire not only heated homes and cooked break-fasts, dinners, and suppers, it was essential to dairying, it heated water for laundering bedding and clothes, and its warmth helped bread rise and beer ferment. While boys in agricultural communities like Esther's elder brothers John, age thirteen, and eleven-year-old Samuel were expected to assist men with tasks performed largely out of doors like farming, herding, main-taining farm tools and equipment, and sometimes hunting and fishing, girls like Hannah and Esther worked side by side with their mothers, sisters, and women servants and slaves at the endless rounds of domestic labor re-quired to maintain a middling Anglo-American household. Cooking, wash-ing up, and milking too—if the family kept cows—had to be done at least daily, if not two or three times a day, while other tasks needed biweekly, weekly, monthly, or only seasonal attention: baking, brewing, gardening, butter and cheese making, food preservation, washing, mending, sewing, and knitting, for example, were skills that took years of practice before most girls would be proficient at them. While men's and boys' work was more frequently outdoors, women's and girls' work was not necessarily less physical, considering the strength and stamina needed to work with large animals, beat or grind dried whole grains into meal and flour, and boil laundry in enormous kettles—sometimes all in the same day. The work that women and girls did was equally arduous, but more confined, bounded as it was by houses, kitchen gardens, barns, and perhaps larger yards for messier tasks like laundry and food processing.[8]

Esther's world was restricted in other ways less visible than stays, walls, or palisade fences. Both male and female children worked as soon as they could be reliably helpful to their parents, and neither really had much of a choice of what work they would do for the rest of their lives, especially if they remained in an agricultural community. Wells, Massachusetts, was a farming community, like most of the other small towns of colonial British America, and most people made their principal living from the soil, although they eagerly supplemented it with profits from trading with the Wabanaki and New Englanders alike. Both girls and boys could be apprenticed or indentured to work for other families, although usually only boys had the opportunity to learn a skilled trade or craft. When girls were indentured, in the vast majority of cases they would be expected to perform the same round of domestic chores they had assisted with all their lives. Families in bigger towns or cities like Boston in the eighteenth century might not keep cows or engage in as much food preservation because of the provisions available in urban markets, but otherwise girls' work routines would have been pretty much the same in both rural and urban environments. Because domestic labor was at the center of women's work lives, women's work was seen as less skilled, more repetitive, and worthy of less compensation than men's work.

Although their labor was largely hidden indoors or inside fences—and was largely uncompensated—the actual value of girls' and women's labor was tremendous. Kitchen gardens, contrary to what their name suggests, were nutritional and medicinal workhorses, providing critical vitamins, minerals, and calories to the diets of colonial New Englanders. There are no records of the fruits and vegetables grown in Mary Wheelwright's kitchen garden, nor are there details of the foods she and her servants and slaves prepared for her family's table, but we know that there was a remarkable diversity of plants grown in other New England kitchen gardens with similar climate and resources.

Kitchen gardens were assiduously cultivated to offer both food and medicine. New World squashes and pumpkins were probably central to most gardens, because they were simple to grow, packed with vitamins, and easily stored through the winter. However, English imports probably made up the majority of garden crops at the turn of the eighteenth century: several kinds of cabbages and greens, root vegetables like onions, carrots, beets, parsnips, and turnips, as well as celery, cucumbers, and many varieties of melons, were regularly grown in kitchen gardens like Mary Wheelwright's. Even vegetables regarded by many now as fit for haute cuisine were cultivated by New England's goodwives and their daughters and servants: asparagus, leeks, mushrooms, fennel, and endive. Fruit trees were planted alongside the garden, in order to provide a shelter from northern and eastern winds, and perhaps to provide shade for cool-weather crops like cauliflower and broccoli. Apple trees were critical for cider production, but cherry, plum, and pear trees were popular, and strawberries and blackberries were garden regulars too. Besides fruits and vegetables, herbs were garden regulars prized for their medicinal powers as well as their flavors: basil, dill, parsley, rosemary, mint, savory, and thyme, among many others. By shrewdly storing hardier root vegetables, and pickling others, an industrious New England goodwife and the girls and women she supervised could make their hard work in the garden enliven the daily staples of beef, dairy products, cornmeal, and dried peas through the winter until early spring crops of lettuces, greens, and fresh peas were available again.[9]

By providing their families with this hefty supply of nutrients and calories, the labor of girls and women in kitchen gardens may help to explain the paradox that although New England had the poorest and least fertile soil of any region of colonial America, Anglo-Americans there had the greatest health and longevity. Perhaps one of the reasons that families like the Wheelwrights were so large and healthy—nine of their eleven children survived to adulthood and both parents lived into their eighties—is that women and girls assiduously cultivated the soil in their kitchen gardens. The emphasis here must be on the labor of free women, servants, and enslaved women alike: only the improvement of the soil and dedicated attention to their gardens made them so beneficial and productive. Only after years of women and girls working compost, wood ashes, and various animal manures into the soil, as well as watering their gardens with specially treated water (either a compost or dung-enriched "tea," or in coastal towns like Wells, water that had been limed by oyster shells), would these gardens produce their legendary bounty. Although the kitchen garden may have felt like a relatively open space in which to work, where Esther's lungs could breathe fresh air instead of wood smoke, there is no doubt that it was a place of hard work for even the littlest girls, who would have been enlisted in seeding, weeding, and carrying compost and water as soon as they could follow their mothers' instructions. Their contributions may have seemed small, but collectively women and girls of all ages contributed to the survival and health of their families. New England's successes in creating large and healthy Anglo-American families vindicated their belief that America should naturally be peopled and ruled by them.[10]

While women's work was confined and restricted in some ways, it was exhausting and endless, in the busy Wheelwright garrison as in other homes. Although they lived on intimate terms inside palisade fences and fortified doors, many Anglo-American homes in colonial Massachusetts were in fact open to strangers as well as family members. Aside from the thirteen people who lived there, the Wheelwright home was also a "Publick house of Intertainment & retayling all Sorts of Liquors" through the 1690s. This was a popular way to supplement family income in colonial Massachusetts, and there were several men and women granted licenses every year in small towns like Wells, York, Kittery, and Saco. Depending on the license granted to individual householders, they might offer meals, beverages, and a place for weary travelers to sleep. With a more limited license, they might just sell "Bear [beer] & Syder" to anyone who needed a drink. From the 1680s onward, several families in Wells, as in many other small towns nearby, had licenses like these that would have generated extra income for their families. Esther's father John had a license from 1693 to about 1700, as he and his wife Mary began raising their large family, and it probably supplemented their income as they strove to make a living on the New England frontier.[11] Passersby and travelers who stayed a night or two kept even frontier outposts like Wells connected to Boston and beyond, individual links in a human chain that brought news, information, and trade goods. Thus, in this world that was bounded in so many ways, children like Esther and her brothers and sisters were accustomed to strangers stopping by and even living with their family temporarily. Travelers, traders, and passersby; regular customers and strangers; Wabanaki traders, enslaved or free Africans or African Americans, and Atlantic sea captains and sailors undoubtedly found their way to John and Mary Wheelwright's garrison.

This diverse array of visitors meant not just extra income, but also extra work for the women and girls who produced and served the food and drink. Because Mary was nearly always pregnant or nursing the newest baby through the 1690s and 1700s, the work of female servants or enslaved women was absolutely critical to running a tavern or "ordinary," or taking in overnight guests. The use of hired or enslaved labor was especially important in the 1690s, because the Wheelwright daughters were still far too young to contribute much productive labor to the household. Therefore Mary probably relied on the labor of servants and enslaved women. Although we don't know exactly how many servants and slaves worked inside the Wheelwright garrison around the turn of the century, we know from a pair of depositions left in court records that they had at least two servants in 1703, Thomas Wormwood and Elizabeth Goodale. We also know that they owned an enslaved man named Sambo in 1712, and their ownership of slaves appears to have spanned well over half a century. Evidence from Wheelwright wills shows that Esther's grandfather Samuel left his wife "one Negro Servant named Titus" when he died in 1700. When Esther's father, John, died in 1745, he left Mary, among other things, "all Kinds Negro or Molatto Servants," and when Mary died a decade later, she left her daughter Sarah "a negro boy named Asher" and decreed that "my Negro Servant Woman named Pegg" might live with any daughters or granddaughters "which She Shall choose to live with after my Decease." Casual references to "all Kinds Negro or Molatto Servants" suggests that perhaps the number of enslaved women and men owned by the Wheelwrights was greater than the number of their Euro-American servants.[12] Given that slaveowning was a family tradition of the Wheelwrights, and that they owned slaves of various ages and both sexes, it's probable that Elizabeth Goodale worked alongside at least one enslaved woman inside the Wheelwright garrison.[13]

As bounded as the world of Wells, Massachusetts, was for free little girls like Esther, enslaved men and women were held in a much more restrictive institution of law and customs that stole their labor and their children away from them. Moreover, slaveowning was not just an affectation of the Wheelwrights—a nineteenth-century historian of Wells lists dozens of slaves owned by Anglo-American families through the eighteenth century. While enslaved Africans or African Americans were not a large part of the workforce in early New England, they were hardly unusual, even in small towns in northern New England. Although slavery never became central to the economy of rural New England, that was due more to the fact that New Englanders practiced mixed agriculture in a short growing season instead of staple-crop cultivation as in the Caribbean and the mainland colonies of the upper and lower South. Enslaved men and women were a notable part of the urban labor force in cities like Boston and Newport.[14]

Although it may seem hard to square with popular visions of Pilgrims sharing a multicultural and egalitarian Thanksgiving feast with the Wampa-noags, white New Englanders practiced slavery until its state-by-state abo-lition in the North around the time of the American Revolution. Neither religious nor civil objections to slaveholding were articulated by white New Englanders until later in the eighteenth century. In fact, slavery, like servi-tude, fit neatly into a Puritan worldview that was rigidly hierarchical: age above youth, male above female, free above unfree, human above animal, Christians above non-Christians, and rich above poor. In this way of think-ing, inequality was not a problem, it was in fact a positive good that might ensure God's blessings (or at least help to avoid His divine wrath).[15] As the founder of the Massachusetts Bay Colony, John Winthrop, put it more than sixty years before Esther Wheelwright was born, "God Almighty in His most holy and wise providence hath so disposed of the condition of man-kind, as in all times some must be rich, some poor, some high and eminent in power and dignity, others mean and in subjection."[16] Of course, men who were "high and eminent in power and dignity" like Winthrop—or even John Wheelwright inside his garrison—found this model of society much more tolerable than those who were poor or in subjection to the powerful. Then as now, individuals frequently refused to conform to the expectations of society—women publicly scolded their husbands, men in-sulted their ministers and magistrates, and servants and slaves stole or ran away from their masters, for example—but at the turn of the eighteenth century, there was no discourse on civil rights or human rights that could have made those individual acts of resistance into a political movement.

Enslaved women working in the Wheelwright garrison wore their status on their bodies regardless of their skin color, because they typically wore just a shift and a petticoat and went without stays or gowns. This was probably not just a practical measure meant to liberate their lungs and backs for physical labor—after all, in the Wheelwright household, Mary, her daughters, and white servants would probably have participated in the same or a similar round of wearying household chores that she assigned to her slaves. The bodily discipline of wearing stays, although confining and certainly uncomfortable for active girls and women, was still a mark of status and a privilege reserved for free women only.[17] The bodies of enslaved women were disciplined in other ways too, with whippings, beatings, brandings, and other bodily mutilations always a possibility. Furthermore, slaves had no legal right to bodily integrity, and could be raped and abused sexually as well. Because masters owned their bodies, any children enslaved women had were not theirs legally, but rather were the property of their masters.

This is the crucial difference between servitude and slavery in colonial America: When a master hired or signed a labor contract (or indenture) with a servant, he owned only her labor. When a master bought a slave, he owned not just her labor but her body too, for the rest of her life. While white servants were subjected to corporal punishment through the seventeenth century, increasingly through the eighteenth century they came to identify these bodily humiliations as fit only for "negro" bodies, not for white bodies, although their bodies were otherwise treated the same. Well into the eighteenth century throughout colonial America, especially on family farms of modest size, servants and slaves performed the same work, ate the same food, and slept in the same beds, but white servants successfully redefined the boundaries between servants and slaves by arguing that corporal punishment was wrong for white bodies of any status by the mid-eighteenth century. Elizabeth Goodale would eventually outlive her servitude, but her African American coworkers would never claim ownership of their bodies or their children.[18]

The reality of these differences between slaves and servants—and their potentially deadly consequences—was made frighteningly clear to enslaved women and men in what's now southern Maine in 1694 when a woman named Rachel was murdered by her master in Kittery, a town just south of Wells. Because African Americans were relatively few in number, slaves in the Wheelwright garrison may have at least known of her, even if they didn't know her personally, and they would surely have heard about her murder. If they did know Rachel personally, they may have known about her master's brutal behavior, but because of their shared status, they could offer her little more than their sympathy. While her master Nathaniel Keene (or Caine) was initially accused in court of "Murdering a Negro Woman," in the end the jury found him guilty only of "Cruelty to his Negro woman by Cruell Beating and hard usage." The penalty exacted of him was a five-pound fine—which was suspended—and five pounds, ten shillings in court costs. In order to put this punishment into perspective, people convicted of fornication or of bearing a child out of wedlock in 1694 and 1695 were regularly fined between twenty shillings and five pounds, substantial but not crippling sums. The same court that adjudicated Rachel's murder also convicted Walter Burks of "lifting up his hand" against one of the justices of the peace "and giving threatning speeches," and fined him nearly five pounds for that offense plus court costs.[19] By their calculation, the mere threat of physical violence against a magistrate was worthy of harsher punishment than beating to death an enslaved woman. While the court recognized that Keene was cruel, repeating the word twice over in their sentence, it refused to defend the value of Rachel's life by holding Keene accountable for her murder in any meaningful way.[20] We can only imagine the effect Rachel's murder and her killer's virtual acquittal had on the other enslaved people nearby, scarcely any of whom left traces of their lives. While slaves lived on intimate terms with free people, and may well have formed bonds of friendship with other laborers and even sometimes their owners, Rachel's miserable life and unavenged death was a reminder close to home that they had no rights before the law.[21]

While court records don't record people's inner lives, we can see a snapshot of the busy Wheelwright household around 1703 through depositions collected in a 1707 lawsuit concerning disputed charges and payments on behalf of regular guest Benjamin Mayers (or Mairs), who was killed in a 1703 attack. This was a lawsuit between two men—the administrator for Mayers's estate, Richard Carr, was suing John Wheelwright for some cash Mayers left with Wheelwright before his death—but the depositions give a detailed account of the women's work that the Wheelwright tavern license depended on. Mayers was such a regular guest that one former Wheelwright family servant, Thomas Wormwood, testified that Mayers "did Constantly take Mr John Wheelwrights house as his home as he passed to & from on his Business at all Lett times Sometimes thre or four Dayes or a week or more together & made it his dwelling place." This meant that "he was Entertained with victualls & Lodging in the house & also mended & made him cloths and mended his wollin cloths & had his cloths washed in the house & sd Wheelwright took a great deal of Care & pains for him." Wormwood might have been the servant who cared for Mayers's horse, which also lodged in the Wheelwright garrison "both in the winter & summer time with pasturing in the Summer & in the winter with hay & Sometimes with provender & that for about four or five years time." Additionally, when Mayers suffered a lengthy illness, he was "Entertained Attended & Nursed in Mr Wheelwrights house by [Wheelwright's] wife & Servants." One of those servants, Elizabeth Goodale, also testified on the Wheelwrights' behalf in the lawsuit, swearing that Mayers had not one but "two fitts of Sickness in sd Wheelwrights house & that sd Mairs was Entertained for about Eight years at times." She very clearly remembered the volume of extra laundry he brought for the women of the household to wash, as Goodale claimed that Mayers "brought his linin from Saco and other places & had them washed in Mr Wheelwrights family & mended by her mistress." Mayers and other guests kept Mary, eldest daughter Hannah, servants like Elizabeth Goodale, and probably enslaved women busy with extra demands for food, drink, comfortable beds, clean laundry, mending, and even nursing from time to time.[22]

As this account of Mayers's life with the Wheelwrights suggests, colonial taverns and "ordinaries" were indeed ordinary places where people could purchase their comfort and safety by the day. Tavernkeeping was not a disreputable undertaking in colonial New England, nor was it unseemly to have a family of young children underfoot while keeping a house of "public entertainment." Growing up in a home that also served as a tavern or "ordinary" was almost certainly more interesting than being isolated on a farm. Patrons might break into rounds of song and dance, or engage in illicit lawn bowling on the warm afternoons and evenings of summer and early autumn.[23] The Wheelwright children would not only have been accustomed to strangers and neighbors dropping in for a drink or a meal, they may well have welcomed the variety of guests who might bring new tales to tell them at night before bed.

Modern readers might wonder about the propriety of raising children in a tavern, but we should remember that drinking wasn't just an adult occupation. Everyone in colonial America—men, women, and children—drank alcoholic beverages, and they drank them all day long, although lower-alcohol drinks ("small beer" and cider) would have been their mainstay rather than distilled spirits. People believed that it was healthier to consume fermented beverages rather than cold water, because water—especially in urban areas before modern sanitation—was (probably correctly) considered unhealthy. Fermentation killed most of the harmful germs that fresh water might harbor, like cholera, giardia, or other intestinal infections, and beer and cider probably offered stimulating flavor to palates that were bored much of the year by a cuisine based on reconstituted dried grains, beans, and salted meats or fish. Additionally, people believed that alcohol wasn't just healthier than cold water—they believed that beer, cider, and especially hard liquor, in reasonable amounts, offered health benefits beyond the avoidance of diarrhea. Beer and wine were integral to the preparation of home herbal remedies, serving as the base for all manner of soothing potions and purgatives alike. Rum, and later in the eighteenth century, gin, were believed to offer nutrients and medicinal power, and they were credited with relieving or curing a variety of ailments, from fevers and snake-bites to broken limbs and the common cold. In contrast to the prohibition-ist advice that pregnant North American women receive today from their obstetricians, colonial midwives urged their patients to continue their same diets when pregnant, and indeed, even prepared caudles and mulled wines, beer, and rum punches for their patients who were laboring.[24]

Although friends and strangers could bring excitement and news to the Wheelwright garrison, they could also bring trouble. The dangers of over-indulging in drink were as well known in small-town Massachusetts as anywhere else in colonial America. Although Wells had much less traffic than cities like Boston or Portsmouth, the socially disruptive potential of alcohol was something that the local magistracy was well acquainted with. Drunkenness was a frequently prosecuted misdemeanor in York County, and usually resulted in a public whipping or payment of a fine for the miscreants.[25]

In the winter of 1690, a county court proclaimed that because of "excessive Drinking of rum, flipp, &c.: the Il consequence whereof is publickly seene in the misbehaviour of severall persons in the presence of authority," tavernkeepers were forbidden to sell "any rum or other strong liquor or flip" to any of the townspeople, "Except in Case of great nesessity as in Case of sickness &c." They were also forbidden to "sell unto any stranger more then one gill [of hard liquor] for a person at one time." Considering that a gill of rum was a measure between four to eight ounces, this was still a generous allowance of spirits—enough to refresh any weary traveler, and then some. While the local courts granted householders licenses to retail beer and liquor, they also prosecuted people for selling without a license, and hauled licensed tavernkeepers before the court for permitting excessive drunkenness, or condoning gambling and illegal games like cards, dice, ninepins, shuffleboard, and billiards.[26]

Childhood in a Frontier Town

After she helped the grown women with the breakfast dishes and tidying the hall, most mornings Esther may have stolen a few moments to play with her younger siblings, and perhaps some neighbor children. At seven, her labor wasn't nearly as helpful or as necessary to her mother as that of her elder sister, who perhaps had to stay closer to home to help Mary Wheelwright and the other women in the household with some late-summer tasks like tending the garden, food preservation, or perhaps laundry before the chill of autumn would make that chore more arduous than it already was. If Esther was at liberty, she may have played marbles with the younger children, or with a toy called a "whizzer," a notched disc strung on a loop that made noise when the string was pulled to make the disc spin quickly. Jew's harps were also common in early New England, so she may have learned to play one from her older siblings, or perhaps from a guest in the family tavern. She may also have had a doll—homemade out of cloth, or a poppet carved of wood, and perhaps shared with her sisters.[27]

Then again, seven was of an age when she might have been expected to spend some time learning to read, with her mother's or older sister Hannah's assistance. Because Puritans were Protestants who emphasized the necessity for all believers to read the Word of God for themselves, both girls

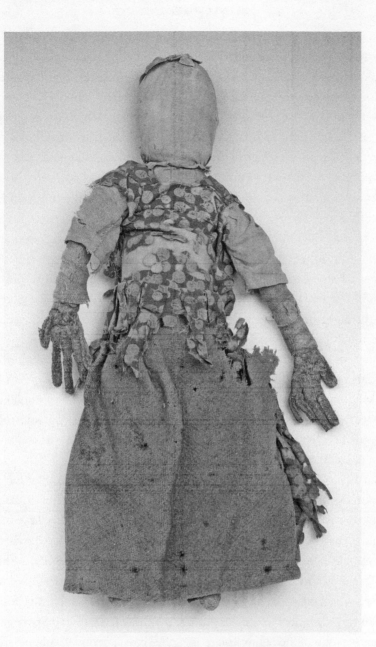

Bangwell Putt rag doll, Moses Field and unknown, ca. 1765–75, 15.25″ h ×
5.5″ w × 2.5″ d, Northfield, Massachusetts. Most children in colonial America
played with simple dolls made by their families, but these dolls were probably
too common and/or too well loved to survive more than a few decades.
Photograph courtesy of the Pocumtuck Valley Memorial Association,
Memorial Hall Museum, Deerfield, Massachusetts

and boys were taught to read in early New England, usually at home or in privately run "dame schools," akin to modern nursery schools or kindergartens, whose main function was teaching reading. But even in her opportunities for education, Esther's world was restricted.

Only boys were taught to write, and this precious skill was taught in boys-only Latin grammar schools, which were intended to train boys in skills they would need in college instruction, or in less ambitious reading-writing schools that for the most part admitted only boys. (This latter schooling is probably all that was available to Esther's brothers in Wells around 1700.) In truth, most boys received only the equivalent of a few years of elementary school education, so that they could attain some basic reading, writing, and arithmetic skills, and only elite boys were permitted to undertake advanced study in Greek and Latin in the grammar schools. Girls (and women) were permitted to be passive consumers of knowledge as readers, but through the seventeenth century and well into the eighteenth, they were not permitted to generate new knowledge as writers. This separation of reading and writing skills, and of girl and boy students, was beginning to change around the turn of the eighteenth century, although it's highly unlikely that Esther Wheelwright and her sisters would have benefited from the beginnings of this transition to full female literacy education. In any case, at the time she was taken captive at age seven, she was only just old enough to hold a quill pen.

Her first instruction in reading would probably have come at her mother's knees, her sister Hannah holding a hornbook for her to see. The hornbook was a tiny wooden paddle with a handle that held a piece of paper secured under a translucent sheet of horn—a primitive experiment in lamination, about three inches wide and four inches high. In addition to an alphabet and a basic syllabary (an early exploration of phonics, with nonsense syllables like "ab eb ib ob ub / ba be bi bo bu"), the hornbook commonly included a copy of the Lord's Prayer. Simple, durable, and inexpensive (about one penny apiece if "gilt," half a penny if "plain," in 1700), they were the primary bearers of literacy skills in early New England.[28] Girls like Hannah and Esther may have spent an hour or so reading in the morning after their chores, but at seven and nine they would have probably moved beyond hornbooks. They were at prime ages for somewhat more ideological reading material, such as inexpensively produced didactic primers or catechisms, which were thick on the ground in early New England. Catechisms were written as a dialogue between an adult instructor and a child that emphasized obedience to authority and fealty to Protestant Christianity. In the rhythm and content of the rote questions and responses, they reminded Puritan children of the limits they needed to live within, because there was only one right answer to each of these questions.[29]

One that Esther might have read, Benjamin Harris's *The Protestant tutor for children* (1685), is an instructive example. On the first page it asks, "What Religion do you profess?" and provides the correct answer, "The Christian Religion, commonly called the Protestant, in opposition to Popery." In the late seventeenth and early eighteenth centuries, with border warfare waged by and against French Canadian Catholics and their Algonquian-speaking allies, this was a vitally important lesson to teach New England children. Only one copy exists today at the American Antiquarian Society, and that one is badly worn—an indication perhaps that Harris's catechism was extremely popular and well used in its day. Esther and Hannah may also have read an old favorite, John Cotton's *Spiritual Milk for Boston Babes*, published originally in 1646 in London, but reprinted in both English and Algonquian in 1684, in 1691, and throughout the eighteenth century. Early on in the book, Cotton rehearses an important commandment for New England children to know and heed, especially little girls:

Q. *What is the fifth Commandment?*
A. HONOUR thy Father and thy Mother, that thy dayes may be long in the land, which the Lord thy God giveth thee.
Q. *Who are here meant by Father and Mother?*
A. All our Superiors whether in Family, School, Church, and common wealth.
Q. *What is the honour due unto them?*
A. Reverence[,] Obedience, and (when I am able) Recompence[30]

John Cotton was not just an author of a popular catechism but the most revered minister of New England's founding generation. Esther might not have been told the full story, but John Cotton's acquaintance with her great-grandfather Wheelwright was one of the reasons the Wheelwrights now lived at the margins of Puritan New England rather than in Boston, and why her grandfather and father became farmers, traders, and a tavernkeeper instead of Harvard-trained ministers. Her great-grandfather, also called John Wheelwright (ca. 1592–1679), emigrated with his second wife and family to Massachusetts as part of the Great Migration of religious dissenters who came to New England in the 1630s. Boston proved to be only a short-lived refuge, as he was banished in 1637 as a so-called antinomian (the equivalent today of calling someone an anarchist) in the first major theological and political crisis in the Massachusetts Bay Colony since its founding in 1630. John Wheelwright, an ordained minister, and his sister-in-law Anne Hutchinson preached and taught publicly that Boston's ministers put too much emphasis on good works over faith—a charge that recalled the initial Protestant complaints against the church of Rome. The one minister they exempted from this criticism was John Cotton, as they had come to Boston as his followers and acolytes.

It would have been difficult enough for Wheelwright to weather the accusations of theological irregularity that followed, but he at least was a man and an ordained minister, and thus authorized to preach. Just as only boys and men were taught to write, only they were permitted to speak publicly to a large audience.[31] In early New England, women were not permitted to speak publicly in meeting, let alone to lead a congregation, but Hutchinson dared to preach to men and women alike, and (most offensive of all) she and Wheelwright were popular and had attracted a sizable following in Boston. When Hutchinson proclaimed, "It is said, I will poure my Spirit upon your Daughters, and they shall prophesie, &c. If God give mee a gift of Prophecy, I may use it," New England's all-male magistracy and ministry heard that as an outrageous act of insubordination, not as the divinely inspired words of a Prophet.[32]

The spiritual leadership that Wheelwright and Hutchinson offered started to have real-world effects by the spring of 1637. Wheelwright amplified his defiant rhetoric, declaring that New England's churches were the "antichrist," and in particular criticized pastor John Wilson. Hutchinson's male followers then refused to serve in the militia in the Pequot War because Wilson was the Boston company's chaplain. This angered the ministerial establishment and proved to be the last straw for Governor John Winthrop, who banished Wheelwright and then focused his ire on Hutchinson. Cotton was then put in an awkward situation because he remained a supporter of Hutchinson, testifying on her behalf when she was brought to trial in November 1637. Cotton was unable to prevent Hutchinson's conviction and sentence of banishment. Wheelwright moved north to Exeter, New Hampshire, and Hutchinson moved south to Rhode Island, then eventually to Long Island. Wheelwright obtained a deed for land in what's now Maine in 1643, eventually receiving permission to erect a sawmill on the shores of the Ogunquit River in Wells. He did not remain long in Wells, however, because in 1643 he also petitioned Governor John Winthrop for a repeal of his sentence of banishment. After receiving Winthrop's and the General Council's blessing in 1644, he took a position as assistant minister at Hampton, Massachusetts (later Hampton, New Hampshire), in 1647, then eventually moved to Salisbury, and never again settled in Wells. In contrast, Hutchinson paid a far greater price for speaking out. In 1640 she produced a "monstrous birth," which Winthrop and her enemies in Boston seized on as evidence of her alliance with the devil. Then shortly after moving her family to Long Island in 1643, she was slain in a Native attack on her village.[33]

Some of his partisans in the Antinomian Controversy followed John Wheelwright to Exeter and then to Wells; some remained there, while others followed him on to Hampton. Two who stayed in Wells were Wheelwright's sons Joseph and Samuel, and his grandson and namesake John, Samuel's son and Esther's father, grew up there and remained to raise his family. By 1675, the descendants of John Wheelwright were still immersed in conflict, although not religious conflict among other Protestants. The following Wheelwright generations had traded religious conflict with Anglo-Americans for almost fifty years of continuous warfare with Native neighbors and their French Canadian allies.[34]

"If wee have not Imeadiate help Wee are a lost people."

Despite the dangers of living on the margins of New England, the Wheelwrights showed a remarkable commitment to Wells. Not just Samuel and the younger John Wheelwright but many of the Reverend John's grandchildren stayed to raise their families there, although it was hardly a bucolic hamlet. By moving perilously close to Wabanaki lands and the Jesuit missions on the Penobscot and Kennebec Rivers, they endangered themselves and their children for generations. At the time French and English invaders began making fishing camps and missions in coastal Maine in the early seventeenth century, Wabanaki people had been making their living for thousands of years off of the rich forests, ponds, and ocean fisheries connected by the Saco, Androscoggin, Kennebec, and Penobscot River Valleys. Wabanaki is an umbrella term encompassing a number of ethnically and linguistically related sovereign tribes that live in what is now Maine, New Brunswick, and Nova Scotia: Abenaki, Penobscot, Passamaquoddy, Maliseet, and Mi'kmaq. East of the Kennebec River, hunting, fishing, and gathering seasonal produce were the mainstays of the Wabanaki economy. Only the climate south and west of the Kennebec (now southern Maine) was suitable for the cultivation of summer crops. Politically independent but connected via kinship and friendship, Wabanaki bands of fifty to perhaps a thousand people tended to remain within the same tributary or bay, moving up country in the fall and winter, and down toward river banks and seashores in the spring and summer. As Algonquian-speaking people, they were also related linguistically and culturally to the other Algonquians along the Atlantic coast and in the interior of North America surrounding the Great Lakes to the Ohio Valley.[35]

French Jesuits had some success among the Wabanaki, establishing several missions in the seventeenth and early eighteenth centuries scattered throughout Acadia (now Maine and the Canadian provinces of New Brunswick, Nova Scotia, and Prince Edward Island). English migrants, true to their national style of colonial settlement, attempted to cultivate trade relations with the Wabanaki, but otherwise made little effort to ingratiate themselves with their new neighbors. Unlike the Jesuit fathers, Anglo-Americans never bothered to learn their languages, and unlike French fur traders, they refused to intermarry and join Wabanaki families. Thus neither the French nor the English were surprised that the Wabanaki consistently allied with the French, to the hazard of some of New England's smallest and most vulnerable settlements.[36]

At the turn of the eighteenth century, two families dominated Wells's martial, economic, and political life: the Wheelwrights and the Littlefields. In a census of the town's military readiness taken in 1711, twenty-six of the town's forty families lived in garrisons owned by men with those surnames, which together housed more than sixty percent of the entire town. The Wheelwrights alone counted 92 people within their garrisons—more than a third of Wells's 267 inhabitants and soldiers.[37] Indeed, the pages of the provincial records of these decades are filled with letters by various Wheelwrights and Littlefields and their neighbors, always begging for reinforcements. To live in Wells, Massachusetts, at the turn of the eighteenth century meant to live in constant fear of Natives who "have been Lately & are now Lurking about" and to believe that "if wee have not Imeadiate help Wee are a lost people," "faire for ruin." A steady stream of correspondence flowed from Wells to Boston as generations of Wheelwright and Littlefield men pleaded for Massachusetts to send soldiers to defend Wells.[38] Just as busily, letters flew between French governors and intendants relaying military intelligence about the state of English colonial settlements in northern New England. One French spy's report filed in 1703 at the beginning of Queen Anne's War (1702–13) reported on "la baie Ouel" (Wells Harbor), specifically noting that "there are four little forts . . . to which the families who live on this river withdrew at the beginning of the war." This spy estimated that there were no more than 20 men in the main garrison, along with their households.[39]

The French and Wabanaki made their interests in northern New England clear as early as the 1670s. What's now southern Maine (from York to Falmouth) was a major front in King Philip's War (1675–78), and English settlements there were attacked repeatedly in the summers of 1676–77 by the Wabanaki.[40] Accordingly, English settlements on the northern New England frontier became heavily militarized, and colonial records contain accounts of towns divided not by neighborhoods or salt marshes but by garrisons like John and Mary Wheelwright's. In 1690, Wells reported that it had six garrisons, or strong houses, and only four of the province's soldiers to help the householders in their defense.[41] The area was under attack again during King William's War (1688–97), and nearly all of the English settlements between Wells and Falmouth were sacked and burned. The most shocking and brutal raid happened in a town just to the south, at York. On February 5, 1692, a combined force of Wabanaki warriors and French soldiers attacked the town and laid it to waste. Estimates of casualties vary considerably, but at least forty-eight residents of York were killed, and seventy-three were taken captive. Wells was attacked too that summer, although the Wabanaki and French were distracted by the arrival of some English sloops, which drew away their fire. Queen Anne's War (1702–13) was far worse for Wells. A raid on August 10, 1703, resulted in the loss of thirty-nine friends and neighbors, including Esther Wheelwright: approximately twenty-five people were taken captive, and about fourteen killed, and the town suffered threats of regular attack throughout the war. At the end of this war in 1713, Wells was effectively the easternmost frontier of English colonial settlement in Maine, aside from a tattered remnant of a fort with just a few soldiers at Falmouth (just east of modern-day Portland).[42]

In spite of frequent attacks by French-allied Wabanaki, John Wheelwright strove for both wealth and status to ensure the well-being of his growing family, and by and large, he was a successful householder and local official. As a young man, he offered military service to the colony, beginning as a lieutenant in the militia, and then eventually earned promotion to captain, major, and finally colonel. The Wheelwright name still spoke volumes, of course. His father, Samuel, had served as a judge at county court sessions from 1692 until his death in 1700, and John served on grand and petit juries through the 1690s, including sometimes as the jury foreman. After Samuel's death, John followed in his father's footsteps as a justice of the peace from 1700 to 1732 and as a county judge from 1702 to 1729, and also served as a selectman and town clerk for forty years.[43] After 1700, he apparently didn't seek to renew his license for tavernkeeping, and turned his attention instead to town affairs and developing trade connections with the Wabanaki.[44]

The attack of 1703 wasn't the last Wabanaki attack on Wells, and remarkably, Esther's capture wasn't the only time captivity visited the Wheelwrights. In the summer of 1712, two men from the Wheelwright garrison spent a day or two in captivity. First, John Wheelwright's enslaved man Sambo was taken by the Wabanaki in July, and escaped at the end of the day. Then in September, another Wabanaki attack on the Wheelwright garrison interrupted Esther's older sister Hannah's wedding to Elisha Plaisted. The morning after the festivities, when three men from the garrison went out to look after their horses, they were attacked. Plaisted was among the townsmen who responded to the crisis, and he was taken into captivity by the fleeing Wabanaki. Hannah, who had probably shared a bed with Esther, spent a few mournful nights wondering whether the Wabanaki had taken yet another bedmate of hers forever, but fortunately, her new husband returned just a few days later.[45]

It may be difficult to understand why a family who suffered repeated attacks on their village and their own home would remain in Wells, especially because much of New England to the south and west was more thickly settled with other Anglo-American families and would remain unscathed by the wars that scorched and destroyed Native and New England families in Maine, New Hampshire, and western Massachusetts up to the eve of the American Revolution. After witnessing the deaths of children, friends, and neighbors, or watching them being taken into captivity generation after generation, why didn't the Wheelwrights leave? One reason might have been that they enjoyed status as a founding family of Wells: Samuel and his son John owned land and a sawmill and had invested years of their labor and their family's labor in the town. They probably would not have been able to enjoy the same status had they moved to one of the safer, long-settled towns in New England.

Another factor keeping the Wheelwrights in Wells may have been religious ideology. Most English colonialists believed that God intended for them to take possession of New England—after all, they reasoned, why would He have visited the Native people with terrible epidemics, and at the same time not only spared English bodies, but allowed them to flourish in New England's rocky soil?[46] By all accounts, Esther's father, John, was a devout Puritan, and men in seventeenth- and eighteenth-century New England inherited a particularly militant brand of Christianity that was built around their status as warrior husbands and fathers protecting their homes and families. They heard sermons that admonished "how much it is a Duty for men to become Expert and Valiant Souldiers: that they may be able to answer that noble Exhortation of Joab to the Souldiers of Judah, 2 Sam X 12, *That they be of good Courage, and play the men for their People and for the Cities of their God.*"[47] Believing that they served God as "valiant soldiers" even as He allowed Anglo-American families to suffer was perhaps the only thing that allowed men like Esther's father to continue in "the Cities of their God."

In the final analysis, however, remaining in Wells turned out not to be such a disastrous decision for John and Mary Snell Wheelwright because they were unusually successful in having and raising a large family of extraordinarily healthy children. Mary gave birth to eleven children, nine of whom lived to adulthood, and eight of whom had their own children, so the Wheelwright family was a smashing demographic success. By contrast, even wealthy and prominent families living in Boston faced epidemics of deadly infectious diseases and chronic tuberculosis through the eighteenth century, and accordingly suffered the loss of children on a regular basis. Life in a busy seaport city was exciting, but the concentration of people and ship traffic were also vectors for infectious disease. Recent demographic studies indicate that there was a decisive advantage to living in rural northern New England in the eighteenth century, not the least of which was avoiding the terrible measles outbreak in 1713 and a 1721 smallpox epidemic in Boston.[48]

Compare, for example, the John and Mary Wheelwright family with the families of Cotton Mather (1663–1728) and of Samuel Sewall (1652–1729), two prominent Boston ministers who were raising young families around the time of the Wheelwrights. Of the fifteen children born to Mather and his first two wives from the 1680s through the 1700s, only two outlived him; while some lived to adulthood, many more were carried off by childhood diseases or in the measles and smallpox epidemics mentioned above. Of the fourteen children born to Sewall and his wife Hannah Hull Sewall, only six lived to adulthood and only three outlived him. Boston grew tremendously in the eighteenth century, but it was clearly no healthier than at the beginning of the 1700s. Jane Franklin Mecom (1712–94), the sister of Benjamin Franklin, who was nearly two generations younger than the Wheelwrights, gave birth to twelve children in Boston from the 1720s through the 1750s. Ten survived infancy and grew to adulthood, but the chronic tuberculosis that probably killed her husband and so many of her children and grandchildren meant that Jane outlived all but one daughter and a small handful of grandchildren.[49]

By contrast, the only child of their first nine the Wheelwrights lost was Esther, and she was also their only child who, because of the path she would eventually choose, never married or had children of her own. The only infants the Wheelwrights lost were the last two, born in 1708 and 1710, when Mary was probably over forty, so it is possible that these children suffered from genetic conditions related to her advanced maternal age. Demographic studies indicate that the average number of children a woman had in early New England in these same years was 4.6, only half the size of the John and Mary Wheelwright family.[50] While John and Mary could not have known as they began their married life, in the long run, their decision to stay in Wells was a sound one in spite of its location on a volatile international border. Their family was a striking demographic success, in spite of the permanent loss of one of their children to captivity.

August 10, 1703

Where was Esther that day, August 10, 1703, when the Wabanaki attacked and took her away with them? Where did she wander off to after she finished her chores and her reading lesson with Hannah? Esther was the only member of her immediate family taken, which probably means that she wasn't inside or even close to the Wheelwright garrison. One possibility is that she was visiting her aunt Hannah Parsons, playing with her cousins and even perhaps assisting the eldest daughter, six-year-old Abigail, in looking after four-year-old William, two-year-old Hannah, and Samuel, eighteen months. Abigail escaped with her parents, but William and Samuel were killed on the spot, and Hannah, like Esther, was taken alive.[51] Because Natives in a war party usually killed only toddlers who were too big to carry and too little to keep quiet on the trail, it's strange that little Hannah Parsons survived while big brother William was killed. Perhaps Esther held tightly on to her little cousin and agreed to carry her quickly on the Wabanaki retreat, saving Hannah's life.

Another possibility is that she was visiting the Storer girls, Mary, Priscilla, and Rachel, who were also all taken in the raid, and who were near neighbors of the Parsonses', just across the King's Highway.[52] Joseph Storer kept the longest-standing "house of public Entertainment" in Wells, probably because he had a surfeit of female labor. In 1703, he had four daughters between fifteen and twenty-three, and two teenaged cousins who may have helped out. His daughter Mary had just turned eighteen earlier that summer, and her cousins Priscilla, nineteen, and Rachel, sixteen, probably seemed very grown-up and glamorous to a seven-year-old, and a seven-year-old admirer was a good excuse to take a break from their labors at home—sewing, or laundry, or perhaps stooping constantly to weed and water their garden as it reached the height of its summer bounty. Esther didn't have any teenaged sisters, so perhaps she was their little tagalong.

Maybe she found them working in their garden and planning supper, or maybe she found them outside the Storer garrison out for a walk in the woods and a gossip.[53] None of these girls would marry men from Wells, or anywhere else in New England. All three of the Storer girls taken captive that day ended up staying in Canada, converting to Catholicism, and marrying French Canadian men, the path most commonly followed by female victims of captivity who were brought to markets in Montreal or Québec and sold to the French.[54]

Although the taking of captives, especially child captives, seems like an intolerable cruelty, it made sense in terms of both Wabanaki cultural practices and their specific, pressing needs during the border wars of the late seventeenth and early eighteenth centuries. Like all eastern woodlands Natives, the Wabanaki took captives in war—in fact, the taking of live captives was more characteristic of Native warfare than killing people, as in European-style warfare. In fact, Native people were frequently appalled by the bloodiness of European-style warfare, whether as allies or enemies. Mohegan allies of the English during the Pequot War (1636–37) protested the English insistence on running down their enemies to their deaths, crying *"mach it, mach it;* that is, it is naught, it is naught, because it is too furious and flaies too many men."[55] Taking captives made more sense to Native people, because it simultaneously weakened the enemy and strengthened their numbers if the captives could be adopted into their families. Children like Esther were the likeliest candidates for adoption. Occasionally, adult male captives would be selected to endure a ritual torture and then death, and adult men and adolescent boy captives might have a finger cut off or be forced to run a gauntlet to endure a ritual beating, but after having proved themselves as men, they would be adopted after a fashion, too.

In the 1690s and early 1700s, more and more Anglo-American captives taken in the border wars were taken into Native families only temporarily, wintering over with their Wabanaki captors only until they could be brought to Montreal or Québec and sold to the French. Because the critical summer season of gathering and farming foods was interrupted in times of war, Wabanaki people had to find another way to sustain themselves, and captives were a good substitute for corn. The lively trade in captives in these decades served Wabanaki economic needs as well as Native and French political and military interests, binding them to each other as allies.

At the conclusion of each war, an effort was made to return the New England captives who wanted to go back home—but in many cases, whether they were with the Wabanaki or the French, they didn't want to return. Children especially were likely to have forgotten their natal families and New England, and even how to speak English. In their view, they were already living with their families, and regarded their families back in New England as strangers.[56]

What were the first signs that something was wrong the day that Esther and so many of her family, friends, and townspeople were taken captive? Esther was born after the attacks on Wells in 1690 and York in 1692, but she was old enough to have heard stories about them and to have been warned by her parents to find shelter in a garrison at the first sign of trouble. Were the Wabanaki quiet, or did they announce their arrival in town with a chilling war cry? Did Esther hear gunshots, or just the sickening, wet thud of a war club meeting flesh and bone? Did she try to hide, or run away, or did she grimly submit to captivity? We don't know exactly what happened during the attack that day—all we have to reconstruct the events are a few letters describing the damage the town sustained, and lists of people killed or marched away by the Wabanaki. The most dramatic event in the lives of the people of Wells at the turn of the eighteenth century is unrecorded in any significant detail.

Thus we are left with Esther at age seven, at a critical dividing point in a child's life. Most Anglo-American children faced transitions from play to work and school life around this age, and boys anyway were permitted the freedom of breeches and of no longer wearing stays. But Esther was now faced with a series of harder choices and more wrenching transitions: Would she try to run away from the Wabanaki, or see what awaited her whenever they got where they were going? Would she be adopted, as she knew so many children had been, or would they trade her away immediately? Should she try to learn their language, or resist accommodation to their culture? Although she couldn't have known it, Esther was fortunate that her age and sex gave her these choices. She probably would be adopted and loved like a natural child, and she was young enough that membership in a Wabanaki family would have helped her forget the pain and fear of losing her New England family. Her seven-year-old brain, still mastering spoken English and learning to read English letters, was plastic and highly capable of learning new languages and new ideas rapidly. Whether she was awkwardly holding Hannah Parsons and trying to stop her crying and keep up with the others, or whether one of the Storer girls was holding her hand and comforting her as they made their way quickly northeast of Wells, we know one thing for sure, something Esther herself couldn't have known: she was never coming back.[57]

CHAPTER TWO

MALI AMONG THE WABANAKI

The Norridgewock Wabanaki

The morning she awoke in Norridgewock after her long journey, Esther would have first been aware of the presence of other children sleeping in the dwelling with her. Because of her age and sex, she would have lived with a Wabanaki family from the start. Waking up with a Wabanaki family was probably not too much different from waking up with her family in New England: there were probably at least five or six other people who shared the wigwam with her—adults and children, and more than likely, a few dogs. The woven straw mat she slept on would have felt cooler, smoother, and harder than the straw mattress and linen sheets she left behind in Wells, but she probably shared a blanket with another child, just as she had shared her covers with her sister Hannah. Smoke would have permeated the indoor space so strongly that even in late August, without a lighted fire in the center, the walls, mats, and blankets the Wabanaki family shared would still have smelled heavily of wood smoke. Then again, her new family may have left a few logs smoldering all night long in spite of the heat, because the smoke was useful in driving away biting and stinging insects like black flies, mosquitoes, and fleas. The same sounds of coughing, scratching, rolling over, sniffling, and sighing would have reminded her of waking up in the Wheelwright home in Wells.[1]

Most Euro-Americans probably would have viewed the sleeping arrangements inside an eighteenth-century Wabanaki wigwam as a jumble of tangled mats, people, blankets, and dogs, but it was in fact a highly regulated space. Although she would have been liberated from the stays that bound her body under her English clothing, Esther would soon learn that there were just as many rules for Wabanaki bodies both inside and outside the dwelling, and this etiquette was divided along lines that Esther would have recognized immediately. For example, proximity to the fire, and the posture and placement of one's body whether awake or asleep, was determined by a person's sex, age, and status. Esther would have been shown to her mat and told in which direction to lay her head by one of her new Wabanaki sisters.[2] She probably figured out the working order of her new home and what she was expected to contribute to it fairly quickly, because although it may have seemed very strange at first, there were powerful similarities to the ordering of her home in Wells. Life inside the Wheelwright garrison was also highly regulated along the lines of age, sex, and status. In some ways, it was a short journey to the mission village the Wabanaki called Narantsouak, and the New Englanders called Norridgewock, more than a hundred miles north and east of Wells on the Kennebec River.

In other respects, of course, she was a world away from her home with the Wheelwrights. Esther became a part of a Catholic Wabanaki community that had ties to the missions of Sillery and St. Francis in the Québec suburbs and to the new mission at Odanak nearly two hundred miles up the St. Lawrence River, the great river into the heart of Canada. For more than sixty years mission priests had come to Narantsouak and gone, and the village frequently decamped for the missions on the St. Lawrence River more than two hundred miles away depending on the courses of epidemic diseases and warfare with New England for the previous forty years.[3] Norridgewock by the turn of the eighteenth century was less a fixed physical location than it was the name of a Wabanaki band composed mostly of Eastern Abenakis who were also called the Kinnibeki by the

French (after their location on the Kennebec River), the Canada Indians (probably because of their frequent flights to the St. Lawrence missions), or just Norridgewocks.

The frequent and wide-ranging moves of the Norridgewock Wabanaki were due entirely to the pressures of colonialism after European invasion a century earlier. Historical and archaeological evidence suggests that the village itself had relocated from the western to the eastern side of the Kennebec sometime in the 1690s, and that it was deserted shortly after Esther's arrival in the late summer of 1703 because Queen Anne's War (1702–13) made life in mission towns in what is now Maine—those nearest English colonial towns—very dangerous. This was perhaps especially true for a band of Wabanaki harboring recently taken Anglo-American captives like Esther Wheelwright. The deserted town of Norridgewock and its chapel, schoolhouse, and twelve wigwams were looted of "a few Household Utensils of little value" and "a few old Popish Relicks" before it was burned to the ground by New England volunteer soldiers in 1705. Therefore Esther's acquaintance with that particular location, if any, was brief indeed. Her new family was much safer on the move than at a fixed location.[4]

Although not continuous in the lives of the Norridgewock Wabanaki, the letters and sacramental records left by Jesuit missionaries Jacques and Vincent Bigot offer us a window into the world where Esther lived for five years, from ages seven to twelve. Frustratingly, however, none of the records they left behind mention Esther by name, and she appears not to have attracted much notice before her arrival in Québec in 1708. In his sermon at Esther's clothing ceremony at the Ursuline convent in 1714, Father Vincent claimed that it was "la divine Providence" that rescued Esther from both Protestant heresy and Native savagery, but the letters documenting his and his brother Jacques's work in missions in Quebec and Acadia over twenty years suggest that it wasn't Jesuit leadership or divine Providence that turned Esther Wheelwright into a pious Catholic girl.[5] It was Wabanaki women who initiated Esther in the beliefs and ritual practices of the church, which were of course modified and experienced in their particular context in Wabanakia in the late seventeenth and early eighteenth centuries. Wabanaki women were also a more continuous presence in the lives of their mobile families and communities, more continuous than the mission priests who moved around almost as frequently as the Wabanaki themselves. Esther wasn't a Catholic with a French teacher and confessor—at least, not yet. As with everything else she learned in Wabanakia, Esther was initiated into Catholicism by women first.[6]

The journey from Wells of at least 120 miles northeast to Norridgewock on the Kennebec River would have taken a minimum of a week over land. Even with canoes hidden carefully on the banks of the Saco and Androscoggin Rivers and numerous other rivers and streams, the journey would have been relentless and exhausting. As soon as the Wabanaki got Esther out of reach of immediate English recapture that first day, they took away her English shoes (if indeed she had been wearing any—her mother may have permitted her to go barefoot that day in August) and gave her small moccasins, which were more comfortable and more practical for walking long distances. We can't know for sure, but it's almost certain that at age seven, she would have been expected to march the entire distance on her own two feet. Her captors would have tried to move the party as quickly as possible, so that they could evade capture by New England volunteers and return in time for the autumn hunt. John Gyles, a New England boy of about nine from Pemaquid, taken captive by the Wabanaki in 1689, reported that a canoe journey of about 150 miles from the English colonial settlement at Pemaquid eastward up the Penobscot River to the village of "Madawamkee" took only "a few days," which suggests how much speedier canoe travel was compared to overland journeys. Gyles was able to go by canoe because Pemaquid was the easternmost English settlement when he was taken in 1689, so coastal travel eastward from there was quite safe for his captors.[7]

It's possible that Esther's captors fled Wells by canoe the whole way along the coast, but traveling by water would have been risky for Wabanaki fleeing eastward from Wells, where they might have been sighted by inhabitants of other Anglo-American villages. Esther's captors probably would have taken advantage of the thick forests of southern Maine to provide cover for their flight, although it meant a longer and more exhausting journey for everyone, especially for small children like Esther. If she was sometimes carrying little Hannah Parsons and trying to jolly her into walking alongside her occasionally, the trip would have been even more wearying.

"The village was truly an infirmary"

Fleeing with captives was a challenging feat for captors and captives alike. Because war parties typically traveled light, carrying just a few bags of cornmeal that they could either consume dry or cook into a porridge, they often resorted to eating what they could forage or hunt down quickly while in flight. Father Sebastien Râle, the long-standing Jesuit missionary at Norridgewock at the turn of the eighteenth century, tells a story that sheds light on how the Wabanaki survived on the run without supplies. In one of his letters, he writes of fleeing the village in a hurry in midwinter because New England soldiers had been sighted "at the distance of half a day's journey." The English repeatedly attacked Norridgewock, and this incident probably took place during their 1722 expedition. "'Our Father,' said [the Wabanaki], 'there is no time to lose; thou must go away.'" He and his guides took only a few days' worth of provisions, and when they had eaten them all, they killed a dog that had followed them and ate it. While dogs were not an everyday food source, they were consumed in a variety of different everyday and ritual circumstances in Iroquois and most Algonquian communities. John Gyles reported that his Wabanaki captors ate dog frequently, because "the Indians imagine that Dog's Flesh makes them bold and courageous!" He details a prewar feast of a dog stew and ritual use of the dog's head in inciting the men of the community to go to battle: "When the Chief hath Sung, he so places the Dog's Head as to grin at him whom he supposeth will go his Second: who, if he accepts, takes the Head in his Hand and sings, but if he refuse to go, he turns the Teeth to another; and thus from one to another 'till they have inlisted their Company." Perhaps this dog feast fortified Râle's protectors' spirits as well as their bodies.[8]

After the dog was consumed, they had only leather goods and plant materials found in the winter woods on this particular flight. Râle said the Wabanaki ate the "sealskin pouches" that presumably had held their supplies, but since he could not choke down the cooked leather bags, he ate instead "a kind of wood which they boiled, and which when cooked is as tender as half-cooked radishes." Sometimes he and the Wabanaki shared "certain excrescences of wood" on trees "which are as white as large mushrooms: these are cooked and reduced to a sort of porridge." Other times they ate green oak bark that had been dried, pounded, and made into a porridge. When they returned to Norridgewock, Râle says that he fell upon a store of uncooked cornmeal at his house, "and I ate of it, wholly uncooked as it was, to appease my pressing hunger" after this desperate, impromptu camping trip.[9]

Esther's party would probably have found more and better edibles in the Maine woods in August than Râle's party found in winter—for example, the seasonal offerings may have included wood sorrel leaves from the forest floors, and watercress and river beauty near streams. If they were truly fortunate, there might have been ripe berries—bunchberries, creeping snowberry, bearberry, wild raisins, gooseberries, currants, blueberries, and cloudberries, all of which are in season in late summer. Even with the refreshment of ripe berries where they found them, it would have been a hard and hungry living for everyone in the fleeing party, given the miles they had to travel every day. Once they arrived at their destination, if they were fortunate their bellies were filled. John Gyles's captivity narrative describes the Wabanaki diet at the end of the seventeenth century as that of semisedentary agriculturalists typical of other Algonquian-speaking peoples on the Atlantic seaboard: built around the cultivation of corn and beans, gathered plant foods, and fish in the spring and summer, and supplemented richly by autumn and winter hunts of deer and feasts of moose and bear meat.[10] Esther and her fellow travelers might have looked forward to a corn and bean pottage or bread made of green corn, perhaps accompanied by roasted salmon or mackerel.[11]

On the other hand, they might have looked in vain for such a welcoming meal in 1703. At that point in time, the Wabanaki had been exposed to Europeans and their deadly pathogens for nearly a century. Maine and Acadia lost perhaps 75 percent of their precontact population in the great smallpox epidemic of 1616–19, which devastated Algonquian-speaking peoples from the Penobscot River to Cape Cod. Other highly contagious diseases, too, recurred through the seventeenth century, further weakening the survivors of earlier epidemics with new bouts of hepatitis, measles, plague, cholera, and whooping cough. From the 1620s on, the Wabanaki found themselves increasingly pressed between French claims to the north and east, and English colonial settlements to the south and west, complicated by Mohawk raids and the growing alliance between the English and the Iroquois nations (which included the Mohawks). Twenty-five years of almost uninterrupted warfare from King William's War (1688–97) to the end of Queen Anne's War in 1713 caused a great deal of hardship among the Wabanaki who lived in mission towns in Acadia, so the plenty and variety of harvest foods that John Gyles found in the late 1680s and early 1690s may not have been in evidence in 1703. Disease and warfare were both vicious cycles that weakened their survivors and made it difficult for populations to recover—even more so when they struck in tandem.

Much of the evidence we have from the years immediately before Esther Wheelwright was taken suggests that Wabanaki mission towns in Quebec and Acadia were less havens for the living than refuges for the hungry, sick, and dying. For example, in a 1699 letter from the Acadian mission at Naurakamig, Jacques Bigot wrote that because the village "ha[d] been but recently established, I must confess that I had to endure some discomfort as regards lodging and food." Even if the Wabanaki had not themselves been victims of warfare directly in a given year, their wary mobility between mission towns would have prevented them from planting, tending, and harvesting crops according to the seasons. Later in the letter, Bigot noted that he had accompanied the Wabanaki in the fall of 1699 on a journey to treat with New England authorities. Father Jacques wrote, "The journey fatigued me greatly; and, moreover, we were almost without food on account of the bad weather. I had brought a little with me; but, on the very first night, a Christian who had a good appetite ate the leathern bag in which I had put it, and did not spare the contents. We regale ourselves with oysters, which we procure when the tide is low; that is, indeed, all that we have had to eat for some time." These comments about the scarcity of food are especially disturbing considering that Father Jacques reported arriving in the village "on the vigil of the Nativity of the Blessed Virgin" in early September, in what should have been the harvest season and a time of relative plenty. War was a plague that visited many harvests in this period: when New England soldiers attacked and burned Norridgewock in February of 1705, they reported that near the village "was a Field of Corn ungathered, which may be imputed to the Enemy's desertion by the consternation that seized them at the Ransacking of the Eastern French & Indian Settlements the last Summer."[12] If oystering was their primary means of provisioning themselves, Father Jacques and his Wabanaki hosts were facing a desperate starving year.

When hunger turned to malnutrition, the results were deadly, especially for babies and growing children like Esther. Father Vincent Bigot reported from one of the Wabanaki missions in early autumn 1701, "We had all last winter a large number of women and young children all sick with scurvy" so widespread that "the village was truly an infirmary."[13] These shocking accounts of scurvy among agriculturalists suggests that the privations of the flight into captivity might not have ended for Esther upon her arrival in Norridgewock. Scurvy, a vitamin C deficiency that attacks soft tissue, was much more common among sailors in this period because of the absence of fresh fruits and vegetables in a seafaring diet. That the Wabanaki on dry land were watching their children languish and die of scurvy means that chronic hunger and disease were a fact of Wabanaki life at the turn of the eighteenth century.[14] They came to mission towns not because the priests had food or medicine, but because they offered baptism, and with it the hope that their families might be reunited in heaven after death. For the generations of Wabanaki people who came of age suffering from the pressures and dislocations of colonialism, and for parents who had already lost a child or children to disease or malnutrition, it was a desperate comfort to know that if they and their remaining children were baptized, all might not be lost.[15]

One of the few stories to be told in New England specifically about the captives taken from Wells in 1703 illustrates the hardship of the journey for captors and their captives alike. Perhaps unsurprisingly, it revolves around extreme hunger. This gruesome and undoubtedly embellished tale of would-be cannibalism may have its origins in a scene that Esther herself could have witnessed. The chronicler in this case was clearly not an eyewitness to the story he reported. Cotton Mather was a Puritan preacher and one of the most energetic writers of his day. He pumped out anti-Native screeds and pro-war propaganda from the comfort of his home in Boston. In a hastily slapped-together pamphlet about the attacks on Wells in 1703 and on Deerfield the following February called *Good Fetch'd out of Evil*, Mather wrote that "a Crue of Indians had been Three Days without any manner of sustenance [after fleeing Wells with captives in tow]. They took an English Child, and hung it before the Fire to rost it for their Supper . . . they would Roast it *Alive*." There is little evidence that any eastern Algonquians like the Wabanaki ever practiced cannibalism—either ritually, or for nutrition even in situations of extreme privation. Mather's story seems to be a willful misreading of this encounter, if indeed it ever happened at all. Moreover, a live child delivered to Québec or Montreal would surely have brought a ransom that might have fed an entire village for a week. Mather went on to explain that "[a] Cannoe arrived at that Instant, with a *Dog* in it. The *Lesser-Devils* of the Crue, proposed their taking the *Dog* instead of the *Child;* They did so; And the Child is *yet Living!* Her Name is, *Hannah Parsons.*"[16] Yes—the same little cousin that Esther Wheelwright might have been visiting when Wells was attacked, and the same Hannah Parsons whose life Esther might have saved by carrying her along the trail. As we have seen, dog meat was both an everyday food and one with ritual significance in wartime especially, so it's likely that the Wabanaki would have consumed the dog they traded her for.

The source for (and legitimacy of) Mather's story is unknown, although many Wells captives eventually came home again. But neither Hannah Parsons nor Esther could have been Mather's source: as Mather reported correctly, Hannah survived her journey into captivity, but like Esther and so many other New England girls, she remained in Canada and never returned to Wells or saw her natal family again. At some point, if not on this very river bank, Esther's and Hannah's paths diverged, as Hannah appears to have been brought directly to the mission town of Sault-au-Recollet, and her baptism was recorded at Ville Marie near Montreal seventeen months after her capture. The priest who baptized her, Father Henri-Antoine Meriel, wrote in the record, "The name of Hannah, which she had in her country without having been there baptized, has been changed to that of Catherine, to which the savages add the surname of [Tsiosenneco]." The woman who sponsored her baptism was a Native woman, Hélène Tekaeronta of Sault-au-Recollet, who may have become Hannah/Catherine's mother. Like most adopted captives who were baptized as Catholics, Catherine appears not to have stayed in the mission town past girlhood. A twelve-year-old "Catherine Parsons" of Montreal became a naturalized citizen of New France, but beyond that, her adolescence and young adulthood is a mystery. At the age of twenty-eight, she married a titled military officer and son of an important judge, Claude-Antoine de Berman, and she gave birth to ten children over the next sixteen years.[17]

A critical reading of Mather's shocking story suggests that by the turn of

the eighteenth century the practice of taking captives was less about inflicting pain on the encroaching English colonial settlements than it was about
basic survival and the maintenance of mutually beneficial economic, diplomatic, and military ties between the French and the Wabanaki and other
Native allies.[18] (Although if it had the effect of discouraging further Anglo-
American migration and expansion, so much the better.) Like so many
colonial practices, the taking of captives started out as a Native institution
whose purpose and goals were redirected to serve the needs of the new
colonial world of shifting alliances with European as well as Native trade
partners and allies. Captivity was a military tactic that long predated European contact in the northeastern borderlands, and in fact taking war
captives appears to have been a greater goal than killing warriors on the
battlefield. Captivity served both to deplete the numbers of one's enemies
and to enhance the strength in numbers of one's own tribe or nation. This
was still a major goal of captivity as practiced by the Wabanaki in the early
eighteenth century, but because many captives were no longer adopted by
Wabanaki families but rather traded to their French allies for money and
supplies, captives were in fact a substitute cash crop for Native people
whose villages lay between the St. Lawrence River valley and the rapidly
expanding borders of English colonial settlement. When we consider that
the growing season and the season of warfare almost exactly overlapped—
mid-spring to early autumn—the urgency of taking captives to trade for
cash and supplies becomes even clearer, because people living in war zones
can't count on being able to plant, maintain, and harvest their crops according to schedule.

Harvesting captives instead of corn and trading them to the French served
everyone's interests but those of the captives themselves, and their families
that were left behind: the Wabanaki enhanced their status as French allies
and benefited economically from the exchange, and the French strengthened their ties to the Wabanaki, whom they could rely on to attack the
English colonial towns and settlements that threatened to encroach upon
the mission towns they had already established in Maine.[19] But, only some
captives were traded—many, especially children, were adopted into Wabanaki families, perhaps to take the place of a child who had died. With
Wabanaki families in tatters because of the ravages of warfare, disease, and

starvation, a child like Esther may have presented a Wabanaki family with the opportunity to be restored.

Becoming Wabanaki

Just as fairy tales like "Hansel and Gretel" evoke the mystery and fears of the Black Forest for Europeans, Wabanaki folklore is clearly rooted in the northeastern woodlands of North America. The protagonist in many Wabanaki stories is a young hero named Gluskap who fights the forces that together represent the antithesis of humanity and nature: cannibalism and winter. Many of these stories turn on the transformative power of human communities to turn outsiders, and even hostile enemies, into insiders through hospitality and generosity. These stories may have had special resonance among the Wabanaki of Acadia from 1688 through 1713, twenty-five years of nearly uninterrupted warfare. There are several variations on the story of a Windigo, a cannibal giant, who comes to call at a Wabanaki wigwam. He is received with generosity and warmth, treated like a kins-man instead of a monster, and thereby is transformed into a human being. This Wabanaki belief in the ability to turn strangers into kin was clearly fundamental to their embrace of captives, who like the Windigo were ini-tially hostile outsiders but were gradually transformed into family mem-bers.[20] Moreover, Wabanaki hospitality was something women offered to strangers—food, clothing, and a place near a warm fire.

When Esther and the rest of the war party arrived at Norridgewock, the women of the community would have come out to greet the captives, be-cause they played a key role in deciding their fates. When eastern wood-lands Natives returned to their villages after a battle with captives in tow, women were responsible for deciding which captives would be adopted, which might be tortured a little beforehand, and occasionally, which of them might be ritually executed. Women and girl captives were spared the pain and suffering of ritual torture and execution—only men ever experi-enced those more terrible fates. Unfortunately, Esther Wheelwright never published a captivity narrative describing her experiences among the Wa-banaki, and if she ever wrote anything about it, no record of her experi-ence of captivity survives. But, John Gyles's experiences at Madawamkeag

fourteen years earlier records in some detail the Maliseet welcoming ceremony that greeted the returning war party with their captives, and documents the central role that women played: "I expected some kind Treatment
here: but soon found my self deceived, for I presently saw a Number of
Squaws got together in a Circle dancing and yelling; and an old grimace-
Squaw took me by the Hand, and lead me to the Ring, where the other
Squaws seiz'd me by the Hair of my Head, and by my Hands and Feet, like
so many Furies." But, Gyles says, at that moment "my Indian Master presently laid down a Pledge and releas'd me." He goes on to explain that "a
Captive among the Indians is exposed to all manner of Abuse, and to the
utmost Tortures; unless his Master, or some of his Master's Relations, lay
down a Ransom, such as a Bag of Corn, or a Blanket, or such like: by
which they may redeem them from their Cruelties for that Dance, so that
he shall not be touch'd by any."[21]

Throughout his narrative, Gyles makes it clear that Wabanaki women
took a leading role in hazing and sorting out war captives—some were destined for adoption, others for torture, and some would be sold to the French
or to other Native groups. Shortly after the ceremony at Madawamkeag,
he was brought to Medoctack Fort (now Woodstock, New Brunswick) on
the St. John's River, where he received harsher treatment. At first, he was
welcomed by "two or three Squaws [who] met us, took off my Pack, and
led me to a large Hutt or Wigwam, where Thirty or Forty Indians were
dancing and yelling round five or six poor Captives, who had been taken
some Months before." He reports that he was "whirl'd in among them,"
and described a variety of tortures to which they might subject boys and
men: "Sometimes an old shrivell'd Squaw will take up a Shovel of hot
Embers and throw them into a Captive's Bosom; and if he cry out, the
other Indians will Laugh and Shout, and say, What a brave Action our old
Grandmother has done!" Other forms of nonlethal torture were beatings
(including at the hands of a gauntlet of Native men beating the captive
with war clubs), and even being shaken upside down "'till one would think
his Bowels would shake out of his Mouth." Gyles was himself again saved
from any torture by the actions of "a Squaw and a little girl," who "laid
down a Bag of Corn in the Ring; the little Girl took me by the hand, making Signs for me to go out of the Circle with them," according to the tradition of captive redemption he had experienced at Madawamkeag. At

another stop along his journey, he reports that "an old Squaw saluted me with a Yell, taking me by the Hair and one Hand; but I was so rude as to break her hold and 'quit myself:—She gave me a filthy Grin, and the Indians set up a Laugh—so it pass'd over."[22]

Perhaps women were so instrumental in making decisions about captives because it was they who would have been responsible for clothing them, feeding them, and educating many of them in Wabanaki ways. Married Wabanaki women (like Anglo-American women) were responsible for ensuring that their households ran smoothly and that the needs of everyone in the household were met.[23] Most captives were ritually stripped of their English clothing and then re-dressed in Native garments, which by the late seventeenth century included European or Euro-American-made wool blankets and linen shirts or shifts. These were worn by both sexes and all ages, in addition to traditional aprons, wraps, and leggings made of deerskin. The hair of male captives may have been cut or plucked, and their skin painted or tattooed. So too, their bodily movements and utterances were remolded to match their new appearances: singing and dancing were a central aspect of Wabanaki captivity rituals. Gyles wrote that "when any great Number of Indians meet, or when any Captives have been lately taken, or when any Captives desert and are retaken, the Indians have a Dance." For the captives, however, these dances were sometimes another form of torture. Gyles recalled his own experience with dancing for the Wabanaki: "Three or four Indians drag'd me to the great Wigwam, where they were yelling and dancing round [another captive]. . . . They soon came to me, & tossed me about till I was almost breathless, & then threw me into the Ring to my fellow Captive." After a while, "I was hal'd out again by three Indians, by the Hair of my Head, and held down by it, till one beat me on the Back & Shoulders so long that my Breath was almost beat out of my Body. And then others put a Tomhake into my Hand, and order'd me get up and dance and sing Indian: which I perform'd with the greatest reluctance." (Unfortunately for Gyles, his master and mistress had gone to Canada, and weren't available to intervene to protect him as they had in the past—his tormentors were "Cape Sable" or Mi'kmaqs, not the community of Maliseets that took him in.)[24]

As a girl of only seven, Esther would not have been subjected to the public trials and rituals that greeted Gyles. Her Wabanaki mistress—perhaps the

James Peachey, *A Plan of the Inhabited Part of the Province of Quebec*, ca. 1785 (detail).
This watercolor illustrates the ways in which Wabanaki and French colonial
material culture were combined by Wabanaki people in distinctive ways. The
hood on the woman on the left is of distinctive Wabanaki style, and was probably made of red wool trade cloth and decorated with embroidery and glass or
metal beads.
Library and Archives Canada, acc. no. R9266-334, Peter Winkworth Collection
of Canadiana

woman who became her mother—would have performed a much gentler
initiation into Esther's new way of life. She would have taken off Esther's
woolen skirt or petticoat, her stays, and her shift in private. Her filthiness
might have shocked the Wabanaki woman—after all, Europeans and
Euro-Americans in the seventeenth and eighteenth centuries thought it
unhealthy and perhaps even dangerous to bathe by immersing their bodies,
whereas Native people commonly indulged in cold-water baths in ponds,
lakes, rivers, and streams. So Esther's new mother or big sisters might have
first insisted that she bathe, and then that her body be rubbed with the bear
grease that Wabanaki people used as an emollient and that may have
soothed or offered some protection from insect bites. She was then probably

Desrais del.   Mixelle sculp.

femme Acadienne.

Jean Marie Mixelle, after Claude Louis Desrais, *Femme Acadienne*, from Costumes
civils actuels de tous les peuples connus, accompagnés d'une notice historique
sur les costumes, moeurs, religions, etc., 1787. This Wabanaki or Métis Acadian
woman wears European cloth and clothing in a distinctive hybrid style.
Picture Collection, New York Public Library, Astor, Lenox
and Tilden Foundations

dressed again, given a shift or other woven shirt worn loose, and probably little else since it was still August. Her mother may have had a skin apron or woolen blanket, moccasins, and snowshoes ready for her use come autumn and winter. By the turn of the eighteenth century, Wabanaki women's clothing was a mixture of European cloth and clothing and traditional moose- and deerskin garments, and frequently decorated in a distinctive fashion. Women's woolen hoods or peaked caps were cut in a distinctive style and elaborately decorated with ribbons, beads, and colorful needlework. Women and men alike wore trade silver brooches, rings, earrings, cuffs, and medals along with Wabanaki-made copper beads.[25]

All of these rituals—singing and dancing, stripping and re-dressing, cutting hair, applying tattoos and body paints, and even cutting, mutilation, and savage beatings—were ritual practices focused on the body: its movements, its voice, its presentation, and its sensations. In the absence of a shared language, eastern woodlands Native rituals for captives seem to have been designed to turn outsiders' bodies into insiders' bodies from the outside in, perhaps so as to bind them more effectively to their new families.[26] These physical sensations and ordeals were probably highly effective in teaching captives the ways of Wabanaki life and the roles they were expected to play in their new families. Language would come more slowly, but learning to dress, sing, move, and sit like a Wabanaki was a good place for most captives to start. One bit of language may have been given to her shortly after her arrival, as she was undoubtedly renamed. Esther, with its hard *r*-finish, is a name that would not have sounded right or been pronounced easily by either Wabanaki- or French-speaking peoples. In the late seventeenth and early eighteenth centuries, most Catholic Wabanaki women who were baptized seem to have been named either Catherine (as Hannah Parsons was) or Marie—although they pronounced Marie as "Mali," like the English name Molly, because in fact, there is no *r*-sound in Wabanaki. At this point in the story, Esther becomes Mali for the time being.[27]

Because most captives (like Mali and John Gyles) were taken in the late summer or early autumn, they had to spend at least several months living among the Wabanaki, usually until the following spring, after the rivers were freed of their ice and the hazards of winter travel in Maine and Quebec had passed.[28] Even those who weren't destined for permanent adoption would have had to learn how to live like a Wabanaki girl or boy at least until they could be sold in the town of Québec or Montreal, and to perform work suitable to their age and sex. As in the Wheelwright garrison in Wells, work was the most visible distinction between men and women, although in Norridgewock, there were few finished products that were produced solely by one sex or the other. Traditional Wabanaki gendered divisions of labor were complementary and the work collaborative in some respects: Women planted corn after men had cleared their fields. Men hunted for meat, and women processed it either by cooking it for immediate consumption or by cutting it into thin strips and drying it for storage. Men built the frames for canoes and snowshoes, but women stitched the birch bark rind and knotted the webbing on snowshoes. In peacetime, Mali would probably have been expected to help her Wabanaki mother and sisters in the late summer corn, squash, and bean fields, and with the work of the harvest— not just picking vegetables, but the arduous task of processing crops so that they would help sustain the community through the winter and spring. Boiling, scraping, and drying corn, shucking and drying beans, and storing them in bark-lined underground caches would have been their primary tasks in September and October. Little girls would have been expected to help with these major tasks, but they were also probably useful for chasing away birds and picking worms from stalks of ripening corn.[29]

As in Wells, Mali probably was old enough to help her Wabanaki mother prepare and serve food too, when they had enough to eat—and the daily fare probably looked reasonably familiar to Mali. Gyles said that a typical meal was "Fish, Flesh, or Indian Corn and Beans boil'd together—, or Hasty-Pudden made of pounded Corn," both of which sound remarkably similar to the boiled cereals either made savory with meat and vegetables or sweetened and enriched with milk, raisins, and spice that Anglo-American women served for breakfasts and suppers. It's unlikely she would have eaten much bear or moose meat in Wells. She may have acquired a taste for moose and bear quickly, since it probably wouldn't have been long before her family left for the late autumn and winter hunt.[30] But, because so many Wabanaki missions appear to have been so starved and desperate around the time of Mali's capture and adoption, we must assume that the agricultural and hunting calendars of Maine and Acadia in the eighteenth century were severely disrupted. This description of Wabanaki foodways may represent a best-case scenario that wasn't representative of Mali's diet during Queen Anne's War.

Work was perhaps the most obvious manifestation of gender differences in Wabanaki communities, but it was hardly the only one. Not only were Wabanaki work roles for men and women complementary, but sex segregation at different times played a role both in preserving complementarity and in performing difference. While whole families would go on the hunt together, and women prepared the meat for both consumption and storage, traditional Wabanaki sex segregation seems to have revolved around hunting, eating, and reproduction, three interconnected activities involving death and life that were centrally important to the health and livelihood of a band or tribe. For example, Wabanaki women practiced menstrual seclusion because of the belief that fertile women harbored destructive power during their menses. A menstruating woman could sap a hunter's power by serving food to him, touching his weapons, or simply looking him in the eye. As blood rituals, hunting and menstruation were linked, the one taking life and the other central to giving life. Although we might find hunting to be the more dangerous and disruptive activity, colonial-era Wabanaki believed that menstruation too was a powerful experience, and they exercised great caution lest a woman's blood ritual threaten a hunter's potency. During menstruation, women retreated into rituals and prayers taught them by their elders in an effort to mitigate the potentially destabilizing effects their bodies could have on their communities.[31] Mali was too young for menarche, but she surely noticed that older girls and women separated themselves from the community during their periods. Having lived with a mother and women servants and slaves, she was likely familiar with menstruation, and would probably have seen stained linen rags put in the last of the dirty wash water and hung up to dry in the Wheelwright garrison in Wells. Wabanaki and English menstrual traditions both hid and revealed this function of women's bodies, although in different ways.[32]

Menstruating women had to be kept apart not just from hunters but from warriors as well. All of the corrupting powers of menstrual blood could disarm warriors as it could hunters—and with more immediately dire results for the community. Since Mali lived among the Wabanaki in wartime, perhaps the most obvious aspect of sex segregation after menstrual seclusion was the withdrawal of warriors from the community. But even in peacetime, Wabanaki men retreated into other forms of segregated sociality, although their gatherings sound considerably more festive and convivial than women's menstrual seclusion.

The men of the community gathered separately from the women and children when a feast was given, and although women cooked the food, they were not the first to taste the feast they had prepared. The Wabanaki observed an elaborate order of service that reveals a great deal about Wabanaki hierarchies of gender, age, and authority, and once again a cautious regard for women's fertility. "An Indian boils four or five large Kettles full," John Gyles observed, "and sends a Messenger to each Wigwam-Door; who exclaims, *Kub Menscoorebab!* i.e. *I come to conduct you to a feast:* The Man within demands whether he must take, a Spoon, or a Knife in his Dish which he always carries with him." Gender was not the only operative variable in the choreography of a feast—age too was important, since according to Gyles, the men of the community were served first by other, younger men: "They appoint two or three Young Men to Mess it out, to each Man his Portion according to the number of his Family at Home; which is done with the utmost exactness. When they have done eating, a young Fellow stands without the Door, and crys aloud *Menscommook,* Come & fetch!" After the men have eaten from the portion for their entire family, "each Squaw goes to her Husband and takes what he has left, which she carries Home and eats with her Children. For neither married women nor any Youth under twenty Years of Age are allowed to be present" at the feast. Mali would have eaten with her mother and siblings inside their wigwam.

After the remaining food was distributed, "the Indian men continue in the Wigwam, some relating Warlike Exploits; others something Comical; others give a Narrative of their Hunting; the Seniors give maxims of Prudence and grave Counsels to the Young Men." There was a clear etiquette that guided the order and reception of these speeches. Gyles writes, "tho' every ones Speech be agreeable to the run of his own Fancy, yet they confine themselves to Rule, and but one speaks at a Time. After every Man has told his Story, One rises up, Sings a Feast-Song, and others succeed alternately as the Company see fit." While sex and age were clearly the central means by which each community member found his or her place in a feast, status was also important. Most fascinating is the fact that some people in these communities didn't fit clearly into one category or the other because of their age or their status as outsiders: "Old Widow-squaws and Captive Men" were permitted to "set by the Door," while inside the Wabanaki men continued their segregated meeting. Both captive foreign men and post-menopausal women were seen as a third sex, deserving of proximity to the men without all of the privileges of full manhood. The placement of post-menopausal women at the door of the men's feast furnishes more detail about Wabanaki menstrual seclusion, and suggests that they were interested in regulating not all women but fertile women in particular. The liminal position of captive men and older women—neither at the feast with the adult men nor in a wigwam with the women and children—symbolized their gender ambiguity.[33]

These sex-segregated rituals would have looked familiar to Mali, since the people of Wells used sex segregation in community ceremonies and ritual practice too. Civil society in Wells was dominated by men, who regularly gathered to perform the functions of town government and who served on juries and as judges ruled in civil and criminal trials. As residents of a garrison town, the men of Wells would have gathered at least twice a year for militia training, and only men were charged with walking the watch around the perimeter of the town. Mali had herself been baptized barely two years earlier as Esther in the Wells meetinghouse, whose seating was probably segregated, with men and boys sitting to the right of the pulpit and women and girls sitting to the left.[34] Life among the Wabanaki would have seemed alien in many ways, but a perceptive child like Mali would have seen its many connections to the family and town she left behind.

Perhaps because life inside Wabanaki wigwams was so intimate, and because families worked closely together to ensure their mutual survival, there was an elaborate and even more intimate etiquette of the body—how one carried oneself, how one sat down in the wigwam, and in what proximity to the fire—that Mali would have needed to master quickly. This etiquette too was articulated by sex, age, and status. When seated, men sat cross-legged (or "man fashion"), women sat with their knees twisted around to one side, and children were expected to sit straight up with their legs extended. Men may have slept with their feet pointing toward the fire, while women slept with their heads toward the fire. As with so much else involving the incorporation of captives into Wabanaki households, women were probably responsible for introducing most captives to Wabanaki ways inside the wigwam. Because of their traditions of sex segregation, one of the guiding principles of this etiquette was a strong sense of modesty and propriety between the sexes, even between brothers and sisters. Evidence or discussion of bodily or digestive functions like burping, farting, or elimination were considered especially taboo in mixed-sex company. One story from Wabanaki folklore involves a brother who farted in front of his sister and instantly died of shame; in another version of the story, the brother cleaned himself imperfectly after a bowel movement, and when his sister noticed this offense, he hanged himself out of confusion and shame.[35] Mali may have had some older sisters in the wigwam she could model herself after—or who could shame or punish her for her infractions of Wabanaki etiquette.

Infractions of etiquette may have been painful or even dangerous for captives. John Gyles wrote about "an old Squaw who ever endeavored to outdo all others in Cruelty to Captives. Where-ever she came into a Wigwam, where any poor naked starved Captives were sitting near the Fire; if they were grown Persons, she would privately take up a Shovel of hot Coal, & throw them into their Bosom; or Young Ones, she would take by the Hand or Leg, and drag them thro' the Fire &c." This shocking story reinforces Gyles's message about the central role that Wabanaki women played in deciding captives' fates, but this anecdote may also (unbeknownst to Gyles) have been an illustration of the importance of observing wigwam etiquette. Perhaps those captives were indeed too close to a fire that Wabanaki women were using to prepare a meal, so they needed to get out of the way. Perhaps their bodies were positioned incorrectly or they were sitting improperly for their sex, or maybe the woman wanted to let captives know that because of their status, they had no claim to warmth from the fire. Maybe these captives were too open about their bodily functions in mixed company. Whatever the reason, captives who would survive would heed the lessons she taught, for they were only the first of many lessons that Wabanaki women would teach their captives.[36]

Becoming Catholic

The elaborate etiquette of life inside Wabanaki wigwams was perhaps one way of regulating life in a community that had dealt with the ravages of colonialism for a hundred years. The people of Norridgewock had spent time in other Catholic mission towns in Quebec and Acadia since the mid-seventeenth century, and it's likely that Mali spent more time during her captivity in other mission towns than she did at Norridgewock, because of its desertion in 1703 and its destruction by the Anglo-Americans in early 1705. The mission at Sillery in the suburbs of Québec featured Wabanaki Catholics beginning in the 1640s, although it didn't become almost entirely populated by Wabanaki until the 1660s and 1670s. This mission moved to St. Francis de Sales on the Chaudière River in the mid-1680s, after the soil at Sillery was exhausted, and then many Native people affiliated with St. Francis moved again to the west to settle at the mission called Odanak, near Montreal. By the time Esther Wheelwright was taken in 1703, St. Francis on the Chaudière had been abandoned, so the other main Wabanaki mission town she would have known would have been Odanak. She may have also spent time in other mission villages as her family and community moved back to Norridgewock from Odanak, an overland journey of more than two hundred miles.[37] In this respect, her introduction to life among the Wabanaki in the march from Wells to Norridgewock was a good introduction to the life she could expect to lead as a Wabanaki girl and woman in the eighteenth century: always alert to the fortunes of war and frequently moving to avoid the worst. The Wabanaki she lived among were chiefly concerned with maximizing their ability to survive and nurturing important political, diplomatic, and spiritual alliances with the French.

The histories of all four mission towns—Sillery, St. Francis de Sales, Odanak, and Norridgewock (among other mission towns) from the 1680s to the 1710s—are interwoven with the lives and careers of two Jesuit priests who were also brothers, Jacques and Vincent Bigot. From Father Jacques's first posting at the mission at Sillery, a suburb of Québec, he and Father Vincent were intimately involved in the lives of Native peoples. They were also probably the first Jesuit priests that Mali would have met, and Father Vincent would eventually deliver the sermon at the novice Mali's/Esther's clothing ceremony. The brothers' letters from the 1680s and the sacramental records at Sillery and St. Francis de Sales are full of baptisms, so Jacques and Vincent Bigot could think that their work in Canada was a great success. What success they had was largely due to the efforts of Wabanaki

women. For example, Father Jacques's letter of June 1681 from Sillery records in great detail the influence of Wabanaki women in bringing their
children and other family members to be baptized and Christianized. This
relation, the first of many letters reporting on his missionary activities, establishes two themes that are key to understanding Wabanaki Catholicism:
the importance of movement in the lives of the Wabanaki at this point in
their history, from Norridgewock or other Acadian villages and missions,
up to Sillery or St. Francis and back again; and the central importance of
women to nurturing and sustaining Wabanaki Catholicism. After all, it was
they who were the experts in turning strangers into kin. Wabanaki women
also seem to have been the expert mediators between a foreign faith and
their own communities, and Mali's likely first teachers in the faith.[38]

In his 1681 letter, Father Jacques reports that "the relatives belonging to
the Cabin of a woman named Margueritte have come from the country to
receive the same grace"—all twenty-five of them (or nearabout). Father
Jacques goes on to state, "I do not Think that there can be any fervor
greater than that displayed by all the savages of This Cabin. As They who
had gone to get them in their country had begun to Instruct them in our
mysteries during the Journey, as soon as they all arrived They Continually
urged me to finish teaching them what was necessary." This education was
instrumental—perhaps it's more accurate to describe the baptisms in Margueritte's family as being to her credit rather than to Father Jacques's credit.
He continued, "I begged That same Margueritte and her daughter, Named
Agnes, whose piety and fervor are Known to you, to do so in my stead.
They did it for a month, so assiduously that all these fervent Catechumens
learned in that short space of time Everything that the older Christians
knew."[39] Throughout the Bigots' letters, there are tantalizing hints that the
Wabanaki attached to Sillery didn't live there all the time or all year round:
they appear to have moved around between the missions on the St. Lawrence River and Norridgewock, on the Kennebec River. The passage above
makes a brief reference to those Wabanaki "who had gone to get them in
their country" (perhaps Norridgewock, or another Wabanaki mission or
town) and who "had begun to Instruct [these migrants] in our mysteries
during the Journey."[40] The family that adopted Mali probably had long
experience traveling between Norridgewock and the Jesuit missions on

the St. Lawrence, and as Father Jacques reported, they were perhaps "Instruct[ed] . . . in our mysteries during the Journey" by women like Margueritte.

Father Jacques's account of Susanne in the same 1681 letter further illustrates the connections between the Wabanaki of Acadia and Sillery, as well as furnishing more evidence that Wabanaki women were some of the Bigot brothers' most enthusiastic Catholics. Father Jacques is quick to note that Susanne is a daughter of "the most noted of all The Captains of their country," who along with twenty others was catechized and brought to Sillery by her. "Previous to her arrival I had been told admirable things respecting the fervor that she had displayed in their country in Instructing all the people,—giving no rest, especially to her kindred, until they had learned all the prayers." Father Jacques and Father Vincent were impressed with the eagerness and "holy dispositions" displayed by the newcomers, who although as yet unbaptized eagerly attended prayers in the church, where the Sillery mission Natives were encouraged by Father Vincent to "sing as devoutly as they could, to inspire the New-comers with great respect for our religion." Then after the songs and prayers, "they all withdrew to the Cabin of a devout Christian woman, where the most fervent of our men began to chant the litanies of the Blessed Virgin," and where they all repeated the same prayers flawlessly. Said Father Jacques, "I have endeavored to maintain the practice established among our Savages, of saying their prayers Slowly and distinctly; and They have so thoroughly Instructed one another in this manner of praying, that from the evidence of all our fathers,—and chiefly of those who have seen all the different savage nations,—There have yet been none who have prayed as devoutly as these."[41]

Clearly, Father Jacques was thrilled that women like Margueritte and Susanne were so enthusiastic and encouraging of Catholic devotion in other family and community members. While he was eager to note that there was some interest in baptism among Wabanaki men, especially the among high-status men, his most detailed descriptions of the behavior and fervor of his catechumens describe Wabanaki women much more often than Wabanaki men. Father Jacques reported that two other (unnamed) women "continue their practices of devotion and mortification; and When other savage women, who are not yet so virtuous, sometimes scoff at their devotion, and even offend them by some slander, they content themselves with coming to ask me what remedy they should employ to stifle the Inward resentment Caused Them by Those slanders and raileries." Two more women, both named Jeanne, "Preserve an admirable modesty and purity. They continually wish me to remind them of God, and I assure you that I have no difficulty in believing What you said to me last year respecting these two—that there are few persons, even in religious orders, who better regulate their inner life, who better discern all that passes within their hearts, or who explain themselves better to Those who Guide them, than they do." Furthermore, "a woman named Catherine Continually preaches patience, for she passes hardly a moment without suffering. When this poor woman feels any regret with regard to her illness, or the harshness with which her husband treats her, she accepts it with admirable resignation, and at once comes to ask me what she should do to drive away Those Regretful thoughts; and whether we will let her practice Continual mortifications, in order to make atonement to God for The sins that she thinks she Commits by not repelling them promptly enough."[42] While we don't have letters from the mission priests that specifically mention Mali, it's likely that her first introduction to Catholic ritual was through her Wabanaki mother and sisters.

We might wonder why it is that the letters of French Jesuits are so intent on invoking a world of Wabanaki women. After all, given Wabanaki traditions of sex segregation, why were these foreign men so privy to the lives of Native women? The letters never comment explicitly about the fact that their authors apparently crossed the traditional gendered divisions of Wabanaki society. In part, this may be because of the fact that these letters were written in wartime, when Wabanaki warriors were frequently either on raids or engaging in skirmishes with New England volunteers. Additionally, priests may in fact have been viewed as less-than-men, or as ambiguously gendered. After all, they refused marriage and all sexual relations with women, and they didn't hunt or go to war, while sex, marriage, hunting, and warfare anchored Wabanaki manhood. Although Jesuits didn't conform to Wabanaki ideals of manhood, priests weren't the only people in Wabanaki society at the turn of the eighteenth century whose gender identities were ambiguous. Recall the postmenopausal women and New England men (in John Gyles's telling, the "Old Widow-squaws and Captive

Men") whose place was in between the warriors at the feast and the fertile women and children awaiting their meals inside their wigwams. The priest may have been just another liminal kind of person who inhabited one kind of body but who performed the social roles of the other sex (like post-menopausal women sometimes, or Anglo-American male captives like John Gyles), or just some of Wabanaki men's social roles (like the Jesuits, who were spiritual leaders but neither political leaders, nor warriors or hunters).[43] Because they eschewed sex, hunting, and warfare, French priests may have been permitted more contact with Wabanaki women than Wabanaki men enjoyed.

Whatever the explanation, the letters from the brothers Bigot unmistakably focus on Wabanaki women. Early on in their mission work, they make it clear that some women took their devotion to such extremes that their behavior appears to be modeled on French *devôtes*—cloistered nuns—or on the example of the mission priests themselves. The priests were simultaneously eager to initiate new Christians in ascetic practices and shocked by the zeal for mortification among some Wabanaki women. Father Jacques notes that "when They obtain permission to practice mortification, They treat Their Bodies so harshly that I have been surprised at it, and have often been alarmed at the Blows of the discipline that I have heard when they had withdrawn secretly to some Spot remote from the cabins." Not only did the women beat themselves and one another with branches, but they appear to have been given appliances for mortification by Father Jacques and other priests: "I have found some who were weakened by iron Girdles,—one especially who is the wife of the Captain. Not knowing what made her ill, I compelled Her to tell me. She admitted that it was an iron Girdle [*ceinture de fer*] which she had been permitted to wear, and which she had again put on that day."[44] In his letter of 1702 from St. Francis de Sales, Father Jacques says that such a zeal for mortification in one of the young women at the mission would be surprising in France, let alone at a Native mission. "All of my effort goes to moderating the desire she has to do all of the mortifications of those of the most austere religious." He continued, ascribing to this young woman another nunlike virtue: "She has such a great love of purity that she doesn't want to go into Cabins with men inside unless it's necessary."[45] If Mali witnessed these activities, it was probably a memory she took with her into her life as a *réligieuse*.

Cilice Fragment from the Fort St. Joseph Archaeological Project at Michigan State University. Like an iron girdle, this fragment of a cilice was manufactured specifically as a penitential instrument and might have been used either by a French mission priest or by any of his Native catechumens. Worn on the body or tightly wrapped around a limb, its wire hooks and barbs were intended to lacerate the skin and cause chronic irritation in imitation of the wounds of Jesus Christ.
Photo by John Lacko, and courtesy of Michael S. Nassaney

Can we trust these reports from Jesuit fathers that Wabanaki women engaged voluntarily in self-mortification? After all, it would be understandable for hopeful French mission priests to write in the language of the European Catholic tradition and ascribe nunlike virtues to Wabanaki women and girls. There are several reports in the *Jesuit Relations* in the seventeenth and eighteenth centuries of other Natives (and of women in particular) from different parts of North America who engaged in these practices.[46] They were guided by their confessors—after all, someone had to be supplying them with appliances like the *ceinture de fer* and illustrating their uses. There is even a suggestion in one *Relation* of 1665 of the *réligieuses* guiding a Native woman in the use of an iron girdle. She was described in a letter from the Ursulines of Québec as "a good widow, quite old, named Geneviève, an Algonkin," who lived among the Ursulines and engaged in notably faithful and fervent worship with the nuns: "When she chanced upon any instrument of mortification, she desired to use it, and sometimes she did, especially a girdle of iron points, the pain of which is very acute. But we did not let her do all that she would have liked."[47]

Native people embraced pain and took pride in bodily ordeals at least as much as European flagellant Catholics. Facing pain and bodily discomfort stoically appears to have been a shared ideal among Catholic Europeans and Native North Americans in this period. Men in battle, and even when selected for torture and execution, ideally faced searing pain and certain death with dignity, and even offered songs and dances while being tortured so as to display their bravery and worthiness as warriors to their enemies. Perhaps engaging in self-mortification was an opportunity for these Wabanaki women to experience pain and demonstrate their own worthiness. Besides the stoic ideal, Wabanaki women were themselves the experts in using somatic experiences to teach strangers how to adapt to a new culture. It was they who selected captives for adoption into their families, they who had to feed and clothe the new family members, and they who had to teach their charges how to live in Wabanaki wigwams—and they sometimes used humiliation and physical pain to accomplish this. The "old squaw" who would "privately take up a Shovel of hot Coal, & throw them into [the] Bosom" of the "poor naked starved Captives" in her wigwam was very familiar with the uses of pain for teaching lessons about cultural priorities.[48]

More commonly than reports of self-mortification, the letters of both Fathers Jacques and Vincent from the 1680s through the early 1700s report that Wabanaki women also displayed monastic behavior in rejecting marriage (or, if widowed, remarriage). In fact, the trope of the virginal young Native girl or woman who wants to marry Jesus—like a *religieuse*—instead of a young warrior almost becomes a stock figure in their letters, as she is in the letters of many other contemporary Jesuits in Canada.[49] In 1699, Father Jacques reported that there were two young women at the mission at Naurakamig, one a virgin and the other a widow, who told him they did not want to marry. The never-married woman specifically "begged me to enjoin her parents not to speak to her again of marriage," but in the case of the widow, Father Jacques felt that she didn't enlist his advice soon enough: "When I blamed her for doing so without speaking to me, she said quite simply that when she possessed Jesus Christ in her soul after communion, she could not refrain from saying to him: 'I now belong wholly to you, my divine Jesus, and I will have no other spouse but you.' I cannot tell you all that this fervent christian wished to do for the repose of her husband's soul." In 1701, Father Vincent reported that an unnamed young widow enjoyed "a beautiful death" after resolutely refusing other offers of marriage. "I have absolutely no doubt, and I have very great conviction, that she asked the Virgin to die before she would be married. . . . A happy death liberated her from all this."[50] And in a 1702 letter, his brother Jacques praised a pious young woman because "she doesn't want to hear talk of being married." In some cases, the exemplary piety of a young woman was so impressive that virginity wasn't even necessary. A twenty-two-year-old married woman at Sillery in 1684, Agnes Pulcherie, was so impressive that Jacques wrote, "I cannot help, from time to time, on considering The manner in which this savage woman receives the Things of God, saying to myself: 'Could one see aught more in the Religious persons who Begin to serve God in great fervor?'"[51] We can't know to what extent the priests' praise for these Wabanaki virgins may have influenced Mali's eventual decision to become a professed nun herself, but they may have had some influence on her.

These stories sound almost too good to be true—pious Jesuit propaganda rather than anything resembling Wabanaki experiences. However, we must consider these stories in light of what one eighteenth-century chronicler reports about a particular Wabanaki reverence for virginity. Father Joseph François Lafitau—himself a Jesuit—suggested in his 1724 *Customs of the American Indians* that northeastern woodlands Natives "have a high opinion of virginity and, among all the Indian tribes, there is either in their customs or language, something to indicate the esteem in which they hold it." In particular, he cites the Wabanaki and the Iroquois as valuing the condition for its spiritual power, writing that "they attribute to virginity and chastity certain particular qualities and virtues and it is certain that, if continence appears to them an essential condition for gaining success, as their superstition suggests to them, they will guard it with scrupulous care and not dare to violate it the least bit in the world for fear that their fasts and everything that they could do besides would be rendered useless by this nonobservance."[52] Given what we have already learned about the role of sex segregation and ideas about modesty among the Wabanaki, this interest in virginity is not surprising. Native reverence for virginity and chastity must certainly have motivated the Wabanaki virgins that the Bigot brothers wrote about at least as much as their reported Catholic conversions.

Lafitau's observations not only link respect for virginity to Native people, but also connect this kind of spiritual power to the material application of healing powers as well. Native ideas about chastity extended beyond human beings and into the natural world. He explains that some Native people believe that certain plants are associated with "a feeling of modesty as though they were animate," so therefore "to be effective . . . they expect to be employed and put to work by chaste hands, lest they lose efficacy. Several . . . said to me often, speaking of their illnesses, that they knew very well secrets for curing them but that, being married, they could no longer make use of them." Among the Wabanaki, he suggests that it's female virginity that is most highly prized: "The term signifying virgin in Abenaki is *Coussihouskoue* which translated literally means 'the respected female,' from *Coussihan,* a term which designates not only a respect of inner esteem but also a respect outwardly shown in behaviour." A modern reader must note with irony the Jesuit missionary calling Native reverence for virginity and chastity a "superstition," given the spiritual power the Catholic tradition had assigned to chastity for centuries. By using the word "superstition," he implicitly recognizes that Native chastity was connected to spiritual power and efficacy, even as he worked to exoticize this belief and to deny it in his own religious tradition.[53] This must have been something that impressed Mali as she continued her transformation into Wabanaki Catholicism.

Finally, the nunlike virtues the Bigot brothers praised referred to the Wabanaki women's modesty about clothing and bodily adornment. Father Jacques in 1681 reported that a woman named Jeanne and her sister "placed in my hands some ornaments that they wear on their clothes. They told me that they well knew that Christian women should not be fond of such trifles, and that they would not take them back. Jeanne, in particular, begged me to have a dress with a border of gold braid changed for a plain one for her."[54] The introduction of Catholicism in their lives appears to have shifted the energies they once devoted to creating elaborately decorated garments and personal adornments to using these skills to ornament their chapels instead. They also embraced simple clothing, much like the Catholic *réligieuses* and other religious women throughout modern history. Wabanaki women spent hour after hour creating elaborate items with which to decorate the altar of the mission church after its move from Sillery to St. Francis. In his 1684 letter, Father Jacques wrote that "an altar was set up in The Church of our Mission, where was exposed The Image of the Saint [Francis], which [they] adorned with everything most beautiful in their possession. The whole Altar was covered with a great number of Collars, made in all sorts of designs; Bugle beads and strings of porcelain; and ar-

MATRI VIRGINI ABNAQUÆI DD

Wampum belt. This may be the belt sent from the mission at Sillery to the cathedral in Chartes, France, on the suggestion of Father Vincent Bigot in 1699 with the inscription MATRI VIRGINI ABNAQUAEI DD (gift to the Virgin Mother from the Abnaquis). These "porcelain collars," as mission priests called them, are a hybrid creation of Wabanaki women who worked Latin words expressing Catholic piety with precious Native North American materials. Its size— nearly seven feet long and six inches high—and its substantial weight made it a significant devotional gift.
Photo courtesy of the Penn Museum

ticles worked with glass Beads and porcupine quills." These elaborately woven and decorated belts were wrought with wampum (not porcelain, as the priests mistakenly called it), made from the purple and white clamshells found on the shores of Long Island Sound far to the southwest of the Wabanaki homeland. Father Jacques goes on to explain that "there was placed below The Image of the Saint a very large porcelain Collar, adorned with porcupine quills, which our savages have had the Devotion of sending to the Tomb of their Holy Father and Patron at Annecy, where the Body of St. Francis De Sales lies. It is the most beautiful Collar that I have seen made here. I wished, some Days ago, to recompense a savage girl, named Ursule, for about one hundred porcelain beads that she had Contributed for this Collar. She begged me to give her nothing, and told me that she was expecting her recompense from her Father, to whom she was making this little present." Several other women and girls probably contributed to the materials and artistry in making this collar: "Tall Jeanne, who made the whole Collar, and Colette, who set the porcupine quills in it, have done so with a great zeal for honoring that Saint. The Inscription on the Collar is: *S. franc salisio Abnaq. D. [Sancto francisco salisio Abnaquiis Donatum*—Presented to St. Francis de Sales by the Abnaquis]."[55]

The brief biographies of Wabanaki women drawn by Fathers Jacques and Vincent were portraits of women living in very difficult circumstances: as they fled death, warfare had probably chased them into mission towns where they nevertheless saw death all around them. The admirably patient Catherine—whose husband treated her "harshly" in spite of her illnesses—

was not the only sufferer in Sillery in 1681. Babies, children, adolescents, and young and older adults alike gathered together to die of smallpox, influenza, and other infectious diseases to which Native people had little acquired immunity. Father Jacques's letter of 1681, in which he so lavishly boasts of and praises the piety of the Wabanaki women as students and effective missionaries in their own right, also records the deaths of two young warriors, a girl who was her mother's only daughter, an "Old Captain," and a boy of nine or ten years. This is certainly not a complete census of the dead at Sillery in the spring of 1681, but it suggests that infants, children, vigorous young warriors, and the aged were all vulnerable to infectious disease. The burial records for Sillery in 1680 and 1681 record the deaths of twelve Catholic Natives, most of whom were either very young (fourteen and younger) or very old (eighty and older—Andre Neseghitto-ant and Louise Tchipai both died at age one hundred) between June of 1680 and the following June, when Father Jacques composed his *Relation*. The fact that there were many more unbaptized, uncatechized Native people at Sillery suggests that these deaths were a fraction of the total. Father Jacques admits that "a great many savages have died in this mission," in part because of "a very poor [crop] last year." Father Jacques confessed to severe despair in his letter of 1684 because of his inability to alleviate the suffering at the mission at St. Francis de Sales: "The diseases here, . . . would Fill an ordinary hospital [and] give me, I assure you, much trouble sometimes, and throw me into a sort of dejection. Seeing myself unable to give them the little alleviations which they might need, I must content myself with exhorting them to patience; but, without relieving them otherwise, these exhortations appear to me very barren." He concludes, "I told [the Bishop] that we had in our mission a hospital no less crowded than that of the Nuns at Kebec."[56]

Tragically, the changes from Wabanaki to Christian ritual practice for coping with sickness and death of which Father Jacques writes approvingly may have spread disease and exacerbated the suffering inside Sillery and beyond. He boasts that "they no longer change Cabins at the death of a person, as they used to; and I make them give in public the articles Left by the Savages when they die." Presumably, Father Jacques was pleased to see them cease burying material objects with their dead, which he took as a sign that the Wabanaki accepted the Christian vision of the afterlife. However, abandoning a cabin in which a diseased person died and burying personal items used by the dead were two practices that would have contained infectious diseases more effectively; dispersing the possessions of the dead may have helped to spread infection, and Catholic Wabanaki who gave up these traditional practices may have spread the epidemic outside as well as inside Sillery. In the same letter, Father Jacques reported that "a woman who lost Her only daughter . . . gave me her handsome robe when she died, to be sent to Lorette, and to have the Hurons there pray to God for her." This vessel for her daughter's remembrance might also have brought a disease that would deprive Huron mothers, fathers, sons, and daughters of their loved ones at the Lorette mission.[57]

Autumn 1708

From the time she was taken captive as a seven-year-old in 1703, Esther became Mali, a Wabanaki girl, and because she joined a community of Native peoples who migrated between mission towns in Quebec and Acadia, she became a Catholic Wabanaki as well. She was hardly the only New England captive to live among the Norridgewocks—indeed, like most other Wabanaki bands, the Norridgewocks had been taking Anglo-American children captive for years and teaching them to pray as Catholics. These captives were probably present most years in most Wabanaki villages from the late 1680s through the end of Queen Anne's War in 1713, but Fathers Jacques and Vincent mention them only occasionally (and unfortunately, they never mention Mali specifically or by name). In a 1699 letter by Father Jacques, he notes that "our Abnaquis have begun during the past few days to restore, by exchange, the New England prisoners whom they had taken in war; and in this, my reverend Father, the Catholic religion has triumphed over heresy in the very persons of its children. In accordance with the compact made between the two nations, those who are over fourteen years of age are free to remain with the enemy, but both sides have the right to take back those who are under that age, whether they like it or not." Father Jacques was correct that age played a role in determining who was repatriated and who was permitted to choose either to stay or return, but the age of discernment fixed in the treaty was in fact twelve, not fourteen.

This made for some painful and upsetting scenes with some of the older children who were obligated to return to their natal families. At least according to the Jesuits, their spiritual distress was extreme. As Catholics returned to a Protestant nation, they believed their souls would be doomed to perdition. As Father Jacques reports, "When they came to take away a poor boy of twelve or thirteen, you could not have restrained your tears had you seen how he begged the savages to keep him. 'I shall be lost,' he exclaimed, with sobs. 'Keep me with you, so that I might not be damned.'" Additionally, he told the story of "four English girls [who] positively refused to return to Boston, and preferred to live with our Savages rather than run the risk, they said, of being perverted by the ministers. Another came to tell me that she was resolved to do the same; for she said that she thought nothing of enduring the hardships of the miserable and wretched life led by the Savages, provided she remained in the true religion." Additionally, "seven little English boys, who heard of the exchange that was to be effected, hid themselves in the woods, through fear of being taken away." Because of this danger to the souls of returned captive children, Father Jacques saw in death a mercy for "two others who were older, and who died some months ago after making their first communion here, [who] had assured me positively that they would not return."[58] Father Jacques concludes his letter by emphasizing the importance of Wabanaki ways in bringing New England children over to Christ: "This fervor of the English among us does honor to our good Savages, who display an admirable care and zeal in bringing them to the missionaries, and in themselves instructing them as soon as they take them. At first I find them greatly prejudiced against us, but they gradually allow themselves to be persuaded by the devotion of our Abnaquis and their zeal for prayer—which they do not find, they say, in their colony." He elaborates further on the persuasions of the Natives in a 1702 letter, when he reports on a parley the Wabanaki had with New England, in which the Wabanaki protested Anglo-American dealings with them. Father Jacques says that the Wabanaki complained, "we gave you back all the English that we had taken in war, we treated them like our children and like ourselves, instead of mistreating them as you treated us ill when you had taken some of our people."[59] Immersion and incorporation into Wabanaki family life, as we have seen in this chapter, was the key to encouraging New England Protestant children to adopt Wabanaki Catholicism.

Five years after her arrival among the Wabanaki, Mali faced the same fate—she was taken from her family or encouraged to leave it behind in Norridgewock or Odanak and to travel to Québec. Unlike the English children who faced a return to Protestant New England, and therefore eventually to eternal damnation, the journey to Québec was probably less traumatic for Mali, since she would be living in a Catholic colony and encouraged even further in her faith. But after five years of living with, teaching, and perhaps loving Mali, how could her family have parted with her? Why would they have voluntarily relinquished her to Father Jacques or Father Vincent, and eventually to the governor of New France himself?

The possible explanations are almost limitless, but the historical record yields a few clues that may lead us to a plausible understanding of her move. First, Father Jacques, the Bigot brother most active in missionary work, was recalled to Québec in 1708 to work at an administrative post. In his report on the Canadian missions in 1711, Father Joseph Germain wrote that "after working for over 25 years in the Abnaquis missions—at Sillery, at St. françois, and in Acadia—with Results proportionate to [Father Jacques's] zeal, he was brought to Quebec to take charge of the greater congregation, which gives considerable occupation here; and he performed the duties of that office for 3 years, with all possible zeal and edification." Father Jacques left the Wabanaki and returned to Québec the same year Mali arrived in the city, so it's likely that she traveled with him. For the past twenty-five years at least he and his brother had put several Wabanaki girls in the Ursuline school—Mali may have followed in their well-worn path to Québec.[60] But why would her family permit her to go? And, perhaps more important, why would Mali have wanted or agreed to leave her Wabanaki family, after losing her New England family so painfully and dramatically only five years before?

Perhaps the simplest hypothesis is that Mali wasn't taken from her family —her family may well have been taken from her by death. As we have seen, life among the Catholic Wabanaki of Quebec and Acadia was desperately compromised by imperial rivalries between the English and the French, the attending wars that rent Wabanakia, and the hunger and privation that accompany warfare—all of which made the Wabanaki even more vulnerable to the epidemic diseases that so dramatically reduced their numbers in the previous century. These interrelated cycles of depopulation, warfare, and starvation would surely have afflicted Mali's family. If Mali lost key relatives—her Wabanaki mother and sisters, most likely, or perhaps her father too—who would look after her? Who would continue her education as a Catholic and as a Wabanaki girl? Father Jacques's call to Québec may have come at the exact moment that her Wabanaki family fell apart, sometime in the summer or fall of 1708.

There is another possible reason for Mali's move to Québec that fall, however. At the end of the previous Anglo-French war in North America (King William's War, 1688–97), both sides agreed to return child captives under the age of twelve to their home countries regardless of their own wishes because "they are not in a condition to choose their religion." Children past their twelfth birthday, however, were viewed as having liberty of conscience, and so they could decide whether they wanted to return to their birth families, or to stay with their adopted Native or French Canadian families. King Louis XIV had ruled in 1699 that Anglo-American Catholics who refused to return to New England for religious reasons would be granted letters of naturalization. As it turned out, 1708 was a long way from the peace treaty that ended Queen Anne's War in 1713, and in any case, Mali had passed her twelfth birthday in March of 1708. It is perhaps unlikely that either her fears of having to return to the Wheelwrights in Massachusetts, or the fears of her confessors, were the sole motivation for bringing her to Québec and therefore under the supervision and control of the French Governor de Vaudreuil. But can the timing of her move at the age of twelve be just a coincidence? It's unlikely that either Mali or her French confessors could prove that she was already twelve if an English colonial governor or officer demanded her return, especially if her adopted family had disintegrated.[61]

If she did go back to Massachusetts, what would Mali have faced when she returned to her family there? One of her cousins, Abigail Parsons, was returned to Wells not long after she was taken captive. Her father had been killed and her mother was still in captivity, so Mali's parents, John and Mary Wheelwright, took her into their home until her mother returned in 1706 or 1707. The Wheelwrights' care for Abigail seems very similar to the Native custom of adopting a captive to replace a missing or dead family member. Abigail was only a year younger than Mali, so perhaps her presence in the Wheelwright home soothed John and Mary by filling a little bit of the place left in Mali's absence.[62] In the meantime, Mary Wheelwright had given birth to three more children in the five years Mali had been gone: Nathaniel, who was four in 1708; Sarah, age two; and the newborn Job, born that September. The traumas of warfare and the loss of a child didn't interrupt the Wheelwrights' fertility, which subsided only with maternal age when Mary reached her forties. The contrast with Esther's Wabanaki family could not be more stark: Native families were sickening and dying in the colonial era, while Anglo-American families in the borderlands were teeming with healthy children, flourishing amid the dangers of the frontier.

Father Jacques may well have feared that the Wheelwrights would succeed in claiming Mali, and this may have motivated him to bring her to the seat of French colonial and ecclesial authority upon his recall to the capital. The Ursulines to whom he had brought so many other young Wabanaki girls probably relied on Father Jacques for her approximate age, which they recorded as one to two years younger than she actually was throughout her long life there.[63] It would of course have been in Father Jacques's and the Ursulines' best interests, if they wanted to keep her in Canada, to record her as older than she actually was, but they may honestly have believed that she was younger. Malnutrition, the privations of war, and her lack of Euro-American education may have made her appear younger to them, as she would probably have been much smaller and less developed than a typical Québec twelve-year-old.

As with the day Esther Wheelwright was taken from her Anglo-American family in Wells, so we have no specific evidence about Mali's departure—forced or voluntary—from her Wabanaki family and community. It was autumn, and if she still had a father and brothers, they would have been preparing for the hunt. She may have been a part of the hushed conversations between Father Jacques and her remaining family members about what was best for Mali and more important, what would serve God best.

Unfortunately, we can only imagine—but all of the realistic possibilities we might imagine suggest another unhappy ending to a chapter of Mali's young life.

CHAPTER THREE

ESTHER *ANGLAISE*

Québec, 1708–9

We don't know exactly what Mali's arrival in Québec was like, but the transition from a starving Wabanaki mission village to the security and even luxury of life among the noblesse of New France was among the most startling experiences of her life. Québec was, and still remains, North America's most impressively fortified city, surrounded by enormous earthworks and enclosed by thick stone walls and gates. Its massive fortifications and two- and three-story stone houses would probably have impressed her, because until she arrived she had lived only in one or two rooms in wood-framed houses and wigwams. Mali probably passed through the city's stone gates accompanied by Father Jacques Bigot, recalled to Québec in 1708. He probably is the individual who delivered her to the Château Saint-Louis, the large and richly appointed home of the elderly governor general of New France, Philippe de Rigaud, Marquis de Vaudreuil. With his significantly younger Acadian-born wife, Louise-Élisabeth de Joybert, Marquise de Vaudreuil, he spent most of the 1690s and 1700s filling up their châteaux in Montreal and then in Québec with their eleven children, so

84

Guillaume de l'Isle, *Carte de la Canada ou de la Nouvelle France* (detail), Paris, 1703.
This fanciful cartouche from a turn-of-the-eighteenth-century map illustrates
French ambitions for New France: at the top, scenes of French priests baptizing
and preaching to Native peoples, who sit or kneel in submission; in the middle,
the gendered depiction of a woman at left with a cradleboard on her back and
a man on the right holding up an enemy scalp; and at left on the bottom,
the animal on which the wealth of New France was built, the beaver.
Niagara Falls appears behind the scale of the map.
Henry E. Huntington Library, San Marino, California

Mali would have been in the company of a number of children close to her in age.[1]

When Father Jacques brought Mali to Québec, it was an errand in many respects like many others that he and his brother Vincent Bigot had performed throughout their work in various Wabanaki missions in Quebec and Acadia from the 1680s through the turn of the century. The Bigot brothers served as conduits between the Wabanaki missions and the colonial officials and religious orders in the city of Québec, including the Ursuline convent founded there in 1639 by Mother Marie Guyart de l'Incarnation. The Ursulines were a post-Reformation teaching order, and Marie de l'Incarnation had come to Québec to found a school dedicated to the instruction of young Native girls. But as a cloistered order, they depended on their connections with men like Jacques and Vincent Bigot to bring Native students to their house in Québec for more than twenty years.[2] In the summer of 1683 (just four years after his arrival in Canada from France) and in the winter of 1688, Father Jacques was credited with bringing to the Ursulines six different "*abenaquises.*"[3] The connection between the cloister and the Bigots was even more extensive—both of the brothers preached sermons at the clothing ceremonies of young nuns. Perhaps at first, Mali was much like the other Wabanaki girls that he had brought to Québec aiming to enroll them in the Ursuline school.

Mali was different in one important respect, and that was in her Euro-American origins. This doubtless helps explain why she was brought to the Château Saint-Louis to live with the governor and his family rather than deposited immediately at the Ursuline convent. She had been only an adopted Wabanaki daughter, a difference that meant a great deal more to the people of Québec than it had probably made to her Native family members. After living from the ages of seven to twelve with the Norridgewock Wabanaki, she entered Québec looking and sounding like a Wabanaki girl. However, her new French Canadian hosts had no interest in treating her like a Native girl. As we shall see, Mali was quickly shorn of her Wabanaki identity, and she was described in contemporary documents as purely *Anglaise,* English. This distinction would make all the difference in her life among the Ursulines.

Once again, the men in Mali's life provided the connections and the transportation she needed to move across one border and into another nation. Just as it was Wabanaki men who took her from Wells and brought her into their villages, so it was Father Jacques and Governor Vaudreuil who had the freedom of movement and the connections to take Mali again from her family and put her into a new home. But upon her arrival it was the women of Québec who educated and cared for her, just as her Wabanaki and New England mothers and sisters had looked after her before them. Yet another community of women would reach out, treat her as a daughter, and make Mali their own.

The Château Saint-Louis

The Château Saint-Louis was in every respect a fittingly grand home for a noble French governor, much larger and finer than any of the homes of the Anglo-American governors to the south. While Anglo-American colonial governors were some of the foremost elites in their provincial jurisdictions, governors of New France were drawn only from the French nobility. Even the celebrated Samuel de Champlain is remembered only as the founder of New France; although he effectively served as its first governor, he was never given the title or commission of governor because he was not of noble birth. Acutely aware of this fact, Champlain added the "de" in between his family and given names and began (spuriously) signing legal documents as a *"noble homme"* and *"ecuyer"* (esquire) in the 1610s, shortly after he founded the colony in 1608. Vaudreuil spent most of the years of his long governorship of New France (from 1703 to his death in 1725) completing the rebuilding of what was in fact the second governor's château to occupy the same site, which is still perhaps the most significant piece of real estate in Québec. There has always been one château or another on the face of Cap Diamant going back to 1648: the foundation of the Château Saint-Louis lies beneath the Dufferin Terrace along the walls of the *haute ville* overlooking the St. Lawrence River. Now an archaeological dig of the seventeenth- through nineteenth-century châteaux, the site is also in the shadow of the Château Frontenac, Québec's grand old nineteenth-century hotel of the Canadian-Pacific Railroad era. Champlain has the last laugh, because this public square is dominated by a huge bronze statue of himself, not of any of the noblemen who succeeded him.[4]

An inventory of the Château Saint-Louis completed the year after Vaudreuil's death indicates that it had at least twenty rooms, in addition to storage chambers and antechambers, not to mention a suitable number of outbuildings to support the lifestyle of a large noble family in New France. The inventory itself took nearly three full days and recorded an extraordinary number of luxury goods in several rooms: dozens of chairs and settees, some of which were upholstered with fine fabrics or embroidered cloth; multiple tapestries, mirrors, and pictures for the walls; comfortable beds with all manner of sheets, coverlets, pillows, and curtains to fight Québec's everlasting cold; a dazzling array of kitchen items, serving dishes, and hundreds of pieces of silver cutlery; coffee pots, porcelain cups, and special coffee spoons; hundreds of candles, several quarts of olive and nut oils, and several pounds of pepper; yards and yards of fabric, thread, and ribbons. The array of material goods and their specialized uses must have been striking to Mali, if not overwhelming.[5]

A household of this size furnished with such extravagance was run only by the labor of a dozen or more domestic servants and perhaps some slaves, both women and men, although the enslaved people at the Château Saint-Louis were Native captives given or traded by other Native allies rather than African or African American. Although they were greater in number than the servants and slaves at the Wheelwright garrison, Mali probably recognized them and the roles they played in the Château Saint-Louis: cleaning, cooking, and waiting on the dozens of guests who were always in residence. The Château Saint-Louis was less a home run on a family scale than a political and diplomatic mission run on an institutional scale, offering hospitality to forty people or more in the fall and winter busy season— military officers, visiting diplomats, and even captives like Mali. All of these guests required lodging, meals, and laundry service, not to mention the ongoing needs of the large Vaudreuil family.[6] Although Mali was not among the most prominent guests, borderlands go-between and diplomat Peter Schuyler wrote to Governor Vaudreuil in the late autumn of 1708 letting him know that the Massachusetts Governor Joseph Dudley "is waiting to have the daughter of Mr. Whielieright" in exchange for Louis, "son of Mr. de Verchères, the *Sieur de Beaumany*," who was taken captive by Anglo-Americans in a French and Wabanaki attack on Haverhill, Massachusetts, in August. This was an important letter because it identified Mali as the equivalent of the son of an almost-noble: Louis Jarret de Verchères was the

George Heriot, *Dance at the Château St. Louis*, 1801. Although this scene at the Château Saint-Louis was painted ninety years after Esther Wheelwright lived there briefly, it suggests the scale and kind of entertainments found there under ancien régime French governors. The Château remained an exemplar of European-derived wealth and style under the British as well.
Library and Archives Canada, George Heriot collection [graphic material] (R13927-0-0-E), acc. no. 1989-472-1

son of a man who was granted a fief with *seigneury* rights and for whom the previous governor, Louis de Buade, the Compte de Frontenac, had sought (unsuccessfully) letters of nobility.[7] Although the Wheelwright family of Wells was prominent in its small town and Esther's grandfather Samuel and father, John, served on juries and as justices of the peace from time to time, her New England family was not especially wealthy or elite. But they were among the biggest fish in the small pond of Wells.

Mali would have quickly become intimately familiar with the material goods enjoyed by the nobility of New France, as she was surely dressed and groomed as a Wabanaki girl upon her arrival at the château—swathed in trade cloth blankets, deer- or mooseskin leggings, and moccasins, and covered with bear grease. In the seventeenth century, the founding mother of the Québec Ursulines, Marie de l'Incarnation, described one of the first steps in the process of *francisation* (Frenchification) at the Ursuline convent just a few steps from the front door of the Château Saint-Louis: "When they are given to us, they are naked as a worm, and one must wash them from head to foot because of the grease that their parents have smeared all over their bodies." Mother Marie elaborated on the effort this took, noting that "no matter how diligently one does it or how often one changes their clothes, it takes a long time before one can get rid of the vermin caused by the abundance of their grease. One sister spends part of each day at this." Vermin—lice and other infestations and infections—were a big part of eighteenth-century life among both European settlers and their Native neighbors, but wiping the girls down and dressing them in shifts and simple gowns was probably the first step to begin transforming Native girls into Frenchified students.[8]

The Marquise de Vaudreuil would have directed a chambermaid to set about grooming and dressing her *à la Française,* like a French girl. Hot baths were considered dangerous as well as impractical, so she would have been dry-wiped as clean of the bear grease as possible and then dressed once again in Euro-American clothing.[9] The marquise had only one little daughter in the household when Mali arrived, so she would have needed to have a suitable wardrobe made for her. Mali would have required a chemise and corset, which functioned like the shift and stays she had worn upon her arrival at the Wabanaki village five years earlier. Then she would have worn a petticoat or skirt, or perhaps both, with a gown on top of that which was open in front to reveal the petticoat or skirt underneath. Even wives and daughters of elite colonial officials wore an apron on top of their petticoats and dresses, and around their necks a kerchief (called a *fichu*), which might have been made of soft muslin or perhaps even silk. This was the basic wardrobe for adult French women and girl children in the last years of the reign of Louis XIV, with rank expressed by the coarseness or fineness of the cloth, the absence or abundance of fancy accessories like lace collars or cuffs, and whether or not the cut of the dress or sleeve was au courant.[10]

Once again crossing political borders required cultural transformation.

As Mali was stripped of her Wabanaki clothing and bear grease and re-dressed *à la Française,* was she happy to be dressed again as a Euro-American girl, bound in a stiff corset and draped in several layers of fitted clothing, or would it have felt strangely restrictive? Would her new habit have felt too fussy and complicated? We can't know, except to acknowledge the differ-ence down to her skin that this border crossing meant for her.

More likely to have been welcome to Mali would have been the three daily meals laid out for the family and their many official guests: breakfast, dinner—the main midday meal—and supper. Colonial accounts suggest that the Québécois, from peasant farmers to the wealthiest military officers and colonial officials, took great pleasure at the table, and put enormous effort into cultivating and enjoying a wide variety of nutrient-dense foods.[11] This was a real challenge in their northern climate, with its short growing season, but the Canadian diet was based on locally cultivated grains, veg-etables, fruits, and meats, supplemented with luxury imports like coffee, chocolate, brandy, and wine for those who could afford them. Although Swedish traveler Peter Kalm visited Québec forty years after Mali's arrival in the city, from his detailed description we can get some sense of the rich variety of foods that she might have enjoyed while dining at the governor's table. In a travelogue from August 1749, Kalm described the Canadian table as a garden of sensual pleasures. One wonders about the impression he might have had of food in Québec if he had visited in February or March instead of August—but we can clearly perceive and perhaps share in his hungry delight at what he found during his well-timed summer visit to the city.

Breakfast probably involved the consumption of the highest percentage of imported foodstuffs among those who could afford them. Kalm writes that "they breakfast commonly between seven and eight, for the French here rise very early, and the governor-general can be seen at seven o'clock, the time when he has his levee." *Le petit déjeuner* was typically a simple meal enhanced by imported beverages: "Some of the men dip a piece of bread in brandy and eat it; others take a dram of brandy and eat a piece of bread after it. Chocolate is likewise very common for breakfast, and many of the ladies drink coffee. Some eat no breakfast at all." Because of the number of cups, saucers, spoons, and pots listed in the inventory of the Château

Saint-Louis as specifically designated for the preparation and consumption of coffee, we can assume that Governor Vaudreuil and his guests enjoyed coffee with breakfast as well as after their dinners.

Dinner was the largest and most elaborate meal of the day. Kalm reported that "dinner is exactly at noon. People of quality have a great many dishes and the rest follow their example, when they invite strangers." Here is where the bounty of Québec was on display, especially in August: "The loaves are oval and baked of wheat flour. . . . The meal begins with a soup with a good deal of bread in it. Then follow fresh meats of various kinds, boiled and roasted, poultry, or game, fricasees, ragouts, etc. of several sorts, together with different kinds of salads. They commonly drink red claret at dinner, either mixed with water or clear; and spruce beer is likewise much in use. The ladies drink water and sometimes wine." Although bread was served at every meal, "butter is seldom served, and if it is, it is chiefly for the guest present who likes it. But it is so fresh that one has to salt it at the table." Kalm continued, "After the main course is finished the table is always cleared. Finally the fruit and sweetmeats are served, which are of many different kinds, viz. walnuts from France or Canada, either ripe or pickled; almonds; raisins; hazel-nuts; several kinds of berries which are ripe in the summer season, such as currants, red and black, and cranberries which are preserved in treacle; many preserves in sugar, as strawberries, raspberries, blackberries, and mossberries. Cheese is likewise part of the dessert, and so is milk, which they drink last of all, with sugar." A fortifying jolt of caffeine finished the meal: "Immediately after dinner they drink coffee without cream."

Kalm also reports on other customs of the Canadian diet, describing the table as set with "a plate, napkin, spoon, and fork" for each person, adding that "sometimes they also provide knives, but they are generally omitted, all the ladies and gentlemen being provided with their own knives." The inventory of the Château Saint-Louis lists no forks, as they were probably not yet in widespread use in Québec even just twenty years before Kalm's visit. However, the governor was able to offer his guests a wide variety of knives for their own use—knives of various sizes and with different purposes; knives with silver, wood, or porcelain handles. Salt and pepper were on the table at each meal, and instead of saying a prayer before or after their meals, Québécois "only cross themselves, a custom which is likewise omitted by some." Supper was usually served between 7 and 8 P.M. (although presumably earlier on shorter winter days), and Kalm says that "the dishes [were] the same as at dinner."

Kalm described a Canadian table as one nominally governed by religious practice but dominated by secular, even sensual pleasures, especially during his late summer visit, when the bounty of French Canadian gardens and orchards was evidently on display at every dinner and suppertime. The Québécois who entertained him observed the fast at the end of the week, although Kalm (a Protestant) suggests that fast days were no real sacrifice: "Friday and Saturday, the 'lean' days, they eat no meat according to the Roman Catholic rites, but they well know how to guard against hunger. On those days, they boil all sorts of vegetables like peas, beans, and cabbage, and fruit, fish, eggs, and milk are prepared in various ways." He also notes that cucumbers and melons were very popular in season: "They cut cucumbers into slices and eat them with cream, which is a very good dish. Sometimes they put whole cucumbers on the table and everybody that likes them takes one, peels and slices it, and dips the slices into salt, eating them like radishes. Melons abound here and are always eaten without sugar. In brief, they live just as well on Fridays and Saturdays, and I who am not a particular lover of meats would willingly have had all the days so-called lean days." If the bounty of well-to-do tables in Québec was evident to an elite and sophisticated traveler like Kalm, whose sighs of satisfaction we can practically hear in his description of his visit to Québec, what would a malnourished twelve-year-old Mali have thought or felt as she ate meat on most days, fresh vegetables, and perhaps even sweetened fruit and sugared milk? It is difficult to imagine just how welcome food security was for a girl like Mali.[12]

After a few months in the Château Saint-Louis and presumably more instruction in spoken French, it was time to enroll Mali in school. Besides, the Marquise de Vaudreuil was about to embark on a journey to France, where she would pursue the interests of her family and Canada (and in that order) at the court of Louis XIV. Just as her own parents had enrolled her at the Ursuline convent school years earlier, someone walked Mali two city blocks from the Château Saint-Louis to the Ursuline school to enroll her as a boarder on January 18, 1709. The marquise had spent a few years as a boarding student there nearly thirty years earlier: The daughter of a French officer, she was enrolled for a year in 1680–81 from ages seven to eight, then returned after a year and a half away for another seven months when she was nine. Mali's enrollment wasn't a mark of her difference from the Vaudreuil family, as the marquise would enroll her own eight-year-old daughter there later that year, and then again in 1712 when she was eleven. All the military officers, the colonial officials, and the townspeople who could afford it sent their daughters to board at the Ursuline school. Like the marquise and her daughter, they would usually board for just a term or two, and would often return to board again for perhaps another six months or a year. Mali's entry in the student register reads "Mme. De Vaudreuil gave us a little English girl named Esther to be our pensioner," adding that the Marquise had paid her fees of forty écus. The record of her enrollment does not list her surname, but rather calls her by just her first name and her ethnic identity—much like the Huron, Iroquois, and Wabanaki girls enrolled in the boarding school. If the Ursuline recorder were inclined to treat her as a Native girl instead of a Euro-American girl, this is the only archival evidence of it.[13]

From now on, we'll see the Ursulines engage in the process of *blanchissage,* of bleaching or whitening Mali's identity in their records by emphasizing at nearly every turn her Anglo-American roots and ignoring her Wabanaki past. She reclaimed her birth name when the marquise enrolled her in the Ursuline school, and she retained the name Esther as part of her identity for the rest of her life. Although her New England origins would not always be an unqualified advantage to her in the convent, Esther's teachers and future sisters in religion were much more interested in commemorating her ties to an Anglo-American family and community than they were in remembering her connections to the Wabanaki. As we'll see, both Esther and the Ursulines had their reasons for wanting to rewrite the story of her life to play down her Wabanaki identity.

L'École des Filles

The Ursuline convent school in 1709 was a very different school from the one that the founding generation originally envisioned upon their arrival in Québec in 1639. The pioneer generation of Ursulines came to Canada in the mid-seventeenth century full of evangelical zeal and optimism about

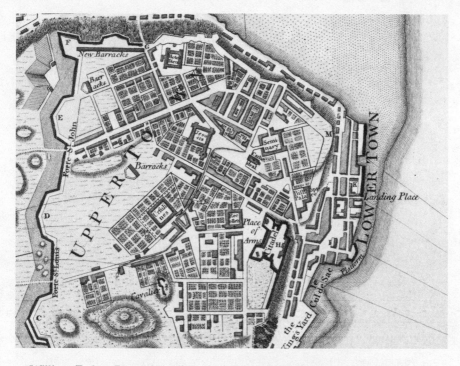

William Faden, Plan of the City and Environs of Quebec with its Siege and
Blockade by the Americans, from the 8th of December 1775 to the 13th of May
1776 (detail), London, September 12, 1776. In this detail of the upper and lower
town of Québec drawn shortly after Benedict Arnold's failed siege of 1775–76,
the Ursuline convent, surrounded by the orchards and gardens that allowed it
to feed its nuns and boarding students a rich and varied diet, appears large
in relation to the other religious houses. The home of the governor, the
Château Saint-Louis, is called "Citadel" on this map.
Henry E. Huntington Library, San Marino, California

the power of their religious faith to change the lives of Native girls and
women. Mother Marie de l'Incarnation was an enormously charismatic
woman who labored for the rest of her life in Québec on the conversion
and *francisation* of Native girls. She was also a prolific writer of letters and
chronicler of her work in early Canada, which makes her especially attrac-
tive as a subject for historians. Arriving with two other Ursulines, an assistant and an aspiring nun, and their lay benefactor, Madeleine de la Peltrie,
Marie de l'Incarnation set about building a monastery that included both
a boarding school (or *pensionnat*) and a day school (the *externat*). The vows

future *réligieuses* took would include, besides the traditional poverty, chastity, and obedience, a fourth to "employ themselves with the instruction of French and Native little girls."[14]

The eighteenth-century Québec Ursulines have received a great deal less scholarly attention, probably because their history couldn't possibly live up to the idealism of the founding generation. However energetic and optimistic the order was about its missionary outreach, Native girls were only a minority of the boarding students at the Ursuline school from the first, and by the turn of the eighteenth century they were only occasionally enrolled. Although some of the records for the seventeenth-century monastery were destroyed in the fires of 1650 and 1686, one scholar has identified only a total of 69 Native students and 6 *métisses* (girls with one Native parent and one French or French Canadian parent) enrolled in the *pensionnat* between 1639 and 1686, compared with 514 French Canadian girls in this same period. By the time Esther arrived in the winter of 1709, both the *externat* and the *pensionnat* included just an occasional Native student, such as Louise Sauvage and Marianne Ailleur, who entered as boarders in 1707 and 1708, respectively, and Marie Angelique Sauvage, who began her studies in 1713. Ethnicity was, and remained, one of the only identifying characteristics of these girls, as the Ursulines usually enrolled the girls with the surname *Sauvage* or *Abnaquise*. Using the girls' French baptismal first names and assigning them surnames according to European tradition served the Ursulines' goal of Frenchification. Yet at the same time, they chose to give Native girls surnames that marked them as different from French Canadian girls.[15]

But by the time Esther arrived in 1709, much more common than the *Abnaquise* or *Sauvage* were the girls described as *Angloise* or *Anglaise:* English. Again, ethnic origin served as a default surname for many, if not most, of these students who were captives taken in war: Marie Catherine Angloise, Marie François Angloise, another Marie Catherine Angloise, Marguerite Langlois, Agathe Langloise, and Marie Louise Angloise, for example, were all enrolled as boarders between 1691 and 1701. Like Esther, dozens of other captive Anglo-American girls spent at least a few months at the Ursuline school during their captivity in the decades from 1690 to 1714, during King William's War and Queen Anne's War.[16] Esther and all other New England–born students at the school were marked every time they appear in the archival record, just as the Native girls were. Even the way her birth name is recorded bears the stamp of her foreign origins: Esther Wheelwright's aggressively English name—so difficult to pronounce in French, with the hard "r" in her first name, and the odd "Wh" at the start of her family name—meant that the convent's record keepers often came up with different and idiosyncratic spellings of her name: "Villereth," "Vullereth," "Wullereth," "wheelwrihet," and "Marie Esther Houilleret."[17] Esther was neither the first nor the last captive Anglo-American girl to be educated at the Ursuline *pensionnat*. Because the school rolls record her name as Esther in 1709, and because of the Ursuline interest in forgetting her Wabanaki background, we can assume that she was probably called by the name Esther again, in spite of that hard-to-pronounce hard "r" at the end of her name.[18]

Ursuline education was a tremendous bargain if families could spare a daughter's time and labor for a year or two, as tuition was free of charge for both the day and boarding students. However, the cost of room and board at the monastery meant that for the most part, only noble and merchant families could enroll their daughters in the *pensionnat*. In the mid-seventeenth century, boarding a student cost 120 livres per year, or about a year's pay for a skilled male laborer. By the 1760s, the price had doubled or even tripled to between 260 and 360 livres, depending on how many months of the year a student was enrolled, so the cost of boarding a student would have been prohibitive to all but the colony's social elites—prosperous merchant families, noble families, and the families of military officers and highly ranked civil officials.[19] This helps explain the absence of Native girls among the boarding students. The few Native and New England–born captive students before 1759 enrolled as boarders were sponsored by a French donor or by "*la fondation*," the scholarship fund started by their founder, Madeleine de la Peltrie, later supplemented by an occasional donation from the king. The Ursulines of Québec were far from rich, but they clearly had resources to share with numbers of Anglo-American, Native, and French Canadian girls alike whose own families couldn't enroll them as boarding students without a scholarship.[20]

Perhaps because the French Canadian boarders were elite girls accustomed to a rich and varied diet, the Ursulines had to provide generously for their students. Even accounting for fast days and the seasonal availability of fresh foods, the girls and women in the Ursuline monastery enjoyed a strikingly rich diet much like the meals described by Peter Kalm above, and a high degree of food security as well. In the seventeenth century, the Ursuline refectory offered a variety of nutrient-dense foods, such as meat-enriched soups and/or fish plus something else served alongside, depending on the season and availability—salads, vegetables, fruit (raw or cooked), or milk. In the eighteenth century, the menu appears to have been literally beefed up, when in 1710 the mother superior and her council decided that five days of the week (provided that they were not fast days), the boarders' evening meal should include veal or beef. "When they do not get roasted veal, they get beef disguised several ways namely *à la mode*, stewed, or fried, Grilled, or on a spit . . . sometimes they will get fricassee . . . [or] braised meat." In short, "A sufficient piece of beef will be in available if needed, so that the boarders are always well fed. For dinner when they only get boiled beef, the cook will try to add some dessert. The boarders will get snacks according to what we previously decided."[21]

While her Wabanaki family undoubtedly fed Esther as best it could, the scarcity of food in wartime Acadia took its toll on everyone. As we saw in chapter 2, children suffered most particularly from starvation. Some of the Ursuline sisters used food (or rather, the refusal of food) to mortify themselves in the eighteenth century after Esther made her final profession, but perhaps unsurprisingly, she was not remembered for that particular virtue over the course of her life within the convent. To move from a community that may have suffered from hunger to the extent that women and children were dying of scurvy, to a community in which the boarding students were guaranteed beef five days a week, plus desserts and "snacks," would likely have meant a deep and thrilling relief from chronic hunger. Although the wars and sieges that plagued Québec in the eighteenth century periodically interrupted local agriculture as well as transatlantic trade and therefore Ursuline access to imported goods, they don't appear to have led to either involuntary caloric or nutritional deficits for the women and girls inside the cloister. The Ursulines maintained a garden "stocked with all sorts of kitchen herbs and fruit trees," according to Peter Kalm. It provided not just the crucial vitamins and nutrients found in seasonal fruits and vegetables, but also herbs for medical uses and pharmaceutical preparations.[22] Their excellent diet doubtlessly helps explain the extraordinarily low death rate

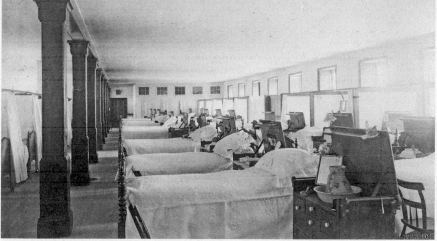

Refectoire des Élèves (*pensionnat* refectory), ca. 1850, and Dortoir des élèves (*pensionnat* dormitory), ca. 1890–1910. Although from the later nineteenth and early twentieth century, these photographs of the living spaces set aside for the boarding students suggest a crowded but refined lifestyle that Sister Esther would have recognized. The famous cleanliness of the Ursulines, and especially the tremendous dedication and hard work of the converse sisters in keeping all of these linens clean, white, and neatly pressed, is evident in both photos. PDQ, 0, MQ, 1/P, 003, 000, 000, 016, 0188; PDQ, 0, MQ, 1/P, 003, 000, 000, 016, 0129. Photo courtesy of the Archives du Monastère des Ursulines de Québec among their boarding students—out of hundreds of students, only four girls died at the convent from 1700 to 1759.[23] The rich and varied diet offered to students in the *pensionnat* doubtlessly played a major role in ensuring the health of the girls entrusted to the care of the Ursulines of Québec.

Gender, Race, and Intellectual Authority

At the turn of the eighteenth century, the education of girls was a political problem both in western Europe and in the European colonies of North America. Most elite Europeans and Euro-Americans recognized that a basic education was probably a practical and necessary good for middling and elite girls as well as boys, but at the same time they preferred a different curriculum as well as a different timeline for their daughters and sons. From the time girls were first instructed in European convent schools in the fifteenth century, they were limited to an elementary education. Secondary education as well as the study of Latin, the language of humanistic scholarship as well as the Catholic Church, was reserved for boys and men. Because Europeans and Euro-Americans recognized that education was powerful, great care was taken to exclude girls and women from the community of learned scholars and priests. Elite European and Euro-American boys were meanwhile instructed in both reading and writing in their own language as well as in Latin as a matter of course.[24]

Literacy for girls was grounded in reading, and may or may not have included the ability to write. Writing is a generative act, one associated with the production of new knowledge, which was considered an unfit activity for most women in the early modern period. The pen was, after all, a highly gendered tool. An "instrument of generation" (much like the penis), the pen was not fit to be deployed by girls or women who were meant to be merely consumers of ideas and information. Instruction in the eighteenth-century Ursuline convent probably included writing, as all of the teaching nuns could write, and all of the elected officers of the convent would have been expected to write in order to carry on necessary correspondence and to keep their financial and archival records. Furthermore, their boarding students were well-off daughters of the leading families of New France, and so were of a class of young women who would be expected to write. Therefore, the Ursulines' writing skills were another thing that set them and their students apart from most women in colonial North America.[25]

The most highly and uniformly educated group of women in Euro-American society were probably Catholic religious women. Early modern convents were divided into two classes: lay sisters (*soeurs converses*) performed the domestic labor of cooking, cleaning, and laundry for their order and would not necessarily need to be literate, while choir nuns (*soeurs choeurs*) were taught to read and write so that they could perform the official and administrative work of their orders, if not also to work in a teaching order like the Ursulines. But even these accomplished, elite, and devoutly Catholic women were kept ignorant of Latin except for what they needed to know to chant the liturgy, also known as the canonical hours or Divine Office. Both Ursuline founder Angela Merici and the pioneer leader of the Québec Ursulines, Marie de l'Incarnation, were "infused" with a divine understanding of Latin, but aside from God's intervention, women in North America were generally not permitted to study or teach Latin. Occasionally, bright girls with extraordinarily sympathetic parents would be allowed to be tutored alongside their brothers, and some of these girls learned Latin and even Greek, but European and North American educational practices remained highly segregated throughout the seventeenth and eighteenth centuries.[26]

Nearly seventy years after Esther was enrolled at the Ursuline convent school, in the spring of 1776, John Adams learned that his ten-year-old daughter, Abigail (Nabby) Adams Jr., was studying Latin. In a break from his responsibilities in the Second Continental Congress, he anxiously wrote to her, "I learned in a letter from your mamma, that you was learning the accidence" a popular Latin primer by the famed New England schoolteacher Ezekiel Cheever. "This will do you no hurt, my dear, though you must not tell many people of it, for it is scarcely reputable for young ladies to understand Latin and Greek—French, my dear, French is the language, next to English—this I hope your mamma will teach you." He had instructed his wife in a previous letter that Nabby, "by Reason of her sex, requires a Different Education" from her brothers.[27] Even revolutionary fathers and feminist mothers felt pressure to bow to convention when it came to educating their daughters.

The curriculum of the Ursuline boarding school in the seventeenth and eighteenth centuries was built around the catechism and composed mainly of elementary-level instruction in reading and writing French, basic mathematics, music, embroidery, and deportment. The emphasis on deportment —the correct way to dress, hold, and move one's body—would have felt familiar to Esther, after having had to learn the elaborate etiquette of the Wabanaki wigwam. The Ursulines too emphasized modesty and bodily discipline—the "careful and perpetual control of their eyes, . . . hands, head, and body"—everything from how to speak, walk, and behave at home as well as in church and school, not to mention table manners, how to write letters, and how to address strangers. The curriculum for the Native girls was nearly the same as for the Euro-Americans, although the Native girls had a separate schoolmistress, and their curriculum emphasized speaking French and living "*à la Française.*" (Because the day school students varied from day to day, their curriculum was undoubtedly simpler and focused on the catechism and French-language instruction.) The students of the *pensionnat* were usually between the ages of six and fifteen, and because their teachers were all Ursulines with vows to keep and hours of prayer to observe, they adhered closely to the same schedule. The nuns were up at 4 A.M. while students were permitted to sleep until 5:30 or 6, when they were called to prayer, Mass, breakfast, and then school. Dinner was at 10:15, followed by an hour of recreation. Their afternoons were filled with more prayer, vespers, more school, supper, another hour of recreation, and then hours of silence that would last until the next morning. Bedtime was at 8:15 or 8:30, depending on the time of the year.

But even on this exacting and demanding schedule, the Ursulines offered most girls only an elementary education. Nearly three-quarters of Canadian boarding students in the seventeenth century were enrolled for less than a year, and all but a handful studied for no more than two years. Peter Kalm noted that the Ursuline school offered only a basic education when he visited in 1749, claiming that "when [the students] have learned reading and have received instructions in religion they return to their parents again."[28] All in all, the Ursulines offered most of their students in New France a useful but elementary education in the brief time they spent in the monastery.

Esther was unusual, in that she would spend more years in the Ursuline school than the majority of her classmates in the boarding school, mostly French Canadian girls who returned to their natal homes after a term or two of basic instruction. This was due in part to the fact that Esther had no family in or near Québec, as well as the probability that she was educationally behind her peers. Although it is likely that she had received some instruction in basic English literacy in Wells before her abduction at age seven, it is uncertain how much of this she would have remembered after five years of speaking Wabanaki, years that were also filled with trauma and dislocation. Evidence from later in her life suggests that as a middle-aged woman she could speak some English, but that she needed a translator for written English documents. This may also have been the case for Esther at age twelve. Her French education probably began either on her journey to Québec or upon her arrival there at age twelve, although Catholic education would have been central to her life in a Wabanaki family. Therefore, by 1709 Esther was already a practicing Catholic who probably needed only intensive French language and literacy training.

Esther was probably an eager and successful student, but however expertly she learned to speak and write in French, however successful she was at overcoming her Wabanaki accent, she would be marked inside the convent for the rest of her life by her foreign origins. Significantly, the archives suggest that it's not her Wabanaki origins that the Ursulines were eager to remember. Instead, signal events and recitations of her biography are consistently stamped with the word "*Anglaise*" (English), as though to erase her years with the Wabanaki and yet still mark her as a foreigner. From her first appearance in the records in 1709, she is identified as someone whose origins were different. When she first became a novice, her name was entered into the official register of novices as "Esther Anglaise" (or "Esther Angloise"), not as Esther Wheelwright.[29] Although Esther had been living, speaking, and worshiping as a Wabanaki girl for the previous five years, the fact that she was not born a Wabanaki child was of decisive importance in her life. Her New England origins marked her as different from the Canadian-born girls and women she lived among for the rest of her life, but it was usually a distinction from which she benefited, compared with the Native girls who were her classmates.

Racial hierarchies were characteristic of all New World societies in the seventeenth and eighteenth centuries, so ethnicity was just as centrally important in French colonies as it was in the English colonies to the south. The economy of New France was famously dependent on intermarriage with Native families in the *Pays d'en Haut* for its lucrative successes in the fur trade. French mission priests thought it better (after St. Paul) for French men to marry Native wives than to burn, but intermarriage and cultural hybridity were not celebrated in the cities of the Laurentian Valley, where racial and class lines were more strictly drawn. Montreal, Québec, and Three Rivers were islands of French Canadian ethnic homogeneity by comparison with the Great Lakes region and the Mississippi Valley, and the women who entered religious life in these cities were not for the most part the kind of women who grew up in fur trader or *métis* families.[30] Therefore, it is unsurprising that Esther's English origins rather than her Wabanaki background were the roots that the eighteenth-century Québec Ursulines preferred to remember and emphasize. This whitening, or *blanchissage*, of her name and reputation is something that the Ursulines would continue not just for a year or two, but through the rest of her life.

"mr whellrits dafter is with child by an indian"

Another reason that the Ursulines might have preferred to emphasize Esther's Anglo-American heritage instead of her years with the Wabanaki is a rumor that was repeated by at least two former captives in Deerfield, Massachusetts, in the winter of 1709–10. Esther Williams, a former captive herself and the sister of the famous "unredeemed captive" Eunice Williams, wrote her brother Stephen a letter about the return of another Deerfield captive, John Arms, and the news he brought about other captives still in Canada, including their sister. In a letter dated February 28, 1710, Eunice wrote that "mr whellrits dafter [daughter] is with child by an indian."[31] Some historians have left open the possibility that this might have been true, although there is no corroborating evidence that Esther was ever pregnant or gave birth.[32]

Although historians cannot generally declare a proposition impossible based on historical evidence alone, this rumor is as close to impossible as we can reasonably determine. First, Esther was enrolled at the Ursuline convent the previous winter of 1709, and we have no evidence that she left the school at all in 1709. Second, she would have been merely thirteen years old in 1709 and early 1710, far too young to marry or to engage in sexual experimentation, according to either Wabanaki or French custom. The rape of adult women and children was not the practice of northeastern Native peoples when they took war captives, so it's highly unlikely that Esther, as someone almost certainly adopted as a daughter, would have suffered a sexual assault among the Wabanaki.[33] Among the French Canadians, however, sexual assault was probably more common, and certainly a possibility for many women in a town like Québec, which was crawling with young (and not-so-young) military men, merchant mariners, and fur trappers and traders. There were probably a number of men living in the Vaudreuil home in the months that Esther lived there because the governor entertained a large number of military officers as well as other former captives of Native people, and Euro-Americans had fewer scruples about the sexual abuse of either adult women or children.

Even granting the slim possibility that Esther was involved in a romance or the victim of sexual predation, she was almost certainly still sexually immature. A girl who had suffered the likely nutritional and caloric deficits of Esther's diet from ages seven to twelve would probably not even be menstruating yet at age thirteen, let alone capable of sustaining a fetus to the point of quickening (the detection of fetal movement), which is when most pregnancies were publicly acknowledged.[34] As we have seen, perhaps as a result of this chronic malnutrition in her critical growing years, the Ursulines and the Bigot brothers thought Esther was a year younger than her actual age, another clue that this pregnancy rumor was mistaken. Besides, even if Esther had had the occasion of becoming pregnant and of sustaining a fetus at least to the quickening at approximately twenty weeks—both highly unlikely scenarios—would Jacques and Vincent Bigot and the Ursulines as well have been interested in making her a choir nun? All available evidence about Esther's age and the conditions of her childhood suggest that Arms's news about Esther Wheelwright was either mistaken or a malicious rumor.

We can only speculate as to why Esther Williams would pass along the rumor of Esther Wheelwright's pregnancy to Stephen Williams. It may have been expressive of the Williams family's own anxieties about their sister Eunice, who in fact would marry a Mohawk man and would several times be "with child by an Indian" in the course of her lifetime. Did the rumor originate in English fantasies about the sexually suspicious nature of celibate nuns and conventual life? English Protestants were astonishingly puerile on the subject of Catholic celibacy, and there was a rich cultural tradition of assuming that convents were sexually degenerate spaces in the English and Anglo-American imagination.[35] Unfortunately, historical documents can't tell us any more than the words scrawled upon the page, and Eunice Williams's secondhand news that "mr whellrits dafter is with child by an indian" is the only source we have that claims that Esther Wheelwright was ever pregnant.

Aside from this improbable rumor, adolescence is a perilous time in a girl's life even if she is not the object of international diplomacy. Esther was at a potentially dangerous crossroads and she probably knew it. The Esther we meet in the Ursuline archives was an eager schoolgirl who expressed a desire for a religious life among the Ursulines by the autumn of 1710. However, Queen Anne's War (1702–13) was coming to a close, and traditionally living war captives in the hands of the French were returned to New England at the conclusion of the peace treaty. Esther's name (along with those of other New England captives) appears in letters between New England and New France in the early 1710s that suggest that John and Mary Wheelwright were interested in bringing Esther back to her natal home, and the Ursuline convent records confirm this.[36] No correspondence from the Wheelwrights on this topic survives. In the fall of 1710, Esther was fourteen—a bit too young to be accepted as a novice, especially without parental approval, but she was clearly old enough to decide which side of the border she wanted to live on. As we saw in the previous chapter, New France and New England had agreed in 1698 that children under the age of twelve would be returned to their parents, regardless of their own preferences. However, the law said that children twelve and older would be permitted to decide for themselves whether they wanted to return to New England or to live and work in New France for the rest of their lives. As a fourteen-year-old, then, Esther was empowered by law to make up her own mind. Furthermore, taking religious vows was like marriage—once Esther had taken sacramental vows, they were irrevocable. No one, not even parents, could reach across the border and take her back.[37]

Although parental consent might not have been legally necessary in Esther's case, consent was desirable because it usually came with some kind of material support—an inheritance, or a dowry that could help launch a daughter in marriage or in religious life. Although Esther had no need of the former, she would absolutely need a dowry to enter religious life. The Ursulines' Assemblée des Discrètes, which functioned as an executive committee for the monastery, gathered on October 1, 1710, to discuss her fate. They reported that the parents of "Esther Vullereth *Angloise*" were "desperately trying to get her back to them in *Baston* New England, and *they appear resolved never to spare her*" (emphasis mine). From the Ursulines' point of view, and with eternity in the balance, permitting Esther to remain in a Catholic country was her salvation, and would "spare her," whereas a return to "Baston" would have meant alienation from her faith and therefore perdition. But of course from the Wheelwrights' point of view, it was they who offered Esther both earthly redemption and the possibility of eternal life through their Puritan faith. The Wheelwrights' interest in their daughter was concerning too, as the Ursulines acknowledged that Esther had "a vocation for religious life, and many good qualities for admission here."[38] But a nun without a dowry, or *dot*, was of no use to the Ursulines, who barely survived on their modest holdings and the charges for the boarding students.

Why were the nuns apparently worried about the "Vullereth" parents and their alleged determination to take her back to New England when Esther was already fourteen? Throughout her life, the Ursulines appear to have thought her a year younger than she actually was.[39] Additionally, she had recently spent five of her growing years among people who were frequently suffering from starvation and disease, both of which might have meant that Esther was a very small and underdeveloped fourteen-year-old. Given the nutritional deficit she endured plus the fact that she had almost certainly not reached menarche, the Ursulines might not have been certain that she had passed her twelfth birthday. Another explanation is that her Jesuit benefactors, Vincent and Jacques Bigot, were confused about the terms of prisoner exchange at the conclusion of King William's War. In a letter written in the autumn of 1699, Father Jacques wrote, "In accordance with the compact made between the two nations, those who are over fourteen years of age are free to remain with the enemy, but both sides have the right to take back those who are under that age, whether they like it or not." This letter is a window into the Bigot brothers' understanding of the rules of border diplomacy, and perhaps offers insight into the caution exercised by other Catholic officials in the case of Esther's entry into religious life.[40] If the Ursulines thought she was only thirteen in the fall of 1710, and they also were confused about the minimum age for refusing repatriation, then they may well have feared the influence of the *Anglois* "Vullereth" parents, who might induce Esther to return to New England with them.

Money, Race, and Status Among the Ursulines

In the same 1710 meeting records, the Discrètes report that "Father Vincent Bigot of the Society of Jesus helped us with the sum of fifteen hundred *livres*" toward a dowry for Esther. The typical dowry offered in this period by the families of future choir nuns was between three and four thousand livres, and Father Vincent offered barely half that sum. The only women who were admitted to the Ursulines for less than two thousand livres were women who served as converse sisters, who neither taught nor prayed all of the hours but rather performed the heavy domestic labor required to keep the dozens of choir nuns and their boarders warm, well fed, and in clean linens. Because of this discrepancy in the dowry required of most choir nuns (*soeurs choeurs*), "the Discrètes had some difficulty in accepting this proposal, but they did nothing to reject it," and rather referred the matter to the full congregation.[41] Perhaps their concern for the fate of Esther's everlasting soul motivated their charity; perhaps their loyalty to the Bigot brothers persuaded them to accept her with a smaller dowry than usual. Or perhaps they recognized the political value of bringing a New England convert into religious life. In their own account of her arrival in the monastery, her sisters claimed that they "took in consideration all her good qualities and the risk of going back to her country, . . . and accepted her for 1,500 *livres*."[42]

Esther was neither the first nor the last Anglo-American captive admitted as an Ursuline choir nun. Moreover, two Ursulines of Native descent were taken into the order in the eighteenth century, one in Québec and the other in New Orleans. How does Esther's experience compare with those of the other two New England–born captives, and the only two nuns of even partial Native heritage yet found to have been accepted as women religious in the history of New France? Perhaps a comparison will offer insight as to why the Ursulines were willing to admit Esther into religious life, as well as some clues about her rise through the ranks to become mother superior. Although we have only a few examples of Ursulines who had lived among Native people or whose mixed-race heritage meant that they embodied the French encounter with North America, comparing Esther with these other eighteenth-century nuns is instructive in helping us untangle the entwined issues of race, class, and status among the Ursulines. Esther's nationality as well as that of the order's two other foreign-born nuns is noted repeatedly, and almost obsessively, in the margins of the Annales—the institutional history kept by the Ursulines themselves—and throughout the convent's records. Take, for example, the entry for Dorothy Jordan, another New England–born girl who lived among the Wabanaki before coming to Québec and becoming a nun. In the margin next to her name is a large cross with the notation "*Bostonaise*," just as Esther is marked in the Annales with a cross and the words "*Englois de nation*."[43]

How did Esther's career compare with those of the two other New England–born nuns who made their way to Québec after a time in captivity? Quite simply, there is no comparison beyond their origins in New England: although the other two nuns were admitted as choir nuns, neither was ever entrusted with work that was central to the Ursuline community's teaching apostolate, and neither was ever elected to an office or a leadership position in the community. Both of these women—Mary Ann Davis, who became Sister St. Benoit in 1699, and Dorothy Jordan, who became Sister Marie Joseph (or St. Joseph) in 1719—had been Wabanaki captives longer than Esther, and both were older when they came to Québec and began to learn French. Each had an obituary written about her that emphasized her cleanliness, thereby associating each with menial domestic labor rather than teaching or leadership positions. Davis was praised as someone who was "very clean, tidy and orderly and managed with much order in everything she did. She liked to decorate altars, so she was several times *sacristaine* which she performed with satisfaction as well inside as outside. This dear sister was skillful and enjoyed [needle]work." Jordan's obituary damns with even more faint praise: "She worked and fulfilled all the services she could do"—in the laundry, and some needlework, more like a converse sister than a choir nun.[44] Were the nuns unable to eliminate the sheen of bear grease from the skins of these sisters? Was their French simply too poor to entrust them with anything but menial labor? Were they somehow intellectually inferior, either from birth or through injuries or illnesses they may have suffered in captivity? Presumably knowledge of Algonquian languages would have been an asset among the Ursulines, who still had a few Native students at the turn of the eighteenth century, but for whatever reason, Ursuline leadership did not think Davis and Jordan fit to teach. We can only speculate on the differences the Ursulines saw in Esther versus her other New England–born sisters, but she may have been recognized for having special talent and intelligence for teaching.

Just a few years after Mary Ann Davis was admitted to her novitiate, the Ursulines of Québec accepted as a choir nun one Marie Anne DuBos (1678–1734, alternately Dubo, Dubocq, or Duboct) in 1703. She was the daughter of Laurent DuBos and his wife Marie Félix, described oddly in a nineteenth-century Ursuline history as "both friends of education." The same account remembers Marie Anne DuBos, who became their Mother St. Marie Madeleine, for her gentleness, perseverance, and obedience to authority. She had been put into the Ursuline boarding school at age six and left there for seven years; upon her parents' return, she informed them that she wanted to become a nun. Her father was said to have responded "very calmly, acknowledging that the monastery had been a peaceful and happy" refuge for his daughter. "He didn't disapprove of her desire to return there, but that having been separated from her for seven whole years, he demanded restitution, and that it was only fair that she stay the same number of years in the paternal home. Mlle Du Bos didn't think the price was too high," considering that after this delay she could have the happiness of entering religious life.[45]

Although it wasn't unusual for girls to be left in the convent school for a few years at a time, usually their parents were nobles, rich merchants, or colonial officials with business in France to attend to, but Laurent DuBos was none of these. In fact, I came across his story only by accident, as someone mentioned as a case of mistaken identity in another man's entry in the *Dictionary of Canadian Biography*. DuBos was probably a rich but obscure fur trader, and his family's prosperity probably had at least as much to do with his Huron wife and her well-connected family as it did with his own energy and industry. That helps explain why Laurent DuBos's daughter Marie Anne was able to offer a dowry of two thousand livres to join the

Ursulines as a choir nun, one of the smaller dowries in these years, but as we have seen with Esther's dowry, far from the smallest. Men who had Native wives prospered the most, because they could mobilize their wives' kin connections in the service of their trade. In marrying a Huron woman, DuBos would have benefited greatly from the access to the substantial calories provided by his wife's and her female kin's agricultural labor, and access to furs hunted by her male kin. So, too, Native families benefited from having a French trader in the family, their own personal conduit to highly valuable European trade goods like guns, gunpowder, knives, and cloth. Laurent DuBos's and Marie Félix's absence of seven years might be explained by a long expedition into the rich hunting grounds of the Great Lakes.[46]

Nothing in the manuscript Ursuline records or in the nineteenth-century French- or English-language histories of the order suggest that Marie Anne DuBos was of Native descent, although her mother, Marie Félix, is described in a nineteenth-century genealogical dictionary of Québec as "Huronne," with the maiden name of "Arontio," and as the daughter of "Joachim de la Conception." Evidence from the *Jesuit Relations* also corroborates her mother's Huron identity. In a journal of the year 1662, Father Jerome Lalement wrote, "On the 19th [of August], the marriage of Laurent du boc and Marie Felix, a huron girl, took place. The sum of 500 livres was given to her as marriage-portion out of the property of her deceased mother, an excellent Christian, which had been well looked after." Furthermore, the family's entry states that their daughter Marie Anne was baptized at Sillery, the early Jesuit mission in the Québec suburbs, in addition to pointing out that she became an Ursuline nun called "St. Marie Madeleine." Marie Félix was a Christian who served as godmother to at least one French Canadian infant, which suggests the degree to which she was knitted into the fabric of early Catholic culture in Québec. This erasure of her daughter's Huron heritage is a fascinating although unsurprising omission considering the Ursuline interest in whitening their sisters like Esther who lived among the Wabanaki, insisting they were "*Englois de nation*" rather than "*sauvage.*"

The *Jesuit Relations* offer more clues about this intriguing family. Marie Félix's father may have been the "Joachim Annieouton" (a name plausibly similar to "Arontio") whose conversion and death were recorded in near-hagiographic detail by Father Claude Dablon in 1672. He is portrayed by Dablon as a charismatic and powerful leader of the Hurons near Québec at Ste.-Foy who had been baptized twenty-five years earlier "although he had still remained an infidel at heart, and was a Christian only in name, occasionally, bearing a fair outward appearance." Dablon claimed that "his vices were impurity, intemperance, and impiety," which was vexing to the priest "because he was esteemed for his valor, his intelligence, and his good sense. These fine qualities gave him the foremost rank in all their affairs, and no step was taken without his advice." Dablon's story of his true conversion and death has him suffering imprisonment and a brutal stabbing in a case of mistaken identity, and persisting in agony for fifty days as he forgave his attackers and persuaded some of his younger kinsmen not to avenge their assault on him. Dablon then connects the story of Joachim Annieouton explicitly to the Augustinian hospital nuns at the Hôtel-Dieu in Québec, suggesting that "the consolation of this good Savage would have been complete had his wounds permitted him to be carried to the Hospital at Quebec, where the Hospital Nuns . . . render aid, with all possible charity, not only to the French in their ailments, but also to the Savages, of whatever Nation they may be." In fact, their care for the physical and spiritual needs of their patients was such that "it is enough to die in the Hospital at Quebec to give very evident signs of one's predestination." Regardless of nation or background, "all these Peoples are received there with open arms, and provided, during their illness, with beds and treatment after the French custom; and even whole families who come from other countries to make their abode at Nostre-Dame de Foy among the Hurons, or at Sillery with the Algonquins, are welcomed there, lodged and fed, until they see their way clear to a permanent home."[47]

With these suggestive connections between Joachim Annieouton, Marie Félix Arontio, and nuns in Québec, it's likely that Sister St. Marie Madeleine was Joachim's granddaughter as well as Marie Félix's daughter. But why would the Ursulines have chosen to forget or to suppress her Huron heritage, given her distinguished Christian pedigree going back two generations? Why, when it would only have fulfilled Marie de l'Incarnation's dream of *francisation* to its fullest to have the daughter and granddaughter of high-status, devout Hurons become an Ursuline choir nun? Although many beliefs and practices in the monastery seem timeless and unchanging, the fact of the matter is that by the turn of the century, when Marie Anne DuBos and Esther Wheelwright entered the convent as students and then as choir nuns, Marie de l'Incarnation and Madeleine de la Peltrie were no longer part of the living memory of the convent. No one was left from the founding generation of Ursulines in Québec, so the energy for missionary work among Native peoples was greatly diminished. Rather than trumpet the arrival of a *métisse* choir nun from a distinguished Christian Huron family, it was easier by 1703 to accept her as a French Canadian girl. The example of Marie Anne DuBos may have offered a useful template for incorporating an Anglo-Wabanaki daughter into the convent a decade later.[48]

The life of our last Ursuline, a generation younger than both Marie Anne DuBos and Esther, might help us understand why the Québec Ursulines might have accepted a *métisse* choir nun but also have chosen to suppress or deny her mixed heritage. Marie Turpin was also a *métisse*, born in Illinois in the late 1720s to a wealthy French merchant and his Catholic Illinois wife. Marie Turpin was not raised in trading cloth and bear grease; her mother, Dorothée Mechip8e8a, had been previously married to another French man before she married Louis Turpin, the royal storekeeper and a militia lieutenant in Kaskaskia. She and Turpin raised their family of at least seven daughters *à la Française* in the largest house in town, a three-story stone mansion with stone chimneys and a shingled roof. Although theirs was a frontier family, the Turpins lived in high French colonial style by comparison with the dislocation and poverty of Acadia during Queen Anne's War, which Esther and other war captives knew. Like the Wabanaki family who raised Esther, though, the Turpin family were devout Catholics, especially Dorothée Mechip8e8a, who was "known for her exemplary merit and piety and who was filled with religion." In spite of her family's wealth and renowned piety, Turpin was admitted as converse sister by the Ursulines of New Orleans in 1749, and significantly took the name of Sister St. Marthe (St. Martha is the patron saint of servants and cooks because of the hospitality and service she offered Jesus in the Gospel of Luke). When she died in 1761 at the age of thirty-two, she was remembered as Dorothy Jordan and Mary Ann Davis were upon their deaths—for possessing the virtues of a converse sister: "vigilant, strong, adroit, and of great cleanliness." In her thorough biographical analysis, Sophie White argues that

Turpin's life illustrates "the limits of Frenchification in mid-eighteenth-century New Orleans," the stain of Native blood being so much more difficult to remove than ochre and bear grease.[49] The Ursulines of both New Orleans and Québec were unprepared to admit women of even very wealthy and high-status mixed-race heritage on anything close to equal terms: Marie Turpin was admitted only as a *soeur converse* among the Ursulines of New Orleans, a servant-sister who would perform only lower-status domestic labor in an order with a teaching apostolate. Marie Anne DuBos was permitted to serve as a choir nun, but the Ursulines of Québec were careful to scrub her biography free of any mention of her Native heritage.

What explains the differences in the lives these five religious women led? The life of Marie Turpin suggests that by the middle of the eighteenth century, race was centrally important when the Ursulines of Québec and New Orleans considered candidates for choir nun status, even in the case of a pious and wealthy *métisse* like Turpin. The life of Marie Anne DuBos, the French Canadian and Huron choir nun in Québec, suggests that this obsession with status and race was already prominent in the public face the Ursulines wanted to present around the turn of the century. In Québec, European heritage appears to have been necessary if not entirely sufficient, as the cases of Dorothy Jordan and Mary Ann Davis suggest. Esther Wheelwright may have possessed personal qualities that suited her to teaching and prayer, qualities that the nuns saw in her as a slight adolescent with a Wabanaki accent as early as 1710. Just as important, it was only her accent and appearance that were Wabanakified—underneath it all, she was a Euro-American girl, one who was brought to them by the governor's wife, not a Native or a *métisse*. The bear grease and the accent could be washed away by more years of study and preparation in the monastery.

Before Esther could start her life as an Ursuline, the question of her status as a war captive had to be resolved. Although she turned fifteen in March of 1711 and therefore had been legally free to choose her religion and nationality for three years, Governor Vaudreuil may have had other reasons for continuing to consider repatriating her. She left the convent in 1711 in the company of the governor as he traveled from Québec to Three Rivers and then to Montreal in his efforts to begin the exchange of prisoners at the end of yet another decade of warfare in the northeastern borderlands. Traveling in the company of a man yet again, Esther probably wondered whether she'd ever be able to live *une vie Religieuse.* In spite of her legal right to self-determination, she was still in the hands of a powerful man whose motives she probably did not entirely understand.

CHAPTER FOUR
SISTER MARIE-JOSEPH DE L'ENFANT JÉSUS

Québec, January 1713

As Esther entered the richly decorated Ursuline chapel for Mass on Sunday, January 3, 1713, she prepared herself for a ceremony as elaborate as any she had ever witnessed before. Most remarkable, this was a ceremony in which she was the center of attention. The chapel was the finest in Québec, a glittering display in candlelight of the Ursulines' own gilt work with gold thread woven into the altar frontals, and gold paint decorating the many brightly painted wooden sculptures and architectural features of the interior. For all of its finery, however, the unheated chapel was freezing cold, something Esther would have known intimately as she knelt on the stone floor before the mother superior to ask her blessing as she whispered the name she would take in religious life. The voices of the chantress and the other Ursuline sisters were joined in singing *O Gloriosa Virginum* as Esther walked slowly to the grille, the iron gates that separated the nuns' choir from the rest of the chapel. At the end of the long procession of nuns ordered by rank, two by two, came the cross bearer and then Esther, with

Mother Superior Marie Le Maire des Anges holding her right hand and the assistant holding her left hand. As the cross bearer left the cross on the steps of the grille, Esther curtseyed and knelt before the blessed sacrament with her hands joined in prayer.[1] This was just the beginning of a long Mass filled with song, supplication, and prayer for the entire community.

The ceremony in which novices take the white veil is called, significantly, a clothing ceremony or a *vêture*, emphasizing the role that costume plays in the transformation of the young woman entering a monastery. In the modern West, "taking the habit" became synonymous with "becoming a nun," the clothing and the vocation interchangeable. For a sixteen-year-old like Esther, whose many border crossings had featured other ceremonies in which she was stripped of her clothing and re-dressed, first among the Wabanaki, then upon her arrival at the Château Saint-Louis, this rite of passage was perhaps one that she looked forward to with the greatest excitement. This was the first time she was stripping and redressing herself entirely voluntarily in the habit of an Ursuline novice. The white veil and black robe that she wore as a novice symbolized her rejection of the world and would continually announce her decision to serve God and to live in community with other girls and women. Accordingly, as with other important civil and religious ceremonies, clothing ceremonies were open to the public, and the people of Québec were eager to see this living trophy in their struggle against New England and Protestantism publicly embrace French Catholicism as a professed *réligieuse*.

As the community of professed nuns and the wider Québec community gathered to see Esther's *vêture*, the name she whispered to the mother superior was *Marie-Joseph de l'Enfant Jésus*. Did she choose this name, or was it given to her by the Ursulines? Is it a pious extension of what her Wabanaki name, Mali, might have been? (I have inferred that she might have been called Mali because of the popularity of Marie as a Christian name for Wabanaki converts, as well as my knowledge that Esther would eventually take Marie as part of her religious name.) Was her new name taken in fond remembrance of her New England mother, Mary Snell Wheelwright? No matter where she went or which borders she crossed for the rest of her life, Esther would carry a family with her, the Holy Family contained in her very name: Mary, Joseph, and the infant Jesus. Sister Marie-Joseph de l'Enfant

Jésus, like her fellow Ursulines, cast aside her birth name and previous identities when she became a choir nun and took on a new life not as an individual but as part of a community dedicated to the service of God.

"The daughter of the governor of a small place"

About eighteen months earlier, at age fifteen, Esther left the convent for what she must have hoped would be the last time. She probably left in the summer of 1711 and returned that autumn, although as in the case of her first journey as a captive in 1703, there are few clear dates by which to measure her trip to Three Rivers, Montreal, and back to Québec. She probably made the journey by water, perhaps even in a canoe, on the St. Lawrence River. Three Rivers is seventy-five miles upriver from Québec, and Montreal another eighty miles southwest, so this would have been a trip of at least a few months' duration. The Ursuline Annales cover Esther's three hundred–mile adventure in just one convoluted sentence: "M. le Governor sent her back to our sister the R[everend] Mother de L'Hôtel Dieu in Montreal, took her back from there and sent her with our sisters in *Trois-Rivières* but God seeing her good intentions sent her back to us as a nun."[2] In this telling, the Ursulines emphasized not Governor Vaudreuil's role or motives but rather the protection and support of women's communities that Esther enjoyed along the way.

Esther was fifteen—well beyond the age at which she would have had to return to her family in New England—and she had already indicated a sincere interest in becoming a nun. Why did Vaudreuil take her away from Québec when he knew she wanted to remain in Canada, and when she was in fact legally entitled to make that decision herself? The Ursuline archives suggest that Esther's parents were "desperately trying to get her back to them in *Baston* New England, and they appear resolved never to spare her." Although no letters from the Wheelwrights to Esther or Governor Vaudreuil survive, there is evidence that toward the end of the war, the Wheelwrights and New England officials were pressing the government of New France to return their war captives, Esther included.

If Esther knew about these efforts to effect her return, what meaning would it have had to a young woman who hadn't lived in Wells since she was seven, and who had more recently been attached to a Wabanaki family?

She had probably been praying as a Catholic for more than half her life, so Esther may have agreed with the Ursulines that the Wheelwrights represented a threat to her spiritual well-being. She might have looked at a possible return to New England not as a redemption but as yet another involuntary border crossing, another kind of captivity—one that surely would endanger her soul as well as alienate her from the family of students and religious women in the convent. She knew what she wanted, and had expressed her will clearly in the fall of 1710: she wanted to become an Ursuline choir nun.

Like all politicians, Vaudreuil wore one mask in his dealings with the enemy government and quite another when dealing with his own. Vaudreuil regularly corresponded with governors of Massachusetts about the fates of New England captives in New France, Esther Wheelwright included, throughout his long rule as governor of New France (1703–25). He was a tough negotiator as there were more New England captives in New France than French Canadian captives in New England, and most of these had converted to Catholicism. (The fact that many captives remained in Native communities and were beyond his authority was true, although New England governors were doubtful.) Just before he took her to Montreal in June 1711, Vaudreuil wrote to Joseph Dudley proclaiming that "Mr. Wheelwright's daughter is no longer considered a prisoner here." He insisted that "this young lady's change in religion will never be sufficient reason for me to detain her," explaining that he was merely abetting the captive's own preference to remain in New France.[3] Vaudreuil remained consistent in his reasoning over the course of three years discussing the return of Anglo-American prisoners, from June 1711 through the summer of 1714, as he and Dudley worked out the implications of the Peace of Utrecht, which ended another decade of war: he would not return those who didn't want to go, and assisted those who preferred to stay in Canada by procuring letters of naturalization and noting their sacramental obligations like religious vows and marriages.[4]

While Vaudreuil appears to be the devout champion of both the former captives and the Catholic Church in his correspondence with New England, his official correspondence with the Court of Louis XIV indicates that he had little personal interest in Esther or the other war captives or in their personal preferences of nation or confession. He had a clear financial interest in getting rid of Esther, such that well before 1711, Vaudreuil was looking for someone else to maintain the teenager. In addition to feeding and housing several English officers in the course of their attempts to retrieve other prisoners, Vaudreuil complains, "There is also the food and lodging . . . for more than a year, [for] the daughter of the governor of a small place. This was at great cost, without having been reimbursed a *sol*" (one-twentieth of a livre). Both the governor and his wife mention Esther briefly in letters to the court seeking recompense for their expenses in 1709. The Marquise's letter of 1709 deploys much the same language, and adds that "[Governor Vaudreuil's] predecessors had been paid at the rate of 4 l[ivres] per day for the English officers he had had at his house, and which is easy to justify."[5] The Vaudreuil family had paid for Esther's first term at the Ursuline school, and they were probably interested in finding someone else to foot the bill. It may be that he took her from Québec in hopes that he could either ransom her back to her family or at least leave her in someone else's care.

The governor's letter is of particular interest because in calling her "the daughter of the governor of a small place," he amplifies the notion that she was from an important New England family. Although it may sound slighting to us, calling her father a "governor"—even if of "a small place"—was important because in New France, only noblemen could be appointed governor. Peter Schuyler's letter to Vaudreuil of 1708, which suggested an exchange of Esther for a son of a minor noble, probably influenced Vaudreuil's opinion about Esther. Or perhaps he merely thought he might be reimbursed for his expenses more generously if he reported housing New England nobility for "more than a year . . . at great cost."[6]

If the governor general of New France supported Esther "at great cost," she was only one of a large number of captives, military officers, and diplomats staying at the Château Saint-Louis. In keeping with his own performance of nobility, Vaudreuil entertained his guests lavishly. A travel journal kept by John Livingstone, a New England diplomat sent to retrieve prisoners of war from the French governor in 1710, details the hospitality extended to official guests at the château, including several parties over the Christmas and New Year's holidays. Upon his arrival, Livingstone reports that Vaudreuil "received me with all imaginable marks of civillity, and ordered me lodgings in the fort in his house," in addition to the loan of his sleigh and one thousand livres "to buy my selfe and servant cloaths." (Livingstone had lost his wardrobe in a canoe accident on the way.) He knew he'd need something fresher than the shirt on his back, which he reports having "worne 44 days," because of the weeks of winter festivities ahead. He reports that he "supped at the Intendants," a top colonial administrator, and there "was very hansomly entertained, the Governor, Gentlemen, and Ladies of the town were guests, and were diverted with musick and dancing." The following night, "the Governor treated nobly with musick and dancing." Ten days later, Livingstone "sup't this night at the Intendants, had a splendid entertainment with musick and dancing, and had the drums and musick at my door." On Christmas, "the Govr. Genll. [Vaudreuil] had a supper this night where were at least 50 persons of distinction, and the whole entertainment in great splendour." The following night, both Livingstone and the governor were back at the intendant's, "where was much company, great plenty, with dancing and musick to admiration."[7]

Livingstone's journal supports by its omissions the notion that Vaudreuil had no specific diplomatic use for Esther, in spite of reporting that she was the daughter of a governor (of however small a place). Although Livingstone's mission was to procure New England prisoners, he never mentions Esther by name, further complicating our understanding of how her status was understood at this time. (In the winter of 1710–11, she was at the Ursuline *pensionnat*.) Livingstone mentions some captives by name, including another young woman, Eunice Williams, who was taken captive in the attack on Deerfield nearly seven years earlier, and the only child of Reverend John Williams still remaining in captivity. He wasted no time in inquiring after Eunice Williams, as his journal reports that shortly after his arrival at the Château Saint-Louis, "I demanded of the Governor Mr. Williams daughter," and notes a visit from Johnson Harmon, who was only recently taken at Winter of Harbor in Maine. Livingstone's demand for Eunice Williams highlights her importance in Anglo-French diplomacy and the insignificance of Esther Wheelwright by comparison. After all, Eunice Williams was taken from Deerfield to Sault St. Louis, a mission town near Montreal 155 miles to the southwest. The fact that he might (reasonably) expect Vaudreuil to know of her whereabouts and well-being is extraordinary, let alone that he "demanded" Eunice's return to him. Alas, Livingstone's demand was refused. Vaudreuil "told me it was not in his power to gett her; she was among the Indians, and as for the prisoners in their hands, he could not ingage for their exchange, for they were his Allies."[8] A little recompense, rather than political advantage, was the only clearly articulated interest the Vaudreuil family ever had in Esther.

Esther's desire to become an Ursuline choir nun may have increased Vaudreuil's interest in keeping her in New France. She was potentially much more valuable to him as a professed *réligieuse*. In the fall of 1711—perhaps while on his journey to Montreal and Three Rivers with Esther—Vaudreuil wrote to the court to ask for compensation again (in the third person) "for the purchase of many Anglo-American prisoners he made whom he removed from the hands of the Natives, who are made Catholics, of which there are two girls who took the veil of the Ursulines, for which he also put up 8,000 l[ivres]."[9] We know from the Ursuline records of 1710 that Father Vincent Bigot had already secured 1,500 livres toward a dowry for Esther at the convent—maybe Vaudreuil promised more, but he was surely exaggerating the extent of his support, if not outright lying in the hopes of greater reimbursement from the crown.

Vaudreuil here claims to have supported not just one but two young Ursuline novices. As we saw in the previous chapter, Mary Ann Davis, the first of the three New England captives to become Ursuline choir nuns, entered the convent in 1699, four years before Vaudreuil became the governor general of New France. Dorothy Jordan, the third and final New England captive to become an Ursuline, didn't profess until 1719, eight years after Vaudreuil's claim. He was probably thinking of Mary Silver, a captive at whose baptism Vaudreuil served as a godfather. Silver became a hospital nun in Montreal in 1710, a fact that Vaudreuil repeats in other letters, and 1710 was the same year that the Ursulines and Vincent Bigot began making arrangements for Esther to become an Ursuline nun. Vaudreuil had a lot of English officers and prisoners to look after, in addition to the larger problem of managing Canadian forces in Queen Anne's War and preparing for an invasion of combined British and New England forces in 1711, and he also served as a godfather at a number of baptisms.

Although Esther lived in the Château Saint-Louis with the governor and his family in 1708, and although she was enrolled at the Ursuline school alongside his young daughter in 1709, Governor Vaudreuil appears not to have paid all that much attention to the details of her case unless he could bother a New England official with her. He may also therefore have incorrectly remembered the details of Mary Silver's profession. In other correspondence with the court over letters of naturalization, both he and the king's minister failed to call Esther by the correct family name, referring to her as "Esther O'Wellen" and "ester owelin."[10] Wondering too much about Vaudreuil's motives is a mistake, given his inattention to her case outside of asking for reimbursement for the (exaggerated) expense of her upkeep. Forty years later, Esther herself would deny that the governor had anything at all to do with her profession—in fact, she was to insist that Vaudreuil contributed nothing whatsoever to her dowry, although she says ruefully that he was happy to take credit for her religious profession.[11]

When we broaden our view beyond the machinations of the Vaudreuil family and look at Québec as a whole, 1711 was a traumatic year for the city. First, after years of warfare and a poor grain harvest in 1709 "bordering on famine," a contagious febrile disease struck down hundreds of city dwellers and thousands of habitants in the countryside in the spring of 1711.[12] "This year there were pestilential diseases that took away a lot of people and saddened many entire families," including most of the city's religious communities. The Ursuline records list seven priests who died in May or June 1711, "every one of them excellent missionaries committed to charity and caring for the sick were afflicted with [the] horrendous and contagious fever which killed a lot of people." No Ursulines died of the fever, and although dozens of the hospital nuns of the Hôtel Dieu were desperately ill, remarkably, only one of them died of the contagion. The death that affected the Ursuline community and Esther herself most was the death of Father Jacques Bigot, the missionary who had brought her to Québec in 1708 and who had worked for decades with his brother Vincent as a conduit between the Wabanaki and the Ursulines. The Ursuline Annalist writes that "he surrendered to fever and fatigue from assisting the sick. He was consumed by fever in seven days. He was missed by everybody and it is an irreparable loss for the country." Bigot died on April 7, one of the earliest to succumb to the disease.[13]

In addition to a virulent epidemic, colonial officials were warned that New England forces bolstered by the arrival of a British fleet were planning a naval invasion of Québec from the east and a simultaneous land invasion of Montreal to the west. This undoubtedly is what preoccupied Governor

Vaudreuil in the summer and early autumn of 1711 while he was traveling with Esther. The attack scheme was abandoned when eight British troop transport ships in Admiral Hovenden Walker's fleet were dashed to pieces in the fog off of Isle aux Oeufs at the end of August. Nearly nine hundred men drowned in the icy waters at the mouth of the St. Lawrence River north of the Gaspé Peninsula. When word of Walker's humiliation reached Colonel Francis Nicholson, he wisely abandoned his plan to attack Montreal as well.[14] The British would not attack the Laurentian Valley in 1711 after all, but this was a plan they would attempt several more times during Esther's lifetime.

There is one other scrap of evidence that tells us something about Esther's whereabouts and activities during her flight from Québec with Governor Vaudreuil. She appeared as a witness at the baptism of Dorothée de Noyon (or Desnoions), the daughter of the former Abigail Stebbins and her husband, Jacques de Noyon, at Notre Dame de Montreal on October 3.[15] Abigail Stebbins (rebaptized now as Marguerite de Noyon) was a New England–born woman from Deerfield, Massachusetts; in keeping with his interest in New England captives, Governor Vaudreuil himself had been a witness to her baptism in Montreal in 1708. New England birth and conversion were all she had in common with Esther—otherwise they had no connection. Stebbins had married de Noyon, a fur trapper and trader nearly twenty years her senior, in Deerfield, presumably with her parents' consent. De Noyon was taken captive with the rest of the Stebbins family in February 1704, and by the autumn of 1711, they were living in or near Montreal. Dorothée was their second daughter and the third child of a union that would eventually produce at least twelve children. The other witness was Nicholas Le Moyne de Longueuil, a son of a military hero, trusted ally of Governor Vaudreuil, and governor of Three Rivers and Montreal himself, Charles Le Moyne de Longueuil. The elder Le Moyne de Longueuil was the only native Canadian ever made a baron of New France. He is described in the baptismal record as "Baron and Esquire, Knight of the Order of St. Louis, Lieutenant of the King in Montreal," while Esther's father John Wheelwright is described with the wildly inflated title of "Justice of the Peace at York and Member of the Sovereign Council of Boston, New England." But of course, it was in everyone's interest to suggest that Esther was a peer of the young Le Moyne de Longueuil. In addition to Governor Vaudreuil, who had brought Esther to Montreal and who probably knew of the younger Le Moyne de Longueuil, the other individual who brought all of these young people together was probably the presiding priest, Henri-Antoine Mériel, a Sulpician who baptized an astonishing number of New England captives in Montreal. He also spoke English and was eager to introduce new captives to other New England–born Catholic converts.[16]

What Esther brought to the baptism, aside from her shared identity with the infant's mother as a New England native and a Catholic convert, was perhaps the spiritual power of her vocation, something that Vaudreuil knew and that either he or Esther must have shared with Father Mériel. She didn't come from a noble family, but perhaps her identity as a future religious woman was significant and prestigious enough. After all, Governor Vaudreuil himself tried—falsely—to take credit for having placed her in the convent as a nun. Although religious women couldn't say Mass, their presence was powerful and something that the parents of a new infant may have appreciated for the spiritual protection they could confer.[17]

Esther's whereabouts for the rest of 1711 are unclear, but it's likely that she returned to the Ursulines of Québec later in the autumn of 1711. On October 2, 1712, almost exactly a year after she witnessed the baptism of Dorothée de Noyon and two years after the Discrètes first discussed her desire to remain with them as a choir nun, she was entered into the Ursuline record as a postulant who had been accepted as a novice. (Postulants were women who petitioned for admission to an order while they prayed and tried on the hardships of religious life; novices were those who were admitted to an order but who had not yet taken final vows.) Although in the records of the Discrètes back in 1710 she was discussed as "Esther Vullereth *Angloise*," now that the Ursulines' work to erase Esther's Wabanaki background was well under way, and now that their victory over the Wheelwrights' potential claim on their daughter was in sight, they entered her name into the book as "Esther Anglaise," shorn of the family name in preparation for her joining a new family composed only of sisters and mothers.

Making a New Nun

Before she was permitted to take religious vows, Esther had to endure a novitiate meant to test her piety, faith, and fitness for religious life. While the majority of women admitted as Ursuline novices persisted in their vocations, some left before taking final vows, or in some cases, before their clothing ceremonies, during which they officially took the white veil of the Ursuline novice. One historian of French *réligieuses* has compared the novitiate to a "military boot camp," in which the novices slept, prayed, and ate separately as a class. They were forbidden to communicate with their families or with anyone besides the novice mistress, the professed nun whose charge it was to accustom her postulants and novices to the piety and discipline required in religious life. This "boot camp" was apparently effective, in that the women who weren't entirely committed to religious life appear to have been discouraged before they took final vows. Among the postulants and novices who left the Ursulines of Québec in the seventeenth and eighteenth centuries, most left within eighteen months of their admission. From 1647 to 1785, 127 women were admitted as novices for the choir, and 20 (just under sixteen percent) left before final vows. Furthermore, there is no record of a professed nun leaving the order. Most girls and women left because they "lacked a vocation," meaning that they were not sufficiently drawn to the rigorous schedule of work and prayer that structured life in an Ursuline community. A few of these left because of illness, although only one woman died as a novice. Most of the women left within months of beginning their novitiates. The only indication of a woman leaving for extraordinary reasons was in the case of Marie Elizabeth la Croix, who was admitted as a novice in March of 1757 but removed from the convent sometime after the fall of Québec in 1759: "She left our community because of the war and the capture of Québec. . . . Her mother is bringing her to France with her."[18]

After a period of time—several months to a year, usually—a novice would be invited to take part in the clothing ceremony (or *vêture*), in which she would take the white veil. There is no detailed record of Esther's *vêture* in particular, but Abigail (Nabby) Adams Jr., the daughter of John and Abigail Adams, recorded her impressions of a clothing ceremony she attended in Paris in 1784 at the age of nineteen. Although Adams witnessed the profession of two Augustinian nuns more than seventy years after Esther's *vêture*, her lively observations confirm several of the elements of the ceremony that awaited Esther in Québec. Adams reported that she was invited by "Mr. [Thomas] Jefferson . . . to see the ceremony of taking the veil, in the convent where his daughter is to receive her education." Martha Jefferson was indeed enrolled at the Abbaye Royale de Penthemont, a prestigious convent school that educated only the daughters of French and visiting English aristocrats, and her younger sister Mary (Polly) Jefferson would follow her there, too. Adams reported that "this is considered the best and most genteel convent in Paris. Most of the English who send their children here for their education, put them into this convent." Like many convent school girls through the generations, "Patsy" Jefferson, as she was nicknamed, was so taken with her teachers' example that she briefly contemplated conversion to Catholicism and a religious life. (Similarly, like many alarmed Protestant parents, Jefferson withdrew Patsy and Polly from the Abbaye shortly thereafter.) Upon arriving at the church for the event, Adams noted that "we found a number of persons of our acquaintance." Like the Parisian ceremony that Adams witnessed, Esther's 1713 clothing was attended by many prominent community members. Nevertheless, Adams reports that she and the rest of the congregation of witnesses in Paris were "separated from the place of the nuns and those of the convent, by iron gates." In other words, the nuns remained behind their grille, physically and visibly separate from the world, just as they had in Québec at the beginning of the century.[19]

Esther's future sisters in religious life did not preside alone at her clothing ceremony. Because women are still forbidden ordination as priests in the Roman Catholic tradition even today, a male priest had to be there to celebrate the Mass for Esther. Preceded by assistants swinging Parisian silver censers and incense boats, Father Vincent Bigot was perhaps wearing a cope and maniple of silk brocade embroidered in silver and gold twist in the Ursulines' own workshop. The death of his brother Jacques in the epidemic that had struck Québec in the spring of 1711 meant that he would have the honor of presiding at Esther's *vêture*. Both of the Fathers Bigot had worked toward the day when one of the girls from their Wabanaki missions might be accepted not just as a student but as a choir nun, Jacques by bringing her to the Ursulines in the first place, and Vincent by securing the funding for Esther's *dot*. Father Vincent stepped up to light a candle, sprinkled it with holy water, then presented it to Esther, who remained kneeling on the chilly steps before the grate while a prayer was said. Then Esther was directed to a seat nearby so that she could be addressed by Father Vincent in his sermon.[20]

Vincent Bigot was clear about the meaning of Esther's profession: only divine Providence could explain how she had come to be an Ursuline choir nun. Esther was not just a fortunate child: her very life to this day bore witness to supernatural truth and divine guidance: "Thy hand, Lord, shall lead me; thy right hand shall sustain me." His sermon represents the first time anyone attempted to explain Esther's biography, and in so doing he laid out a Catholic and French nationalist explanation of divine Providence that would continue to be popular for nearly three centuries. Bigot began his sermon by explaining that "by the marvels of his good will, you find yourself today happily transplanted from a barren and ungrateful land, from a land where you had been a slave to the demon of heresy, to a land of promise and of blessing, where you are about to enjoy the sweet liberty of the children of God." Bigot was referring to her life in an English colony; nearly two centuries after the Reformation, Catholics still regarded Protestant beliefs as "heresy." We can see here how Bigot followed the script that the Ursulines had drafted, which was to emphasize Esther's Anglo-American roots rather than her Wabanaki childhood. Therefore, although he noted the "savagery" in which he first encountered her, his emphasis was on her providential escape from Protestant "heresy." So, too, Bigot emphasizes the role that he and other men played in her rescue from this "heresy," which he credits to the patriarchal Christian God ("the father," "the Lord") rather than to the Wabanaki women who taught her how to cross herself and how to pray as a Catholic. Bigot lectures the Ursulines: "You are interested here: it's a matter of a bride that he has chosen himself the Spouse of Virgins, your immortal Spouse; it's a matter of a sister that he has given you, who being a stranger you must not regard as any less dear or less agreeable."[21]

When Bigot notes the conditions of her captivity, he uses her Wabanaki background as a foil for her supposed "polite" (although heretical) education at the hands of her New England family and for the rewards of French civilization and religion she later enjoyed. Addressing her directly, Bigot proclaimed that "providence drove you out of your nation. . . . Alas! How many captive children died on the way at the age you were! No, my dear

Sister, I can't but be affected by an extreme compassion for you." Esther was in his telling "a young child of six or seven, violently torn away from a house where you were tenderly raised, plunged into the bitterness of the loss of everything that you held most dear in the world; there you were, all of a sudden, reduced to a life wandering in the forest, obliged to follow new masters who didn't care that your legs couldn't keep up with theirs. . . . You followed them nevertheless (as you had yourself told me in a manner so lively and eloquent), charming your troubles in the middle of these awful miseries, in the vain hope that you would be rewarded one day." When he first saw Esther, "the marks of a polite education were detectable through the tatters that covered you, and I could not have stopped myself from shedding tears." But "it is there nevertheless, my dear Sister, in this place so apparently sad and so dreadful that God was going to show himself to you; it was here that he was going to work to make you capable of the great things for which he destines you."[22]

Bigot's sermon describing Esther's captivity and life among the Wabanaki is the only direct testimony we have about her experiences. Although clearly an ideologically and religiously charged document, the sermon offers glimpses of Esther's childhood and even her character. "There you were, amidst a savage people whose language is barbarous and whose manners are coarse and so different from yours": Bigot portrays her as suffering the inconveniences of Wabanaki life stoically. "I will always remember, my dear Sister, the sad appearance you made the first time I met you in these villages," in an outfit that reflected so little Esther's age or "the delicacy in which you had been raised." He continues, "You devoured all the scraps, all of the inconveniences of a life so hard," but instead of crediting the Wabanaki women who cared for her or even her own character, Bigot of course credits the hand of God. Esther was also a hard worker, a gifted linguist, and an eager convert in his telling: "Already doing a little work, you rendered service in your *cabane* which, a little before, you had performed in your paternal home." Fortunately, "[God] granted you an admirable facility in understanding a barbarous language, the privilege of which he had granted Joseph in his captivity. . . . Therefore, little by little naturalized to a foreign country," Esther became aware of the "holy exercises of a Christian life, of which a good number were practiced in these lonely wild places."[23]

Notice how differently Bigot describes Catholic religious practice in the Wabanaki missions here compared with his and his brother's descriptions in the *Jesuit Relations* that we saw in chapter 2, in which they boasted endlessly of their successes among Native converts. Here in his sermon at Esther's *vêture*, his successful Wabanaki women converts and teachers of the faith are erased, and somehow daily Catholic devotions "were practiced" passively in "lonely wild places." All of this served further to erase Esther's Wabanaki background and her likely first instructors in Catholic devotional practice. Bigot remarked that "nothing gave you more pleasure than to follow [Catholic rituals] yourself every day." He doesn't try to take the credit of teaching her himself, but he withholds his knowledge of the fuller story of Esther's conversion. Astonishingly quickly, Bigot shifts his narrative to describe the young catechumen as no longer merely a student but a teacher of the faith who "would assist the other children in the village" in their devotional practice. Bigot emphasizes what he calls Esther's "precocious wisdom," turning the young student into a teacher within two paragraphs of his sermon. Esther was joining a teaching order, after all, so Bigot's pivot is understandable. Eliminating any specific reference to Esther's other teachers in the faith was also a choice.[24]

After the sermon, Father Bigot asked a ritual series of questions about her intent to enter religious life, and Esther and the superior answered:

Q. My child, What do you demand?

A. The mercy of God, the holy habit of religion, the charity of the order, and the society of the mothers and sisters.

Q. It is with your free will and consent you demand the habit of religion?

A. Yes, my Rev. father. . . .

   Turning to the superioress, he says, Rev. mother have you inquired into the other points necessary to be known for those who enter into religion, and are you fully satisfied?

   Yes, Rev. father.

Q. My dear child, have you a firm intention to persevere in religion to the end of your life; and do you think you have sufficient strength to bear constantly the sweet yoke of our Lord Jesus Christ, for the love and fear of God alone?

A. Relying on the mercy of God, and on the prayers of the mothers and sisters, I hope to be able to do so.[25]

At that point she was led away by the mother superior and assistant to be stripped of her gown and re-dressed as a nun. Much as she had been stripped and re-dressed as a Wabanaki captive, so she participated in the Catholic rituals of religious profession in which clothing was laden with symbolic and spiritual meaning. Nabby Adams describes the two novices she saw take their final vows as dressed in "fine, white woolen dresses, made like a parson's robes, loose and flowing; their veils were white . . . their hair shaved off; a white cap and veil." Novices were dressed in white veils, to signal their special status; only when she took her final vows as a choir nun would Esther receive a black veil. As Esther removed her clothing, a new robe, wimple (loose, white fabric that covered the neck and breast), cap, and veil were brought to the grate and blessed by Father Bigot with a special prayer and sprinkled with holy water. While the cap, wimple, and robe were for Esther to put on herself, Father Bigot continued with the blessing of the veil, with another special prayer and more holy water, before it was returned to Esther. Then the nuns sang a psalm until Esther returned in her new tunic and black robe, cap, and wimple, carrying the candle she had been given earlier. When she appeared before the choir, the chantress began an antiphon which the other nuns joined in singing until Esther arrived once again at the grate. She was then left alone by the superior and the assistant at the grate to genuflect to the blessed sacrament and kneel again. Although the rite was much less violent than many Native ceremonies in which captives were beaten, stripped, and re-dressed, the principle was the same in monasteries as among the Wabanaki: through her new clothing, Esther was completely transformed into a novice of the Ursuline order.[26]

There were two elements of her costume that she was not permitted to put on herself, but rather were set aside for her superior to put on her during the Mass: the cincture, a leather strap that she would wear as a belt around her waist on top of her robe, and the veil, which along with a cap, linen band, and the wimple would cover most of her head and face, leaving visible only her eyes, nose, mouth, and chin. Upon her return, Father Bigot rose to make the sign of the cross over Esther and then turned to make the sign of the cross over the cincture and recited more prayers. The assistant

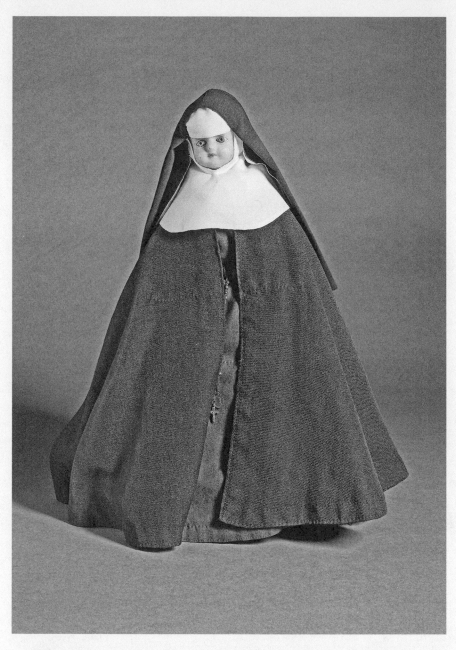

Wax doll in choir nun costume. Made in the Québec convent, this late-eighteenth-century doll was not meant for children but rather was an instructive tool to show novices the correct way to dress as an Ursuline choir nun according to the Rule.

Photo courtesy of the Musée des Ursulines de Québec

handed the cincture to the mother superior, who then placed it around Esther's waist as Father Bigot said: "When thou wast younger, thou didst gird thyself, and didst walk where thou wouldst: but when thou shalt be old, another shall gird thee. In the name of the Father, and of the Son, and of the Holy Ghost." Then the superior took the already-blessed veil and put it on Esther's head while Father Bigot said, "Receive the white veil, the emblem of inward purity, that thou mayest follow the lamb without stain and mayest walk with him in white. In the name of the Father, and of the Son, and of the Holy Ghost." Thus with both her body and her mind symbolically enclosed within a cincture and under a veil, Esther was prepared to become the bride of Christ.[27]

Taking a few steps back from the altar, Esther said, "I have chosen to be an abject one in the house of my Lord Jesus Christ." Then, in the most dramatic moment of the ceremony, Esther prostrated herself on the floor of the Ursuline Chapel, making her entire body into the sign of the cross, and demonstrating complete submission. Nabby Adams describes this moment in the ceremony as "they laid down on their faces, and there was brought in, . . . a pall of black, crossed with white, which was held over them. . . . This was an affecting sight; I could not refrain from tears; everyone seemed affected around, particularly the French." Adams went on to explain that "this ceremony lasted half an hour, while these poor girls were lying on their faces; and when they rise, it is called rising to the resurrection, after having been dead to the world." The use of the funeral pall in fact indicated the nun's symbolic death to the world, and her rebirth in her new conventual life.[28]

Esther bowed and knelt again, and there followed more prayers, more holy water, and more solemn chanting and response between the new nun and her sisters. As she knelt to sing the hymn *Veni Creator Spiritus*, she was immediately aware of how constricting her new wardrobe was, enclosing her body and head in yards and multiple layers of stiff fabric. Muffling her hearing and permitting almost no peripheral vision, the veil in particular encouraged her to turn inward, and her voice may have sounded particularly loud and solitary in the Mass. The other choir nuns continued *Veni Creator Spiritus* as Esther set aside her candle and then prostrated herself on the floor of the chapel in the form of a cross. After this and yet still more prayers, more calls and responses, and more holy water, Esther bowed to her superior and then to signify her entrance into the community, she in turn embraced each of the other nuns while they sang the uplifting hymn *Ecce quam bonum*. Then led by the cross bearer, all of the nuns including Esther departed the choir in reverse order of their entrance.[29]

This was to be Esther's final change of habit—at the age of sixteen, she submitted voluntarily to the discipline of her bishop, her priest, her superior, and her fellow Ursulines. Her hair was cut off shortly after the clothing ceremony. Upon taking her final vows, she would receive and wear a black veil, but otherwise her transformation was complete. The name she whispered to her superior was *Marie-Joseph de l'Enfant Jésus*—the entire Holy Family.

What are we to make of Esther taking the names of Mary, Joseph, and Jesus all at once? Mary was her New England mother's name, and "Marie" sounded like "Mali" among the Wabanaki, who didn't have the *r* sound in their language, and so the name may have been the means to a connection back to her life as a Wabanaki and a New England girl and a way of honoring her families there. And then there was that reference to Joseph in the Old Testament that Vincent Bigot made in his sermon at her clothing ceremony, citing Esther's gift for learning new languages. It's tempting to see her adoption of this name as an effort on her part to reconstruct a family, but that sounds too pat, too much the fashionable cultural studies analysis. After all, taking final vows in a religious order meant ostentatiously leaving behind one's birth family with a symbolic death to be reborn into a religious family, and young girls who had problems with this requirement didn't stay in the convent to take final vows. Of the four other girls who like Esther started their novitiates in 1712, two left within five months. One girl, Charlotte Vaucour Pinguet, lasted barely two weeks with the Ursulines. The language the nuns used in their convent register to describe novices who didn't work out emphasized this duty—or failure—to renounce the things of this world, including family. They would write "*retournée au monde*," or "returned to the world" next to the name of a girl who didn't remain to take final vows.[30] The material world—the world of love, passion, and riches, but also of cruelty, pain, and loss—was outside the convent gate.

Moreover, the evidence in the convent records suggests that Esther was someone who knew what was expected of her, someone who followed the rules. This is perhaps unsurprising—after all, a New England girl who survived a long, hungry trek to be adopted by a Wabanaki family, and who then for five years endured privations and disease to an extent we can hardly imagine, was most likely an intelligent observer and probably a gifted linguist and mimic as well. We can't know whether the name Marie-Joseph de l'Enfant Jésus was selected for her by one of her fellow Ursulines, by the mother superior, or by Vincent Bigot or even the bishops, or whether it was her own effort to embrace the kind of family that could never be taken from her, or an expression of her spiritual devotion, or some combination of these things. But her conformity to religious practice, perhaps the scrupulous zeal of the convert or outsider, is the strongest personal characteristic of hers that we can see in the archival record.

We can also guess about another strong aspect of her character: by the time she turned sixteen, she was an expert in leaving behind the things of this world.

Gender, Rank, and Age in the Monastery

The Ursuline convent that Esther joined in eighteenth-century Québec was a world that represented stability, tradition, and order, and one that was at the same time dramatically countercultural. The monastery was the creature of a patriarchal church, and enclosure—the segregation and cloistering of religious women—was increasingly enforced by bishops in Québec over the course of the eighteenth century. Although part of a deeply patriarchal institution, women's religious orders also challenged the gender hierarchy imposed by the church. They were, after all, self-governing women's communities that offered women leadership roles inside and even outside the walls that were not open to secular North American women until the nineteenth century. Gender was not the only hierarchy that was potentially disrupted by women's religious orders. Class and status hierarchies were simultaneously upheld by both the teaching and hospital nuns among themselves, and disrupted by the education and care work they offered to the community they served.[31] This was especially true in the rustic environment of New France, as at the turn of the eighteenth century the sex ratio within the French Canadian communities in the St. Lawrence Valley was still unbalanced in favor of men. Women's religious orders offered a variety of institutional services in New France that were performed by sisters, wives, mothers, and daughters in the family-based settlement patterns of the English colonies. Instead of receiving education, poor relief, nursing, and hospice care in a family, children were educated by the Jesuits and the Ursulines, and the excess male colonists who were sick, wounded, disabled, or terminally ill were cared for by the Augustinian hospital nuns at the Hôpital-Général (hospice) and at the Hôtel-Dieu (hospital), the other two convents in Québec, which were entirely separate from the Ursulines.[32]

Consider the inversions of status and gender in these religious communities and the multiple ways in which they challenged and reinforced the hierarchies that structured everyday life in New France: The hospital nuns at the Hôtel-Dieu offered intimate body care to soldiers wounded in the wars with the Iroquois and the English, and to people in their community confronting the various infectious disease outbreaks that struck the city on a regular basis. Most of their patients were men of the lower social and economic classes to whom they were unrelated, and as nursing remains today, the care they offered was astonishingly intimate. They removed pus-soaked bandages and filthy bedding, washed and dressed wounds, fed the men who could eat and attended to their toileting needs. The nuns at the Hôpital-Général opened their doors to those wounded in battle when the wars returned to Québec in these years too, but they also offered long-term care to the mentally and physically disabled members of the community who were without family to care for them. Furthermore, all inmates of these institutions were subject to the rules and policies set by the mothers superior rather than by a commanding officer or any of the priests who said masses in the convent chapels and stood by the infirmaries in order to hear confessions or perform extreme unction.

The education of little girls and adolescents might appear to be relatively clean intellectual labor by comparison with nursing, but anyone who has taught or cared for even healthy young children knows that there are opportunities for contact with blood, vomit, and other eruptions on a regular basis. The Ursulines followed the example of their founder, Marie de l'Incarnation, and lived and worked with their charges on sometimes very intimate terms. They bathed and dressed the Native girls *à la Française*, fed them, and slept with them in the dormitory. They nursed them in an infirmary when they were sick, through fevers and epidemics of infectious diseases, and they doubtless had to instruct generations of girls who reached

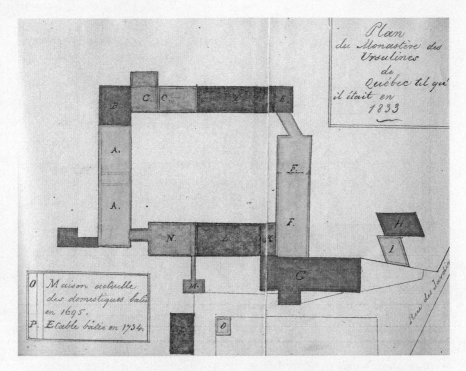

Plan du Monastère entre 1723–1840, in Notes Sur L'Erection Primitive du
Monastère des Ursulines de Québec, sur les divers changements, additions de
bâtiments, etc. This drawing from 1833 shows the convent as it was repaired and
enlarged between the fire of 1686 and the centenary celebration year of 1739,
and therefore as Sister Esther would have known it in her lifetime. The hierarchy
of space in the convent was expressed by proximity to the church (G, lower right,
with the protruding transept) and the choir (FF), both completed in 1723, with
spaces for boarding students (N) and novices (D) protectively flanked by choir
nuns (AA) and the superior (L). Classes for the day students were held entirely
separately from the walled enclosure that formed the cloister above. They met
in the small buildings labeled (H) and (I). The other outbuildings surrounding
the cloister were a little entryway to the *pensionnat* (M), a stable (P), and a tiny
dwelling for *domestiques* (servants) outside the order (O).

menarche at the convent about their monthly cycles and how to use linen rags to absorb their menstrual blood. Religious women in Québec performed care work requiring intimacy with the bodies of the young, the old, the injured, sick, or the chronically disabled that otherwise would have been performed for the most part by wives, mothers, sisters, servants, and slaves in the Protestant colonies of North America. Moreover, they performed this work in service to God and the French colonial state in institutions over which they alone had administrative authority.

Perhaps because their apostolic missions required them to offer Christ-like service and succor to the lowly, social status was carefully noted and guarded among the choir nuns themselves. Wealth and social prestige was something that most of Sister Marie-Joseph de l'Enfant Jésus's peers in the choir enjoyed at birth and continued to evaluate among themselves inside convent walls. The other girls and young women who became Ursulines in the seventeenth and early eighteenth centuries were daughters of the elite of New France. Their mothers and fathers, grandmothers and grandfathers, brothers and sisters, were nobles, governors, military and civil officers, and wealthy merchants of early fur trade society.[33] Although the parents of professing Ursulines are identified by titles like *Sieur* (Sir), *Seigneur* (Lord), *Écuyer* (Esquire), and *Noble homme* (nobleman), several of them lived lives that were clearly Canadian rather than French. Their French-descended families were sometimes interwoven with Native families, and sometimes with individuals sent from France as part of the crown's efforts to discourage these *marriages à la façon de la pays*. For example, both a daughter and three granddaughters of Pierre Boucher (1622–1717), a soldier, interpreter, and eventually governor of Three Rivers, became Ursuline choir nuns: Geneviève Boucher (Mother St. Pierre, ca. 1676–1766) was his daughter by his third wife, but his daughter's profession was hardly his first contact with the Ursuline convent. Pierre Boucher's second wife was Marie Ouebadin-skoue, also known as Marie-Madeleine Chrestienne, a Huron girl who had been educated in the Ursuline convent school. The marriage lasted only long enough for Marie-Madeleine to die shortly after giving birth to a child who also did not survive.[34]

This mixture of fur-trade families with nobility was controversial among some nobles in New France, a tension that is apparent in the stories of the marriages of some of the parents of our eighteenth-century Ursulines. The parents of Marie-Françoise Hertel (Mother St. Exupery, ca. 1680–1770) were part of an experiment by the French crown in the pronatalist engineering of French Canadian families. She was the daughter of Joseph-François Hertel de la Fresnière, a king's lieutenant and military hero whose exploits eventually earned him a noble title, and of Marguerite de Thavenet, who was probably one of the daughters of the bourgeoisie or of the minor nobility sent by Louis XIV to marry French officers. (Women like Thavenet represented about twelve percent of the *filles du roi* sent to help populate New France with French women, and eventually, French Canadian babies and children.) In the case of the Hertel-Thavenet match, the pronatalist experiment was a smashing success, as their marriage gave the colony fifteen children.[35] When the parents-to-be of two Ursulines, Geneviève-Françoise de Lantagnac (Mother St. Henry, ca. 1725/26–65) and Angélique de Lantagnac (Mother St. Marie, ca. 1730–69), fell in love and decided to marry in 1720, Governor Vaudreuil himself opposed their marriage. Their father was King's Lieutenant Gaspard Adhémar de Lantagnac and the grand-nephew of the governor, while the bride's father was merely a respectable bourgeois, not a nobleman. Bishop Saint-Vallier married them anyway, and in spite of the governor's decision to exile his grand-nephew to a post on Cape Breton, they managed to have eight children who lived to adulthood. Their marriage was especially fruitful for the sake of the local women's religious communities; aside from the two Ursulines, four of their five other daughters also became professed nuns in Québec and Montreal.[36]

In terms of both wealth and status, the former Esther Wheelwright just couldn't compare with these daughters of colonial elites. Little wonder that she (and perhaps her senior Ursuline sisters) conspired to make her family sound as distinguished as Governor Vaudreuil had when he described her as "the daughter of the governor of a small place." Even that description was generous, if not fanciful—John Wheelwright had built one of the four strong houses in Wells, but he was a tavernkeeper, a small trader, and an occasional juror, selectman, and justice of the peace—nothing like a governor, even of a "small place" in Maine.

Some of the women who received the most attention in the convent's own records were daughters of the highest-placed families in Québec and Montreal, in part because they tended to become the elected officers and mothers superior of the convent. This was probably due to a combination of status consciousness within the convent with some native ability and early encouragement in leadership in the women elected to leadership roles. Raised in families who governed the colony, these women probably bene-fited from familial connections to church and civil officials as well as from lessons in leadership learned at their mothers' and fathers' knees. Among Esther's contemporaries in the convent was Mother Marie Anne Migeon of the Nativity (1685–1771), who served several terms as mother superior from 1735 to 1760. Her mother, Catherine Gauchet de Belleville, was from a noble family, and her father, Jean-Baptiste Migeon de Branssat, was a Montreal merchant who held a variety of colonial appointed offices. (He also had the good fortune of regulating the fur trade on which he built his fortune.)[37]

By comparison, we can only imagine the leadership lessons Esther Wheel-wright learned either in her garrison in Wells or among her adopted Wa-banaki family or families. The spiritual and community leadership demon-strated by Wabanaki women as their families were suffering and dying from the ravages of colonialism, and the example set by her senior Ursulines as her teachers and mentors, were probably the most significant examples of authority and leadership she was exposed to. As fortifying and inspiring as these examples might have been, they had no currency even in the rustic capital of New France. Esther went to school and joined the Ursuline con-vent with girls who were not just houseguests of governors, army officers, merchants, and titled landowners; they were blood relations to these elites.

Of course, rising to monastic leadership requires not just social status but also—and perhaps most important—longevity. The Ursuline records clearly show that the women who achieved the top elective offices in the convent were nearly always among the oldest sisters.[38] Other daughters of elite fam-ilies died too young to assume high office in the monastery, although they were often extravagantly praised for their obedience, their humility, and their zeal for self-denial, especially considering their wealthy family back-grounds. Their love for discomfort, hard work, the oldest and thinnest gar-ments, and meager amounts of the lowest quality food was remarked upon, presumably because of the contrast with their well-nourished and even luxurious childhoods. A contemporary of Esther Wheelwright's, Catherine Madeline de des Méloizes (Sister St. Borgia, 1697–1725), had a difficult child-hood in spite of her wealthy and entitled family. Her father was François-

Marie Renaud D'Avène de des Méloizes, ensign on the king's ships and a captain of colonial regular troops. Her mother, Françoise-Thèrese Dupont, was the daughter of Nicolas Dupont de Neuville, who had been ennobled by Louis XIV in 1669. He also served on the Conseil Souvrain (sovereign council) of New France, a kind of executive governing board that included the governor and bishop, and which decided policy matters and served as the supreme court.[39] Her mother died on December 5, 1698, just a week after giving birth to Catherine's youngest brother or sister, an infant who did not survive the day. Her father followed his wife and baby to the grave the following spring, when Catherine was barely twenty months old. She was raised by a grandmother who "took particular care with her education, raising her with everything imaginable," but above all "to have a taste for virtue." Catherine was described by the Ursuline Annalist as "pious, humble, charitable," detached from the world, and someone who manifested a "surprising mortification."

Perhaps the Dupont–des Méloizes family just wasn't constitutionally hardy, or perhaps it was Sister St. Borgia's "surprising mortification" that led her to a "happy death" at age twenty-seven. Although her time in the convent was short, barely more than five years from her first days as a novice in the late summer of 1719 until her death in the winter of 1725, she was well remembered and praised extravagantly not only in the contemporary Annales but also in both of the nineteenth-century French and English-language convent histories. Significantly, the *dot* that Mademoiselle des Méloizes offered was much higher than average—4,500 livres at a time when 3,000 or 4,000 was the standard offering.[40] This *dot* was also three times the size of the dowry offered by Vincent Bigot on behalf of Esther Wheelwright just seven years before Sister St. Borgia began her novitiate. As we will see, the small size of Esther's *dot* as well as her family's relative obscurity would be issues that would follow her for the rest of her life.

"Petites filles françoises et Sauvages"

After the clothing ceremony, Ursuline novices like Sister Marie-Joseph de l'Enfant Jésus had time to get used to life behind the veil before they took their final vows. They were required by the Rule to let at least a year pass between the clothing ceremony and making their final profession, although the Ursulines of Québec throughout the ancien régime appear to have preferred to let novices wait two full years. Sister Marie-Joseph de l'Enfant Jésus was among the very few exceptions to a two-year novitiate. As the Annales explained, "At the beginning of her second year of novitiate, some English people from Boston brought her some letters from her family and we started to fear that her parents should try to get her back." Both church and civil authorities, including the bishop and Governor Vaudreuil, "listened carefully to what the English dignitaries had to say and they decided to speed up her vows which the Chapter couldn't refuse and she took her vows April 12 1714 in the church of the Monastery," just fifteen months after her *vêture,* the elaborate clothing ceremony. None of these letters from her family still exists. However, considering the concerns that church officials had all along about Esther's age and her legal right to self-determination, moving forward with her final profession made sense with or without any pressure from the Wheelwright family: the war in which she had been taken was officially over, and the Treaty of Utrecht had been signed in the spring of 1713.

Thus church and state collaborated to keep the eighteen-year-old Esther where she preferred to be, and where her identity as an Anglo-Wabanaki convert was most politically and symbolically useful. Few adolescents could resist the rush of special attention that Sister Marie-Joseph de l'Enfant Jésus received in advance of her final profession. This slight teenager was proof of God's favor for Catholicism and the French that he rescued her from Wabanaki "savagery" and English "heresy" and led her to a religious life. After her final profession, she still wouldn't have been considered a full choir nun yet; like other newly professed women, she would have had to keep company with the novices for another three years after her profession. Only then would she be permitted to eat, live, and speak with the other choir nuns. (Novices were kept strictly separate from the other nuns and especially the boarding students, even having a separate fire for their warmth apart from the choir nuns.)[41]

Since the Council of Trent (1545–63), religious orders were careful to ensure that their novices were entering religious life entirely voluntarily, asking them to answer eight questions attesting to their understanding of the requirements of religious life, their health, and their soundness of mind. Above all, however, these questions were meant to confirm that no one was coerced to take a religious vow. Three weeks before her final profession, Esther sat down with the bishop of Quebec, Jean-Baptiste de la Croix de Chevrière de St. Vallier, who asked her a series of questions required by the Tridentine reforms and recorded her answers precisely. These questions and answers, along with those of all of her predecessors from 1689 and her successors through the turn of the eighteenth century, are recorded in a folio-sized volume called "Examination of Novices," whose leather cover is slowly crumbling to dust but whose parchment pages remain entirely clear and legible. The questions appear to have been written out for the bishop's convenience in advance of the meeting, as the answers Esther offered him are recorded in a completely different hand, a blocky script of "OUI" or "NON," as the question may have demanded. The top of the page announces that this is the examination of "Sister Marie Joseph Esther Whillereght, (known as) the Infant Jesus," further suggesting that the Ursulines still had problems pronouncing her aggressively English name, with its "Wh-" beginning and its "ght" ending, none of which are found anywhere in French spelling or pronunciation. This was possibly the first time Esther's religious name was recorded—Sister Marie-Joseph de l'Enfant Jésus—with her birth name inserted in the middle. On March 21, 1714, a few days before her eighteenth birthday, she signed the document with a hybrid of her given and religious names: Sr. Esther de l'Enfant Jésus.

The first question was forboding but perfectly clear: "Are you totally determined to leave the World and to Live and Die as a Nun?" Esther answered "yes." The second question of the bishop was "Have you been influenced or induced to do so at all by your parents or someone else?" Esther, of all novices, could answer this question with a most emphatic "no." "Have you read and understood the rules and constitution of this Institute carefully, and are you entirely resolute to obey them?" And "Will you be satisfied to live in perpetual enclosure and to fulfill the functions which your Superiors will give you in accordance with the Monastic Institute you committed yourself to?" Of course Esther answered "yes" to both of these questions.

The next questions pertain to the physical and emotional readiness of the novice for religious life: "Do you have any undisclosed, contagious, incurable disease?" (she answered "no"), and "Will you be satisfied to stop talking to your father, your mother, your parents and friends without your

Superior's consent?" Perhaps that last question gave her pause, as she hadn't seen or spoken to her natal family for more than a decade. And what of her Wabanaki family, her first Catholic family? Were there any of them left among the living? Esther had long since been separated from both of her families, so she probably answered "yes" more easily than other young novices. Finally, the last two questions were about her legal eligibility for religious life. "Are you engaged at all to someone on the promise of marriage, or any other obligation?" and "Do you have any debts without your parents' knowledge?" Of course she answered "no" to both questions. Therefore the bishop concluded that "after questioning Marie Joseph Esther Wheelwright Sister of the Infant Jesus according to the conventions of the Council of Trent I declare to the Superior that she may be received in the Monastery and make her profession."[42]

The final vows that the Québec Ursulines took were initially slightly altered from the vows that French Ursulines took. For most of their first century of existence, the Québec Ursulines promised "in the name of our Lord Jesus Christ and in honor of the very sainted mother of our Good Father St. Augustine, and of the Good St. Ursula, I . . . vow and promise to God; poverty, chastity, obedience, and to teach little French and Native girls, according to the Rule of our Good Father St. Augustine and according to the Constitutions of this monastery." The additional vow that Québec Ursulines took promising to teach "*des Petites filles françoises et Sauvages*" lasted into the eighteenth century, and this is the one that Sister Marie-Joseph de l'Enfant Jésus took on April 12, 1714. By 1700 Native girls were still enrolled in both the day school and the boarding school, although their presence was only occasional rather than the central mission of the convent. The number of Native girls continued to drop over the first few decades of the eighteenth century, in the years that Esther was enrolled there as a student in 1709, then as a novice in 1712, and then as a young choir nun in 1714. These are also approximately the same years that the Ursulines accepted their only choir nun of Native descent—Mother St. Marie Madeleine (1678–1734), the former Marie Anne DuBos, whose mother Marie Félix Arontio was a *Huronne,* in 1703. In these two decades, they also accepted two other New England–born captives of the Wabanaki, Mother St. Benoit (the former Mary Ann Davis, ca. 1667–1749) in 1699, and Mother Marie Joseph (or St. Joseph, the former Dorothy Jordan, 1693–1759) in 1719.

As limited as the Native presence was among the Ursulines either as students or sisters by the eighteenth century, the years between 1699 and 1719 represented the high-water mark for the Native presence and influence in the monastery among the novices and nuns. Mother St. Joseph took her final vows in 1722 and promised to teach both French and Native girls, but the next novice to take her final vows, Felicité Poulin (Mother of the Assumption, ca. 1695–1754) promised only to teach "little girls according to the Rule" in 1724. The next professed nun, Marie Joseph d'Ailleboust de Manthet (Mother St. Nicholas, 1701–49) promised once again to teach "little French and Native girls" in 1725, but the tradition ended there. By 1726, the Québec Ursulines had stopped promising to teach both French and Native girls, and at that point the *pensionnat* was entirely populated with French Canadian students.[43] Although Mother Marie-Joseph de l'Enfant Jésus would live on through most of the eighteenth century and would serve in a variety of elective leadership positions in the convent, she would be the last living relic of the Ursuline experiment in teaching First Nations students. Beginning in 1725, the Ursuline mission shifted from sharing the word of God with Huron, Iroquois, and Wabanaki girls to ensuring that the daughters of New France were sufficiently French and thoroughly Catholic.

Inside the Walls

Although the decision to drop the vow to teach both Native and French Canadian students represents a narrowing of the Ursuline vision and mission, Sister Marie-Joseph de l'Enfant Jésus entered the convent in the busiest decade of its existence from its foundation in 1639 to the fall of Québec in 1759. Twenty-four young women were accepted as novices in the 1710s, and all but three stayed to take their final vows. By comparison, the next-busiest decades were the 1770s, with fourteen novices and ten who took final vows; the 1750s, with twelve novices and nine who took final vows; and the 1740s, with ten novices admitted and nine who took final vows.

Is it purely a coincidence that the Ursulines would have more girls and young women looking for a vocation in these years—that is, decades in which war visited Québec? There are different ways of interpreting the growth of the monastery in these war-torn years. Queen Anne's War, the war in which Esther Wheelwright was taken captive from Wells, lasted from 1703 to 1714; King George's War, from 1744 to 1748, included the devastating 1745 loss of the fortress at Louisbourg to the English until it was returned to the French with the peace; the Seven Years' War officially lasted from 1756 to 1763 but was unofficially waged on the frontiers of New England, Acadia, and Quebec throughout the 1750s; and the war of the American Revolution (1775–83) included Benedict Arnold's foiled attempt to capture Québec. No wonder that the convent was the refuge of more young women in these years—some of them undoubtedly war orphans like Sister Marie-Joseph de l'Enfant Jésus or her fellow Wabanaki captive Dorothy Jordan. The security and predictability of life inside convent walls must have appealed to the girls and young women who came of age in this century of war. The food security of the monastery alone was undoubtedly a huge consolation to those sisters who had lived among the Wabanaki in times of extreme famine. What to many modern people might look like confinement and restriction may have felt more like security and stability in a desperately unreliable world.

But we should hesitate to see women only as victims or seekers of safety in perilous times. We might see the Ursulines and other religious women as volunteers in the imperial struggle for the dominion of North America, and religious life was the only way that most women of New France could directly serve the church and the French state. As we have seen, most nuns were from elite families in Québec, Montreal, and Three Rivers—the descendants of men who ventured into Canada with Samuel de Champlain and initiated the fur trade; the daughters of army officers, merchants, professionals, and noble landowners; and the sisters of brothers who supervised Jesuit missions or were commissioned to fight the English. Given the fact that many Ursulines were from families with notable records of service in church, state, and military offices, we might view female monasticism in early Canada as a means by which women could serve God and France through an institution that offered women opportunities for leadership and achievement. There were no other opportunities for most women to demonstrate their patriotism or to give their lives in military, civil, or religious service.[44] Women who married men and gave birth to large families were certainly serving the goals of the French state in New France, but only a very few, very elite married women like the Marquise de Vaudreuil had opportunities to influence politics or policy, let alone to wield real authority.

With France and Great Britain engaged in more than a century of warfare in the seventeenth and eighteenth centuries, enflaming North American proxy wars with the assistance of their Native allies against their Native and Euro-American enemies, what better way to contribute one's talents and energies to the nation than to become a nun? The Ursulines contributed to the spiritual strength and eventual salvation of the citizens of New France by offering Catholic educations to girls and young women of Native, New England, and French Canadian descent. Sister Marie-Joseph de l'Enfant Jésus could have done no better than to turn the fortunes of war into an opportunity to serve God and the king as an Ursuline choir nun. The Augustinian hospital nuns at the Hôpital-Général and at the Hôtel-Dieu in Québec offered even more immediate service to both church and state by caring for wounded and dying French soldiers and colonial regulars. Beyond the specific work they did in the service of the French state in North America, religious women in leadership roles could use their positions and family connections to advance French political and diplomatic goals as well as the interests of their orders.

Prayer and Work

Daily life in the Ursuline convent was organized according to the recitation of the Divine Office, the daily round of prayers and psalms known as the liturgy of the hours. Prayer was at the heart of monastic life from its beginnings, and it remained the source of its power and prestige. The prescribed routine of psalms, hymns, and prayers that made up the hours—matins and lauds, the morning prayers also designated as major hours; then prime (midmorning), terce (midday), and sext (midafternoon) prayers; followed by vespers (the evening prayer, also a major hour) and compline (night prayer)—gave structure and meaning to the sisters' days, and offered moments of rest from their other work. Only choir nuns were expected to observe all of the hours, amid their teaching and administrative responsibilities. *Soeurs converses* (lay sisters who performed the domestic labor necessary to the institution) did not have the honor of reciting all of the hours. The nuns arose at 4 A.M. to recite the first of the prayers of the day, matins

Reconstruction, ca. 1990s, of a nun's cell before 1759. This re-creation of an
Ursuline nun's cell with its cupboardlike enclosed bed suggests the realities of
living in unheated rooms in Québec.
PDQ, 0, MQ, 1/P, 003, 000, 000, 016, 0245. Photo courtesy of the Archives du
Monastère des Ursulines de Québec

and lauds. They awoke their boarding students at 5:30 or 6 A.M., and the
whole community attended Mass at 7:15 A.M., followed by breakfast. School
and work occupied the remainder of the morning. The midday meal was
served at 10:15, followed by prayer and an hour of recreation, which might
include free conversation, strolls in the garden, reading, writing, and needlework. Afternoons were filled with more work, school, and prayer until
supper was served at 5:15 from mid-October until mid-April, or 5:30 during
the warmer months. After supper, they had another hour of recreation, vespers and compline, and then bedtime at 8:15 or 8:30, according to the season, followed by hours of silence that would last until the next morning.[45]

Teaching was the apostolate of the Ursulines from their beginnings, but
the Ursulines of Québec were also famous for their gilt work, painting, and

embroidery, especially the gold and silver embroidery of various items used in Catholic devotional practice: altar frontals, banners, copes, chasubles, and altar cloths, among many others. The nuns' expertise in embroidery and the high levels of artistry are remarkable. Although much of their work was wrought in colored silk on silk and muslin cloth, the Ursulines were so skilled that they became famous for their incorporation of silver and gold thread and even jewels into their designs.[46] Modern-day visitors to the Musée des Ursulines at the convent can marvel at the needle- and brushwork of the seventeenth- and eighteenth-century Ursulines, and wonder at their painstaking labor and sacrifice for the production of such elaborate devotional and decorative items—which is all the more impressive, considering the short, cold days and even colder dark nights that dominate Québec for at least six months of the year. Many of these items decorated Canadian chapels in the colonial period, and gold embroidery and giltwork are clearly central to the aesthetic of the Québec churches even today.

Convent histories as well as architectural and artifactual evidence document the nuns' communal emphasis on artistry from their earliest days in Québec.[47] The founder of the Québec Ursulines, Marie de l'Incarnation (1599–1672), is remembered as excellent in "all kinds of needle-work and embroidery, as well as in painting and gilding. While she sanctified these talents by working for the altar, and contributing to the decoration of chapels and churches all over the country, her young Sisters, as well as the pupils, loved to take lessons of the amiable Mother, and were happy to aid her in her toils." As though supervising this happy workshop of young artists weren't enough, "even in sculpture and architecture, this indefatigable Mother was skillful. It was she who directed the workmen, employed in decorating the interior of the church with architectural ornaments, guiding them for the proportion of the columns, capitals and entablature, as well as in the minute details of the art."[48] Training in painting, embroidery, and gilding continued through the eighteenth century, serving as a source of both income and spiritual inspiration inside convent walls.

When Sister Marie joined the Ursulines in 1712, the Ursuline commitment to artistic expression would have felt familiar to her. She had been surrounded by examples of women's piety and devotion from the time she arrived in Wabanakia as a captive, and by their insistence on creating something of lasting beauty and value for their new religious traditions—

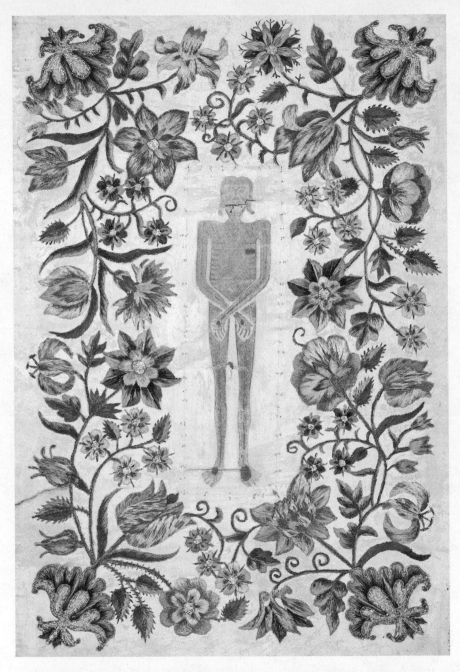

Eighteenth-century embroidery of Jesus Christ, silk thread on stiffened fabric. This figure of a crucified Christ surrounded by an elaborate and still brilliantly colored floral border demonstrates the kind of artistry that was part of everyday life in the Ursuline convent. The elaborate interplay of different stitches, textures, and colors brings the flowers to life in three dimensions. Photo courtesy of the Musée des Ursulines de Québec recall all of those devotional wampum belts and the intricately decorated items for personal adornment that Wabanaki women created. The artistic expression Sister Marie found among the Ursulines of Québec would expand over the course of her lifetime, and would become one of the main skills for which the Ursulines were known outside their monastery.

The large number of professions in the 1710s was accompanied by a dramatic expansion of the physical and spatial layout of the monastery in the 1710s and 1720s, increasing in its intensity as the convent approached the hundredth anniversary of its founding in 1739. The monastery had been twice burned down and rebuilt in the seventeenth century. According to Father Pierre de Charlevoix, "Their funds are so small, and the dowries they receive with the girls in this country are so moderate, that after their house was burnt down for the first time, it was resolved to send them back to France. They have, however, had the good fortune to recover themselves both times" through their own hard work as well as a few royal donations. By the time Father Pierre visited them in the 1720s, he reported, "They are neatly and commodiously lodged, which is the fruit of the good example they set the rest of the colony by their oeconomy, their sobriety and industry."[49]

When the convent was enlarged in the peaceful prosperity of the 1710s and 1720s, the nuns themselves continued in the tradition of their founder and assisted in building and decorating the new church themselves: "At the hours when the masons were absent for their meals, we used to mount the scaffolding, carrying up the stone and the mortar, our Mother Superior leading the way." When the masons returned to their work, the nuns "all returned to their respective labors, some to painting, gilding or embroidery; some wrought tapestry, or bark-work, others made artificial flowers. Their earnings served to augment our revenues and to aid in paying the workmen." The gilding in the chapel of the enlarged convent, finally completed in 1735, "of which there is that profusion required by the taste of those times, was all executed by the patient toil of the nuns themselves." A remembrance of the life of a late-eighteenth- and early-nineteenth-century nun praised her talents as a florist and "an artist of unrivalled skill in gilding," crafts that were at their heights around the turn of the nineteenth century.[50] Marie de l'Incarnation's talents were taught and preserved for at least two centuries.

Hagiographic insider accounts are not the only records that noted and praised Ursuline artistic skills in this era. Both Catholic and Protestant foreign visitors to the Ursuline chapel in the eighteenth century frequently attended a Mass as part of their tour of Québec, and most commented on its striking beauty and ornamentation shimmering in the candlelight. Father Charlevoix, who visited amid the busy rebuilding and enlargement of the convent in the 1720s, noted that the Ursulines "gild, embroider, and are all usefully employed, and what comes out of their hands is generally of a good taste." Peter Kalm remarked on his visit in 1749 that the chapel included an "apartment or small chapel dedicated to the Virgin Mary," and noted that the nuns did "all sorts of neat work there, gild pictures, make artificial flowers, etc."[51]

Captain John Knox, an officer in the British Conquest of 1759, kept a journal that commented several different times on the Ursuline chapel and Ursuline artistry. Five weeks after the British marched triumphantly into Québec to claim it, he reports that he and several British officers attended a Mass at the Ursuline chapel: "High Mass was performed this day in the church of St. Ursula, in commemoration of her birth; I went, with several other Officers, to see their ceremonies, where we saw all their finery and different vestments displayed, and were very agreeably entertained." Knox apparently sampled Masses at various convent chapels during the autumn of 1759. He singled out the "Ursuline and Hôtel de Dieu convents with their churches" as public buildings which "carry a striking appearance," although he later went on to say that the Hôtel-Dieu chapel afforded him "a view of many other paintings of angels, saints, &c. but they are too indifferent to deserve any notice." He also contrasted the Ursuline chapel with that of the nuns of the Hôpital-Général, saying that the latter chapel was "small and extremely neat, void of all superstitious pageantry . . . but whatever may be deficient in this is amply compensated in that of the Ursulines, within the city; where no art has been spared to render it, throughout as ostentatiously glittering and captivating as possible."[52] Later that fall, he noted that a significant gift of Ursuline artistic handiwork was "presented [to] the Governor and other officers . . . a set of crosses of St. Andrew curiously worked, they were displayed in compliment to this day: in a corner of the field of each cross was wrought an emblematical heart, expressive of that attachment and affection which every good man naturally bears to his native country."[53] Clearly, Ursuline artistry was a significant part of their apostolic mission and their devotional practice.

Teaching, artistry, and performing all of the psalms, hymns, and prayers of the liturgy of the house was the work of choir nuns, while the work of lay sisters (*soeurs converses*) was the ongoing housekeeping and maintenance of the large household that was the monastery. These sisters were typically admitted to the convent with much smaller dowries than the choir nuns, and they were from more modest family backgrounds as well. The work of the lay sisters in the Ursuline convent involved food preparation, laundry, cleaning, and the nursing care involved in operating a household that in the eighteenth century typically housed dozens of nuns and boarding students at a time.[54] Imagining the mountains of laundry alone is enough to make the modern reader quail at the arduous tasks of eighteenth-century *soeurs converses*, let alone the demands of cooking and keeping house for perhaps sixty to seventy-five girls and women at a time. Lay sisters had to be physically strong as well as undaunted by the daily routine of two or three hot meals a day for the teachers, students, and themselves. While the choir nuns were the teachers, the lay sisters oftentimes had even more intimate relationships with the boarding students as they nursed them when they were ill and performed the other daily labor that mothers (or servants) typically performed for children in New France.[55]

Cleaning fireplaces and building and tending fires; drawing and carrying all of the water used in the convent, as well as stirring boiling pots of soap and giant copper kettles of stinking linens; or even just baking the daily bread and roasting or braising the beef that was served on most days of the week—it was difficult, hot, and frequently dirty work. Laundry must have occupied the majority of the lay sisters' time, as convents appear to have had unusually high standards for personal cleanliness in the early modern period. In fact, the Rule dictated that each week all sisters must have two chemises, two caps, two veils, and two wimples apiece freshly laundered, not to mention their stockings, aprons, nightcaps, handkerchiefs, and menstrual cloths. The Ursulines' black woolen habits were laundered twice a year. Linens were also subject to a remarkable scrubbing for the seventeenth and eighteenth centuries: napkins in the refectory were changed weekly, tablecloths twice a month, sheets monthly (those in the infirmary as needed), and shared towels two or three times a week. Food preparation

Soeur Converse Ursuline de la Congrégation de Paris, 1792, from Pierre Hélyot's *Histoire des Ordres Religieux et Militaires* (Paris, 1792). This converse sister is not shown wearing the shorter sleeves and gown, compared with those of a choir nun, that would have signaled her station. Long sleeves would have made domestic chores like housekeeping, laundry, tending the infirmary, and barn work especially messy. However, the hierarchy of religious life is otherwise evident here, as she will wear forever the white veil of the novice rather than the black veil of the professed choir nun.

Wellcome Library, London

was probably the next most time-consuming task for the *soeurs converses*, as they prepared three meals a day for dozens of Ursulines and their students. In the late seventeenth century, it was typical for the convent to have forty or more boarding students, in addition to a dozen or so choir and lay sisters. By the middle of the eighteenth century, the Ursulines had forty-five lay and choir sisters combined and perhaps thirty or forty boarding students per year, so the Ursuline kitchen crew had to feed at least eighty people three times a day.[56]

Because of their heavy workload, lay sisters were set apart visually from their sisters in the choir and reminded throughout their lives of their lower rank in the convent. Their habits were typically of a coarser fabric and hemmed a little shorter at the bottom and on the sleeves to facilitate their physical labor. They also retained the white veil of the novice rather than the black veil that professed choir nuns wore. Additionally, just as they did not teach, they were not permitted to say the Divine Office with the choir nuns, nor were they permitted to vote in the order's triennial elections. Finally, while choir sisters were generally "promoted" from the title of Sister to Mother after twelve years of profession, lay sisters continued to be called Sister for their entire lives. In short, they were servants at a time and place where the privileges of class and rank were strictly observed. However, working as a lay sister in a convent offered several advantages that servants in secular homes did not enjoy, such as membership in a community, liberty from the sexual predation of men, and finally, a guarantee of care in sickness and old age. These were considerable advantages when we look at the much more vulnerable position of women workers, and especially servant women, in the rest of colonial North America. Considering that most of the lay sisters would probably have been destined for household service outside the convent, lay sisters were fortunate by comparison.[57]

Secrets of the Convent

Ursuline piety and devotion to the arts were not the only connection between Catholic Wabanaki women and religious French Canadian women in the eighteenth century that Sister Marie would have recognized. One final thing united them besides work and prayer, and that was the practice of bodily mortification, which we saw so vividly in chapter 2 via descriptions of Native women's mortification practices recorded in the *Jesuit Relations*. Although there is a little more evidence of these practices in the Ursuline records—the practice of self- or possibly mutual flagellation; the use of haircloth, cilices, and iron girdles; the withholding or limitation of food, clothing, or warmth; and other practices meant to inflict pain or discomfort on the body—none of these is described in detail or addressed directly in the monastic records. Like most women's religious orders in the late medieval and early modern era, French Ursulines still engaged in a variety of ascetic and penitential practices. Seventeenth-century Ursulines and other women's religious orders in France were caught between a medieval monastic ideal for women that praised saints and martyrs for their endurance or self-infliction of bodily misery, and a new emphasis on apostolic mission (especially a zeal for teaching young girls) and service characteristic of post-Reformation religious life.[58] While the Ursulines of Québec clearly had a strong apostolate and offered many services to the French Canadian and Native communities, they brought with them a range of practices (and probably appliances) designed to mortify their flesh even as they taught and served. The traditions of penitence and the use of the body to channel the divine were too well established and respected among women religious for them to be set aside entirely. Mortification appears to have been a part of ritual Ursuline practice in Québec at least through the mid-eighteenth century, and may have continued well into the nineteenth century.

Official monastic obituaries commemorating the work and lives of deceased seventeenth- and eighteenth-century Ursulines suggest some of the ways they used their bodies to affirm communal "virtues" and to channel the divine. (Indeed, sometimes these penitential practices were credited with hastening deaths.) While some ascetic practices were of an external and more public nature—denying oneself food or proximity to warm fires, for example—other mortifications like the use of haircloth, appliances worn under the clothing, or flagellation—weren't apparent or remarked upon until nuns were called to wash a sister's body and prepare it for burial.

The founding mother of the Québec Ursulines, Marie de l'Incarnation, exemplified both the Ursuline devotion to ritual mortification and the early modern imperative to conceal it at the same time for fear of being judged mentally unstable. She beat herself with stinging nettles, used haircloth to further irritate the wounds, wore chains under her robes, and slept on a plank. We know about her efforts to make herself like a "slave" or a "dead person" because she wrote it all down herself and sent her *Relation* of 1654 to her son, a Jesuit back in France. Yet at the same time she revealed these extreme expressions of her piety, she wrote that she must conceal her mortification from everyone, "otherwise they would think I was crazy."[59] This game of engaging in mortification and concealing it while also allowing others to know about it appears to have continued long after Marie de l'Incarnation's death, and it appears to have become interwoven into Ursuline ritual practice. Like their work and prayer, mortification was a shared set of sensual (if not obviously pleasurable) practices that set them apart from the world and bound them together. Unlike their public work, however, ascetic practices were secrets known only to the community of religious women.

What evidence is there for the mortification practices among the Québec Ursulines? Out of the 109 obituaries recorded in the *Livres*, which record the lives and deaths of the first choir nuns of the order from its foundation in 1639 until 1830, 10 obituaries list mortification specifically as a virtue possessed by the late nun, or describe notable ascetic behavior. This is a significant minority, especially considering that the deaths of seven of the ten are clustered within the same twenty-five years from 1725 to 1750.[60] The timing of this cluster is probably not coincidental. In preparing in 1738 for the one hundredth anniversary of their foundation, the Ursulines instituted a number of special observances for the centennial year 1739, including a number of ascetic Catholic practices beyond their usual Rule. The Ursulines "prolonged nearly all [their] ordinary pious exercises," and "on Fridays, three were appointed in turn to observe silence, refraining from the usual recreations, and adding several acts of mortification and of other virtues."[61] Even two generations after the centennial, mortification was still listed as central to the Rule in an anecdote from 1789, and it was even praised in an Ursuline who died in 1883—nearly 250 years after the arrival of Marie de l'Incarnation in Québec.[62]

In manuscript records and convent histories in both French and English, the word "mortification" appears occasionally to describe a virtue Ursulines might embody as well as to praise the zeal for mortification of some individual sisters. It is in the manuscript evidence, however, that we find the more detailed descriptions of mortification and other ascetic practices, and can begin to explore their meanings in the life of this religious community. In the obituary for Mother St. Ignatius, the last survivor of the original congregation of Ursulines who arrived from France in 1639 and who became the first professed nun of the order in Québec, she was remembered as "animated by a spirit of penitence. This friend of austerity treated her body like her paramount enemy" until her death in 1701.[63]

Other eighteenth-century obituaries repeat some of the same language —nuns were honored for choosing only the basest of work assignments, for refusing bodily comforts and medical treatment, and for having "always treated her body like her greatest enemy."[64] The rejection of food and the embrace of poor clothing and hard work were described in more detail and appear to have been more common than more aggressive ascetic practices. Mother Marie Madeleine de Lauzon de St. Charles (ca. 1654–1731) was praised for her "principal virtues," which were "humility, charity, patience, and mortification." The annalist continues, "Her charity was universal, as much for people outside as for those inside the monastery. She appeared everywhere in the school for the little Native girls where she worked for several years. She had the tenderness of a mother for her students [who were] somewhat disgusting, washing them upon their arrival in their cabin with an affection that showed well that she regarded the little creatures as souls redeemed by the blood of J[esus] C[hrist]." With this embrace of low-status labor in caring for the bodies of Native girls, Sister St. Charles's mortification "went hand in hand, always taking the lowest quality clothing and food that we had for herself." Even today, this kind of intimacy with poor outcasts is a Catholic virtue, as Pope Francis has recently commemorated Jesus' washing of his apostles' feet before his crucifixion by washing the feet of patients, prisoners, and juvenile detainees on Holy Thursday.[65]

Some of the sisters clearly damaged their health through their ascetic practices, and even then some avoided medical attention so as to prolong or deepen their suffering. One extreme example of this was Mother Angelique Roberge de St. Marie (1676–1750), who was remembered for having been "sickly almost her whole life. . . . The illness that took her from us was scurvy, which rotted her head and all her entrails, [an] illness that made her suffer inexpressible pain which she bore with a patience that we had to admire a great deal." How would one develop scurvy, a severe vitamin C deficiency that attacks the soft tissue of the body, amid the relatively high food security of a convent with its own orchard and gardens? Only by denying herself food and even water: "She spent several days without taking anything, not even a taste of water to refresh her mouth which was completely dry, and also her throat."[66] In witnessing these pious devotions, did Sister Marie-Joseph de l'Enfant Jésus think of the starvation and suffering of the Wabanaki women and children she lived among as a child?

Although the denial of food and other bodily comforts is most often discussed explicitly in the obituaries, the "chain of traditions" brought by Marie de l'Incarnation and Mother St. Ignatius clearly included more aggressive practices, and probably included cilices or iron girdles (*ceintures de fer*)—barbed chains or belts that were wrapped around thighs, arms, or waists to inflict constant pain and irritation. Mother Marie Genevieve Baudoüin de St. Augustin (1693–1739), who died at age forty-six, was remembered for being "fervent and very mortified . . . which we confirmed again after her death by the penitential instruments which we found covered in her blood."[67] And although the annalists who composed these obituaries over the course of more than fifty years sometimes describe penitential practices in graphic detail, they also hint at a desire to conceal the same practices. The obituary for Mother Louise Pinguet Vaucours de St. François-Xavier (1695–1749) says that she hid her "indispositions and suffering" as "an Arab does his treasure."[68] This was an especially unusual turn of phrase, because the vast majority of obituaries avoid any reference to the world outside the monastery, let alone to another part of the world entirely.

By comparison with other contemporary New World religious women's communities, the Ursulines of Québec may have been unusual in their circumspection. (Perhaps they internalized the style of their founder in the extreme—to borrow the words of Marie de l'Incarnation, "otherwise they would think [we were] crazy.") In a recent study of Ursulines of New Orleans, one of their most prominent mid-eighteenth-century members was remembered for her mortification practices in great detail. Charlotte Hebert's obituary said that she "gave herself with zeal to all the austerities which a spirit of penance could invent." These austerities for Hebert included a hair shirt and belts of horsehair, iron chains, iron cuffs, daily self-flagellation, and an austere diet of a daily meal of only the "most common and crude" sort. Similarly, the records of the Congrégation de Notre Dame in Montreal, a teaching order like the Ursulines, are much franker about the ascetic practices, particularly in the life and writings of Marie Barbier (1663–1739). Another recent book includes Jesuit Father Claude Chauchitière's detailed record of Iroquois women's ascetic practices at the Mohawk mission of Kahnawake, where exposure to extreme winter weather, beating with willow switches, and the use of iron girdles were encouraged and monitored by the mission priests.[69]

Although lacking in the graphic detail other historians have found, references to mortification practices continue through the eighteenth-century Ursuline records. For example, the obituary for the young and aristocratic Mother St. Borgia (1697–1725), formerly Catherine Madeline de des Méloizes, describes her as an Ursuline whose devotion is all the more praiseworthy because of her rejection of worldly wealth and comforts: "Her piety was most exemplary, her charity unbounded. Her detachment from self and from everything earthly; her mortification, her fidelity to the observance of the rule and her holy engagements, rendered her a bright example of what is meant by religious perfection." Perhaps because of her aristocratic background, she was described in her obituary as having a "surprising mortification, always seeking to find and remove" anything that "might give her any satisfaction." Mother St. Borgia's only fault was overzealousness in her detachment and mortification, because "it was necessary, on more than one occasion, to moderate her fervor which always exceeded her strength." Perhaps this is why she "pass[ed] from the novitiate, her earthly paradise, to that above, just as she was completing the fourth year of her religious profession" at the age of twenty-seven.[70]

References to mortification drop off dramatically in the Québec Ursuline records after the centennial celebration, but it is clearly included as a "virtue" among the Ursulines through the monastery's first century, and perhaps for some time beyond. We cannot know whether mortification ceased to be practiced regularly in the late eighteenth or nineteenth centuries, or whether the convent annalists grew even more circumspect in mentioning it at all. Mortification among the Ursulines may have ceased or gone entirely underground as of the mid-eighteenth century because of its continuing associations with medieval immoderation and barbarism, especially given the unfavorable climate for religious women and men in both New France and old France: First, there were challenges to monasticism in

France through the eighteenth century. Next, we must consider the jeopardy to Catholicism and monasticism more on Québec specifically in the fifteen years between the British Conquest of 1759 and the passage of the Québec Act of 1774, which declared the practice of Catholicism legal there. And finally, at the end of the eighteenth century French monasteries were seized after the Revolution.[71] In any case, the Ursulines faced bigger problems at the end of the eighteenth century than whether or how to engage in and conceal mortification practices.

What was the meaning of inflicting hunger, discomfort, pain, and even skin-piercing wounds on the body, especially in a century ravaged by warfare and the epidemic diseases that traveled with mobilized armies? Perhaps we should think about mortification and suffering less as a *denial* of pleasures than as an affirmation or embrace of something of value. Significantly, lay sisters were never memorialized for their mortification—that was a privilege reserved for the choir nuns, and as we have seen, it was their elite status (as in the case of Mother St. Borgia) that made their bodily sacrifices even more meaningful to the community, presumably because they were strangers to privation and discomfort aside from their asceticism. Caroline Walker Bynum famously demonstrated that rituals surrounding food and the body—fasting and eucharistic devotion—were a particularly gendered form of piety among medieval women religious, and it appears that the commemoration of the sufferings of medieval saints may have forged bonds among monastic women around the world from the twelfth through the twentieth centuries.[72] In other words, although mortification practices probably were undertaken individually and even secretly, the Ursulines of Québec were linked to one another and to a much larger Christian women's history and tradition through mortification practices.

While there may be broad similarities between sexual experiences and mortification practices, especially in their hidden and forbidden natures, I do not mean to suggest that mortification was a simple substitute for or a means to sexual pleasure. Nevertheless, these practices may have offered relief from stress and may even have been experienced as pleasure. The current medical and psychiatric literature on adolescent self-cutting or self-mutilation—the infliction of shallow, multiple cuts on their bodies, usually but not always in places ordinarily covered by clothing—may help us understand the value of Catholic mortification practices. Not only do modern adolescents report no pain during the self-mutilation, they often report that the mutilation has an analgesic effect and that they get great emotional relief from incidents of self-cutting. This literature also agrees that self-mutilation is a highly gendered activity among adolescents—many more girls than boys report cutting—and it also suggests that self-mutilators report enjoying feelings of power and control. This combination of analgesia and relief may make self-mutilation a repetitive and addictive behavior. Furthermore, the prevalence of self-mutilation today among prisoners and adolescents—people who are involuntarily subject to the authority and power of the state or their parents—suggests a connection to the cloistered women and mission Mohawk women discussed above. While nuns were examined to ascertain that they voluntarily wished to submit to the Rule of their order, one can well imagine that the elite women who became Ursuline choir nuns might have frequently struggled with the vow of obedience. The analgesia and emotional relief offered by self-mutilation appears to offer comfort and release to people who are subject to the will and authority of others.[73] Thus self-mortification among the Québec Ursulines may have served multiple purposes: It may have offered the means to relieve the frustrations of life within the cloister as well as affirming ties among the women who engaged in these practices.

We should also consider what the intentional infliction of wounds and the drawing of blood meant in the specific context of a New World Catholic women's religious community. New World religious—men and women alike—shared an ethic of bodily sacrifice, and believed that bodily suffering, pain, and even torture could be a means of spiritual communion with the divine.[74] They went to the New World not in spite of the danger of martyrdom but because of their eagerness to make the ultimate sacrifice for God. While priests and brothers could engage in mission work and travel to the far corners of a continent dominated by Native peoples, religious women's communities in Canada and New Spain were urban and cloistered. Although many scholars have questioned the extent to which they were effectively cloistered in ways that would satisfy their bishops at all times, it is unquestionable that the women's communities were located in urban spaces, and that any missionary activity they engaged in happened inside their schools and hospitals.[75] They could never go into the Canadian woods like the Jesuits and other male religious orders, who explicitly sought out and reveled in the discomfort of travel and mission life with the Native people, if not mutilation or death at the hands of the Iroquois or Hurons like Isaac Jogues or Jean de Brébeuf, North America's first martyrs.[76] Just as monasticism offered women opportunities to serve the church and the French state like their brothers, mortification practices may have constituted a strategy for religious women to demonstrate their ethic of missionary self-sacrifice.

As to the specific value of blood rituals: modern-day self-mutilators frequently report that seeing the blood they let is a central aspect of the pleasure they experience.[77] The Eucharist is central to Catholic ritual practice, and all masses feature the transubstantiation of bread and wine into the body and blood of Christ. In a family of women religious, it might have been a matter of great personal joy as well as a marker of status within the community to draw blood in imitation of Christ's wounds. The drawing of blood may have had special importance in the eighteenth century in North America, a bloody century for the sacrifice of young men in warfare. Suffering and bleeding for Jesus bound religious women to one another and to holy people throughout church history, and it may also have offered the Ursulines of Québec opportunities for bodily sacrifice and devotion they otherwise could not access.[78]

What does it mean that there is no evidence that Sister Marie-Joseph de l'Enfant Jésus ever engaged in mortification or other ascetic practices? While the daughters of elite citizens of Montreal and Québec might have felt compelled to introduce pain and suffering into their comfortable lives, our sister might have felt that her precarious childhood as a border-crossing war captive, adopted daughter, and refugee was suffering enough. As an adolescent contemplating a religious life, she probably looked at the monastery as a place of extraordinary calm and safety compared with the chaos and fear that had governed her childhood and adolescence from ages seven to fifteen.

We moderns have questions for Sister Marie-Joseph de l'Enfant Jésus that she might never have understood or wanted to answer. Did she ever look back on the communities and families she had lost or left behind with longing or regret? Did she remember some of her sisters and brothers, Wabanaki and Anglo-American alike, better or more fondly than others? Did she ever contemplate a "return to the world" outside the convent? Did she wonder where she would have gone, or how she would have lived, had she not entered religious life? Sadly, for long decades inside the convent from age eighteen to her fifties we have no insight into her inner life—her memories, thoughts, and feelings. Her answer to these questions might have been indirect or slighting, anyway: who was she to question God's plan? Who are we to wonder on her behalf? That she endured two likely traumatic removals from her New England and Wabanaki families and then a last journey away from the Ursuline convent and back was improbable enough; that she survived and thrived in all circumstances was interpreted by Father Bigot as a sign from God of her special destiny. What devout fifteen-year-old could resist that interpretation of her life, appealing as it does both to eighteenth-century providentialism and to the solipsism of most teenagers? What else might God have in store for her? As Father Bigot's sermon suggested, our sister was well suited to the life of a teacher, and we know that she would grow into several leadership roles inside the convent.

Unfortunately, we must leave Sister Marie-Joseph de l'Enfant Jésus in her new black veil and cincture on the cold steps of the Ursuline chapel. Just as a pall was cast upon her as she entered religious life at her clothing ceremony, so a curtain now descends to prevent us from seeing clearly the details of her life as an individual for several decades. We can assume that as she matured and aged, she thrived on the predictable routine of the convent, the Hours, the classes, the dedicated times for eating, recreation, and rest. We can assume this because she chose religious life voluntarily, and as we will see in the next chapter, she defended that choice in a letter to her mother and explained some of the circumstances behind her profession to a Wheelwright nephew who came to visit her. Whatever fleeting memories or emotions might have run through her head at different times in the next three decades, she remained consistent in her desire for a religious life and determined to explain and defend her choices to the Wheelwrights.

We leave our sister in the spring of 1714 after her final vows, but we note one important change to come: according to Ursuline tradition, after a dozen years or so in religious life a choir nun was called by the title Mother, and no longer Sister, and was therefore promoted to the *vocales*, the community of senior nuns who had voting rights in convent government. Following the naming practices of her senior mothers and sisters, Sister Marie-Joseph de l'Enfant Jésus would use a hybrid name composed of her given name and her religious name. (Our status-conscious Ursulines insisted on their peers remembering their family names and connections to the world outside the monastery.) In English, "Mother Esther of the Infant Jesus" is how she typically was referred to in the convent's archival records by the time she reached middle age, and she would use combinations of her given and her religious names in her signatures over the decades. By adopting this hybrid name, Mali/Marie vanished in favor of her given English name, Esther. Did this represent the final erasure of her Wabanaki childhood from her public and perhaps even her personal identity? Did it represent a renewed embrace of her New England family? Did it mean that she hoped one day to renew those connections, or at least to benefit from the perception that she was from an important family in New England? All of these are possibilities suggested by the evidence in the chapters that follow.

Our idyll inside the cloister is over. As we will see in the final three chapters, the Ursulines of Québec no longer had to inflict pain on themselves with iron girdles, switches, or branches. By the second half of the eighteenth century, their daily and spiritual lives were threatened by political, military, and religious domination by outsiders who had only contempt for French Canadians in general and for women's religious communities in particular. War would return to New France again in the 1740s, and it would make itself at home in Québec in the 1750s, even in the Ursuline monastery itself. But as we have seen, although the Ursuline monastery appeared to be a place of stability, food security, and calm compared with the world outside, in many ways the routine of work and prayer would have seemed familiar to Mother Esther, who had become a Catholic first because of her immersion in a Catholic Wabanaki community. The prayers she recited, the work she did in adulthood, and the artistic achievement she would encourage as she rose to convent leadership—in all of these things we can see glimmers of her Wabanaki background, however much the Ursulines of Québec worked to erase them.

The stresses of military invasion and conquest would expose for the first time real evidence of dissension among the Ursulines as Sister Marie became Mother Esther, and as she rose to leadership. As Quebec was conquered by the British, the Ursuline monastery would elevate its only foreign-born nun to mother superior. Although she was elected mother superior three times, some choir nuns resented her authority and struggled with their vows of obedience. In the last three decades of her life, Mother Esther's leadership would be tested by conditions outside the convent as much as questioned from within.

CHAPTER FIVE
MOTHER ESTHER

Québec, January 1754

When Mother Esther de l'Enfant Jésus strode into the parlor to meet her nephew Nathaniel in January 1754, he met a woman of nearly sixty who had been a professed nun for forty years.[1] With the permission of the bishop of Québec, he visited his aunt and gave her a silver place setting and chalice. The place setting was engraved with the Wheelwright coat of arms, which impressed the Ursulines and may have reassured them about Mother Esther's New England family's status. In turn, the Ursulines received Wheelwright as an honored guest befitting a foreign diplomat. He reported in his journal that upon this first visit, "I was very politely received and genteely entertained with Variety of wines & sweetmeats," and "the next morning they sent me a very genteel desart." He would have been initially received by his aunt in the parlor, separated from her by the iron grille. Wheelwright was yet another Protestant visitor who remarked that "the Church is very handsomly adorned and their Chapels, in which are very curious imbroidery, all of their own work." His report suggests a familiarity with parts of the monastery not open to the public, including the private cells of the choir nuns: "They are conveniently Lodged, each one hath her separate appartement, with a small bed, a table, & one Chair, nothing but what is necessary."[2]

As we will see, Nathaniel's call upon his aunt was important in terms of Mother Esther's position in her community and her relations with her fellow Ursulines. But his presence in the convent and what it might have signaled to the Ursulines was complicated: his visit as an ambassador for Massachusetts was evidence of the Wheelwright family's growing importance and wealth in colonial Boston, but he was still *un étranger*, a foreigner in New France.

In middle age, Mother Esther had assumed a variety of offices in the leadership of the monastery, and within a decade of Nathaniel's visit she would become mother superior. Even as she taught both the children in the day school and boarding students and served as the novice mistress three times, as portress (doorkeeper) once, and as assistant to the superior before her election as mother superior, she was engaged in a diplomacy and evangelical outreach of her own from within the walls of the monastery. Her nephew was hardly the first or the last foreigner she met with, spoke to, counseled, or charmed. The previous four chapters began with us following Esther as she moved through time and space from the Wheelwright garrison in Wells to Wabanaki mission villages to Québec as a student and then as an Ursuline novice. These next three chapters will be filled with movement as war returns to Québec in midcentury. Rather than Esther leaving the convent, however, we'll observe different foreigners like New England's Nathaniel Wheelwright and British General James Murray as they tour and invade Québec, ultimately occupying the Ursuline monastery itself.

Nathaniel Wheelwright's Mission

In the autumn of 1753, Massachusetts Governor William Shirley granted Wheelwright a passport and a commission to retrieve some New England captives from the previous war who were living in Iroquois mission villages near Montreal. The North American front of the War of Austrian Succession, King George's War (1744–48), had been fought to a draw by the British and French, while its Wabanaki and Iroquois participants paid a higher price. The one major conquest of the war was the taking by New England regulars of the French garrison town of Louisbourg on the southeastern tip of Nova Scotia, and Louisbourg was returned to the French by the Treaty of Aix-la-Chappelle.[3] Tracking down the captives in this war was taking many years more.

Wheelwright and his companion on the mission, Colonel Nicholas Lydins, were typical backcountry travelers in eighteenth-century North America. They traveled light and relied on the assistance of many other people— Dutch, Native, and African American—to supply and conduct them safely through the patchwork of rivers, portages, French forts, and Native villages that characterized the northeastern borderlands. Leaving Boston in November 1753, Wheelwright and Lydins traveled overland west to Albany, where they purchased supplies and contracted with "Indians, a man & two squaws, to conduct us in a birch Canoo" north toward Montreal. Wheelwright reported in his journal that their departure from Albany was delayed because "the next day being sunday though good weather, the Indian fellow did not chuse to go, giving for a reason that he would serve God as others did that day." Their Christian companions guided the travelers to Fort St. Fréderic, portaging the canoes while Wheelwright, Lydins, and a "negro man Sharper," who had joined them at some point, rode on horseback. The Wheelwrights were a slaveowning family from the late seventeenth century through at least the mid-eighteenth century, so it's possible that Wheelwright owned Sharper; however, he may instead have been a hired man who had joined the expedition in Albany. Wheelwright noted that the many portages were due to previous efforts at military engineering: the creeks were clogged by "the trees which the French cut down in order to fill, or stop the Creek, so that the English might not come that way, as they were apprehensive they would, if they had attack'd Canada last War."[4]

These intentionally clogged creeks were a metaphor for the reception that Wheelwright and his party received as they went deeper into the woods and streams of New France. While on the one hand Wheelwright was offered the hospitality and lodging that would customarily be offered a person traveling under a passport from the governor of a neighboring province, especially one who spoke French as he did, he was at the same time presumed to be a spy. At Fort St. Fréderic, on the southern tip of Lake Champlain, he was detained until the fort's commander could check out his story;

his party was eventually released to continue its journey to Montreal, but only in the company of two French soldiers. The commander supplied the two soldiers from the fort's stores, and permitted Wheelwright to purchase supplies for his company for the next leg of their journey. In Montreal, Wheelwright was received by the governor of New France, Ange Duquesne de Menneville, the Marquis Duquesne, who did not detain him but rather "as he perceived by several officers speaking to me, that I was not a stranger in the place [ordered that] I might go and take Lodgings where I pleased and repose myself." He then says that he stayed with "my friend," François Decouagne. Wheelwright then received a message from Duquesne (whom he called "the General" in his diary) suggesting that "he had been informed that the last time I came in the Country I had with me an Engineer who passed for my domestick, and that I had with his assistance taken a plan of this City, Quebec, and the River." In other words, Duquesne suspected Wheelwright of collecting military intelligence. Wheelwright then "assured the Gentleman it was false and that some ill minded busy person must have raised the report to prevent my having an opportunity to execute the Commission I had the honour to receive." In spite of the open suspicion Wheelwright met with, he nevertheless reported during his stay in Montreal in December and January that "I have had the honour of dining with the General several times, and have been very genteely entertain'd by many of my Friends."[5]

The privileges of his rank on the one hand, and the open suspicion of his mission as an enemy foreigner on the other, continued to whipsaw Wheelwright. His fellow diplomat Nicholas Lydins took ill in late December and died on January 7, 1754. Upon Lydins's death, Wheelwright was informed by his host Decouagne that "if a Protestant dies among them, the Judge as soon as he is informed is obliged to demand the Body and with the same ceremony seal the forehead of the person dead, and order it to be carried without the City & buried." In other words, Protestants in New France were subject to extramural burial, "as though the person had been a thief or a murderer." Decouagne acted to prevent this kind of insult to the Wheelwright delegation: "To prevent any ridiculous thing of this sort, he was kind enough to give a place in his Garden, where [Lydins] was secretly & decently buried." Accusations of spying and dinner with "the General," the threat of extramural burial, and the delivery of "genteel desart"—all of these things characterized Wheelwright's mission to retrieve four captives before the outbreak of fresh hostilities. War was certain to come again —in fact, the Marquis Duquesne's explicit charge during his brief term as governor of New France (1752–55) was to secure the French Canadian fur trade and to drive British traders out of the Ohio Valley. To this end, he had spent the previous winter raising and equipping an army of two thousand men to march on the Ohio Valley at the same time that Nathaniel Wheelwright received his commission in Boston.[6]

Although Mother Esther de l'Enfant Jésus had been in Québec for nearly forty-five years, the events of the 1750s and 1760s were to demonstrate that like her nephew, she enjoyed rank and prominence in the city but was also still regarded by some of her sisters as *une étrangère*, a foreigner even inside the convent she rose to lead after the British took the city in 1759. Her nephew's visits to her in the early 1750s would have been politically useful to Mother Esther in the acutely status-conscious world of the convent, as they offered some of the first real proof her peers would see of the prominence of her extended family in New England. As New England diplomats and British military officers became common sights and eventually the masters of Québec, her sisters may have elected her superior because they were assured of her family's eminence and because of her Anglo-American family and connections, but her status as *Angloise* remained controversial.

In her record of Nathaniel's visit, the Ursuline annalist marked the entry of "Mr. Oüilleret" into the official history of the order with a cross and the words "Englois de nation," an elaboration on "*étranger*."[7]

The Permeable Convent

How is it that a Protestant diplomat from New England, who was threatened with the extramural burial of his companion in Montreal, could get the permission of the bishop to enter the Ursuline convent, and perhaps even to tour the private cells of the nuns? Why, if Protestant foreigners were so contaminating that their flesh could not be permitted to decompose proximate to the Catholic dead, could living Protestant male bodies be welcomed into the most intimate spaces of a convent? Nathaniel Wheelwright's visit to Canada and his two brief visits with his aunt tell us a great deal about the paradoxes and selective permeability of monastic life in Québec in the 1750s.

First, the cloister was in fact more permeable than a strict reading of the Constitution might suggest. Like most other transplanted European social institutions, convents in America offered their inhabitants a greater degree of liberty and autonomy than they were officially allowed according to the Rule. In fact, there is a great deal of evidence to suggest that the Québec Ursuline convent was founded by women whose goal was to escape the strict rule of cloister that was central to the reforms that French bishops were finally enforcing against newer orders of nuns like the Ursulines in the seventeenth century.[8] For centuries after the Council of Trent (1545–63), Reformation-era orders like the Ursulines attempted to evade the efforts of various bishops to impose strict claustration. In fact, Marie de l'Incarnation's and Madeleine de la Peltrie's planting of an Ursuline community in Québec in 1639 fit into the order's pattern of finding new outposts so as to preserve their self-determination far from a bishop's control. Marie de l'Incarnation sought papal approval of the Ursulines' Rule before a diocese was established in Québec specifically to avoid being subject to the bishop's authority. Although the Ursulines of Québec eventually accepted some of the trappings of claustration—they began to wear habits made in France, lived in a walled cloister, and met with others only through an iron grille— for the century between the arrival of a bishop in Québec in 1661 and the British Conquest, they continued to work to preserve their autonomy against the claims of reform-minded bishops.[9]

Strict claustration was nearly impossible for orders like the Ursulines, whose work as teachers required daily contact with young students— boarding students, who lived with the nuns, and were fed and nursed by them when sick, as well as a fluctuating population of day students, who came and went as they wished. Similarly, the Augustinian hospital nuns at the Hôtel-Dieu and the Hôpital-Général who provided care to the mostly male and utterly desperate injured, sick, and chronically ill people of Québec were women who cared for men on very personal terms inside officially cloistered spaces. As we have seen, both the Ursulines as teachers and the hospital nuns of Québec necessarily had very intimate contact with the ailing bodies, bodily fluids, and waste of the people they washed, nursed, dressed, fed, and in many cases among the hospital nuns, prepared for burial. Although teaching may appear to be a less intimate (or at least less messy) activity, teaching and boarding children as young as five or six are activities that still require a great deal of intimacy with the choir nuns, let alone the clean laundry, nourishment, and nursing care provided for the girls by the lay sisters. And as we saw in the previous chapter, the Ursulines' distinctive artistry attracted several Protestant male visitors, many of whom appear to have ventured beyond the grille. Finally, priests were present in the convents on a regular basis—each convent had its own confessor who would say the daily masses, and the bishop of Québec was a regular visitor as he had the administrative responsibilities of examining new nuns, supervising their triennial elections, and dealing with controversies within the convent, as we will see.

Aside from the requirements of their vocations and their openness to tourists, claustration was difficult to maintain given the daily needs of a large institution like a convent. The Ursuline convent in Québec, which housed dozens of choir and lay nuns at a time as well as the boarding students, required the delivery of supplies of food and clothing on a regular basis, as well as materials for their teaching and artistic production. Their own clothing and shoes, as well as art supplies and items stocked in the infirmary, made up the bulk of their imported supplies. A few surviving letters from 1711 and the 1750s testify to the absence of North American cloth production and to interruptions in shipping and trade that the wars of the eighteenth century repeatedly visited on the people of Québec. Large quantities of cloth for the sisters' habits—*toille de Rouen,* broadcloth, *marmazet,* denim, and kersey, for example—dozens of shoes of particular sizes, and sixty or more pounds of white and yellow wax for their candles were required annually. Their infirmary also purchased a great deal of imported supplies as well, spices like pepper, nutmeg, cinnamon, cloves, and saffron; supplies for closing wounds like "good woven cotton" and "fine pig hairs"; pharmaceutical preparations like rhubarb (for constipation), cinchona (for treating malaria and other fevers), and Epsom salts; and luxuries like "white honey," almond oil, and sugared confections, as sweet items were thought to have medicinal properties. Furthermore, both the teaching and the artistry the Ursulines performed relied on imported supplies—paper, psalters, books on "Christian instruction," and dozens of "a b c"s (alphabet books), both *gros* and *petit,* as well as art supplies like embroidery thread, verdigris (a pigment for producing green paint), and two dozen "thrush hair brushes to apply gold, preferably big." The letters of 1757 bear an addendum: "they ask not to take the risk [of sending the supplies] if the war continues."[10]

Besides the occasional delivery of imported goods, the convent's rich diet required regular supplies of locally produced beef, peas, grains, and vegetables. While the nuns kept their own kitchen garden and an orchard, the majority of their food had to be purchased from vendors on the outside, requiring the gates of the convent to be opened to accept deliveries on a regular basis. Carters and draymen were therefore regular visitors inside convent walls. Additionally, we might wonder who, exactly, delivered that "genteel desart" to Nathaniel Wheelwright the morning after his visit with his aunt. The Ursulines probably had a number of male and female non-monastic servants on whom they could call to carry a letter or bring in goods in addition to performing the heaviest labor inside the convent—washerwomen, scullery maids, and gardeners, for example. But even in these small early North American cities, boys and young men could travel safely and more freely through the streets and in between towns and villages than could girls or young women; girls and women who weren't subject to cloister couldn't travel with as much liberty as their male counterparts. This was especially true after Québec became an occupied city in 1759, when the presence of even more young soldiers in the conquering army made the city more perilous for its female residents.[11]

Finally, the convent's human visitors and the material goods they brought into the convent sometimes carried unwelcome microbial guests with them, especially in wartime, when both human beings and diseases traveled more freely across the Atlantic Ocean and throughout North America. Mobilizing soldiers also mobilized epidemic disease, so British regulars, *Troupes de la Marine,* New England regulars, and Habitant volunteers alike became both the victims and agents of deadly pathogens, and the permeability of the convent made it nearly as vulnerable as any other part of the city of Québec. We have already seen the toll of the epidemic of 1711, which killed Father Jacques Bigot. He was probably an indirect victim of Queen Anne's War (1702–13), the same war in which Esther was taken captive in 1703.[12] Similarly, King George's War may have brought at least one epidemic that took an even greater toll in the Ursuline monastery. The Ursuline annalist at the time reported that in the late autumn of 1749, "a common illness . . . spread all over the country and killed a lot of people in cities as well as in the country," and "did not spare our community." The disease—possibly influenza but never described in greater detail than "a common illness"— afflicted "seven of our nuns, four of whom died in a month," a *soeur converse* of seventy-three and three choir nuns, ages thirty-nine, forty-eight, and fifty-nine.[13]

Age and Leadership in the Convent

Just who was making all of the decisions about the comings and goings at the convent? Who was placing orders for locally made or imported goods, and who was paying for them? Along with the daily routine of prayer and teaching, the administration and governance of the convent was another responsibility of Ursuline choir nuns. Ancien régime monasteries were hardly democracies, but the community of choir nuns was charged with self-government, and most major decisions were put to a limited vote. Choir nuns with seniority, the *vocales* (literally, those with a voice), voted on the admission of novices and professed nuns, and they also held triennial elections for the convent offices. The major administrative responsibilities were vested in the superior; her assistant; the zelatrix, or enforcer of the Rule; and the *dépositaire*, or treasurer. The superior was also aided and advised by the Discrètes, an elected executive council.

The kind of women who were selected for leadership by the *vocales* tended to be higher in worldly rank rather than lower, and women elected to the top offices tended to be among the oldest women in the order. There was no exact formula, but some combination of an aristocratic background, longevity, and the wisdom and good judgment that should accompany rank and age were all desirable qualities in convent administration. Besides these officers, cloistered communities also elected a *scrutaine*, a person who oversaw convent election process; a portress, or a keeper of the keys entrusted with preserving the rule of cloister; a novice mistress, who was responsible for training and guiding new nuns; and a sacristan, who decorated the altar according to the liturgical calendar and was charged with preparing the altar, vessels, and priestly vestments for daily masses as well as feast days. Teaching communities like the Ursulines elected mistresses of both the boarding school and the day school.[14]

Worldly rank and experience are essentially secular qualifications for what were offices in a religious community, but age itself authorized women for leadership positions in the convent. In our secular era, old age might appear to be a disqualifying characteristic in leadership positions, for fear that the infirmities of senescence would deplete a superior or her assistant's mental and physical energy. The literature on old age in the Protestant Anglo-American colonies and in early-modern England is consistent with this narrative of decline, especially when we focus on women's lives. When women have only one path in life and one means of staking out an adult identity—through marriage and children—the loss of their fertility meant a loss in status in their families and communities.[15] Women who married and bore children were disenfranchised politically and economically by Anglo-American law to begin with, and in North America they appear to have lost even more power and rank in their families and communities after they completed their childbearing years and outlived a husband. For example, widows past childbearing age were much more vulnerable to accusations of witchcraft, especially if they lacked sons to inherit their property.

Even if they escaped criminal charges and poverty, many Anglo-American widows were resented by their own sons, and this disregard and disrespect appears to have spanned the seventeenth and eighteenth centuries. Seventy-three-year-old Rebecca Cornell was murdered and her corpse half-burned in 1673 in the room she inhabited in the house she shared with her son Thomas and his family in Portsmouth, Rhode Island; he was convicted of her murder, in part because of his reputation for verbally abusing his mother. In 1804, Martha Ballard's violent, impulsive son Jonathan seized her home and forced his aged mother to move into a single room of her own house in Hallowell, Maine, taking advantage of his father's custody in debtor's prison. In these cases spanning nearly 140 years, both Cornell's and Ballard's communities knew full well about their sons' antagonistic or even abusive relationships with them, but no one in either community intervened on behalf of the old women.[16] If they weren't evicted or murdered by their sons, for married or widowed women old age was still a time of loss—of status, of wealth, and of their standing in their communities.

But for women in Catholic religious communities, whose potential fertility was irrelevant to their public identities, old age was not characterized so dramatically by loss. Instead, it was a time in which they might increase in stature within their communities and wield greater influence in the world outside. In this context, women who lived long lives and survived until an advanced age may have been thought of as possessing a kind of spiritual power that younger people did not have. In the Catholic tradition, there were several means by which believers could express their spiritual strength, and all of these involve a kind of mastery of the demands and desires of the human body. Celibacy is one practice associated with spiritual purity and fortitude, one required for priests and for both women and men in religious orders. As we have seen, the intentional infliction of discomfort (through wearing poor clothing, sitting apart from hot fires, and abstaining from food) or even pain caused by flagellation and the wearing of cilices (iron girdles) is another means of both denying the flesh and using it as a means to channel the divine. We might view old age similarly, as a challenge to the weakness of human flesh and evidence of God's special favor for its sufferers.[17]

The eighteenth-century obituaries for elderly Ursulines reflect this view of old age. Those who survived to an advanced age—especially those who also served in high office—were frequently praised in their obituaries for their persistence in observing the hours, saying prayers, and attending masses in spite of their infirmities. When death came, they were praised for conforming to the expectations of a good death—a death characterized by the peaceful acceptance or even enthusiastic embrace of suffering, and consistent affirmations of faith.[18] Nuns were praised for their submission to God's will and complimented on their patience with pain and suffering along the way. When death came for Angelique Roberge de St. Marie in June 1750, she was praised in her obituary by the convent annalist for being "perfectly submissive, seeing death approach without terror." Sister Marie Anne de Boucherville de St. Ignace, a former convent apothecary who cared for many sick and dying women in her lifetime, was praised for her Christlike patience and sweetness, and for enduring "her illnesses without complaint" in her own life. Although Esther Wheelwright was not remembered for the virtue of mortification, like many of her fellow Ursulines she endured the trials of old age with determination. She had in her youth been a skilled embroiderer, "at which she was always perfectly successful," but "many years later her eyes got bad" and she suffered from an ocular fistula, the painful swelling of an eye that becomes engorged with blood. Determined to remain productive although her vision was diminished, "she asked to darn underwear, a task she did skillfully and directed as well."[19] (The ocular fistula might help explain the obvious asymmetry of her eyes in her portrait; the right eye and surrounding tissues may have been chronically swollen.) Those elderly women who could keep up with their sisters in prayer and work from 4 A.M. until after 8 o'clock in the evening may have been seen as especially spiritually formidable, laboring as they did under the increased afflictions of old age.

But aged bodies eventually must fail. Unlike women outside convent walls, nuns were guaranteed a living and nursing care in old age. Most of this work was done by the lay (or converse) sisters, who performed the domestic labor inside the cloister. Toward the end of her second term as mother superior, perhaps feeling all of her seventy years, Mother Esther called a meeting of the *vocales* concerning the acceptance of another *soeur converse*. She asked her sisters "to consider the need we have to take some more sisters to help and care for our elderly lay nuns."[20] Whatever the challenges of life inside the monastery, the sisters would not abandon one of their own. As they aged and weakened, this must have been a comfort to each of them in turn.

Esther at Middle Age

From 1735, at the age of thirty-nine, Mother Esther became part of the Ursuline community's leadership structure and served at the highest level of leadership for more than forty years, occupying most of the offices described above. She was elected *scrutaine* (the overseer of convent elections) seven times from the 1730s through the 1750s, then rose into the ranks of even higher offices. She served a one-year term as assistant starting in 1759, and again after her superiorships she served as assistant from 1772 to 1778. She was elected superior three times, in 1760, 1763, and 1769, and once as zelatrix, in 1778. Her obituary also credited her with serving as novice mistress three times and once as portress, "and she fulfilled all these tasks with application."

Mother Esther's official obituary in the Ursuline archive is among the few surviving documents that give us any hints about her personality behind the providential and politically useful story of her rescue and conversion as told by Father Vincent Bigot and by her sister Ursulines. Unfortunately, her obituary is also almost the only evidence we have to help us understand how she spent the majority of her seven decades in the convent, although it's more information than we have about the vast majority of Native, Anglo-American, and French Canadian women who were wives and mothers in eighteenth-century North America. In this Esther is not alone—convent obituaries are usually the most personal remembrances of long-dead choir nuns, and even then they're encrusted with calcified recitations of various Catholic virtues. But sometimes these obituaries veer slightly off script to permit a more personal glimpse into a life.

Mother Esther's 1780 obituary makes it clear that Esther's long life was spent working as a teacher, work that was central to the Ursuline order and as we have seen, one key to her rise through their ranks. At the same time, it highlights her administrative skills. The obituary reports that "she strived to raise young girls and teach them for a number of years" in both the day school and the *pensionnat*. Additionally, she was an expert needleworker, a significant skill in a convent that was famous for its delicately shaded silk embroidery and elaborately embroidered golden altar cloths, as well as trinkets for the tourist trade. When in old age her eyesight failed her for more skilled needlework, as we have seen, she mended underwear. The obituary also lists the various offices she held in the order, documenting her administrative expertise. (Perhaps this is why she also "directed" the darning of underwear when her eyesight failed her—she was used to being in charge.)[21]

The insights we get into her personality through this document are fleeting but significant. One of the most notable virtues for which she was praised was her devotion to routine—a striking thing to consider in light of her childhood and youth, which were characterized by such trauma and uncertainty. This commitment to observing every rule above all might help explain why she was repeatedly elected *scrutaine*, frequently served as novice mistress, and was also elected to serve as both portress and zelatrix. Furthermore, this regularity was not a typical virtue or habit discussed in Ursuline obituaries, suggesting that her dedication was a notable feature of her personality. She was apparently a marvel of consistency, known for her "ardor and the greatest reliability, with her taste for observances and her punctuality for the smallest rules," which were, "as she said—her happiness and solace and indeed as long as it was for God's Glory, it seemed to kindle and excite her zeal."

Perhaps this was the zeal of the convert, the need for every day to unfold like the previous one, the desire for the comforts of routine? Her obituary notes that "God kept her alive till she was 84 and she kept her zeal and exactitude; even in the coldest winter weather she wouldn't miss a communion and attended mass every day with an extreme devotion to Jesus' sacred heart and the Virgin Mary." The Ursuline annalist concluded, "St. Bernard's words can be applied to her more than anyone about religious life kept with regularity till the end."[22] After a childhood notable for its dislocations and losses, life in the convent offered the prayer cycle of the hours and other daily observances. Catholic liturgy prescribed the same holidays and observances according to the calendar, and the protocols of rank and seniority ordered daily life in the monastery as well. We know what a gifted linguist she must have been to pick up Wabanaki as a child so quickly, and to have learned French well enough after age twelve to become a teacher indicates a real facility for language as well. She must have been a quick study—should we be surprised that like other top students, she became an enthusiast for the regularity and exactitude of the Rule in the convent?

Intriguingly, the obituary also suggests—gently and politely, of course, in the manner of a religious community's official records—that although a skilled administrator, she was perhaps too kindhearted and accommodating: "Although her sweetness and politeness did not allow her all the firmness sometimes necessary, everyone liked and respected her because of her virtue."[23] Does this mean that she was always one to go along to get along? That would be a vital skill for surviving the many cross-cultural dislocations of her early life, but perhaps it made her too eager to please others. This tendency to go easy on those she was supposed to supervise is something for which she would be criticized more openly in the course of her superiorship.

In the 1750s, Mother Esther was herself in her fifties and early sixties. She had built a successful career as a teacher and administrator within the Ursuline convent, but it was the connections she welcomed and maintained outside the convent and even outside of Québec itself that permitted her to live a life like that of the superiors who preceded her. These were women whose fathers, brothers, and nephews were wired into the political and military elite of New France; finally, in the 1750s, Esther Wheelwright had confirmation that she too was connected to an important family in New England, and she would work to maintain ties to the Wheelwrights and other prominent English-speakers over the next twenty years.

Other New England Connections

Nathaniel Wheelwright's diplomatic errands in the 1750s were not the first renewed contact Mother Esther had with her family—she exchanged letters with her mother, Mary Snell Wheelwright, in 1747 after the death of her father, John, in 1745. When he sat down to write his will eight years earlier, John Wheelwright left legacies of land for his four sons, and cash or its equivalents to his four daughters who lived in New England. He also remembered his estranged daughter, although her inheritance came with a catch. John Wheelwright noted that "my Daughter Esther Wheelwright if living is in Canada whom I have not heard of for this many Years and hath been absent for more than Thirty Years," which suggests that before the late 1740s, she was not at all in communication with her family. Nevertheless, he continued, "if it Should please God that She return to this Country & Settle here then my Will is that my Four Sons vizᵗ Iohn Samuel Ieremiah and Nathaniel each of them pay her Twenty five pounds it being in the whole One Hundred pounds within Six Months after her Return and Settlement." In other words, the Wheelwrights would not be making a contribution to Esther's dowry at the Ursuline convent—she could inherit only if she "return to this Country & Settle here."[24]

No copy of Mary's letter to her daughter survives, which means that we can only speculate about its contents and the timing of her outreach. Did she write to inform Esther of her father's death two years earlier and of his remembrance of her in his will? (If she wrote for that purpose, why the delay?) Was she struck with a premonition of her own death, or of a need to write a will of her own? Did the loss of her husband put her in mind of the daughter she had lost as a child more than forty years earlier? An English translation of the letter Mother Esther wrote in response to her mother is in the Ursuline archives, one of only four letters she wrote to have survived to the present and the only evidence we have that she received a letter from her mother at all. However, the response gives us a number of clues as to the content of her mother's letter, as well as a great deal of information about the author at middle age, after nearly forty years among the Ursulines.[25]

Mother Esther opens her letter of September 26, 1747, by thanking her mother for her letter, which she had received just three days earlier. She notes that it had been "faithfully interpreted unto me by a person of virtue," which suggests that she was unable to read English (or that she had forgotten how, if she ever learned in the first place). Mary Wheelwright apparently had expressed worry for her daughter living in another country, but Mother Esther replied in a fashion that echoed Vincent Bigot's sermon from her clothing ceremony. She reassured her mother that "what ought to lessen your cares and concerns for me in beholding me living in a distant country" is the fact that "Providence over-rules and governes all things [and] has had a particular regard unto me and assisted me in all my ways." Mother Esther assures her "lovely Mother" that she made an affirmative decision in becoming a choir nun, and that she is satisfied with her life: "You know, my dear Mother, that the Lot which I have chosen hath been that of consecrating myself wholly unto the Lord, to whom I belong without reserve, being bound by my obligations which [are] impossible for me to break." She even indicates that this was not the first letter she had received from Wells asking her to come back home, declaring that it is an "impossibility" for her to "return to you, which you and my dear Father have so often repeated in times past, but I hope the Lord to whom I have devoted myself will greatly reward me from his infinite goodness." Mother

Esther then reminds her mother that the Lord "himself assures us in his holy word that he who leaves for his sake Father, Mother, Brothers and Sisters, shall have an hundredfold in this life, And Life Eternal in the next." Returning to New England to join her natal family would have meant not just exile from the Ursuline convent, but conversion to Protestantism and therefore—in the eyes of this devout Catholic—an exile from paradise and her heavenly spouse.[26]

Mother Esther's vocation as a teacher and as a missionary is clear when she turns the tables on her mother to ask instead that her mother move to

Québec and become a Roman Catholic: "Oh! what joy, what pleasure, what consolation, would it give me my dear Mother if you had the happiness of knowing this holy religion which a kind Providence hath made me embrace since I left you." She reminds her that it is "an established religion which our Forefathers professed for a long time with much heed and fervour until the Schisme," that is, the Reformation. She closes her letter by noting that "this moment one comes and tells me he is obliged to depart which obliges me to finish sooner than I intended. However I cannot forbear saying that I am greatly affected with the news of the death of my father, whom I loved so tenderly, and whom I shall never forget, and I shall always share with you in the trouble of so grievous separation." Mother Esther then writes, "Be persuaded that I shall not cease daily to pray to the Lord Jehovah to be himself your strength, your support and your consolation during this Life, and that we shall have one day the happiness of meeting together in a blessed and glorious Eternity. This is that which I wish from the bottom of my heart." After more declarations of her love and devotion to "bretheren and Sister whom I embrace a thousand times and *you* more tenderly than anyone, being with all love and possible respect Madam my Mother," she signed her letter "Your very humble and very obedient daughter and Servant, Sr Esther Wheelwright de l'Enfant Jésus." This was a typical style of formal signature, one that followed the conventual custom of combining her birth name with her religious name. However, it may be significant that Mother Esther included "Wheelwright" in her signature, as she tended to sign the other three surviving letters (written to religious authorities in Paris) with just a "Sr. de l'Enfant Jésus," or "Sr. de l'Enfant Jésus, Supre." Perhaps Wheelwright, like other New England captives, was eager both to refresh her family ties and to affirm her commitment to her new family and religion.[27] But the larger message of Mother Esther's letter is clear: she loves her family and will pray for them, but she has no intention whatsoever of abandoning the life she had chosen nearly forty years earlier.

When Mary Snell Wheelwright sat down to write her will a few years later in 1750, she had much less property to distribute to a much smaller family than had her husband just a few years earlier, as two of her daughters had died. Once again, Esther was remembered, "provided my beloved Daughter Esther Wheelwright who has been many Years in Canada is yet living, and Should by the wonder working Providence of God be returned to her native Land and tarry & dwell in it." Although once again the will made it clear that Esther's inheritance was contingent upon her return to New England, Mary called her a "beloved Daughter," as she did the other living legatees in the will. Mary's will differed significantly from John's because aside from her four "beloved Sons," all of her legatees were women— either her living "beloved Daughters" or "beloved Grand Daughters" by her "dear deceased Daughter[s]."[28] Mary had died in 1755, just a year after her grandson Nathaniel made his second visit to his Aunt Esther at the Ursuline convent.

The 1750s brought Mother Esther more opportunities for setting the record straight with the Wheelwrights. After Nathaniel Wheelwright attempted (and failed) to retrieve the war captives on his 1753–54 mission, he returned to visit his aunt once again at the convent in Québec. He offers a valuable judgment of her temperament and character, writing that he "went often to visit my aunt La Mère de L'enfant Jesus at the Convent" in the late spring and summer of 1754, describing her as "of a cheerful disposition." Wheelwright was probably a most welcome guest for Mother Esther, not just as a high-status diplomat but as a rare Anglophone who spoke fluent French. In one of the most revealing primary sources recording Mother Esther's life, Wheelwright writes that "as She thought she might confide in me as a friend and near Relation, she gave me a particular account of her being detained in Canada, after she got out of the hands of the Indians and [of] the Reasons why she was not returned according to the desire of her Father, & the promise of Monsieur La Marquis de Vaudruille who was at that time General of Canada, and who received her as a present from the Indians." Wheelwright continued, "I always understood he was at the expence of her education, and of putting her into the Nunnery, as they are obliged to give a sum of money with every one. He had the credit of this but my Aunt gave me to understand the Contrary—." As amiable and "cheerful" as she was, Nathaniel wouldn't leave Québec without seeing the flash of steel in her temperament.

Nathaniel Wheelwright, always a breathless writer, goes on to tie up a lot of loose ends and questions about Esther's entrance into the convent: "She said she lived some time with Monsr. De Vaudruielle, and as he had given his promise, was or appear'd willing to return her, but finding an opportunity to Reimburse himself; or Reather get money, (as seems to be the principal of most of the French, who have at any time got Captives out of the hands of the Indians) and at the same time have the Credit of doing a Charitable Action" by placing her with the Ursulines. Therefore, "[Vaudreuil] forfited his word, and sold her to a priest who had a sum of money given him by a Lady in France to make a Nun, and who paid Monsr. De Vaudruielle forteen hundred Livres for the expences he had been at as he said for her Ransom and, during her stay with him, as he produced an account which he made amount to that extravigant sum." We saw in chapters 3 and 4 that both Vaudreuil and Mme. Vaudreuil were insistent about being reimbursed by the Crown for the expense of housing and feeding so many official visitors, captives, officers, and diplomats (Esther included), so Mother Esther's explanation for her entry into the convent makes a great deal of sense. The arithmetic also adds up—Mother Esther's dowry was fifteen hundred livres, and Wheelwright writes here about a ransom of fourteen hundred livres. When the average dowry for Ursuline novices was around three thousand livres, could it be that Father Vincent had to pay Vaudreuil fourteen hundred livres ransom for Esther out of a donation of three thousand or so, leaving him just about fifteen hundred to offer the Ursulines, who were persuaded to take her for a lower sum of money? Father Vincent used the money donated by the "Lady in France to make a Nun," but perhaps he had to ransom her from her putative benefactor. "Thus," Wheelwright concludes, "she was put into the Convent without the least Obligation to Monsr. De Vaudreuielle or his Family—."[29]

We might wish that Wheelwright had kept a more faithful account of his visits with his aunt, but as the diary was kept as part of the official record of his diplomatic mission, he may have thought that accounts of all of his visits were unnecessary and perhaps even inappropriate. But were his visits with her purely personal? Wheelwright was young, but the fact that he was entrusted with a diplomatic mission at a time when war threatened to break out again suggests that at least some in New England thought he understood something about New France. If she were just an older relative on whom he paid social calls, why mention her at all in his official diary? Wheelwright probably thought that his aunt, as a former captive who still understood a great deal about the Wabanaki language and people, might be a useful resource. Why else would she tell him the story about the intrigue surrounding her admission to the convent if she didn't also mean to teach him a lesson about the circuitous ways that power and money circulated among wealthy donors, missionary priests, cloistered nuns, and ambitious (or even grasping) governors?

Wealthy donors obviously had the money, and colonial governors clearly had power. Of what use were the priests and nuns, then? We must remember that in the mid-eighteenth century, religious people were perceived as having a great deal of spiritual power. Priests could say masses and therefore were quite spiritually powerful, but choir nuns also prayed the hours. Lives of celibacy and service made female and male religious not just different from most people, but also more spiritually powerful. Why wouldn't a colonial governor want to "have the Credit of doing a Charitable Action . . . without the least Obligation" for any expense he had been at in caring for Esther?

Around this time, we find traces of Mother Esther's work with the current generation of New England captives taken in the imperial wars of the 1740s and 1750s. Other captives, whether they were enrolled in the Ursuline school or not, appear to have held an enduring interest for Mother Esther. Susanna Johnson, an Anglo-American wife and mother of four, was taken into captivity with her entire family in an attack on Fort Number Four (Charlestown, New Hampshire) in the late summer of 1754. In her captivity narrative, she reports visiting fellow captives Mary (Polly) and Submit Phipps when they were enrolled as students in the Ursuline convent by another Madame de Vaudreuil, the wife of the Governor General Pierre de Rigaud, Marquis de Vaudreuil-Cavagnal, the son of the governor and his wife who enrolled Esther in the convent school forty-five years earlier. Johnson writes, "they were sent to the grand nunnery in Quebec, where my sister and I made them a visit; they were beautiful girls, cheerful and well taught. We here found two aged English ladies, who had been taken in former wars." One was of course Mother Esther, while the other Ursuline they met was Dorothy Jordan (Sr. Marie Joseph, or St. Joseph), whom we met in chapter 3. She had spent a much longer time among the Wabanaki than Esther had, and at a much older age, so her French was probably inadequate for her to perform the traditional labor of Ursuline choir nuns of teaching. Perhaps she played some role in working with Anglo-American captive girls—perhaps her Wabanaki language skills held up much longer than Mother Esther's, which might explain her audience with Johnson, as well as her presence with the Phipps sisters.[30]

Johnson explained further that the nun "by the name of Wheelwright . . . had a brother in Boston, on whom she requested me to call, if ever I went to that place; I complied with her request afterwards, and received many civilities from her brother." The brother was probably her eldest brother John, the father of Nathaniel, whose journey to Québec opened this chapter. Why would Mother Esther ask Johnson, a complete stranger and a fairly obscure New Hampshire woman, to remember her to her brother? Her encounter with Johnson was probably in 1758, just a few years after her nephew Nathaniel's visit. Mother Esther wanted both to send greetings and remind her Boston family members of her, as well as to impress her fellow Ursulines (and perhaps Johnson as well) with her connections.

Nearly half a century in the convent meant that Mother Esther had long since adopted the aristocratic values and style of her fellow choir nuns, none of whom would hesitate to remind a visitor of her family status and connections. It had taken more than forty years for a family member to visit her at the convent—perhaps she thought that these connections would finally redound to her credit among her peers and benefit their community. At this point, Mother Esther's concerns might have been mostly intramural, mostly about politics among the Ursulines themselves. However, the geopolitical issues raised by the official declaration of the Seven Years' War would have been of great interest to her as well. As an Anglo-American child, war captive, and Wabanaki daughter, and as someone who (finally) had proof that her New England family had not forsaken her, she would have been intensely interested in the world outside the convent as well. Her very life was proof that the North American borderlands were not marginal, but were in fact central to the geopolitics of the eighteenth century. She embodied the contingent and improvisational nature of her world.[31]

Mother Esther and her sisters couldn't have known in 1756 or 1757 how desperate they would be for connections and assistance in just a few years' time. They didn't know then that Québec and even their own convent would be occupied by the enemy army by the close of the decade. And they certainly couldn't have known how useful it might be under those circumstances to elect a New England–born superior.

The Seven Years' War and the British Conquest of Québec

Early in the 1750s, even before the war was officially declared, the Ursulines knew that an ill wind was blowing. Shortly after Nathaniel's first visit to his aunt in January 1754, the Ursuline annalist began a catalog of doleful events that suggests her unease with the times—naval disasters, devastating fires, and yes, literal strange and damaging winds were all ominous. On May 8, 1754, a house near the Ursuline monastery burned to the ground, although the convent was spared. Then later in the same month, three houses near the Hôtel-Dieu, the Augustinian sisters' hospital, burned down as well, but "by a great Miracle of the very holy Virgin," the fire spared their convent. Mother Charlotte Daneau de Muy de St. Hélène, the Ursuline annalist who left an extraordinary account of the events of the Seven Years' War in the convent's official history, the Annales, noted that "part of the upper city of Québec would have burnt as well without this Miraculous Protection." Then on September 11, one of the king's ships was damaged by high winds, which led to a cargo loss of 100,000 livres. On the same day in Montreal, thirty-three houses burned in the space of four or five hours, apparently because of a dangerously ill-maintained chimney of the Jesuits. Then, on the evening of December 4, "a firey wind with thunder and quaking" blew for two hours in Québec. Houses and barns fell down, and many institutions in the city, including the Hôpital-Général operated by the other order of Augustinian nuns, were damaged as well. "As for us, our church tower fell down but the bell was found to be undamaged." Still, Mother Charlotte de St. Hélène noted that the bill for rebuilding the church tower and rehanging the bell would be 2,000 livres. Finally, on June 1 of the following year, the hospital nuns of the Hôtel-Dieu, who had just endured the terrible wind, lost their entire convent in a fire: "All their Houses, Church, Hospice, Barn, Laundry, Slaughterhouse, Ice House, and lots of other houses in the upper city were consumed by devouring flames." Forty-nine of the homeless nuns sheltered with the Ursulines for three weeks, which permitted the Ursulines to repay the goodwill they had received of the Augustinian nuns when the Ursuline convent burned twice in the seventeenth century, in 1650 and 1686.[32]

Although the prologue to Mother St. Hélène's narrative of the events of the Seven Years' War was portentous, culminating in the great fire at the

Augustinian hospital nuns' monastery on June 1, 1755, the early years of the conflict were full of marvelous providences for a French victory. When news of Major General Edward Braddock's July 1755 defeat on the banks of the Monongahela River in Pennsylvania reached the Ursulines later that summer, the annalist gleefully reported on the events of the battle: "The hand of God was never more visible than in cutting down the pride of a new Holofernes in the person of general bradork who (wished for?) breakfast at *la belle rivière*, lunch at niagra, and supper at montreal." Instead of conquering all of the interior of North America, she concluded triumphantly that "he lost his life and the greater part of his army." Braddock's goal was "not only to take *la belle rivière*, which they call *la rivière Loyau* [the Ohio River], but also all of the country which he regards as his, and it would have been his without the visible protection of God by the intercession of the Holy Virgin and of the glorious St. Joseph."[33]

In spite of the great victory on the Monongahela, the people in the St. Lawrence Valley suffered the deprivations of war through the rest of the decade. Crop failures, the seizure of more than three hundred French merchant ships by the British, and an unusually cold spring meant that by the summer of 1758, the people of Québec were starving and desperate. As one letter from the Ursuline convent put it, "We're in a severe famine. The three scourges rule our country, pestilence, famine, and war. With the grace of God they'll leave us soon." The people of Québec were also fearful that they might suffer the fate of the Acadians, the French-speaking people who had been forcibly marched out of Nova Scotia by the British beginning in 1755. When news of the fall of Louisbourg to the British once again reached Québec, the city was totally cut off from any French support or supplies. They were therefore unsurprised by the arrival of the British fleet in the early summer of 1759.[34] "We leave to our historians the particular details of the pain and suffering that the country felt once again." Instead, Mother St. Hélène preferred "to say a little word regarding our Community in this year of tribulation and misery." Casting the fall of Québec as a manifestation of God's wrath because of the sins of the city, she describes the futile prayers for deliverance ordered by the bishop to be said in all the city's churches. "But," she concludes, "we were not able to appease the Lord. We had to suffer the Chastisement that we had brought upon ourselves."[35]

When the Ursulines had definite word that the British were approaching

Québec, they made arrangements to store securely their most precious objects of worship, "like the sacred vessels and everything seen in the sacristy —the ornaments, linen, and furniture of the church. Everything else we couldn't put in our vault, we left to Providence, in the hope that our house would be spared of bombs and canons." When the British began to bomb the city on the night of July 12, the Ursulines decided that "we had to look for a refuge, to avoid the furor of the bombs and Canons that we had not been spared at all. . . . Nevertheless, ten of our dear Sisters had the Courage to stay" in the Ursuline convent for the duration of the siege, "which never ended until the 13th of September 1759." Three priests stayed with them to pray with them and say Mass.

The rest of the nuns, Esther included, fled the convent to take cover with the Augustinian hospital sisters at the Hôpital-General, which was sheltering the nuns of the Hôtel-Dieu as well as hundreds of other citizens seeking refuge. The Ursuline mother superior, the formidable Mother Marie-Anne Migeon of the Nativity, had secured permission in advance from the bishop to evacuate their monastery if necessary. "Everyone's dismay and anxiety was written all over their faces. . . . We had so little hope of returning to our house," because it was hit every day in the bombing. The Ursulines' central location in Québec's upper city, so close to the Château Saint-Louis and the Cathedral, meant that the siege was very destructive to the monastery. "The house for the day school was ruined, our Sacristy, our Chapel of the Saints, parts of our Choir, and of our Church were knocked over, several rooms in our dormitory were ravaged, our Laundry was ruined by a passing shell, two chimneys were cut down," and other outbuildings were in danger of setting the rest of the city on fire. "All this made us think that we could never see our monastery again."[36]

Let's pause for a moment and consider what it meant for thirty-five women who had taken sacred vows to evacuate the monastery they had promised never to leave, and the unhappy scenes of fire and devastation they beheld on their flight. The blitzkrieg of London in World War II was hardly more effective than the relentless British cannonade of Québec in 1759. The Ursuline convent's stone walls had proved just as vulnerable to British bombs as the rest of Québec, but the sisters' return to "the world" was far from enticing amid a military siege. Instead, the world must have looked like it was coming to a fiery end. The Ursulines left their house in the late afternoon a few days after bombing began, the sun still high and hot in the sky just a few weeks after the summer solstice. Those who could walk or run with their small bundles of personal belongings probably made their way as fast as they could to the Hôpital-Général. A few others, too elderly or ill to make the journey on foot, had to be carried on litters. According to an account of the siege left by one of the nuns from the Hôpital-Général, at six o'clock in the evening, "we saw in our meadows the Ursuline Reverend Mothers who came on foot, seized with fear of the bombs and bullets which had pierced their walls in many places." They were probably eager to get settled at the Hôpital-Général before nightfall, when the bombing would resume. "Although we couldn't doubt that our mission was going to receive all of the wounded during the siege, we received with open arms our dear Sisters of Québec" from the Hôtel-Dieu. After they settled the Hôtel-Dieu nuns into their own cells, "it was necessary to find space for thirty or so [Ursulines] that we could not have received with less than tenderness and with the affection that we had received our dear Hospitallers."

Although their monastery was now crowded with nearly every woman religious in the city as well as scores of the wounded, the Hôpital sisters were grateful for the assistance of the nuns of the Hôtel-Dieu as well as the Ursulines, who also worked as nurses and caregivers alongside their hosts. The siege would last for two more months. We can only imagine the conditions inside the Hôpital-Général for the patients and their caregivers alike, considering that the city was low on food and fuel at the end of the spring of 1759. Not only had the British effectively blockaded the city, the agricultural cycle and harvest were completely disrupted as well. The Hospital nuns paid the Ursulines the highest compliment they knew when memorializing their wartime emergency evacuation: "The cares and fatigues that they wanted to share with us and the patients gave them, under the habit of an Ursuline, the heart of a Hospital nun."[37]

In spite of their immiseration at the Hôpital-Général, only two Ursulines died there during the siege, and all of the sisters and priests left behind at the Ursuline convent survived the siege, as well as the battle on the Plains of Abraham on September 13. (This is remarkable because a dozen of them—more than a quarter of the total—were older than age sixty in 1759.) However, two choir nuns left at the Ursuline convent died immediately after the battle. One of the deaths was that of Dorothy Jordan de St. Joseph, which left Esther as the last surviving former captive who had taken the Ursuline veil. The other death was that of Mother Charlotte Daneau de Muy de St. Hélène, the annalist whose narration of the war shapes my own version of the war as experienced by the people of Québec, and especially by the Ursulines. Both Mother St. Joseph and Mother St. Hélène died September 14, 1759, the day after the brief battle on the Plains of Abraham, a battle in which both the French and the British general lost their lives as well. Major General James Wolfe died on the day of the battle, September 13, while General Louis-Joseph, the Marquis de Montcalm, lasted until the morning of the fourteenth. He was buried in a plain wooden casket set into a crater left by a mortar shell that had fallen on the Ursuline chapel, "in the glow of the flames, mourned by everyone," according to the new annalist who took up Mother Sainte-Hélène's pen to continue her description of the fall of Québec to the British. The cathedral Notre Dame des Victoires in the lower city, like most of the lower city itself, was reduced to rubble and ashes.

The city fell to the British, and on September 18, three companies of grenadiers marched in to commence the occupation, which would eventually include seven thousand troops, suddenly doubling the size of the city's population to fourteen thousand in autumn. The British hoped to winter over their army in the city through the following spring and summer until Montreal could be compelled to surrender, but the winter promised to be a frozen nightmare, with twice the population to house and feed in a city that had been shelled to pieces amid wartime blockades and famine.[38]

Little did the Ursulines know that their service among hospital nuns during the siege would continue to be useful during the occupation of Québec as well. When they "hurried to return" to their monastery a week later on September 21, "we entered joyfully," finding that for the most part, the convent had survived the siege. However, their chapel was damaged, and like the rest of the city, they were low on food and fuel, and winter was fast approaching. In a meeting with the newly appointed governor general of Québec, James Murray, the Ursulines learned that he would install a hospital in part of their monastery and quarter healthy soldiers there as well, considering the large and relatively intact spaces they possessed. The occupation of their convent was fortunate for the Ursulines, as "*Monsieur Murai* our illustrious Governor had the kindness to rebuild our Church, and all of our monastery. They started with the Church, which [was] the only one that was able to serve the Parish, and which serve[d] in this capacity since 24 September 1759." Aside from helping out with building repairs, the Ursulines found that their new role as military contractors and their connections with British command meant assistance with supplies for the winter—soldiers procured fuel for them and shoveled their walks and work-spaces, and King George paid to feed everyone in the convent—officers, soldiers, patients, and Ursulines alike: "Our conquerers knew of our indi-gence and assissted us with a kindness that we hadn't had reason to hope for." They were fortunate in that General Murray saw the value of the spaces and the social services offered by Québec's religious women. He understood the esteem in which they were held by the rest of the city, and their potential value in pacifying its conquered citizens.[39]

The Ursulines were undoubtedly glad for the help in rebuilding their convent, but the price they paid for this assistance was an unprecedented proximity day and night to scores of male bodies—mostly young, Protes-tant male bodies. Although they had returned to their house, we must see the occupation as a continued interruption of their claustration. Moreover, not only were the Ursulines proximate to men living in the convent, but many were working very intimately with the injured or sick men. The con-vent's Annales are mostly silent on this break of their enclosure, and they don't say which women gave themselves over to nursing. It may be that the mistress of the infirmary, a choir nun, was assisted by others in the choir as well as by lay sisters. Nursing was not the only means by which the Ur-sulines cared for their male inmates, who included a regiment of Highland-ers in kilts instead of breeches. Some Ursulines therefore used their exper-tise in working with textiles and set about knitting long and thick stockings for the men. In his journal of the siege and occupation of Québec, one Highlander, Lieutenant Malcolm Fraser, complains on December 1, 1759, that "the winter is now very severe." By December 20, he writes that "the winter is become almost insupportably cold," and "our regiment in partic-ular is in a pitiful situation having no breeches, and the Philibeg [kilt] is not at all calculated to this terrible climate." He was not stationed among the

Ursulines, and had to rely on a commanding officer "doing all in his power to provide trowsers" for his men. The fuel shortage made the Highlanders' prospects especially desperate, considering that "the men are obliged to drag all the wood used in the Garrison on sledges from St. Foy, about four miles distance."[40]

In spite of the efforts of the Ursulines and British military leadership to procure better food and clothing for the soldiers, the winter of 1759–60 was astonishingly hard on them as well as on the people of Québec. The cold was a severe and persistent challenge to the British army camping in a war-ravaged Canadian city at the end of the Little Ice Age. Lt. Fraser complained in December of 1759 that "several" of his men "have already lost the use of their fingers and toes by the incredible severity of the frost," and "some men on sentry have been deprived of speech and sensation in a few minutes, but hitherto, no person has lost his life." That would change by the spring of 1760, when Lt. Fraser reported that nearly half of all men at the garrison in Québec were either sick or dead. Of the 5,653 men stationed in Québec, only 3,341 were fit for duty in the spring; 2,312 were sick, and nearly 700 had died since their triumphal march into the city on September 18. In an echo from Esther's childhood in a war fifty years earlier, Fraser writes in the spring of 1760 that "the Scurvy, occasioned by salt provisions and cold, has begun to make fierce havock in the garrison, and it becomes every day more general. In short, I believe there is scarce a man of the Army entirely free from it."[41] Thus the Ursuline experience of young military men's bodies over this winter was at least as much about their vulnerability to cold and disease as of their powers to intimidate and coerce.

The Ursulines left almost no trace of these men in their convent records, as though one means of restoring the cloister and observing the Rule was to refuse to discuss in any detail the ways in which they cared for the occupying army. This omission is startling, even given the tendency of religious orders to deny or paper over conflict and to promote a vision of community peace and harmony. Aside from the picturesque and motherly detail about knitting stockings for the Highlanders, the men who lived and were nursed in the Ursuline convent in the winter of 1759–60 do not exist in the convent's *Annales*, or in any other record. Were the Highlanders and their fellow inmates brutes, or angels? Did the Ursulines see the men as fellow sufferers, or helpful workers who fetched wood and helped with building repairs? Or were they only impositions on their sisterly communion, and even a danger to their young students? Any other miseries suffered or kindnesses received either were recorded in British officers' journals of the occupation or are lost to history.

The Election of 1759

The rhythms of religious life continued to structure the Ursulines' days and weeks, and in December of 1759, the Ursulines were due to vote in their triennial election of convent leadership. Mother Marie-Anne Migeon de la Nativité had completed a fourth three-year term as superior, and the Rule required the election of another superior. Mother Marie-Anne de la Nativité had served as superior for a dozen years, from 1735 to 1741 and again from 1753 to 1759, and superiors were not permitted to serve more than two consecutive terms. This mother superior was the former Marie-Anne Migeon de Branssat, the daughter of Jean-Baptiste Migeon de Branssat, a fur merchant and attorney from Montreal who bettered his station substantially through marriage to Catherine Gauchet de Belleville, a native of France and a noblewoman. The Migeon de Branssat family was typical among elite Canadians—they were involved in sometimes unscrupulous dealings in the fur trade and local real estate, and a strong tradition on her mother's side of serving in religious orders as well. Marie-Anne's mother Catherine was related to the superior of the seminary at Saint-Sulpice, the wealthy Abbé Gabriel Souart, and after raising a large family and being widowed, Catherine herself became a hospital nun at the Hôtel-Dieu in Montreal, following one of her adult daughters into this order. The business and political acumen for which Mother Marie-Anne is remembered was probably something she learned at her father's and mother's knees. The Ursulines needed an adept and politically astute leader at the moment her term as superior was to expire. In December of 1759, the convent was still in disrepair, occupied by a foreign army and one of their military hospitals. This was not to be a typical triennial election.[42]

When the community of *vocales* assembled in the interior chapel of the monastery, Mother Marie-Anne Migeon de la Nativité followed the tradition for elections directed by the Rule: she symbolically acknowledged the end of her rule by "put[ting] the Keys of the Monastery back in the Hands of the Venerable and Discreet M. Briand, Canon and Vicar General of the Bishop." Father Jean-Olivier Briand, representing Bishop Henri-Marie Dubreil de Pontbriand, told the Ursulines that the bishop had considered what "certain persons who were interested in the good of their Community" had told him. He thought that changing superiors in the present circumstances was not advisable, considering the goodwill the British governor had shown the community, especially considering that "the present Superior was currently known and very well regarded" by the governor, while a new superior would take time to earn his esteem. Therefore, the bishop thought that the Ursulines could continue by one year Mother Marie-Anne Migeon de la Nativité's term as superior by a new election, and then hold the regular triennial election. This suspension of the Constitution was such a momentous event for the Ursulines that they devote almost an entire page in their election records to this proposal from the bishop. The Ursulines agreed, and went on to elect as assistant "Marie Estere hoüilleret" of the Infant Jesus. (Those English "Wh-" and "ight" sounds and those hard English Rs were still too much for the Ursulines.)[43]

Because Mother Esther was elected assistant in this special election of 1759, the community may have had at that point a clear sense of who would succeed Marie-Anne Migeon of the Nativity. Who better to elect as mother superior in the midst of the British Conquest of Québec than the woman memorialized by her order as *"une gracieuse fleur d'Albion,"* their graceful English rose. But why not elect her in 1759? Was there some concern about her readiness for the task, although she had served in several convent offices through her career? She was regularly elected *scrutaine,* the overseer of convent elections, by her fellow *vocales* going back to 1735, when she was thirty-nine years old.[44] For all their efforts to efface Esther's Wabanaki background and insist on her New England roots, was there even fifty years later something about her that was just *too foreign?*

The British were now masters of all Québec. Thousands of soldiers and officers now occupied not just one garrison or the city itself but even intimate spaces within the Ursuline convent. Protestant foreigners were everywhere—even if many were sick and vulnerable, the Ursulines could not escape the invasion and occupation. Would an English-born superior assist the Ursulines in their efforts to survive the Conquest and continue their mission to the people of Québec? Or would she embody the Conquest in ways that were too literal and personal for her sisters to bear? As we will see, Mother Esther's election as superior would create some dissention in the community of women with whom she had lived for the past fifty years.

CHAPTER SIX

ESTHER SUPERIOR

Québec, December 1760

When Mother Esther walked into the chilly choir on December 15, 1760, she was surrounded by her fellow Ursulines, all twenty-nine of them who had survived the siege and the first year of the occupation. Of the three Ursuline choir nuns who had been captives of the Wabanaki at the turn of the eighteenth century, she was the only survivor. She watched expectantly as Mother Superior Marie-Anne Migeon de la Nativité approached the grille that separated the choir from the rest of the chapel, knelt there before Father Jean-Olivier Briand, and said, "In the presence of His Divine Majesty and before all of the community, I resign the office of Superior, my lord, asking very humbly the pardon of God and of the community for the errors I have made, and I beg you, my lord, to give me penance." Having since the previous December served an additional emergency year in her fourth term as mother superior, Mother Marie-Anne de la Nativité may have been relieved finally to resign her leadership position in the convent. After receiving her penance, she kissed the ground, put the keys to the monastery into Father Briand's hands, and then returned to her place among her fellow sisters in the choir, a superior no more. As Father Briand offered the Mass of the Holy Spirit, the candles flickered on the gold and silver decorations of the Ursuline chapel, and shadows danced on its dark walls and gilded statues. Who would next be called to leadership?

The *scrutaine,* or person responsible for the election, put a ballot box on a nearby table, alongside a list of the *vocales* eligible for election to superior, and some paper and ink. This was a routine familiar to Mother Esther, as for the previous twenty-five years she had served as *scrutaine,* in addition to most of the other positions of leadership and elected offices in the convent. Few Ursulines knew the order for elections as well as Mother Esther. For the previous year, she had served under Marie-Anne Migeon de la Nativité as her assistant, the highest-ranking nun next to the superior. In December 1760, Mother Esther was sixty-four years old, soon to turn sixty-five, and perhaps already afflicted by the ocular fistula that affected her eyesight but not her vision for an Ursuline monastery under British occupation. The chantresses then led the congregation in *Veni Creator Spiritus,* an invocation of the Holy Spirit for guidance in their election. Finally, each of the *vocales* walked up to deposit her ballot according to her rank in the convent. When the *scrutaine* announced the results, the most junior member of the *vocales* rang the bell to announce to the rest of the community—the junior choir nuns and the converse sisters—that they had a new superior. Mother Esther became the next superior of the Ursuline convent, and would go on to serve three full terms as superior, as well as two full terms as assistant again.[1]

Because of age, experience, and perhaps her origins as an Anglo-American girl as well, Mother Esther had the confidence of a clear majority of her sisters. But her election didn't mean that she was beloved or trusted by everyone. As we will see, not only did Mother Esther have the challenge of leading the monastery through its poorest and most desperate days, her leadership was questioned from the start and she was attacked from within throughout her terms as superior. Although the Ursuline archive is no different from most monastic records, which usually put the happiest and most consensual face on the challenges of living a communal religious life, there are several letters lurking in the bound volumes of correspondence at the archdiocesan records in Québec that testify to the lingering resentment Mother Esther endured. As she reached the final decade of her life, Mother Esther was still considered a foreigner—and even an arrogant autocrat—by some within her own community.

However controversial, Mother Esther's judgment would prove correct. By the end of her third term as superior in 1772, the convent was more secure under her leadership with more students, more novices, and more money than they could have hoped for in the dark hours of 1759 and 1760. Father Vincent Bigot, who had given the sermon at Esther's clothing ceremony in 1713, nearly fifty years before her election as mother superior, would have been entirely gratified. The truth of his providential explanation for her survival and rescue from both her New England and Wabanaki families—"thy hand, Lord, shall lead me; thy right hand shall sustain me" —would have proved itself a hundredfold.

La Mère "Étrangère"?

As we have seen, the mission of the Ursuline convent had shrunk dramatically from the missionary zeal and optimism of the days of its founders, Mother Marie de l'Incarnation and Madeleine de la Peltrie, in the 1630s and 1640s. Once they had hoped to help evangelize the continent, but as we have seen, by the turn of the eighteenth century urban convents like the Ursulines' had begun to restrict their efforts among Native girls. Instead, they focused on educating French Canadian girls and the occasional Anglo-American captive girls who were placed in the convent school through the mid-eighteenth century. By the middle of the eighteenth century and especially after the British Conquest, the church in Québec was laboring mightily just to nurture and preserve Catholicism among Canadian *habitants* and their families. Perhaps the Ursulines were right to reallocate their energies to French Canadian girls and New England captives who became nuns or married French Canadian men, as they had much better luck with them than they had with Native girls, who for the most part passed through their doors and back again to Native kin networks and marriage to Native men. *Francisation* was much easier with girls and women who remained in Québec and under French colonial government.

The Ursulines (and other women's religious orders in Québec) may have been vindicated in their shift to serve the Franco-American community for another reason: working only in the city of Québec among the Euro-

acquired

American population appears to have bought them grace with their new British masters, who carefully assessed the wealth and human resources of each women's monastery and men's religious order.[2] The Jesuits were singled out as especially dangerous for "their Turbulent and Intriguing Genius." As ever, the British found their missionary work especially objectionable. The British aimed to sever the ties between the French and their Native allies, and the Jesuits were considered historic political and military foes for their supposed "seductions" of the Native people and their ability to nurture ties between the French and the Wabanaki, Huron, and Iroquois. Because the Ursulines had given up on evangelizing the Native people of Québec early in the century, they escaped the scrutiny this kind of missionary work might have brought upon them after the conquest.

The Ursulines were matched in their political acumen by General James Murray, the governor general of occupied Québec, who appeared to be sympathetic to the work of women religious in particular for very practical reasons. In his analysis, he cited the women's communities as offering valuable services to the local population and also suggested that support for rebuilding the city—and in particular the Cathedral of Nôtre-Dame de Québec—might translate into toleration of or even appreciation for the British on the part of French Canadian civilians. He wrote with typical British condescension, "The Canadians are very Ignorant, and extremely Tenacious of their Religion, nothing can Contribute so much to make them Staunch Subjects to His Majesty, as the new Government's giving them every Reason to imagine no alteration is to be attempted in that Point." Furthermore, he recommended that "assist[ing] the People in Rebuilding their Great Church, would much ingratiate their new Masters with them."[3]

Imagine Murray enjoying the relative comfort and security of the tidy, whitewashed cells, classrooms, and common rooms of the Ursuline convent as he wrote an eighty-page report assessing the military capacity, the infrastructure, and the human capital that constituted Québec in 1762. His report emphasized the modest and meagerly self-supporting nature of the women's communities, and noted especially the value of the nursing and teaching they provided to the French Canadian community. But Murray forecast their end in a Protestant colony, even without being expelled: "As they are much esteemed and Respected by the People, the narrowness of their Circumstances will probably prevent their being filled up so easily as

in former times."[4] Cut off from the occasional royal patronage of the court
of Louis XV, their monastery, he predicted, would surely wither and die.
Although their analyses are marred by anti-Catholic bigotry and superstition, British measures of Québec's religious women and men ring true.
They were already seen by hostile invaders as people who were mainly
concerned with the daily affairs and observances of the French Canadian
community.[5] And because of the military occupation of Québec, Murray's
analysis of the relationship between religious women and men and the rest
of the civilian population was essentially correct. The optimism and energy of the seventeenth century gave way to defeat in the eighteenth century, and after the British Conquest the influence of the church turned
inward to focus on the small French Canadian population of Québec.
Ironically, it was a New England–born superior converted by Catholic Wabanaki women who would be among the first to lead the Ursulines under
British rule.

Although succeeding generations of Ursulines have celebrated their
"*gracieuse fleur d'Albion*," Mother Esther's election was controversial among
some of the *vocales*. The official narrative history of the Ursuline convent,
the Annales, betrays no dissention or hint of controversy, but three letters
in the Archives of the Archdiocese of Québec demonstrate that some of
her fellow choir nuns felt entitled to complain and even to raise questions
about the lawfulness of her election to the office of superior. Just a little
over a month after the election at the Ursuline convent in Québec in 1760,
Étienne Montgolfier, vicar general of the bishop of Québec, wrote a letter
to the Ursulines addressing the question as to whether or not "foreigners"
(*étrangers*) could assume "ecclesiastical responsibilities" (*charges ecclésiastiques*),
or whether offices in religious communities must be staffed with people
who are "completely French" (*entièrement françoise*). Mother Esther had been
elected superior the previous month, the first and only mother superior in
the order's history who was born outside of France or New France. In the
end, Montgolfier said that the requirements of the order's Constitution
could be overridden by the bishop, but this was unlikely as Bishop Henri-Marie Dubreil de Pontbriand had died in May of 1760, and the office remained vacant because of the colony's occupation by the British.[6] Other
than evidence of this anonymous complaint, Mother Esther's first superi-

orship was uncontroversial among her sisters. In fact, Esther was reelected in 1763 to serve a second full term. The order's rules did not permit superiors to serve more than two consecutive terms, but she was elected to serve another term in 1769. She must have had the esteem of most of the *vocales*, since she served in an elective office of her order for all but one three-year term of the last forty-five years of her life.

It is unclear who might have asked for Montgolfier's opinion about the legality of Esther's election as superior. By December 1760, the date of her election, she had been a professed nun for forty-six years, and it had been more than fifty years since her arrival in Quebec from the Wabanaki mission towns of Acadia. To all appearances, she was no *étrangère:* she had probably long since forgotten how to speak English; she had been put in the Ursuline convent school at the age of twelve in 1709; and she had remained there as a student, then as a novice, and finally as a naturalized French citizen and professed nun since 1714.[7] Perhaps part of any discontent or suspicion of Mother Esther was colored by the fact that she succeeded an enormously popular and successful mother superior in Marie-Anne Migeon de la Nativité, who embodied the ideal Ursuline through her rich family, noble blood, and connections to the French Canadian Church that went back more than a century.[8] What was it about Mother Esther that made her still "foreign" in other people's eyes?

Mother Esther and the Ursulines no doubt thought her personal history and family connections to New England might influence Murray and incline him to be more sympathetic to the interests of the Ursulines. Who might want to challenge Mother Esther's election, and what would such a challenge suggest about the salience of ethnic and national differences in the mid-eighteenth century? Esther's Anglo-American origins functioned in a variety of ways throughout her life—sometimes they were useful, sometimes they marked her as exotic, and sometimes they may have been held against her. Her New England roots never prevented her full participation in the life of the Ursuline community, although they were clearly a huge part of her identity throughout her life in the monastery, long before they became politically expedient. But even under British occupation, her New England connections were not seen as an unqualified good for the community —or for the nation.

"A correspondence was carry'd on with the French From this Town by a person of Consequence"

Mother Esther's family connections in New England were politically charged, given that their country—and the monastery itself—were occupied by the British. In fact, unbeknownst to anyone in the Ursuline community at the time, rumors were circulating in Boston that Nathaniel Wheelwright was suspected of working as a spy—this time for the French—and by implication, so was Mother Esther! On February 7, 1762, a little more than a year into Mother Esther's first term as superior, a young man named Tuthill Hubbard walked to the imposing Georgian brick building now known as the Old State House in Boston, which was then the seat of colonial government in Massachusetts. This is the historic building now remembered most famously for its role in the protest against colonial government in 1770 that ended with British soldiers firing on an unarmed crowd, the Boston Massacre. But throughout its existence, the Old State House was the seat of power, politics, and intrigue.

There Hubbard testified before the Superior Court about a conversation he had witnessed more than two years earlier in Boston, shortly after the British takeover of Québec. In November 1759, Hubbard recalled that some of the officers who had been at the siege of Québec "say'd they had done themselves and country great honor & more than was expected from them considering the small number of troops they had." Hubbard reported that "Capt. Arthur Loftus made Answer that it was true considering the Disadvantage that they labour'd under For the French very well knew their Numbers & every thing that pass'd & that a correspondence was carry'd on with the French From this Town by a person of Consequence." In other words, this "person of Consequence" was a British or Anglo-American spy for the French. Hubbard continued with his testimony: "Capt. Loftus then say'd it was no less a person than Mr. Nathaniel Wheelwright." Nathaniel, suspected of being a spy for the British in 1753–54 by the Marquis Duquesne, was now rumored to have spied for the French!

Some of the other officers doubted Wheelwright's guilt. According to Hubbard, they suggested that "if a Report prevail'd that the French had Received Intelligence, that as Mr. Wheelwright had been there in a publick character and had a Relation there; his name might be spoke of more familiarly by the French and from thence a Suspicion might arise that he was the Person." Of course Nathaniel "had a Relation there"—she was his aunt, Mother Esther, and he had visited and openly communicated with her on a lengthy diplomatic mission to Québec in 1754. Hubbard continued, explaining that "Capt. Loftus say'd no," there was no mistake as to the identity of the spy. In fact, "there was a better Evidence for there was a Letter not sign'd either taken or deliver'd by the French which the French say'd was Receiv'd From Mr Wheelwright which had been compar'd, [and the] Hand was his Writing." According to Hubbard's testimony, Captain Loftus concluded "that he should not be suppris'd if General Amherst Sent an Order to take [Wheelwright] and hanged him."[9]

Could Nathaniel have been sending information about troop strength and movements to the French through Mother Esther? This story seems too good to be true, with Mother Esther playing Miss Marple crossed with James Bond. It probably is too good to be true, although the allegation that Nathaniel passed intelligence to the French through Mother Esther reflects a few truths that are important to understanding immediate post-Conquest Québec, and to understanding the role of religious women in colonial politics. Fears of spies and spying were legion among both the British and French Canadians at this time in between the military conquest of Québec in 1759 and the 1763 Treaty of Paris, which finally ended the conflict.

Anglo-American and British officers regarded high-ranking religious women with suspicion and fear, because they recognized how connected to colonial elites the women were. Captain Loftus and a Captain Small were only two among many officers to suspect religious women of political intrigue. As we have seen, the women who became choir nuns were from wealthy and even noble families. Their fathers and brothers were governors, colonial officials, and military officers; entering a convent and serving in its leadership were simply a means by which these women could serve king, country, and their faith, and their connections to colonial elites outside the convent were always well known. In fact, at the Hôpital-Général across town from the Ursuline convent at the very same moment, Mother St. Claude, the mother superior of the Augustinian hospital nuns there, was suspected by British Captain John Knox of spreading false rumors of French victories and British defeats among the officers they nursed there on both sides of the conflict. Recognition of their rank and connections outside the convent walls led British officers to suspect religious women, especially mothers superior like St. Claude and Esther de l'Enfant Jésus, of political intrigue.[10]

The allegations that Nathaniel Wheelwright was a spy went nowhere. General Amherst never hanged him, or even sent for him, though his story ends badly not long after Hubbard's accusation. He was rich and married into a rich family, but his young wife died in 1764, leaving behind three children. Nathaniel declared bankruptcy the following year, and because of the extensive web of credit and debt in which he was heavily invested, this caused a regional financial crisis, which exacerbated the recession that had set in after the war. Nathaniel fled from his creditors in disgrace to Guadeloupe, where he died of yellow fever in 1766, an ending all too typical of the white migrants to the Caribbean who were usually either on the make or on their way down.

A final detail about Nathaniel seems significant: It turns out that the coat of arms that was engraved on the place setting that he brought his aunt in 1754 was an eighteenth-century invention by the Wheelwrights in Boston. They were just as eager to conjure a noble lineage for their family as Mother Esther was.[11]

"We have to make do with the little we have"

Economic precariousness and religious uncertainty were the only constants in Québec in the 1760s: Although massive government spending continued in Québec in the early years of the occupation, the city had to rebuild itself almost entirely because of the damage caused by the British bombs in 1759. Until the passage of the Québec Act in 1774, fully fifteen years after the conquest, Catholics in Québec lived in fear of their religion being outlawed and their clergy being banished by their new British masters. The Ursuline annalist remembered the harsh winter and spring of 1760: "Winter had passed with a great deal of pain and misery, [and] on 28 April 1760, we had to endure a second siege: the French came to take the city back. God's anger justly irritated against us was not appeased yet: many were injured and many killed." The occupation of the monastery continued after the British secured their victory in Québec and after the fall of Montreal later that summer. "Our community serves as a room for the officers. Our monastery was a hospital and had hardly enough room for ourselves after these tragic adventures, suffering and moaning all summer long for fear Canada was going to be overtaken, which happened on September 8th 1760."[12] This is the monastery that Mother Esther was elected to lead just three months later.

Even absent the domination of a government hostile to Catholic religious orders, convents were not wealthy institutions. Canadian convents were typically funded through a combination of fees and revenues: most owned land and houses, for which they were paid rent; some hired out the farming of some of their land too. They received no revenue from their mother houses in France, as they were working to support themselves. They might receive occasional gifts from the king—hospital nuns tended to receive more royal largesse because as nurses, they supported the military and the work of colonization more directly than the teaching orders, whose monasteries were filled with little girls rather than ailing soldiers and marines, but even they couldn't rely on government support for their work. The biggest economic advantage that convents had over other institutions was that they were staffed entirely by volunteers who themselves paid for admission in the form of the *dot*, or dowry, which would then be invested for the good of the community. Their collective labor was the most valuable asset they possessed. The fruit of this labor went entirely to support the work of the monastery, be it teaching, nursing, artistry, or a combination of all three as was the case of the Ursulines in the early years of British occupation. As we have seen, teaching orders charged a premium for room and board for the students in the *pensionnat*, and Ursuline workshops produced a variety of devotional items that were purchased and used in churches and chapels across Canada. Québec's sudden occupation by British officers and soldiers, and then the colonial officials and merchants who followed them, led to Ursuline entrepreneurial innovation.

Mother Esther's first success was in maintaining the convent financially through the first few years of the British Conquest. General James Murray's report on the state of Québec in the spring of 1762 gives a brief but clear picture of the dire state of the monastery's finances. He explains that "this is likewise a Community of Women, their Institution is for the Education of Young Girls." He notes that their work was supported to a much lesser degree by the French king than were the other religious houses, male or female, in the city. Whereas the annual allowance from the king to the

Augustinian sisters at the Hôtel-Dieu was seventy-five hundred livres, and two thousand livres for the sisters at the Hôpital-Général, the Ursulines received only fifteen hundred livres, less than any of the religious orders except for the Recollets, a mendicant order of priests. In a 1761 letter to Father Alain de Launay in Paris, Mother Esther asks whether a rumor she had heard is true—"We were just told Peace was made and this poor country was given back to the French. I wish it were true and that we could hear from you by the first ship sailing from France." Father de Launay was in charge of administering the Canadian missions, and Mother Esther was concerned about "where we stand with our small annuities. We really would need them to be more considerable but we have to make do with the little we have." In the same letter, she asks him to send a few necessary supplies they had done without since the British blockade began nearly three years earlier—"Would you have the kindness to send us a piece or two of light [fabric?] for the veils which we absolutely need?"[13]

British bureaucrats and their recommendations for disestablishing the church were perhaps even more threatening to the long-term survival of Ursulines of Québec than were the British bombs and shells of 1759 and 1760. The British approached their occupation like the experienced imperialists that they were, and part of imperial conquest in the eighteenth century included the creation of a bureaucratic state apparatus: censuses of the city of Québec and its suburbs, precise descriptions of the numbers, sexes, and ages of people and animals on particular farms, and analyses of the holdings of each of the religious orders and the best way to contain their influence and shut them down.[14] In his own journal of the occupation, Murray's terse, telegraphic language is that of an administrator who uses language to break the city's geography into governable parts, just as bombs and shells had pulverized much of the city: "I ordered the town to be divided into quarters; set the proper officers to survey the same; see what repairs were necessary." Murray remains concerned mostly with the secular business of keeping Québec's citizens pacified and disinclined to rebel against British rule, as well as keeping his men safe from starvation and frostbite during his first Canadian winter (and occasionally keeping civilians safe from the predations of his men). Other British officers were more directly concerned with controlling the influence of the Church, which they saw as key to breaking any attempts at continued political resistance.

British anti-Catholicism is in full flower in the documentary record of the occupation of Québec, but several officers recognized the importance that religious institutions and people played in the secular and spiritual life of the province. General Murray was among the most sympathetic of British officials, as we have seen. He recognized the esteem the civilian population had for the work of the women's religious orders, and recommended assisting the Canadians in rebuilding their churches to encourage their loyalty, or at least their resignation to British rule. However, Murray also recommended a new regime for the men's religious orders in Québec: evict the Jesuits, tolerate the mendicant Recollet priests until they left of their own accord, and preserve the seminary to furnish Canadian-born priests who would be less likely to foment rebellion than French-born priests. Murray cautioned that more delicate handling was required for the women's orders: "When the Canadians become a little more reconciled to British Customs and Government, it may not be amiss, under Colour of serving these Communities in their distressed situation, to Restrict the admission of any under a Certain Sum; This Regulation with another fixing a Certain Age, under which no vows to be taken, would Probably soon reform the worst abuses of such Institutions."[15] Of course, women's orders all along demanded that novices contribute a substantial dowry and observed their own age requirements, but his comments here probably allude to the widespread English and Anglo-American Protestant fantasy that young girls were coerced to join religious orders at very tender ages or against their wills.

If Murray was strategically sympathetic to Canadian Catholics, other bureaucrats used the language of containment and even urged the abolition of Catholic religious orders. For example, one anonymous letter suggests that the occupation government bear in mind the "possibility of what may happen, should the Times change, should *their* strength increase, and *ours* diminish. In this view it seems advisable that all *Regulars*, all Convents of Men & Women, all Canons, Priests, Deans &c should be *totally abolished*, but that they should have power, before they retire, within a limited time, to sell their Lands & their effects." More typical was the counsel to let the religious orders die out on their own through the imposition of various rules that would limit the number of new postulants. One Anglican churchman recommended in 1765 "that the several Convents and religious Communities of Women be continued upon their present establishment; but that no new professions, Engagements or Admissions whatever in the said Convents or Communities be allowed of, and their Revenues as they decrease in number, and their whole Estates when the Communities are entirely dissolved, be applied & set apart to the Support of a Protestant Ministry and Schools, in the like manner as has been already proposed in respect to the revenues and Estates of the Jesuits and Recollects."[16] With the military and political conquest of Canada under way, British Protestants hoped to effect its religious conquest as well.

In the absence of any assistance from the French king or the Canadian missions, Murray totted up the properties and investments with which the religious orders funded themselves and their work, and the Ursulines once again came up short. In fact, the few meetings of the congregation or of her executive council (the Discrètes) Mother Esther called in her first term as superior speak to their pinched circumstances: she proposed that they decrease the amount of money spent on the boarding students, and sell some land in return for £1,200 and an annuity of £15 (about 30,000 and 350 livres, respectively). The land sale was announced barely a week before Murray issued his report on the state of the Ursulines that spring. While these economies were doubtlessly disappointing, they speak to Mother Esther's shrewdness and determination in maintaining the Ursuline convent and continuing its mission through the uncertain years of the occupation. Selling some assets and making other budgetary reductions would continue through her three terms as superior, as the Ursulines would need to sell other properties and reduce their expenses for the *pensionnat* into the 1770s.[17]

In terms of the Ursulines' financial health, being a teaching order instead of a nursing order had real advantages. Although they had more professed nuns than the other two women's religious orders—thirty-six were at the Hôtel-Dieu and only thirty-three at the Hôpital-Général, compared with thirty-eight Ursulines—Murray's estimation of their wealth was much lower than that held by the other women's orders. He supposed that the Ursulines' real estate holdings and rents brought them only 4,082 livres, hardly more than the amount of money a novice was expected to bring as her dowry when joining the order. The two orders of Augustinian hospital nuns collected at least 6,346 and 6,800 livres each—more than the Ursulines, but barely enough to cover two dowries. Although the Ursulines were poorer in terms of their investments and their occasional allowances from the king, their income was much higher, as they could charge for their services. Whereas the Ursulines charged their boarding students fees, and they could sell the elaborately embroidered and gilded devotional objects they decorated, hospital nuns were in the business of serving those who had nothing—no families to nurse them through illnesses and injuries, or to offer hospice care for (in Murray's words) "Invalids, Ideots or Incurables." (Recall that the education offered by the Ursulines was free, but that the typically wealthy families of boarding students paid for their accommodations.) Therefore, while the Ursulines were poor on paper, Murray concluded that their "Chief Estate . . . Consists in their Boarders."[18]

In fact, the siege and occupation of 1759–60 did not much interrupt the Ursuline teaching mission. A large number of boarding students left the convent upon the beginning of the siege in May and June 1759, but a few stayed with the Ursulines throughout the siege and bombardment. The school admitted a few boarders in 1760, including *"deux petites desmoiselles Angloises"*—two little English misses—and another with an English name and an "English mother" who paid her boarding fees. The school was nearly overwhelmed with students in 1761, when twenty-eight new students—French Canadian and British—enrolled in the Ursuline *pensionnat*. These were the years when girls named Sally, Peggy, and Nancy took their places next to the Marie-Annes, the Marie-Madeleines, and the Marguerites who had dominated the school for the previous century. Sometimes the exotic English names challenged the Ursuline educators, who would write *Becqué et Paulé* instead of "Becky and Polly." The *pensionnat* in these years cost £260 a year—a hefty charge, but one happily borne by British newcomers who aspired to found the city's Anglo-Canadian elite. New students continued to flock to the school—twenty-two in 1762, though only fourteen in 1763, the year that Murray and his men finally left the convent. Presumably, British parents were using the *pensionnat* in much the same way as French colonial officials and military officers had, as a safe place to keep daughters while they were traveling or otherwise on official business. Mother Esther suggested that they drop the boarding fees from £260 to £220, and enrollments rebounded again with twenty-eight new students in 1764, sixteen more in 1765, and nineteen in 1766.[19]

Mother Esther proved herself a sensible businesswoman when enrollment dipped once again after her first two terms as superior and into her third term, when she called the Discrètes, or executive council, to another meeting to propose another reduction in boarding fees in 1771, this time from £220 to £192, and enrollments in the *pensionnat* surged again from an all-time low of four students in 1769 to thirty-three new girls in 1773. Enrollments remained high through the 1770s, with new and returning students numbering in the high twenties to the high thirties. Even at the lower price of £192 per year, thirty to thirty-five students (not all of whom stayed all year) would have brought in perhaps £5,000 to £6,500 a year, making the *pensionnat* a steadier and more stable source of income for the convent than perhaps twelve students at £220 per year.[20]

As at the turn of the century, the Ursuline convent school became a multicultural space in which girls from different ethnic and confessional backgrounds were educated. How much of this is due to the fact that the mother superior of the order from 1760 to 1766 herself embodied part of the seventeenth-century mission of outreach to Iroquois and Wabanaki students? Did she reach out specifically to British officers and church officials and ask them to entrust her with the education of their daughters? Her presence might have been reassuring to some British parents and threatening to others: after all, as a devout convert to Catholicism, she was a living example of the power of Catholic education to turn children against their faith and parents. On the other hand, perhaps the leadership of a woman who had herself been an Anglo-American captive made these parents think that they could work with her, and that she might understand their daughters. We can't know for sure, but there seem to have been many more British girls enrolled during her first two terms as superior (thirteen) than in the interregnum (three) when another superior served from 1766 to 1769. After Mother Esther was again elected superior in 1769, six more British girls enrolled at the school during her final term as superior.[21] The *pensionnat* was clearly a successful business for the Ursulines, as well as an opportunity to resume some of the familiar rhythms of convent life after the conquest. Long after Mother Esther's final term as mother superior, girls with names like Sara Fitzgerald, Betty Kennedy, and Margaret Fraser continued to enroll at the Ursuline school, proof that the British Conquest involved not just an English takeover but an infusion of Irish and Scottish officers and merchants flocking to Québec as well. Several parts of the empire were enlisted in bringing this new, French-speaking colony into the empire.

Education was just one of the means by which the Ursulines were raising money to support themselves. In the same report, Murray noted that the Ursulines were busy making "a Number of little Ingenious Works for which there is a great Demand, by means of which they are enabled to live very decently and Comfortably." These were small objéts d'art—boxes and decorative items—that were a hybrid of European needlecraft and North American materials. Using birchbark embroidered with dyed moose hair instead of silk floss or twist, or decorated with porcupine quills, the Ursulines had made these bibelots since at least the middle of the eighteenth

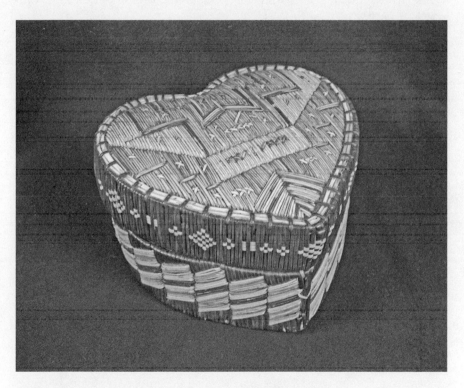

This eighteenth-century birchbark box, overlaid with brightly colored porcupine quills in a design that combines Native and Euro-American design elements, was produced by the Ursulines for the British tourist trade in occupied Québec from the 1760s.
Photo courtesy of the Musée des Ursulines de Québec

century as a fund-raising tool. However, they became much more popular and remarked upon after the Conquest as *souvenirs* for the British officers and merchants who poured into Québec after the 1750s. Mother Esther described these *"petites ouvrages d'écorce"*—little bark works—in a 1761 letter to Father Alain de Launay, the Jesuit who was in charge of the Canadian mission, and noted their financial significance to Ursulines: "As long as the little embroidered objects will be fashionable we will live off this income because we sell them for a high price and the persons who buy them appreciate them so much they are happy to have the privilege to get them, and we never make enough to satisfy everyone." These *petites ouvrages* were not made as a pastime; they were made for profit.[22]

Like Mother Esther herself, they represented North America as a combination of European and Native materials and design, and the Ursulines in the eighteenth century were the only artists who could bring them together in this fashion. Decorated with the European-derived steel needle technology of embroidery, the materials they used and the designs they embroidered were both European and North American. Some surviving specimens at the Musée des Ursulines de Québec, in private collections, and in museums in Britain feature simple, bold geometric designs; others depict floral and vegetal elements in the old-fashioned Mannerist aesthetic of Ursuline embroidery of the era. All were eye-catching, brightly colored, and clearly the product of hours or even days of skillful, patient labor.[23]

Elizabeth Simcoe, the wife of John Graves Simcoe, lieutenant governor of Upper Canada, described a visit to the Ursuline monastery in December 1791 where she almost certainly saw embroidery by Mother Esther: "They make many decorations for their altars and church and gild picture frames. They showed me a fine piece of embroidery worked by an English nun, since dead. Some of them make boxes and pin cushions of birch bark, worked with dyed hair of the orignale, or elk. It is so short that it must be put through the needle for every stich, which makes it tedious." "Orignal" is in fact the French word for moose, not elk, but Simcoe was probably right about the fine embroidery having been wrought by an "English nun." Mother Esther was a skilled embroiderer, and she may have been a skilled painter as well. She allegedly sent the Wheelwright family in New England a copy of the (invented) Wheelwright coat of arms painted on silk, a medium that was key to the brilliant detail that Ursuline embroiderers were able to achieve: First, a design would be painted on silk, then the silk basted to a sturdier material underneath. Finally, the embroiderer could work her design in floss and silver and gold thread as the finer-textured silk on top could showcase a much finer level of detail than the coarser fabric underneath, while the sturdier fabric offered a stiffer and more secure base for the elaborate work. The *ouvrage* that Mrs. Simcoe was shown was probably Mother Esther's work, as she was remembered in her obituary for "works [that] were usually meant for churches"—that is, her work was always of show quality. Furthermore, "she started embroidery when she was young and was always perfectly successful." Of the only other two New England–born nuns, Dorothy Jordan de St. Joseph was remembered in her obituary for doing "some needlework for the good of the community," and Mary Ann Davis de St. Benoit was "very skillful and enjoyed needlework," but neither was praised for producing anything specifically decorative or devotional. (Also, in 1791 Mother Esther was only eleven years gone and also famous as a mother superior, whereas Mother St. Joseph had died in 1759 and Mother St. Benoit in 1749, making it much likelier that Esther's memory would have been foremost.)[24]

Most but not all mothers superior were reelected to serve a second consecutive term. In spite of the evidence of lingering doubt about her "*étrangère*" status, Mother Esther's leadership was acceptable enough to the majority of *vocales* that they reelected her superior on December 15, 1763. The end of 1763 was a happy time for the Ursulines, because after four years of occupation, General Murray and his troops had left, and the sisters finally had their monastery back to themselves. Shortly after Mother Esther's reelection, the order further honored her by planning a large celebration of her upcoming fiftieth anniversary of her final profession. The Ursuline chapel was still serving as the parish church, so attendance must have been high for the celebration on April 12, 1764. Father Briand, the highest-ranking prelate in the absence of a bishop, helped celebrate the Mass, and the Ursuline confessor Father Réché, who had endured the siege of Québec with the nuns left behind in the monastery in 1759, preached "a very beautiful Sermon on the happiness of Religious life, [and we] sang many songs during the Holy mass. Monsieur Réché our very dignified

Confessor played the organ, [and] at the end of the Mass we ended with the *Te Deum*," the moving ancient hymn sung on certain feast days and the celebration of special events like the canonization of a saint, or religious profession. There are no other details about the food and drink they served in the refectory that day, but the Ursulines must have considered this golden jubilee a feast day, as the annalist concludes her description with the notation that "the Community was treated sumptuously, and so were our Priests." Mother Esther was never remembered for the virtue of mortification or for reveling in hunger, so it's likely that she joined in the special feast with great enjoyment. After the previous five years of fear and uncertainty about their future, the Ursulines were probably grateful to have something to celebrate.[25]

The year 1764 was the occasion of other celebrations and returns to normal life within and without the monastery. Shortly after Mother Esther's fiftieth anniversary celebration, Father Jean-Olivier Briand went to Paris to be consecrated as the next bishop of Québec, with the permission of General Murray, a fact that made Roman Catholics there hopeful that the British would permit them to continue to observe their religion and to retain their priests. After having refused new postulants for the previous five years, the Ursulines began to accept new aspirants to the religious life. (Did Mother Esther's large public celebration of her golden jubilee play any role in the decisions made by these young women? It was a good advertisement for the value of religious life in Québec.) After several precarious years, notwithstanding General Murray's prediction that the end of French rule would "probably prevent their being filled up so easily as in former times," the Ursulines accepted three postulants to the novitiate again in the spring and summer of 1764. Mother Esther also had the honor of announcing the return of the bishop to Québec before the expiration of her second term as superior. After a nearly two-year absence, Father Briand returned in June of 1766 as the bishop of Québec in time to preside over the clothing ceremonies of two of the three young novices who had come to the convent in 1764. He lives on in the memory of the Ursulines as the prelate who helped the Ursulines complete their repairs from the damage caused by the siege several years earlier.[26] Bishop Briand would continue to take a personal role in guiding the Québec Ursulines into the next decade.

"Everything I could tell you wouldn't express her hauteur*"*

The late 1760s were happy years for the Ursulines of Québec. They finally completed the repairs from the damage done during the siege in 1759, they continued to attract postulants and to admit novices, and most exciting of all, Pope Clement XIII beatified the order's founder, Mother Angela Merici, in 1768. The Québec Ursulines received the news of their founder's beatification in the spring of 1769, just a few days before her annual feast day of May 31. Beatification, or the limited and often local permission to venerate an individual, is usually the first step on the way to canonization as a saint; the founder was in fact canonized as St. Angela Merici in 1807.[27] Because of Mother Esther's success in leading the Québec Ursulines through their most difficult passage as a community, after serving two consecutive terms as mother superior, she was elected superior again in 1769 to serve for one final term. Her third election clearly put to rest any lingering concerns among the majority of choir nuns about the legality or legitimacy of her service as superior, but her third term was marred by further resentment of her leadership. Why did her leadership remain controversial at all, when under Mother Esther the convent had not only survived but increased its numbers of novices who aspired to become choir nuns, especially considering that Roman Catholics in Québec couldn't even be certain whether their religion would remain legal under British rule, let alone their religious communities allowed to thrive? The admission of new novices was suspended for five full years, from 1759 until 1764, after the Ursulines returned to their home, the soldiers evacuated the convent, and the peace treaty was signed. But once admissions resumed, the novice mistresses were nearly as busy as they had been in the 1710s and 1720s in the enthusiastic years leading up to the convent's centenary: eight women were admitted as postulants from 1764 through 1769, all of whom professed final vows, and another fourteen were admitted in the 1770s, ten of whom took final vows. How then can we understand the whiffs of scandal and resentment that marked Mother Esther's final term as superior?

Was it her age? Esther was seventy-three in 1769; we might consider the Ursuline tradition of electing only the oldest women in their communities to serve as superiors, a practice that may have taxed the health and endurance of even the most energetic septuagenarians. Was it her very success in attracting Ursuline postulants that made the community vulnerable to a breach in the observation of the rules? Or was it, once again, the fact that she was "Esther Angloise," *une étrangère,* someone whose identity as an outsider had been clearly marked from her entry into the *pensionnat* sixty years earlier? While age and infirmity might have played a role in this community scandal, the evidence suggests that she was still regarded as something of an outsider within the community that she led.

Mother Esther's third term as mother superior started with a little scandal. Sometime in the night of July 17–18, 1770, a young novice left the Ursuline convent and returned, and somehow the bishop was notified of this serious infraction of the rules. This was a disturbing lapse of monastic discipline, as novices were tested for their worthiness for religious life in part by strict claustration and a complete ban on seeing or visiting with family members even inside the convent for an entire year. Bishop Briand wrote to Mother Esther—a former portress—to scold her for her lax management of the doors and gates that enclosed the monastery, telling her archly, "It is surprising, my Reverend Mother, that one might be able to go out at 4 a.m." Apparently, he had discussed this problem with her before the novice's nocturnal escape, reminding her that "I often noticed that the main door was left open all day. On that occasion, I told you what I saw at the Ursulines in Saint Brieuc as school boy. Two nuns opened the gate and closed it right away each time carriages went in and out. They went out of their way to follow the rule." He urged Mother Esther that "[this] is what we should recommend here on pain of excommunication. . . . What happened today should only occur once every fifty years. To avoid such a crime and such a scandal would require such an effort every day of one's life. Today, you know I was right: it takes examples to teach a lesson." He concluded his letter with the comment, "I would be justified to punish all those in charge, but I am not doing it. Next time, be more careful. You may receive her, but since she exposed herself to major excommunication, she will not be allowed to come to any church service or talk to anyone but you and the nun in charge of bringing her meals until censure is lifted."[28]

It is important to recall the larger context: Bishop Briand returned in 1766 to Québec, which had been without a bishop for the six years since the previous bishop's death on the heels of the British Conquest in 1760. Times of crisis like the Conquest were particularly likely to inspire early-

modern bishops to exert control over the women's orders under their pur-
view. A bishop attempting to enforce claustration was certainly nothing
new, nor was his emphasis on the gate. Gates weren't just practical security
measures or a means of delineating property lines—when constructing enclosure, they also served as a threshold between religious life in the convent
and *le monde,* the outside world. (Recall that novices who left before they
took their final vows are described in convent records as having *retournée au
monde,* returned to the world outside of religious life.) In post-Reformation
Europe, when church authorities renewed their zeal for a strict enforcement
of claustration, gates of convents became even more powerful symbolic as
well as literal transitions from one world to another. Ideally, perpetual enclosure meant that once nuns entered the convent and took solemn vows,
they would never reenter the world.[29]

This was how it was supposed to work, at least in the minds of bishops
and cardinals—but as we have seen, New World convents were famously
permeable spaces. The Ursuline house of Québec was founded in opposition to these efforts to enforce the rule of cloister. Although the late-
eighteenth-century convent in Québec looked a lot more enclosed than in
its seventeenth-century rustic beginnings, the order had always received
students—day students of both sexes and all ages, as well as boarding
girls—and was even open to Protestant male visitors, not all of whom were
restricted by the grille.[30]

Mother Esther replied to the bishop's letter three days later. She offered
ritual deference to Bishop Briand, assuring him, "We started to carry out
the order your Lordship had the kindness to notify us to our advantage
regarding the closing of the gate. We believe it will be obeyed forever, we
are keeping your letter preciously and I am sending you a copy as you required." (The document in the archdiocesan archives today is not Briand's
original letter, but a copy of his letter that Briand asked Mother Esther to
return to him—perhaps in a didactic effort to ensure that the Ursulines
read the letter and understood his instructions?) But in keeping with the
tradition of independence among New World Ursulines, Mother Esther's
response indicated that she was handling the punishment in her own, rather
sympathetic manner. She told the bishop that the young novice "admitted
to me that she thought she would go out for fresh air for her health and that
she would come right back. I did not make any comment, but all I know is

she feels sorry for it." Mother Esther also reported that per the bishop's orders, she personally goes "to the offender's room three times a day with the one who brings her food to make sure she does not starve herself to death." Mother Esther offered the young woman extraordinary courtesy, especially for someone who had broken the important rule of cloister: "I make sure she gets what she likes. I take it to heart that she will survive the excommunication, because she seems distressed by this last ordeal, and I am trying to explain to her that this is of great consequence and that I cannot take any part in it, that she should submit to the punishment your Lordship imposed on her."[31]

It wasn't only the bishop who wrote letters complaining about Mother Esther's conduct. During her tenure as superior, there were some of her own sisters whom she didn't please. Mother Esther has the distinction of being the only Ursuline mother superior of this era whose sister nuns complained to the bishop about her leadership, at least according to letters preserved in the archdiocesan archives. The petitioners don't specifically identify her Englishness as the cause of their doubt or irritation, and we can never know the extent to which her origins emboldened dissidents to write to the bishop. But given the letter of response which first addressed the question as to whether or not a "foreigner" could assume the superiorship, it may have been at least part of the reason some chafed under her leadership. In 1772, the last year of Esther's third term as superior, Mother Marie Antoinette Poulin de St. François complained that "any advice as well considered, just, and reasonable as it is never gets approval at my Superior's tribunal, mostly when it comes from those whose duty and obligation impose the necessity to give them." Her specific complaint was that Esther moved a young nun into a teaching position prematurely, in her opinion, displacing another young nun. Mother St. François wrote intriguingly to Bishop Briand "to appeal to your Lordship to simply point out a little problem which has been worrying me since yesterday, when I learned a big secret: Sister St. Olivier will be taken out of the class and replaced by the little St Angèle. This big event should take place tomorrow and will be disclosed to the community and to me, so that we will not feel free to express any doubt or bring up the least objection."[32]

Who were Sister St. Olivier and Sister St. Angèle? They were Jeanne Baronet and Marie-Louise Jyncree, two of the new postulants who had been admitted in 1769 within months of each other. Each made her final profession in 1771, Baronet as Sister St. Olivier and Jyncree as Sister St. Angèle, the latter of whom Esther was accused of favoring unjustly. Mother St. François offers some fascinating insights into Jyncree that may help explain Mother Esther's partiality toward her. She writes, "I admit that this poor child's lot touches me much, but she is not yet capable of teaching others." What about "this poor child's lot" was so moving? We can only speculate: was she an orphan, or a refugee of some kind as Mother Esther had once been? We know of her relative poverty because of the very low dowry she paid (one thousand livres, versus the more typical three thousand), but nothing that might explain it or why she was admitted to the choir anyway. Mother St. François continues, "To set things straight, I am begging your Highness very humbly to answer my prayer and grant this young girl the advantage of finishing her novitiate to learn submission before teaching others." Submission is only one among many things young women are supposed to learn as novices, or as new choir nuns who were housed and fed with the novices for another three years after their professions.[33]

What was it about Sister St. Angèle that Sister St. François found unsubmissive or otherwise unseemly in her taking Sister St. Olivier's place as a teacher? We know that the Ursulines of Québec, like other women's religious orders in the early-modern era, were very status conscious and focused on clear hierarchies: Choir nuns were set apart from the lay sisters by additional prayers, inclusion in the *vocales,* and exemption from housework; distinctions in the choir were marked by the order in which the nuns entered and exited rooms and the chapel throughout the day. The last one who professed was always at the back of the line, and she did not move up in rank order unless or until there were newer nuns behind her in line. We know that St. Olivier had started her novitiate three months ahead of St. Angèle, and we know that she was one year older, but even so, the differences between the two young women that we can discern from this distance are minimal except for one. Sister St. Olivier paid a three thousand–livre dowry, whereas Sister St. Angèle had paid only one thousand livres. Mother St. François thought that Jyncree was being advanced ahead of her age, experience, and rank by Mother Esther—perhaps as Esther herself had been?

Just two weeks later, Mother St. Augustin (Marie Elizabeth Richard) wrote to confirm Mother St. François's portrait of Mother Esther as capricious, proud, and haughty. She writes, "Permit me . . . to get a few things off my chest. Last Sunday, we were read the recommendations your highness took the trouble of addressing us, which were not those of a superior's but rather those of a concerned father of our community, and we listened to them with the deepest respect and all of us showed our satisfaction and gratitude for your kindness." However, "we were not given the time to taste its sweetness, because our Mother (Esther) gave us a long lecture, which in everyone's opinion, was quite uncalled for. Here is an example about the only one who stands out in [the] room, with her affected attitude. . . . This is a mix of righteousness and politics which we understand nothing of, and we regret it." Mother St. Augustin related a few examples of Mother Esther's partiality and caprice, from her point of view. She also furnished evidence that she and Mother St. François were collaborators in their complaints to the bishop, saying that St. François would have written herself but she didn't want to bother the bishop again, and reiterating St. François's complaint that Sister St. Angèle was "incompentent." Mother St. Augustin concluded her letter by leveling another charge of arrogance at Mother Esther: "At any rate, it is the general feeling and everything I could tell you wouldn't express her *hauteur*."[34]

Mother St. François and Mother St. Augustin never say why they find Mother Esther so overbearing—but Esther's semioutsider status probably had something to do with it. As we have seen all along, it was important for the Ursulines to see Esther Wheelwright as an English girl and woman—at first, this investment in her New England origins was a defensive reaction against her Wabanaki upbringing between ages seven and twelve. Since the midcentury resumption of warfare with the British and their colonies in New England, as well as the French defeat, Mother Esther's supposed Englishness came to function as something that could make her more diplomatically useful perhaps but also potentially more dangerous. The Ursulines may also have felt as though they were conquered by British invaders within as well as without convent walls: however politically useful Mother Esther's New England roots may have been outside the community, they may also have been the cause of unusually strong resentment of her leadership inside the monastery.

Whatever the causes of their resentment, these letters were a major breach of the respect mothers superior were accorded for several reasons—their advanced age and accomplishments as well as rank in office and in the monastery. There are no other letters from Ursulines complaining about any of their eighteenth-century mothers superior in the files of the Archdiocese of Québec—only these complaints about Mother Esther. The correspondents, Mother St. Augustin and Mother St. François, were in their late forties and early fifties, fully middle-aged but a generation younger than Esther, who was seventy-six in the last year of her superiority. Mother St. François was the *dépositaire,* or treasurer, for the community for twenty-one years, including the years of Esther's superiority, and so served in convent leadership in a high elective office that entrusted her with the community's stores and funds. (She was herself elected superior in 1778 and served one three-year term.) As the treasurer for the community, Mother St. François would have had access to the community's records going back to its foundations, so she might have known not only that Mother Esther was born outside Québec, but also that she was accepted as a choir nun with a much smaller dowry than her peers. No eighteenth-century choir nuns were admitted to the Ursuline convent with a smaller dowry than Esther Wheelwright until Sister St. Angèle. This detail makes their experiences stand out, although it certainly wasn't something to brag about in a religious order that was highly status conscious and perpetually strapped for cash, especially in the unsettled 1760s and early 1770s. The issue of economic and social status may also have been an issue for Mother St. Augustin because her own dowry had been much larger than those of most girls admitted to the novitiate in the 1740s—she paid five thousand livres, far more than the typical three thousand. All of these factors may have made some of Esther's younger Québec-born sisters resent especially her *"hauteur."*[35] Who did this *étrangère* think she was?

The Wheelwrights of Wells and Boston

Although Mother Esther's leadership was challenged within the convent by some fellow nuns and without the convent by the bishop, the years of her superiority coincided with a renewal of her fame in New England. Nathaniel Wheelwright's visit to his aunt was the only thoroughly documented contact with Mother Esther, but Wheelwright family lore holds that two other nephews in military service visited her in 1761 after the British

Conquest and after her election as mother superior. Captain Daniel Wheelwright appears to have sailed his sloop Ranger between Québec and Boston in 1761, and was involved in provincial troop transport to Halifax after the conquest of Québec. Another nephew, Joshua Moody, was the means by which the silk painting of the supposed Wheelwright coat of arms by Mother Esther, as well as her oil portrait, was sent to her family. Mother Esther was apparently pleased to renew the connection with her nephews and their children.[36]

Mother Esther's fame as mother superior spread through parts of New England beyond her family circle. Eighteen-year-old Abigail Smith, during her courtship by future U.S. President John Adams, wrote a letter to her cousin Isaac Smith in which she told him that "by the favor of my Father I have had the pleasure of seeing your Copy of Mrs. Wheelwrights Letter, to her Nephew, and having some small acquaintance with the French tongue, have attempted a translation; of it, which I here send, for your perusal and correction." (Smith uses the honorific "Mrs." as an abbreviation of the honorific "Mistress" offered to high-ranking colonial American women whatever their marital status.) Historians have assumed that this was a letter that Joshua Moody brought back from his visit to his aunt in 1761. If copies of the letter circulated, it was almost surely because of Mother Esther's stature in the British-occupied city of Québec rather than the want of French-language materials for students in Massachusetts. Her conversion to an enemy language and religion was perhaps viewed as less threatening now that she and all of her sisters in religion would live once again under British rule.

Unfortunately, the translation is no longer attached to Smith's letter, but a postscript to her letter suggests that Mother Esther's sex was of special interest to Abigail Smith. In particular, Smith is fascinated by the gender politics of religious women, suggesting to her cousin, "N B. How the Lady abbess came to subscribe herself Serviteur [servant], which you know is of the masculine Gender I cannot devise unless like all other Ladies in a convent, she chose to make use of the Masculine Gender, rather than the Feminine." In March 1763, Mother Esther was completing her first term as mother superior, and would be elected to another term that December. The few letters we have in her hand date from that period, and unfortunately, only two out of three preserve her original signature, which was

"Votre tres humble et tres obeissante servante Sr. de L'enfant Jesus"—Your very humble and obedient servant Sister of the infant Jesus. In one case she omits the feminine "e" at the end of "servant," but Mother Esther never uses the word "serviteur." Perhaps the words "servante Sr." ran together in Smith's eyes to resemble the word "serviteur." Contrary to Smith's claims that "all other Ladies in a convent . . . make use of the Masculine Gender, rather than the Feminine," Ursuline nuns conformed to the grammatical conventions of the French language and used the feminine forms with reference to themselves and others when appropriate.[37] Smith was wrong in her guesses about Esther's signature and the kind of masculine authority she may have assumed or presumed as the mother superior of the Ursulines. But Smith's letter is proof that in her old age, Mother Esther had become an object of fascination and an example of female independence and achievement for Protestant Anglo-American girls like her nieces and grand-nieces.

Joshua Moody brought back more than just the letter that Abigail Smith translated for her cousin Isaac—he also carried the portrait of his aunt to Boston. We know that Mother Esther saw herself as an important person if only because of the existence of that extraordinary portrait that now hangs in the Massachusetts Historical Society. There are skillfully executed oil portraits of other eighteenth-century nuns, and in particular of mothers superior, but they hang in the halls and common areas of the Ursulines of Québec. Mother Esther sent her portrait back to New England; a very inexpert copy of the portrait based on a photograph of the original now hangs in the Ursuline archives, but it was made only in the twentieth century. We don't know who the eighteenth-century artist was, but she was almost surely a younger fellow Ursuline, given the tradition of artistic production within the monastery, as well as the fact that Mother Esther was cloistered and there is no record of an outside painter visiting the convent.[38]

The portrait may in fact be the best evidence we have that Mother Esther—as Esther Wheelwright, as Mali, and as Sister Marie—was the author of her own life. As a devout religious woman, she undoubtedly believed that it was the hand of God, in the words of Father Bigot half a century earlier, that preserved her life in captivity among the Wabanaki and brought her to the Ursulines. She probably also saw the hand of God at work in her election as superior at this dangerous moment for French

Canadian Catholics, and she wanted to mark the occasion so that it would be known by the Wheelwrights in New England. In choosing to commission this portrait and send it back to her family in New England, Mother Esther appears to have made toward the end of her life an almost modern assertion of subjectivity: "*Regardez! C'est moi!* And this is my life's work." That was the message to her mother in the letter she wrote in 1747, and I think this was the message of the portrait.

Mother Esther's distinctive biography as a New England–born Wabanaki convert—simultaneously politically useful but still regarded as an outsider in Québec—marked her entire life. Even as she was able finally to offer evidence of her status and useful connections outside the convent because of renewed communications with her family, some of her peers continued to regard her suspiciously as their city became a British military installation. At the same time, because of these renewed family relationships her fame in New England spread once again. Even after Mother Esther's re-elections as superior, she faced challenges to her leadership from within the convent as she led her community successfully through British occupation and toward an unknown future for Catholicism and for the Ursulines in North America.

After more than half a century at the Ursuline convent, Mother Esther was still viewed by some in Québec as *étrangère*, foreign, a stranger to French Canada. The ethnic distinctions at work at the turn of the century when New England and Native students were assigned *Angloise* or *Sauvage* as their surnames were still at work in the minds of Ursuline choir sisters and other citizens of Québec at the time of the British Conquest. But the rapidly shifting politics of military occupation meant changes in Mother Esther's relationship with both her adopted homeland and the forsaken land of her birth.

It's tragic that the aspect of Mother Esther's life that made her remarkable in her lifetime—her transnationalism as a New England–born Catholic nun in New France—is the very thing that probably doomed her to obscurity in both U.S. American and Canadian national histories. She rose to leadership in her community in a revolutionary era that might have proved a time of fatal decline in women's religious communities. Her years of teaching and artistic creativity were instrumental to her understanding of how the boarding school and making souvenirs for the tourist trade could help support the Ursuline community. But these achievements are largely invisible or irrelevant to both her native and adopted countries. She remains too English or American even now for French Canadians who see the British Conquest as a traumatic divide in their national history, and too foreign and too Catholic to fit easily into the American pantheon of Protestant male heroes. How many people who see her portrait hanging in the Massachusetts Historical Society wonder why there's a painting of a nun there, if they even pause long enough to wonder?

CHAPTER SEVEN

ESTHER ZELATRIX

Québec, November 1780

When Mother Esther de l'Enfant Jésus woke up that morning in the Ursuline infirmary in November 1780, she might have known. After she said her matins and lauds, she walked to the chapel for Mass, perhaps walking on the arm of one of her sisters or a young novice. Did she then take her breakfast in the infirmary, or did she eat in the refectory with her sisters in religion? Did she eat anything at all? On this her last day on earth, she received extreme unction from the Ursulines' confessor, Father Grave. (His name is humorously portentous only in English; "grave" in French means serious, not the *sépulture* in which a body is interred. We can surely say that her bodily condition was grave in either language, her hold on life slipping away.) Mother Esther's obituary forces us to imagine her last days, affirming only that she "kept her zeal and exactitude; even in the coldest winter weather she wouldn't miss a communion and attended mass every day with an extreme devotion to Jesus' sacred heart and the Virgin Mary." Her obituary concludes that "she ended just as she lived, with continuous aspiration to Heaven, repeating [bible verses] and psalms." After the final sacrament, she died on November 28 at 8 P.M. at age eighty-four, undoubt-edly confident about the paradise that awaited her in the afterlife.[1]

In her lifetime, Esther Wheelwright was stalked by war. She survived captivity during Queen Anne's War as a child, and two sieges of the city as an old woman: first the successful British invasion and occupation in the Seven Years' War in 1759 and then Benedict Arnold's unsuccessful 1775 siege at the outbreak of the War of the American Revolution. She survived the effects of these borderlands wars as well at both ends of her life, suffer-ing in childhood from hunger and probably illness among the Wabanaki, and in old age enduring evacuation and then the occupation of her con-vent as the assistant and then the mother superior. Finally, she led her convent through its most difficult years, between 1759 and 1774, when French Canadian Catholics had no idea whether their religion would re-main legal under British rule, and when religious people in particular faced expulsion. With the passage of the Quebec Act—among what American revolutionaries would deem the Intolerable Acts, the final outrages by Par-liament that pushed them toward independence—Catholicism was de-clared lawful in Quebec, and the Ursulines and all religious women in the colony were permitted to remain. Thanks at least in part to Mother Es-ther's leadership in those impoverished and uncertain days, the Ursuline community would persist and continue its work of teaching and artistry up to the present.

Another Siege

After Mother Esther stepped down from the superiorship, she was no longer the object of resentment or complaints from her fellow Ursulines, the majority of whom continued to elect her to important offices in the convent. She was elected to be the assistant to Mother Superior Marguerite de St. Louis de Gonzague twice, in 1772 and 1775. The work of rebuilding the monastery continued even to this late date after the Conquest. It was only in 1775 that the Ursulines finally could report that they had "a lot of repairs done to our house" from the damage done in the siege of 1759. The annalist wrote proudly of the "new windows in the Community room and a shed . . . built to replace the old one that fell into ruins. The roof was fixed up as new."[2]

More important to the long-term security of the Ursulines than their new roof and windows was the passage in 1774 of the Quebec Act, which guaranteed religious liberty to the colony's Roman Catholic majority, permitted them to serve in public office, and extended the use of French civil law (although criminal law would be British). The Quebec Act was undoubtedly rushed through Parliament in a bid to help secure the loyalty of the French Canadians to their British masters as the imperial crisis with the Anglo-American mainland colonies threatened to explode. Although intended to pacify resistance to British rule in Canada, the Quebec Act enflamed Anglo-American opinion, especially in the nearby New England colonies. New England had been at war with New France and its official religion for nearly a century, since before Esther Wheelwright's birth to 1763, and its resentment of the French was inextricable from its reflexive and violent anti-Catholicism. New England's men had volunteered for wars against the French since the 1680s, and hundreds of its women and children, like Esther, had endured captivity with both the Native allies of the French and French Canadians. New England more than any other region in colonial British America had rejoiced at Wolfe's victory in 1759 and at the capitulation of the French in 1760. Its Protestant citizens celebrated the fact that "no more *Te Deums* be sung for Vict'ry gain'd," and expected that "No more, (O may we *prophecy* in Truth!) / Her Priests no more debauch the *Indian* Youth." The Quebec Act of 1774 was perceived by New Englanders as a slap in the face for their decades of loyal sacrifice for English and British interests, and it was immediately classed among the so-called Intolerable Acts by the rest of Britain's mainland North American colonies.[3]

With the protection offered by the Quebec Act for Roman Catholics in this British colony, the Ursulines no longer feared that British laws could upend their work in the monastery. However, the satisfaction that news brought was short-lived, as Colonel Benedict Arnold began his difficult portage up the Kennebec and Chaudière River valleys in September 1775, heading with an army for Québec. Arnold's mission was part of a two-pronged effort to persuade French Canadians to join the American rebellion, by coercion if necessary; General Richard Montgomery left Fort Ticonderoga at the same time in an effort to take Montreal and then join Arnold on the Plains of Abraham, where Wolfe and Montcalm had met their deaths in 1759. As the Ursuline annalist put it, very politely, "I am just going to recount what happened since 1775 when the Americans had the kindness, without being asked, to defend Canada whose upper country and lower country were being attacked simultaneously." The decadelong political war ignited by American opposition to the Stamp Act in 1765 had become a shooting war in Massachusetts in the spring of 1775, with a failed British attempt to seize or disable the Anglo-American store of arms at Lexington and Concord on April 19 and the costly British victory near Bunker Hill on June 17. Although the Quebec Act helped secure the loyalty of church officials and seigneurial elites to the British regime, there were hundreds of *habitant* women and men across the province who were willing to join the American cause. They were caught between two former enemies—the British, whose occupation they resented, and the anti-Catholic Anglo-Americans they had been fighting along with the British for the previous century. The *habitants* willing to join the American rebellion were numerous enough to worry the British, but in the end, not enough to help Arnold's and Montgomery's efforts to take the city.[4]

Arnold's army was in a sorry state, having been frustrated by a journey that was twice as long as Arnold and General George Washington had estimated, and weakened by insufficient food and a want of other supplies along the way. In a telling echo of the Wabanaki desperation at the turn of the eighteenth century we saw in chapter 2, survival in the northern New England autumn for the Americans meant killing and eating dogs and even their own leather shot pouches. Accordingly, they were reduced to just six hundred of the eleven hundred who had begun the trek. Shortly after Arnold reached the city and set up his encampment on the Plains of Abraham with what was left of his army, smallpox struck the Americans, most of whom were boys and men from the interior of rural New England or from the South and who therefore had never been exposed to the virus before. Whereas colonial cosmopolitans or people from colonies that experienced high rates of immigration were exposed repeatedly to *Variola major* through the eighteenth century, rural folks had little exposure to the virus. The isolation that helped large families like the Wheelwrights of Wells see most of their children live to adulthood made their children and grandchildren more vulnerable to epidemics when the serial wars of the middle of the eighteenth century visited the region. When Montgomery arrived from

Montreal with another five hundred men, they too suffered from the disease. As among the Wabanaki seventy-five years earlier, the combined forces of arduous travel, malnutrition, and close living quarters made the contagion all the more ghoulishly successful in infecting and killing the American rebels. Because traditionally colonial militia service was for just one season, from the spring muster to New Year's Day, Arnold and Montgomery faced the likely desertion of the portion of their army who could stand up and march home.

Accordingly, Arnold and Montgomery mounted a futile attempt to take the city in the midst of a blizzard at midnight on December 31. It was a disaster for the already weakened and desertion-prone Americans, and turned out to be a suicide mission for Montgomery, who died early on in the fight. Only thirty men were killed in the battle, but four hundred American officers and enlisted men were taken prisoner. One account of the battle reports that the American prisoners "had slips of Paper pin'd to their hats with these words: *Liberty or Death*." Although these men had survived the battle, death in a military prison was certainly a strong possibility. Conditions for the Americans were miserable beyond measure, whether they were prisoners of war held by the British or were among Arnold's surviving army: smallpox ravaged both camps, as did the Laurentian valley winter and ongoing supply problems. Twenty to twenty-five percent of the American army in captivity as well as in camp outside the city walls were afflicted by the disease, further reducing Arnold's army. Even the arrival of nearly two thousand reinforcement troops in midwinter wasn't enough to make a difference—it just meant an increase in the numbers of the sick and dying outside the city's massive walls.

In spite of their misery, the Americans were still affected by a striking *rage militaire*—one British officer reported that on March 5, 1776, "a red flag [was] seen flying near the Ferry at St. Charles's River, supposed in commemoration of the 5th March, 1770, called by the Yankees 'the Bloody Massacre at Boston.'" Another officer also noted the presence of red flags in the rebel camps, explaining, "In new England the 5 of March is a day of fasting & prayer; anniversary orations are spoken in sad commemoration of what they call the bloody Boston Massacre."[5]

Once again, the Ursulines watched from inside the walls of their monastery as men went to war, imperiling the civilian population of Québec as well. "God protected us and took pity on us, poor nuns who have nothing to do with this war and suffer inevitable losses no matter how hard we tried to survive." Church bells no longer tolled to call the faithful to Mass—"The bells rang only to warn us of imminent bombing: we were the targets of the cannons and we had no shelter but a room which we used as a chapel." The triennial elections were once again set to happen in the midst of a military siege, as in 1759, but this time "the elections took place as they should in spite of the bombing and the cannon balls." The Ursuline annalist writes that the Americans bombed the city steadily from December 4 until their attempt on the 31st to take Québec. "After this victory, we were at peace till February 16, 1776 when they had reinforcements and attacked us twice more." Unhappily, the recently finished repairs to the monastery were at least partially undone in the American siege: "The two first cannonballs hit our infirmary and the novice's dormitory and broke a window and a bed. We [removed?] the windows and the fight slowed down for a while, then we got one which went through two windows of the church and ended up hitting a neighbor's house." The only good news for the Ursulines was that through the siege, "nobody was uncomfortable in spite of the bitter cold of winter." Even more important, smallpox did not breach the convent's walls.[6]

As Arnold and his army retreated after the arrival of British relief supplies and warships on May 6, Mother Esther had survived yet another siege, but her life was nearing its end. Her energy and perceptions were probably dimming rapidly, but in the final election in her lifetime in 1778, she was elected to serve as zelatrix, an office to which she was well suited. After all, her enthusiasm for religion, her "punctuality," and her exactitude in observing the Rule were her strongest characteristics. As the Ursuline annalist would describe her after her death, "She was a living Rule with her punctuality of all the holy observances and her faithfulness to the littlest things." Her election to zelatrix at the end of her life, after serving three terms as superior, is the strongest indication we have that the complaints to the bishop in her last term about her partiality, poor judgment, and *hauteur* were probably minority opinions. If the order as a whole shared the resentments of Mother Marie Antoinette Poulin de St. François and Mother Marie Elizabeth Richard de St. Augustin or were concerned about Mother Esther's attention to details like the open gate of 1770, then surely she would neither have been elected zelatrix nor have been remembered so explicitly for "the greatest exactitude [which] elevated her observances and her punctuality for the smallest rules." These were "her happiness and solace and indeed as long as it was for God's Glory, it seemed to kindle and excite her zeal." One more detail suggests that Mother Esther may have attended mass in the choir on her last day rather than staying in bed in the infirmary or in her cell: the claim in her obituary that "it is true that the Lord gave her a good nature and an excellent constitution," and she "walk[ed] constantly with the same pace till the end of her career with ardor and the greatest reliability."[7]

Punctual, reliable, orderly, and burning with the zeal of a grateful convert, Mother Esther died at the end of November 1780. She was remembered in a loving obituary by her sisters in religion, and her body was laid to rest inside the Ursuline chapel.[8] She was among the last living connections to the Ursulines' original mission "to teach little French and Native girls," the last of the English-born Ursulines, and the last of the three who had come to Québec and *la vie réligieuse* from Wabanaki households and families in wartime.

Esther for the Ages

Mother Esther's death represented the passing of the ancien régime in the Ursuline convent in many ways. The death of the last surviving New England–born nun signaled the end of the colonial era of warfare between New France and New England, an era when Native practices of captivity and adoption turned strangers into family members. Peace between Canada and the United States wouldn't truly be achieved for another thirty-five years. The War of 1812 shifted the center of political and military antagonism to the South and West: instead of Boston and Québec, it was the cities of Washington, D.C., and York (now Toronto) that burned in that conflict. After 1815, the nations remained at peace with each other and turned their aggression on the Native peoples. Although countless Native people suffered and died as a result of military conquest by the United States and Canada through the rest of the nineteenth century, in Canada perhaps the most hated symbol of settler colonialism to this day remains the Catholic and Protestant residential schools that were established across the country.

Much like the school founded in 1639 by Marie de l'Incarnation at the Ursuline monastery, these schools presented themselves as benevolent institutions meant to introduce Native children to the virtues of "civilization," Christianity, and the English language. Because of the example of Esther Wheelwright and hundreds of her peers and students, we know how powerfully immersive boarding schools can be. The nineteenth-century Canadian residential schools are now remembered as the most insidious tools deployed against First Nations languages, religions, and cultures.[9]

In most respects, daily life in the convent continued after 1780 as it had since the days of Mother Marie de l'Incarnation. The Ursuline monastery had grown and been improved, burned, rebuilt, enlarged, bombed, and rebuilt and improved again, but daily life—*la vie quotidienne*—went on much as usual into the nineteenth century. Every day, the nuns rose at four to begin the Hours, their cycle of prayers; every week they fasted and feasted in turn. Every month, new girls came to the day and boarding schools, and every month some left, too. Every year new postulants requested permission to begin their novitiates. Spring, summer, fall, winter; Lent, Easter, ordinary time, Advent. As Mali, as Esther *Anglaise,* as Sister Marie-Joseph de l'Enfant Jésus, and as Mother Esther, she found her purpose in the city walls, inside the monastery, under the belt and veil, and in the predictable routines of religious life. Her life among the Ursulines suited her well, but more important, it permitted her to live the life of work and prayer she believed God had intended for her.

Mother Esther's death put to rest any lingering concerns there may have been about *étrangères,* foreigners in the convent, as she both was the first and remains to this day the last foreign-born mother superior of the Québec Ursulines. But there was another aspect of Mother Esther's life among the Ursulines that her sisters in religion would not give up: the matter of Esther's small dowry, and her inheritance in New England. In a letter dated August 22, 1789, nearly nine years after Mother Esther's death, Mother Charlotte Brassard de St. Claire, superior, wrote to a Dr. Penn in Salem, Massachusetts. She had heard through a "Mr. Latierrier a French Gentelman lately come out from the University of Cambridge where he was gone to study the principles of Phisyc for many month[s]" that "you had told him that you had into your hands as Executor of the last will of a Gentleman father of one of our members born into New England a legacy in favour of his said Daughter and that it appears that in case of her death that Legacy should be reversible to our House." Mr. Latierrier couldn't remember this woman's name; however, Mother St. Claire, through the process of elimination, determined that the inheritance in his hands must be Esther Wheelwright's, explaining that "this Lady died in the year one-thousand seven Hundred and Eighty & had always during her life time hoped that her father would do something in our favour, having promised it himself when he came to Canada, knowing that her Dowry, or portion of his Daughter['s] never had been paid to the Community, as the usual by the constitutional Rules of the order, and that she was indebted still at her death."[10]

Nearly a decade after her death, some of her fellow Ursulines were still concerned enough about Mother Esther's "indebtedness" to the community that they were willing to track down improbable stories and implausible connections to the Wheelwright clan in New England in search of her inheritance, but there are several strange claims in Mother St. Claire's letter that don't accord with what we know about the Wheelwrights and the question of Mother Esther's inheritance. First of all, as we have seen, the terms of John Wheelwright's 1739 will (sixty years earlier!) were quite clear —Mother Esther could receive her inheritance only "if it Should please God that She return to this Country & Settle here," in New England, then she'd receive £100 paid by four of her brothers "within Six Months after her Return and Settlement," so the Ursulines had no legal claim to the inheritance. Second, there is no record of John Wheelwright having visited Mother Esther at the convent—did she tell her younger community members that he once had visited and promised her an inheritance? Did they misremember Nathaniel Wheelwright's 1754 visits to the monastery, thirty-five years past, as visits from her father? The youngest novices and religious women who might have remembered Mother Esther's visitor before the Seven Years' War would have been well into middle age by 1789.

Given the importance of rank and family connections in New France and among the Ursulines in particular, Mother Esther had a strong incentive to suggest to her sisters that an inheritance from the Wheelwrights would be forthcoming. Perhaps she honestly believed she could work her Wheelwright relations and persuade them to send a donation, if not her inheritance. She did reach out after she was elected superior the first time, and was in contact with her relations for a time in the 1760s. In the end, a hundred pounds *was* real money, but it was hardly a life-changing amount of money for the Ursulines in 1789. By comparison, the boarding fees for students at the Ursuline school in the previous decade were nearly twice that amount of money. Unsurprisingly, the Ursuline archives contain no evidence that Dr. Penn ever replied to this query. We can therefore count this letter as evidence of the Ursulines' excellent record keeping, the strength of the management skills of their elected superiors, and Mother Esther's ability to inspire hope among her colleagues that her family would make up for the cut-rate dowry. A hundred pounds was worth the price of writing a letter and having it translated.

For the first century after her death, Mother Esther was remembered only by members of the Ursuline order and within the Wheelwright family in New England. The name Esther continued to be passed down among generations of Wheelwright daughters, and her oil portrait from the early 1760s along with it. The newly professionalizing historians of the nineteenth century were all men, most of whom defined history very narrowly as military and political achievements of other men. They had little use for a story about a little Anglo-American girl who became a Wabanaki daughter and then an Ursuline sister and mother. Anglophone historians in the United States and Canada had inherited the reflexive anti-Catholicism of their English and British forebears, which also likely suppressed interest in her story. Moreover, her nationality and identity changed and re-formed itself though her lifetime. Was she American or Canadian? Was she French, or British, or Wabanaki? She seemed to fit in nowhere, so how could her story be important to the story of the emergence of nation-states in North America and western Europe? Although a Wheelwright family descendant, Edward "Ned" Wheelwright, was a history enthusiast, a Wheelwright family genealogist, and the architect of the Massachusetts Historical Society's landmark 1899 building at 1154 Boylston Street, professional historians remained uninterested in stories like Esther Wheelwright's, and in her in particular.[11]

But at the turn of the twentieth century in the midst of the Colonial Revival, Mother Esther's story was rediscovered by a pair of amateur historians of colonial New England, C. Alice Baker (1833–1909) and Emma Lewis Coleman (1853–1942). In the early twentieth century, they catalogued the daughters and sons of New England who were "carried to Canada" and never returned. Baker also published engaging portraits of the women and men whose lives were reshaped by the border wars between New England and New France in the ninety years of warfare between the French and English colonies. Like Nathaniel Wheelwright, they were unusual New Englanders in their interest in and ability to read the French as well as the English-language archival records, and they traveled to Québec to the Ursuline archives to conduct research there on the three girl captives who as women became Ursuline nuns. The passing years meant that Baker's and Coleman's exploration of New England captives who embraced Catholicism and chose to make lives as Native peoples or French Canadians was less politically charged than it would have been in the late eighteenth century. However, they continued to regard the people they wrote about as curiosities of a preindustrial past rather than people whose stories were central to the creation of the United States or Canada.[12]

In the middle of the twentieth century, another amateur historian by the name of Gerald Kelly became fascinated with Esther Wheelwright's story. A New Yorker who read French, Kelly was also a devout Roman Catholic. His interest in Mother Esther was primarily in her dramatic conversion and her success as a *réligieuse*. After decades of research in the Ursuline convent and a long-standing correspondence with living Ursulines in Québec as well as with other genealogists and historians interested in the colonial wars between New England and New France, Kelly wrote a biography of Esther Wheelwright. He called his biography "Thy Hand Shall Lead Me," after Father Vincent Bigot's sermon at her clothing ceremony, but he never published it. His interpretation of Esther's life agrees entirely with Father Vincent's in 1713: "To those, however, who accept the principle of the working of grace in the human spirit, it will be clear, *post factum,* that the hand of God was guiding the young Captive and that the theme of Pere Bigot's sermon was not merely empty symbolism." Fortunately, he was a dedicated enough sleuth to leave all of his research and correspondence to the Massachusetts Historical Society, as Coleman had as well. Baker had left her papers to the Pocumtuck Valley Memorial Association in Deerfield, Massachusetts, her summer home.[13]

In spite of their care, through the rise of the "new" social history and the rediscovery of women's history in the 1960s, as well as another colonial revival as the 1976 bicentennial of the founding of the United States approached, the Kelly, Coleman, and Baker papers slept undisturbed in their archival boxes, and professional historians continued to overlook stories like Esther Wheelwright's. Her story seems especially difficult to fit into the celebration of American nationalism that was the bicentennial of forty years ago, when the founding of the United States was cast once again as a male affair, with white Protestants playing all of the choicest roles. My hometown of Sylvania, Ohio, hosted a parade in the summer of 1976, part of the Bicentennial Wagon Train that crossed the United States from west to east in a mash-up of Revolution history crossed with a commemoration of nineteenth-century white pioneers. My introduction to eighteenth-century history was being hit in the face at age seven by a dry teabag thrown from a parade float by a "colonist" dressed as a Mohawk in a carnivalesque re-enactment of the Boston Tea Party.[14]

Unlike professional historians, the Wheelwrights have never forgotten Esther. Picking up on the threads of the story left by Ned Wheelwright and the other earlier enthusiasts, a descendant from a Canadian branch of the family, Julie Wheelwright, wrote a biography, as well as a screenplay for a movie codirected by her sister Penny on the life of Esther Wheelwright in 2005. Julie Wheelwright's *Esther: The Remarkable True Story of Esther Wheelwright: Puritan Child, Native Daughter, Mother Superior* (2011) is a beautifully written account of Esther's life, as well as a meditation on the role her story has played in the Wheelwright family in recent generations. Julie's mother, Tish, was an English child "war guest" sent to Canada after the fall of France to the Nazis in 1940, a physical and emotional exile from her family that changed the course of her mother's life, and one that resonated with the story of her ancestor Esther. As Julie writes, "[my mother's] story gave me insight into Esther's motivations, her character, and her ability to survive. When I grew up to become a writer and historian, I knew where to look for documents and how to piece together the scraps of Esther's life. . . . But always, the emotional thread belonged to my mother."[15]

My version of Esther Wheelwright's story is one of sisters and mothers as much as of mothers and daughters. I use her story as a means of understanding the work and lives of the communities of women she lived and worked in her entire life—women like her mother, Mary Snell Wheelwright, raising a large family on the fragile borders of English colonial expansion.

It's also about uncovering the experiences of the Wheelwrights' indentured servant Elizabeth Goodale, their enslaved woman Pegg, and Rachel, the enslaved woman murdered at Kittery a few years before Esther was born. This book is also about the Wabanaki women and girls like the enthusiastic catechists Susanne and Margueritte, who taught entire extended families and communities how to pray as Catholics and brought them to be baptized, and the artists Tall Jeanne and Colette, who made the wampum belts with Latin inscriptions. It's about the dauntless noblewomen of New France like Louise-Élisabeth de Joybert, the Marquise de Vaudreuil, as well as Mother Marie Anne Migeon de la Nativité, Mother Esther's immediate predecessor as mother superior. And of course, it's about the thousands of girls and women who passed through the gates of the Ursuline convent in the eighteenth century, some just for the day school, others to board there, and still others to live there for the rest of their lives.

Above all, Esther Wheelwright's story is about families that are formed by choice as well as by blood. It's the alphabet books and catechisms, the pen and ink, the brush and canvas; it's the moose hair, the porcupine quills, and the shell beads; it's the silken floss and the gold twist that bind the generations of North American women, one to another across the centuries and down to the present, and beyond.

NOTES

Major Archives

Archives de l'Archdiocèse de Québec   AAQ
Archives du Monastère des Ursulines de Québec   AMUQ
Clements Library, University of Michigan, Ann Arbor CL
Library and Archives Canada, Ottawa   LAC
Massachusetts Historical Society, Boston   MHS
Massachusetts State Archives   Mass. Arch.

Other Libraries and Archives Consulted

Bibliothèque et Archives Nationales du Québec
Historical Society of Pennsylvania, Philadelphia
Historical Society of Wells and Ogunquit, Wells, Maine
Huntington Library, San Marino, California
Maine Historical Society
Michigan State Library, Lansing
Morrin Centre Library, Québec

Introduction

1. Personal communications with Anne E. Bentley, curator of art and artifacts at the Massachusetts Historical Society, January 4, 2001, and October 2, 2014; Gerald M. Kelly to Charles D. Childs, March 21, 1975, Gerald M. Kelly Research Materials, box 9, Massachusetts Historical Society, Boston. See also Andrew Oliver, Ann Millspaugh Huff, and Edward W. Hanson, *Portraits in the Massachusetts Historical Society* (Boston: Massachusetts Historical Society, 1988), 116–17.

2. *Les Ursulines de Québec, Depuis leur Établissement Jusq'a Nos Jours* (Québec: C. Darveau, 1864), 2: 75–88; *Glimpses of the Monastery: Scenes from the History of the Ursulines of Quebec during two hundred years, 1639–1839,* 2nd ed. (Québec: L. J. Demers, 1897), 175–84; C. Alice Baker, *True Stories of New England Captives Carried to Canada During the Old French and Indian Wars* (Greenfield, Mass.: E. A. Hall, 1897; facsimile rpt. Bowie, Md.: Heritage, 1990), 35–68; Emma Lewis Coleman, *New England Captives Carried to Canada* (Portland, Me.: Southworth, 1925; rpt. Bowie, Md.: Heritage, 1989), 1: 425–35; Gerald M. Kelly, "Thy Hand Shall Lead Me: The Story of Esther Wheelwright," unpublished manuscript, ca. 1970s, MHS; Julie Wheelwright, *Esther: The Remarkable True Story of Esther Wheelwright: Puritan Child, Native Daughter, Mother Superior* (Toronto: HarperCollins, 2011).

3. I am indebted to Julia Garbus for alerting me to this poem.

4. James Axtell, "The White Indians of Colonial America," *William and Mary Quarterly,* 3rd ser., 32, no. 1 (1975): 55–88, rpt. in James Axtell, *The European and the Indian: Essays in the Ethnohistory of Colonial North America* (New York: Oxford University Press, 1981), 168–206; James Axtell, *The Invasion Within: The Contest of Cultures in Colonial North America* (New York: Oxford University Press, 1985), 302–27; Daniel Richter, "War and Culture: The Iroquois Experience," *William and Mary Quarterly,* 3rd ser., 40 (1983): 528–59; Daniel Richter, *The Ordeal of the Longhouse: The Peoples of the Iroquois League in the Era of European Colonization* (Chapel Hill: University of North Carolina Press, 1992); June Namias, *White Captives: Gender and Ethnicity on the American Frontier* (Chapel Hill: University of North Carolina Press, 1993); John Demos, *The Unredeemed Captive: A Family Story from Early America* (New York: Vintage, 1994); Evan Haefeli and Kevin Sweeney, *Captors and Captives: The 1704 French and Indian Raid on Deerfield* (Amherst: University of Massachusetts Press, 2003); Ann M. Little, *Abraham in Arms: War and Gender in Colonial New England* (Philadelphia: University of Pennsylvania Press, 2007), chaps. 2–4; and Teresa A. Toulouse, *The Captive's Position: Female Narrative, Male Identity, and Royal Authority in Colonial New England* (Philadelphia: University of Pennsylvania Press, 2007). Cf. William Henry Foster, *The Captors' Narrative: Catholic Women and their Puritan Men on the Early American Frontier* (Ithaca, N.Y.: Cornell University Press, 2003).

5. On the enslavement of Native peoples by New England colonists, see Michael L. Fickes, "'They Could Not Endure That Yoke': The Captivity of Pequot Women and Children After the War of 1637," *New England Quarterly* 73, no. 1 (2000): 58–81; Margaret Ellen Newell, "The Changing Nature of Indian Slavery in New England, 1670–1720," in *Reinterpreting New England Indians and the Colonial Experience,* ed. Colin G. Calloway and Neal Salis-

bury, 106–36 (Boston: the Colonial Society of Massachusetts, 2003); and Alan Gallay, ed., *Indian Slavery in Colonial America* (Lincoln: University of Nebraska Press, 2009), esp. 1–146. Newell says that there were more than 1,200 Native women, children, and men enslaved in New England in the seventeenth century alone, 107. By comparison, Alden T. Vaughan and Daniel K. Richter, in "Crossing the Cultural Divide: Indians and New Englanders, 1605–1763," *American Antiquarian Society Proceedings* 90 (1980): 23–99, estimate that there were a total of 1,579 Anglo-American captives taken in New England wars between 1675 and 1763, 392 females and 1,187 males.

6. Bonnie G. Smith, *The Gender of History: Men, Women, and Historical Practice* (Cambridge: Harvard University Press, 1998; 2004); Judith Bennett, *History Matters: Patriarchy and the Challenge of Feminism* (Philadelphia: University of Pennsylvania Press, 2006); cf. Joan Scott, "Back to the Future," a review of *History Matters* in *History and Theory* 47, no. 2 (2008): 279–84. On the fascination with the so-called Founding Fathers of the United States, see Thomas A. Foster, *Sex and the Founding Fathers: The American Quest for a Relatable Past* (Philadelphia: Temple University Press, 2014), "Introduction: Remembering the Founders," 1–9.

7. Allan Greer, *Mohawk Saint: Catherine Tekakwitha and the Jesuits* (New York: Oxford University Press, 2005); Jon Sensbach, *Rebecca's Revival: Creating Black Christianity in the Atlantic World* (Cambridge: Harvard University Press, 2005); Eric Hinderaker, *The Two Hendricks: Unraveling a Mohawk Mystery* (Cambridge: Harvard University Press, 2010); Tiya Miles, *The House on Diamond Hill: A Cherokee Plantation Story* (Chapel Hill: University of North Carolina Press, 2010); Joshua Piker, *The Four Deaths of Acorn Whistler: Telling Stories in Colonial America* (Cambridge: Harvard University Press, 2013).

8. Smith, *The Gender of History*, 157–240; Laurel Thatcher Ulrich, *The Age of Homespun: Objects and Stories in the Creation of an American Myth* (New York: Knopf, 2001), esp. 3–40; Susan M. Stabile, *Memory's Daughters: The Material Culture of Remembrance in Eighteenth-Century America* (Ithaca, NY: Cornell University Press, 2004); Marla R. Miller, *The Needle's Eye: Women and Work in the Age of Revolution* (Amherst: University of Massachusetts Press, 2006), esp. 211–31; Mary Louise Swanson, " 'Let It Be a Woman's Park': Gender, Identity, and the Establishment of Mesa Verde," unpublished paper, Notre Dame University, 2011.

9. Camilla Townsend, *Pocahontas and the Powhatan Dilemma: An American Portrait* (New York: Hill and Wang, 2004); Camilla Townsend, *Malintzin's Choices: An Indian Woman in the Conquest of Mexico* (Albuquerque: University of New Mexico Press, 2006); Marla R. Miller, *Betsy Ross and the Making of America* (New York: Holt, 2010).

10. Laurel Thatcher Ulrich, *A Midwife's Tale: The Life of Martha Ballard, Based on Her Diary* (New York: Knopf, 1990); Nell Irvin Painter, *Sojourner Truth: A Life, A Symbol* (New York: Norton, 1996); Alfred F. Young, *Masquerade: The Life and Times of Deborah Sampson, Continental Soldier* (New York: Knopf, 2004); Catherine Allgor, *Dolley Madison and the Creation of the American Nation* (New York: Holt, 2006); Annette Gordon-Reed, *The Hemingses of Monticello: An American Family* (New York: Norton, 2008); Ava Chamberlain, *The Notorious Elizabeth Tuttle: Marriage, Murder, and Madness in the Family of Jonathan Edwards* (New York: New York University Press, 2012); Cynthia A. Kierner, *Martha Jefferson Randolph, Daughter of Monticello: Her Life*

and Times (Chapel Hill: University of North Carolina Press, 2012); Jill Lepore, *Book of Ages: The Life and Opinions of Jane Franklin* (New York: Knopf, 2013); Marla R. Miller, *Rebecca Dickinson: Independence for a New England Woman* (Boulder, Colo.: Westview, 2013); Terri L. Snyder, "Jane Webb and Her Family: Life Stories and the Law in Early Virginia," in *Virginia Women: Their Lives and Times,* ed. Cynthia A. Kierner and Sandra G. Treadway (Athens: University of Georgia Press, 2015), 55–73.

11. The exceptions here are Nell Irvin Painter, Marla Miller, and Terri Snyder. See also Miller, *The Needle's Eye.*

12. See, for example, Judith P. Zinsser, *La Dame d'Esprit: A Biography of the Marquise Du Châtelet* (New York: Viking, 2006); Greer, *Mohawk Saint;* Hinderaker, *The Two Hendricks;* and Piker, *The Four Deaths.*

13. Susan Ware, "The Book I Couldn't Write: Alice Paul and the Challenge of Feminist Biography," *Journal of Women's History* 24, no. 2 (2012): 13–36; Ann M. Little, "Through a Two-Way Looking Glass, You See Your Alice: Is Feminist Biography Necessarily a Modernist Pursuit?" *Historiann,* June 6, 2012, http://www.historiann.com/2012/06/06/through-a-two-way-looking-glass-you-see-your-alice-is-feminist-biography-necessarily-a-modernist-pursuit/, accessed November 4, 2014; Jill Lepore, "Historians Who Love Too Much: Reflections on Microhistory and Biography," *Journal of American History* 88, no. 1 (2001): 129–44.

1. Esther Wheelwright

1. Alice Morse Earle, *Two Centuries of Costume in America, 1620–1820* (New York: Macmillan, 1903; rpt. Williamstown, Mass.: Corner House, 1974), 1: 304, 316–18; C. Willett and Phillis Cunnington, *The History of Underclothes* (London: Michael Joseph, 1951; New York: Dover, 1992), 11–95; Linda Baumgarten, *What Clothes Reveal: The Language of Clothing in Colonial and Federal America* (Williamsburg, Va.: Colonial Williamsburg Foundation, 2002), on undergarments, 21–22, 26–28, 40; on stays for children, 162–63; on stays for women, 121–22, 133–34; on leading-strings, 166–67; on trousers for boys, 166–68. Baumgarten says that boys were breeched at anywhere from four to eight years.

2. Descriptions of the Wheelwright garrison by nineteenth-century historians vary and conflict with one another, but most agree that John Wheelwright lived in the house originally built by his grandfather in the 1640s, and that it was so inadequate to his needs by 1703 or 1704 that he tore it down and rebuilt it. See, for example, Edward E. Bourne, *The History of Wells and Kennebunk from the Earliest Settlement to the Year 1820* (Portland, Me.: B. Thurston, 1875; rpt. Bowie, Md.: Heritage, 1983), 147, 257–58, 391; C. Alice Baker, *True Stories of New England Captives Carried to Canada During the Old French and Indian Wars* (Greenfield, Mass.: E. A. Hall, 1897; rpt. Bowie, Md.: Heritage, 1990), 42–43.

3. Charles E. Clark, *The Eastern Frontier: The Settlement of Northern New England, 1610–1763* (New York: Knopf, 1970), 193, 220; James Deetz, *In Small Things Forgotten: The Archaeology of Early American Life* (Garden City, N.Y.: Anchor/Doubleday, 1977), 95–107. Clark claims that most seventeenth-century houses (even garrisons) in Maine were probably only one and a

half stories, and the smaller design remained popular even with the emergence of two-story houses in the eighteenth century.

4. The four servants and slaves are my conjecture from other records cited below, along with discussions of them individually in this chapter. The two servants were Thomas Wormwood and Elizabeth Goodale, and the household probably also included at least one enslaved woman and one enslaved man, Sambo.

5. Baker, *True Stories of New England Captives,* 41–44, although Baker exaggerates about the primitive material culture of Wells at the turn of the eighteenth century; Marion Nelson Winship, "Safety and Danger in a Puritan Home: Life in the Hull-Sewall House, 1676–77," in *The American Home: Material Culture, Domestic Space, and Family Life,* ed. Eleanor McD. Thompson (Winterthur, Del.: Henry Francis DuPont Winterthur Museum, 1998), 257–71.

6. Bourne, *The History of Wells and Kennebunk,* 257–58; 391; SC1 45X Massachusetts Archives Collection, hereafter Mass. Arch., 71: 871, Massachusetts State Archives, Boston.

7. See James E. McWilliams's description of a Maryland family and its servants ca. 1650 preparing a dinner of cornmeal mush, smoked meat, and cider, in *A Revolution in Eating: How the Quest for Food Shaped America* (New York: Columbia University Press, 2005), 1–4. McWilliams describes the importance of dairy products to the New England diet, 75–79, and Emerson W. Baker, *The Clark and Lake Company: The Historical Archaeology of a Seventeenth-Century Maine Settlement,* Occasional Publications in Maine Archaeology, no. 4 (Augusta: the Maine Historic Preservation Commission, 1985), reports that even at remote trading posts in seventeenth-century Maine, he found evidence not only of cattle keeping but of glazed ceramic potsherds that were used in processing milk and cheese making: "Cheese, butter, milk, and cream were important parts of the yeoman's diet, with cheese a more important source of protein than meat. Milk pans, colanders, jars, and crocks were used extensively to store and prepare these dairy products. Documents show that Clarke and Lake were raising cattle on Arrowsic and slaughtering them. The widespread presence of these utilitarian redwares suggests that dairying was another important aspect of livestock raising," 27.

8. On women's labors aside from food production and preparation, see Peter Benes and Jane Montague Benes, *Women's Work in New England, 1620–1920* (Boston: Boston University, 2003). On the bounded nature of women's lives, see Winship, "Safety and Danger in a Puritan Home"; and C. Dallett Hemphill, "Sibling Relationships in Early American Childhoods: A Cross-Cultural Analysis," in *Children in Colonial America,* ed. James Marten (New York: New York University Press, 2007), 77–89.

9. James E. McWilliams, "'To Forward Well-Flavored Productions': The Kitchen Garden in Early New England," *New England Quarterly* 77, no. 1 (2004): 25–50.

10. Ibid., 34–35, 42–43. Other scholars have written about the ideological implications of the survival of English bodies and their reproductive successes: Joyce Chaplin, *Subject Matter: Technology, the Body, and Science on the Anglo-American Frontier, 1500–1676* (Cambridge: Harvard University Press, 2001); Trudy Eden, "Food, Assimilation, and the Malleability of the Human Body in Early Virginia," and Martha L. Finch, "'Civilized' Bodies and the 'Savage' Environment of Early New Plymouth," both in *A Centre of Wonders: The Body in Early America,* ed.

Janet Moore Lindmann and Michele Lise Tarter (Ithaca, N.Y.: Cornell University Press, 2001), 29–60; Trudy Eden, *The Early American Table: Food and Society in the New World* (DeKalb: Northern Illinois University Press, 2008); and Martha L. Finch, *Dissenting Bodies: Corporealities in Early New England* (New York: Columbia University Press, 2010).

11. For licensed tavernkeepers in Wells from 1680 to 1718, see *Province and Court Records of Maine*, 3, *Province of Maine Records, 1680–1692*, ed. Robert E. Moody (Portland: Maine Historical Society, 1947); *Province and Court Records of Maine*, 4, *The Court Records of York County, Maine, November 1692–January 1710–11*, ed. Neal W. Allen, Jr. (Portland: Maine Historical Society, 1958); and *Province and Court Records of Maine*, 5, *The Court Records of York County, Maine, April 1711–October 1718*, ed. Neal W. Allen, Jr. (Portland: Maine Historical Society, 1964), passim. John Wheelwright's licenses, 1693–98, are described in 4: 9, 11, 13, 18, 20, 39, 69, 92, 107. The biggest tavernkeeper was probably Joseph Storer, who had a license for more than thirty years, from 1683 to 1716 (see 3: 105, 118, 125, 243, 275, 288, 298; 4: 9, 13, 19, 39, 69, 92, 107, 249, 257, 267, 283, 304, 316, 328, 338, 357, 367, 384; 5: 124, 130, 138, 145, 168, 188). Other Wells tavernkeepers were John Bugg, in 1686–87 (3: 244, 267); Francis Littlefield, in 1690–92 and 1701–02 (3: 288, 305; 4: 257, 267, 280); and Dependence Littlefield, from 1712–17 (5: 130, 138, 145, 168, 197).

12. *Province and Court Records of Maine*, 4: 205–6; see mention of Sambo in the *Boston News-Letter,* July 21, 1712; http://www.mainegenealogy.net/maine_wills.asp?source=probate courtvol1&testator=SamuelWheelwright#Will, http://www.mainegenealogy.net/maine _wills.asp?source=probatecourtvol6&testator=JohnWheelwright#Will, and http://www.maine genealogy.net/maine_wills.asp?source=probatecourtvol9&testator=MaryWheelwright#Will, accessed September 8, 2014.

13. Other girls and women who were owned by the Wheelwright family later in the eighteenth century were Dinah and Zilph, both of whom were described as "Molotto." We know their names because they were baptized as infants in the First Church of Christ in Wells in 1741 and 1764, respectively. Dinah was sponsored by Esther's parents, John and Mary Wheelwright, and Zilph was sponsored by Esther's cousin Joseph Wheelwright and his wife, Mary—perhaps they owned Dinah's and Zilph's mothers, which is why the Wheelwrights had the baby girls baptized. See "First Church of Christ, Congregational, Wells, Maine," coll. 1249, Maine Historical Society, Portland.

14. Bourne, *The History of Wells and Kennebunk*, 276–78, 356, 406–10; Ira Berlin, *Many Thousands Gone: The First Two Centuries of Slavery in North America* (Cambridge: Belknap Press of Harvard University Press, 1998), 47–63; Ira Berlin, *Generations of Captivity: A History of African-American Slaves* (Cambridge: Belknap Press of Harvard University Press, 2003), 81–88; John Wood Sweet, *Bodies Politic: Negotiating Race in the American North, 1730–1830* (Baltimore: Johns Hopkins University Press, 2003), chaps. 2–4; Julie Wheelwright, *Esther: The Remarkable True Story of Esther Wheelwright: Puritan Child, Native Daughter, Mother Superior* (Toronto: Harper-Collins, 2011), chap. 1.

15. See Sweet's commentary on Pilgrim fantasies versus New England realities in *Bodies*

Politic, 1–11, and his discussion of New England's commitment to African chattel slavery ca. 1700, 58–60.

16. Richard S. Dunn and Laetitia Yeandle, *The Journal of John Winthrop, 1630–1649,* abridged ed. (Cambridge: Belknap Press of Harvard University Press, 1996), 1.

17. Baumgarten, *What Clothes Reveal,* 121–22, 133–34; on the European desire to articulate and preserve differences between European and African women's bodies, see Jennifer L. Morgan, *Laboring Women: Reproduction and Gender in New World Slavery* (Philadelphia: University of Pennsylvania Press, 2004), chap. 1.

18. Kathleen M. Brown, *Good Wives, Nasty Wenches, and Anxious Patriarchs: Gender, Race, and Power in Colonial Virginia* (Chapel Hill: University of North Carolina Press, 1996), chaps. 3–4; Kirsten Fischer, *Suspect Relations: Sex, Race, and Resistance in Colonial North Carolina* (Ithaca, N.Y.: Cornell University Press, 2002), 1–11 and chap. 5; and Morgan, *Laboring Women,* esp. chaps. 3–4.

19. *Province and Court Records of Maine,* 4: 34–35. For comparisons, see the cases of John Braun and Annah Langley, 4: 33, 57; John Nelson and Elizabeth Hayly, 4: 37; Abraham and Mary Preble, 4: 38; Alice Metherill, 4: 47; Walter Burks, 4: 42.

20. In fact, Keene used violence against a free neighbor woman eight years later. In 1703, Keene took Joanna Williams to court for hitting him, but the majority of testimony supports her claim of self-defense. Williams testified that the previous summer, "the sd Caine throwed me . . . Down on the Ground and Gave me severall Blowes on the Stomack with his Knees and held my hands that I could not help my selfe and Tooke me by the Throat and allmost strangled me and also hurt my arme," *Province and Court Records of Maine,* 4: 286.

21. For more on the isolation and violence experienced by enslaved women in early New England, see Wendy Anne Warren, "'The Cause of Her Grief': The Rape of a Slave in Early New England," *Journal of American History* 93, no. 4 (2007): 1031–49.

22. *Province and Court Records of Maine,* 4: 205–6.

23. Ibid., 4: 13–14, 51.

24. Sharon V. Salinger, *Taverns and Drinking in Early America* (Baltimore: Johns Hopkins University Press, 2002), 3–4; McWilliams, *A Revolution in Eating,* 241–56; Laurel Thatcher Ulrich, *A Midwife's Tale: The Life of Martha Ballard, Based on Her Diary, 1785–1812* (New York: Knopf, 1990), 184; Rebecca J. Tannenbaum, *The Healer's Calling: Women and Medicine in Early New England* (Ithaca, N.Y.: Cornell University Press, 2002), chap. 2.

25. *Province and Court Records of Maine,* 3 and 4, passim.

26. *Province and Court Records of Maine,* 3: 293.

27. We don't know what toys Esther or her siblings owned, but clay marbles and a lead whizzer were found in an archaeological dig at Arrowsic Island, which was inhabited 1654–76, and is known to have sheltered children during King Philip's War, 1675–76. See Baker, *The Clark and Lake Company,* 23. See also Alice Morse Earle, *Child Life in Colonial Days* (1899; rpt. Stockbridge, Mass.: Berkshire House, 1993), 361–71. Earle writes, "A pathetic interest is attached to the shapeless similitude of a doll named Bangwell Putt," or Put, which is in the

Memorial Hall Museum, Deerfield, Mass., 366, and facing 370. See also *Catalogue of the Collection of Relics in Memorial Hall* (Deerfield, Mass.: Pocumtuck Valley Memorial Association, 1908), 97, and http://memorialhall.mass.edu/collection/itempage.jsp?itemid=5023&img=0, accessed September 8, 2014.

And who can ever forget Laura Ingalls Wilder's loving description of Charlotte, her first rag doll, described in *Little House in the Big Woods* (1932; 1959; New York: HarperCollins, 1971), 74–77. Charlotte supplanted Susan the corn-cob doll in Laura's affections, 20–21.

28. E. Jennifer Monaghan, *Learning to Read and Write in Colonial America* (Worcester, Mass.: American Antiquarian Society, 2005), chap. 1 (especially 40–44 on the sex-segregated nature of schools) and 81–85.

29. For more on the history of childhood at the turn of the eighteenth century, see Judith S. Graham, *Puritan Family Life: The Diary of Samuel Sewall* (Boston: Northeastern University Press, 2000), esp. 61–166.

30. Monaghan, *Learning to Read and Write*, 84–86; Benjamin Harris, *The Protestant tutor for children. The doner thereof [. . .] health and persev[. . .] the Gospel of Jesus Christ. To which is added verses made by Mr. John Rogers a martyr in Queen Maries reign* (Boston, 1685), 1; John Cotton, *Spiritual Milk for Boston babes in either England. Drawn out of the breasts of both testaments for their souls nourishment, but may be of like use to any children. By John Cotton, B.D. late teacher to the Church of Boston in New-England* (Cambridge, Mass., 1656; rpt., Boston, 1684), 5. A copy of Cotton's *Milk for Babes, Drawn Out of the Breasts of both Testaments* (London, 1646) at the Henry E. Huntington Library in San Marino, California, contains a manuscript addition by its former owner, Charles Deane, that claims that "this is the *earliest edition known* of Cotton's 'Milk for Babes,'" and it is nearly identical to the first North American edition, published in 1656.

31. Jane Kamensky, "Talk Like a Man: Speech, Power, and Masculinity in Early New England," *Gender and History* 8 (1996): 22–47; Jane Kamensky, *Governing the Tongue: The Politics of Speech in Early New England* (New York: Oxford University Press, 1997).

32. Marilyn Westerkamp, *Women and Religion in Early America, 1650–1850: The Puritan and Evangelical Traditions* (New York: Routledge, 1999), 35–45, quotation from 35; Michael P. Winship, *Making Heretics: Militant Protestantism and Free Grace in Massachusetts, 1636–1641* (Princeton: Princeton University Press, 2002).

33. Edmund M. Wheelwright, "A Frontier Family," in *Publications of the Colonial Society of Massachusetts, Transactions, 1892–94,* vol. 1 (Boston: Colonial Society of Massachusetts, 1895), 271–82; Baker, *True Stories of New England Captives,* 35–68; Wheelwright folder, Miscellaneous Collections, the William J. Clements Library, University of Michigan, Ann Arbor; Westerkamp, *Women and Religion in Early America,* 39–42; Winship, *Making Heretics,* chaps. 6, 10, and 11.

34. For an overview of seventeenth-century English settlements in Maine, see Edwin A. Churchill, "Mid-Seventeenth-Century Maine: A World on the Edge," and Emerson W. Baker, "The World of Thomas Gorges: Life in the Province of Maine in the 1640s," both in *American Beginnings: Exploration, Culture, and Cartography in the Land of Norumbega,* ed. Emerson W. Baker, Edwin A. Churchill, Richard D'Abate, Kristine L. Jones, Victor A. Konrad, and Harald E. L. Prins, 241–82 (Lincoln: University of Nebraska Press, 1994).

35. Harald E. L. Prins, "Children of Gluskap: Wabanaki Indians on the Eve of the European Invasion," in Baker et al., *American Beginnings,* 95–117; *Handbook of North American Indians,* vol. 15, *Northeast,* ed. Bruce G. Trigger (Washington, D.C.: Smithsonian Institution Press, 1978), 109–59.

36. On the conflict among Anglo-American settlers, French missionaries, and Catholic Wabanaki, see Laura M. Chmielewski, *The Spice of Popery: Converging Christianities on an Early American Frontier* (South Bend, Ind.: Notre Dame University Press, 2012). See also Emma Lewis Coleman, *New England Captives Carried to Canada* (Portland, Me.: Southworth, 1925; rpt. Bowie, Md.: Heritage, 1989), 1: 25–41; John Gilmary Shea, *History of the Catholic Missions Among the Indian Tribes of the United States, 1529–1854* (1883), chaps. 2–3.

37. Mass. Arch. 71: 871, 877.

38. Mass. Arch. 36: 75–76, 447a; 37: 32a, 84a, 144, 259; 51: 182–182a, 241–44, 342–43, 363; 70: 280; 72: 103–4; Coleman, *New England Captives Carried to Canada,* 1: 428.

39. *Collection de Manuscrits contenant lettres, mémoires, et autre documents historiques relatifs a la Nouvelle-France* (Québec: A. Coté, 1883–85), vols. 2 and 3, passim; quotation from "Memoire sur les etablissemens anglois, 1703," *Collection de Manuscrits,* 2: 400–401.

40. See, for example, *Documentary History of the State of Maine,* 4, Baxter Manuscripts, ed. James Phinney Baxter (Portland, Me.: Brown, Thurston, 1889), 348–79, passim; coll. 77, box 1, folder 10; box 2, folders 27, 32, 42; and coll. S-888, misc. box 33, folder 21, both at the Maine Historical Society, Portland.

41. Mass. Arch. 36: 52. For examples of the militarization of Maine in the 1680s and 1690s, see *Province and Court Records of Maine,* 3: 21–22, 36, 62, 86, 153, 155–56, 190, 216, 229.

42. Coleman, *New England Captives Carried to Canada,* 1: 221–27, 395–98; Bourne, *The History of Wells and Kennebunk,* chaps. 15 and 17; Clark, *The Eastern Frontier,* 112–13. Bourne estimates the toll on York in the 1692 "Candlemas raid" as seventy-five killed, eighty-five taken into captivity (211). See also the discussion of the attack on Wells during King William's War in Ann M. Little, *Abraham in Arms: War and Gender in Colonial New England* (Philadelphia: University of Pennsylvania Press, 2007), 41–42, 51–52.

43. *Province and Court Records of Maine,* 4: 395; Bourne, *The History of Wells and Kennebunk,* 390–91.

44. *Province and Court Records of Maine,* 4: 9, 11, 13, 39, 69, 92, 107; Wheelwright, *Esther,* 31–44.

45. *Boston News-Letter,* July 21, 1712; Mass. Arch. 51: 241–44; Bourne, *The History of Wells and Kennebunk,* 276–81; Coleman, *New England Captives Carried to Canada,* 1: 428; Wheelwright, *Esther,* 127.

46. On the environmental and demographic transformation of New England in the seventeenth century, see William Cronon, *Changes in the Land: Indians, Colonists, and the Ecology of New England* (New York: Hill and Wang, 1983); Joyce Chaplin, *Subject Matter: Technology, the Body, and Science on the Anglo-American Frontier, 1500–1676* (Cambridge: Harvard University Press, 2001); Virginia DeJohn Anderson, *Creatures of Empire: How Domestic Animals Transformed Early America* (Cambridge: Harvard University Press, 2004); Thomas Wickman, "'Winters

Embittered with Hardships': Severe Cold, Wabanaki Power, and English Adjustments," *William and Mary Quarterly* 72, no. 1 (2015): 57–98.

47. Little, *Abraham in Arms*, chaps. 1 and 5; quotation from 169–70. On John Wheelwright's devotion to religion, see Bourne, *The History of Wells and Kennebunk*, 284–88, 390–91. He was instrumental in building the First Congregational Church in 1699–1700 and was the first signer of the church covenant in 1701. He also brought five of his children to be baptized in that church. See Wheelwright, "A Frontier Family," 293; and "Wheelwright Families in Maine," *Maine Historical Magazine* 9 (January 1894–January 1895): 76–77.

48. J. David Hacker, "Trends and Determinants of Adult Mortality in Early New England: Reconciling Old and New Evidence from the Long Eighteenth Century," *Social Science History* 21, no. 4 (1997): 481–519; Robert V. Wells, "A Tale of Two Cities: Epidemics and Rituals of Death in Eighteenth-Century Boston and Philadelphia," in *Mortal Remains: Death in Early America*, ed. Nancy Isenberg and Andrew Burstein, 56–67 (Philadelphia: University of Pennsylvania Press, 2003).

49. Kenneth Silverman, *The Life and Times of Cotton Mather* (New York: Columbia University Press, 1985), 261–75, 336–63, 390, 401; Graham, *Puritan Family Life*, 20, 99–108; Jill Lepore, *Book of Ages: The Life and Opinions of Jane Franklin* (New York: Knopf, 2013), 120–26, 280–82.

50. Daniel Scott Smith, "The Demographic History of Colonial New England," *Journal of Economic History* 32, no. 1 (1972): 165–83; Richard Archer, "New England Mosaic: A Demographic Analysis for the Seventeenth Century," *William and Mary Quarterly* 47, no. 4 (1990): 477–502.

51. Wheelwright, *Esther*, 39–44; Coleman, *New England Captives Carried to Canada*, 1: 410–13; *The Vital Records of Wells, Maine, 1619–1950*, ed. Hope Moody Shelley (Rockport, Me.: Picton, 2005), 6.

52. Map by Dorothy Slavin, "Situation of Defensible Houses, 1676–1723," Historical Society of Wells and Ogunquit, Wells, Maine.

53. See note 11 above, as well as James Savage, *Genealogical Dictionary of the First Settlers of New England*, 4 vols. (Boston: Little, Brown, 1862), 4: 210, for details on the Storer family. Mary Storer's three sisters probably all still lived in the Storer garrison, although they escaped abduction by the Wabanaki in 1703: Hannah, twenty-three; Sarah, twenty; and Abigail, fifteen.

54. Coleman, *New England Captives Carried to Canada*, 1: 413–25; Little, *Abraham in Arms*, chap. 4, especially 147–48, 159–65.

55. John Underhill, *Newes from America, or a New and Experimentall Discoverie of New England* (London, 1638), 42–43.

56. James Axtell, "The White Indians of Colonial America," *William and Mary Quarterly* 3rd ser., 32, no. 1 (1975): 55–88, rpt. Axtell, *The European and the Indian: Essays in the Ethnohistory of Colonial North America* (New York: Oxford University Press, 1981), 168–206; James Axtell, *The Invasion Within: The Contest of Cultures in Colonial North America* (New York: Oxford University Press, 1985), 302–27; Daniel Richter, "War and Culture: The Iroquois Experience,"

William and Mary Quarterly 3rd ser., 40 (1983): 528–59; Daniel Richter, *The Ordeal of the Longhouse: The Peoples of the Iroquois League in the Era of European Colonization* (Chapel Hill: University of North Carolina Press, 1992); June Namias, *White Captives: Gender and Ethnicity on the American Frontier* (Chapel Hill: University of North Carolina Press, 1993); John Demos, *The Unredeemed Captive: A Family Story from Early America* (New York: Vintage, 1994); Evan Haefeli and Kevin Sweeney, *Captors and Captives: The 1704 French and Indian Raid on Deerfield* (Amherst: University of Massachusetts Press, 2003); Little, *Abraham in Arms*, chaps. 2–4; and Teresa A. Toulouse, *The Captive's Position: Female Narrative, Male Identity, and Royal Authority in Colonial New England* (Philadelphia: University of Pennsylvania Press, 2007).

57. On the significance of age in the experience of child war captives, see Ann M. Little, "'Keep me with you, so that I might not be damned': Age and Captivity in Colonial Borderlands Warfare," in *Age in America: The Colonial Era to the Present*, ed. Corinne Field and Nicholas L. Syrett (New York: New York University Press, 2015), 23–46.

2. Mali Among the Wabanaki

1. For an imaginative reconstruction of an Innu (Montagnais) childhood and encounter with Catholicism, see Emma Anderson, *The Betrayal of Faith: The Tragic Journey of a Colonial Native Convert* (Cambridge: Harvard University Press, 2007), 11–121.

2. Alice Nash, "The Abiding Frontier: Family, Gender, and Religion in Wabanaki History, 1600–1763," Ph.D. diss., Columbia University, 1997, 76–77, 83–84.

3. John Gilmary Shea, *History of the Catholic Missions Among the Indian Tribes of the United States, 1529–1854* (1883), 135–45; Nash, "The Abiding Frontier," 202–3; Gordon Day, "The Identity of the Saint Francis Indians," Canadian Ethnology Service 71 (Ottawa: National Museums of Canada, 1981).

4. Harald E. L. Prins and Bruce J. Bourque, "Norridgewock: Village Transformation on the New England–Acadian Frontier," *Man in the Northeast* 33 (1987): 137–58; *Boston News Letter* 47 (1705).

5. *Les Ursulines de Québec, Depuis leur Établissement Jusqu'à Nos Jours* (Québec: C. Darveau, 1864) 2: 75–88; quotation from 83. The English-language *Glimpses of the Monastery: Scenes from the History of the Ursulines of Quebec during two hundred years, 1639–1839*, 2nd ed. (Québec: L. J. Demers, 1897), 175–82, is even more aggressive about erasing the influence of Wabanaki women in Esther's conversion. This version of Esther Wheelwright's captivity is told in explicitly racist sentimental language, and any Wabanaki influence on Esther is malign.

6. Susan Sleeper-Smith, *Indian Women and French Men: Rethinking Cultural Encounter in the Western Great Lakes* (Amherst: University of Massachusetts Press, 2001), chaps. 2–3; Allan Greer, *Mohawk Saint: Catherine Tekakwitha and the Jesuits* (Oxford: Oxford University Press, 2005), chaps. 4–6; William A. Clark, S.J., "The Church at Nanrantsouak: Sébastien Râle, S.J., and the Wabanaki of Maine's Kennebec River," *Catholic Historical Review* 92, no. 3 (2006): 225–51.

I avoid using the term "convert" and "conversion" in this book because those terms seem overdetermined and Eurocentric. I use the term "Catholic Wabanaki" and "Wabanaki Catholicism" to suggest what Tracy Neal Leavelle calls the "plural, dynamic, and flexible concept of conversion that accounts for the changes in all participants"; *The Catholic Calumet: Colonial Conversions in French and Indian North America* (Philadelphia: University of Pennsylvania Press, 2012). Leavelle continues, "Such a perspective requires an analysis of religious action—orientation and movement, song and speech, ritual and relationships—more than it does a simple delineation of faith and doctrine" (8). See also Anderson, *The Betrayal of Faith*, 1–10, 235–41.

7. On moccasins, see Ann M. Little, *Abraham in Arms: War and Gender in Early New England* (Philadelphia: University of Pennsylvania Press, 2007), 78–79; John Gyles, *Memoirs of Odd Adventures, Strange Deliverances, &c* (Boston, 1736), 3–5. Gyles reports being taken up the Penobscot River to the village of *"Madawamkee:* which stands on a Point of Land, between the Main River, and a Branch which heads to the East of it," 5. In Maine today, there is a town called Mattawamkeag sixty miles north of Bangor, which features the exact river formation that Gyles describes. The Mattawamkeag River branches east from the Penobscot.

The approximation of Gyles's age comes from a nineteenth-century edition of his narrative, *Nine years a captive; or, John Gyles' experience among the Malicite Indians, from 1689 to 1698,* ed. James Hannay (St. John, N.B.: Daily Telegraph Steam Job Press, 1875), 7. The *Dictionary of Canadian Biography* puts his birthdate at approximately 1680 as well; see W. S. MacNutt, "Gyles, John," *Dictionary of Canadian Biography* (Toronto: University of Toronto/Université Laval, 1966), hereafter *DCB*, 3: 272–73; or University of Toronto/Université Laval, 2003–, http://www.biographi.ca/en/bio/gyles_john_3E.html, accessed September 18, 2014.

8. Letter from Sébastien Rasles to his brother, October 12, 1723, in *The Jesuit Relations and Allied Documents,* ed. Reuben Gold Thwaites (Cleveland: Burrows Brothers, 1896–1901; rpt. New York: Pageant, 1959), hereafter *Jesuit Relations,* 67: 220–25; Gyles, *Memoirs of Odd Adventures,* 28. Denys Delage notes that Native peoples consumed dog meat in times of want, as an everyday food, and frequently as a food with ritual significance in "'Vos Chiens ont plus d'esprit que les nôtres': Histoire des Chiens dans la rencontre des Français et des Amérindiens," *Les Cahiers des Dix* 59 (2005): 185–87; and in "Gazing Across the Divide: Dogs in the Colonial Canadian Context," *Le Journal: Center for French Colonial Studies/Centre pour l'Étude du Pays des Illinois* 23, no. 3, part 1: 3 and part 2: 1, 3. Dog consumption was a widespread practice among Natives of the Americas: Jennifer Fish Kashay has reported that dog was eaten in late-eighteenth- and early-nineteenth-century Hawai'i, and that this practice was viewed negatively by New England Protestant missionaries, in "Missionaries and Foodways in Early 19th-Century Hawai'i," *Food and Foodways* 17, no. 3 (2009): 170–71.

9. *Jesuit Relations,* 67: 220–25.

10. See Lee Allen Peterson, *A Field Guide to Edible Wild Plants: Eastern and Central North America* (Boston: Houghton Mifflin, 1977), 236, 245–46, 249–50, 281–83; Gyles, *Memoirs of Odd Adventures,* 8–12. Harald E. L. Prins, in "Children of Gluskap: Wabanaki Indians on the Eve of the European Invasion," in *American Beginnings: Exploration, Culture, and Cartography in the Land of Norumbega,* ed. Emerson W. Baker, Edwin A. Churchill, Richard D'Abate, Kris-

tine L. Jones, Victor A. Konrad, and Harald E. L. Prins (Lincoln: University of Nebraska Press, 1994), suggests that the Kennebec River was the dividing line for agricultural cultivation in Wabanakia, as the lands north and east of the river had too short a growing season to support the maize, beans, and squash cultivation characteristic of other northeastern woodlands communities (103–4). However, Gyles, who lived in captivity on the Penobscot and St. John's Rivers (well east and north of the mission on the Kennebec River), reported that corn was cultivated among the Wabanaki there; *Memoirs of Odd Adventures,* 6–8, 11, 14, 31.

11. Based on her arrival at Norridgewock in mid- to late August, and on this sample menu provided by Gyles, *Memoirs of Odd Adventures,* 31: "But to return to an Indian Feast, of which you may request a Bill of Fare, before you go; and if you dislike it stay at Home. The ingredients are Fish, Flesh, or Indian Corn and Beans boil'd together—, or Hasty-Pudden made of pounded Corn." In a section of his narrative labeled "Of the manner of the St. John's *Indians* living in the Summer," he describes the manner of corn cultivation and preservation, and other foods available before the corn harvest: "There we planted Corn; and after Planting, went a Fishing, and to look for and dig Roots; till the Corn was fit to Weed: and after Weeding took a second Tour on the same errand, and return'd to Hill our Corn: and after Hilling, we went some distance from the Fort & Field up the River, to take Salmon, and other Fish, and dry them for Food till Corn was fill'd with the Milk: Some of which we dried then, the other as it ripened" (11).

12. Jacques Bigot, letter of October 26, 1699, *Jesuit Relations,* 65: 86–87, 92–95, 263; *Boston News Letter* 47 (1705).

13. Vincent Bigot, *Relation de ce qui s'est passé de plus remarquable dans la Mission des Abnaquis à L'Acadie, l'année 1701* (Manate: de la Presse Cramoisy de Jean-Marie Shea, 1858), hereafter *Relation de 1701,* 11. Naurakamig was on the Androscoggin River, near the present-day town of Canton, Maine.

Jacques Cartier reported that his men suffered and many died from scurvy during the winter of 1535–36 near Hochelaga, which was also gravely afflicted with the disease, but most were saved by a Native remedy of brewing the leaves and bark of "l'épinette blanche," northern white cedar (also called arborvitae for its lifesaving properties). The needles of the white spruce contain sufficient vitamin C to ward off or cure scurvy. See Hiram B. Stephens, ed., *Jacques Cartier and His Four Voyages to Canada* (Montreal: W. Drysdale, 1890), 77–82, 141; Henry Clepper, "Trees That Heal (and Don't)," *American Forests* 97, nos. 1/2 (1991): 8–9. The fact that some, but not all, Native people knew of a cure for scurvy suggests that it afflicted communities intermittently in the northeastern borderlands through the colonial period.

Evidence suggests that scurvy may have been a recurrent disease among Aboriginal North Americans more generally. In an article that surveyed 557 subadult skeletal remains from Florida, the mid-Atlantic region (Maryland and Virginia), the Plains, and the Southwest dating from 950 to 1750, scurvy was evident in the remains from all regions except the Plains samples, and it appears to have afflicted children seven and younger more than older children or adults. (Thus Bigot's report that young children were among the most afflicted appears to jibe with the science.) Furthermore, the authors found a greater percentage of afflicted remains among the two East Coast regions compared with the Southwest; see Donald J. Ortner, Whitney Butler, Jessica Cafarella, and Lauren Milligan, "Evidence of Probable Scurvy in Subadults from Archaeological Sites in North America," *American Journal of Physical Anthropology* 114, no. 4 (2001): 343–51.

14. David S. Jones, "Virgin Soils Reconsidered," *William and Mary Quarterly*, 3rd ser., 60, no. 4 (2003): 703–42, argues that hunger and disease worked in tandem to weaken populations in a "vicious circle" (735), whereby diseased adults can't engage in their usual agricultural work and hunting, which leads to caloric, vitamin, and protein deficiencies, which then further weaken immune resistance.

15. Greer, *Mohawk Saint*, 6–14, 102–10. For an overview of the Jesuit missions and their Algonquian and Iroquois inhabitants, see Allan Greer, *The Jesuit Relations: Natives and Missionaries in Seventeenth Century North America* (Boston: Bedford/St. Martin's, 2000), 1–19.

16. Cotton Mather, *Good Fetch'd out of Evil* (Boston, 1706), 34–35. Joseph François Lafitau singles out "the Abenaki" for their "horror of cannibalism. They alone cannot be reproached with the cruelty of the other tribes"; *Customs of the American Indians*, ed. and trans. William N. Fenton and Elizabeth L. Moore (Toronto: Champlain Society, 1974, 1977), 2: 171.

There is little evidence that cannibalism was practiced by eastern Algonquians, although there is substantial evidence that cannibalism was an Iroquois practice in the seventeenth century. However, it's equally clear that human flesh was usually eaten as one part of the ritual ceremonies surrounding the torture and execution of war captives. See, for example, Thomas Abler, "Iroquois Cannibalism: Fact, Not Fiction," *Ethnohistory* 27, no. 4 (1980): 309–16; Richard White cites one instance of Iroquois cannibalism of captive children in the Iroquois wars in *The Middle Ground: Indians, Empires, and Republics in the Great Lakes Region, 1650–1815* (Cambridge: Cambridge University Press, 1991), 4–5, as well as a few examples of Algonquian cannibalism in the Great Lakes region, 231, 500–501.

17. Emma Lewis Coleman, *New England Captives Carried to Canada* (Portland, Me.: Southworth, 1925; rpt. Bowie, Md.: Heritage, 1989), 1: 410–12.

18. Little, *Abraham in Arms*, 111–12; Nash's "The Abiding Frontier," chap. 5, offers an excellent overview of the multiple practices and meanings of captivity: "In Wabanakia, captivity was a fluid state with a range of possible implications. As with eating moosemeat, captive-taking as a cultural practice persisted through the eighteenth century but changed over time in the context of European colonization. Captives had a rich range of potential meaning, a polysemic quality that made it possible for Wabanaki captors to use them in different ways—as gifts, envoys, hostages, slaves, commodities and status symbols as well as adoptive kin—according to changing circumstances," 263–64. Cf. Brett Rushforth, *Bonds of Alliance: Indigenous and Atlantic Slaveries in New France* (Chapel Hill: University of North Carolina Press, 2012), which argues that Algonquian and Siouxan captivity in the Great Lakes region (the *Pays d'en Haut*) was much more coercive, 15–71, 253–98.

19. Little, *Abraham in Arms*, 111–13; Clark, "The Church at Nanrantsouak." For a description of the Jesuit, Capuchin, and Recollect missions on the Kennebec, Penobscot, and St.

John's Rivers in the seventeenth and eighteenth centuries, see Shea, *History of the Catholic Missions,* chaps. 2–3.

20. Kenneth M. Morrison, *The Solidarity of Kin: Ethnohistory, Religious Studies, and the Algonkian-French Religious Encounter* (Albany: State University of New York Press, 2002), chap. 3. This story presents an interesting counterpoint to "Hansel and Gretel," in which hospitality is offered to the abandoned children in order that the witch may charm, enslave, fatten, and finally eat the children. See also Morrison, "Mapping Otherness: Myth and the Study of Cultural Encounter," in Baker et al., *American Beginnings,* 119–29.

21. Gyles, *Memoirs of Odd Adventures,* 5.

22. Ibid., 6–8, 20. Information on Medoctack Fort and Woodstock, New Brunswick, in W. O. Raymond, "Early Days of Woodstock," in *Proceedings at the Centennial Commemoration of the Ordination of Rev. Frederick Dibblee* (St. John, N.B.: Barnes, 1891), 12–16.

23. Nash, "The Abiding Frontier," chap. 3.

24. Alice Nash, "Antic Deportments and Indian Postures: Embodiment in the Seventeenth-Century Anglo-Algonquian World," in *A Centre of Wonders: The Body in Early America,* ed. Janet Moore Lindmann and Michele Lise Tarter (Ithaca, N.Y.: Cornell University Press, 2001), 163–75; Little, *Abraham in Arms,* chap. 2; Gyles, *Memoirs of Odd Adventures,* 11–12.

25. Kathleen M. Brown, *Foul Bodies: Cleanliness in Early America* (Yale University Press, 2009), 1–80, 156–57. See also Natalie Zemon Davis's description of Marie de l'Incarnation's account of Ursulines in the 1640s stripping their Native pupils of their garments and rubbing the grease off of their bodies in *Women on the Margins: Three Seventeenth-Century Lives* (Cambridge: Harvard University Press, 1995), 95–97. Quoting l'Incarnation, "When [the Native girls] are given to us, they are naked as a worm, and one must wash them from head to foot because of the grease that their parents have smeared all over their bodies. And no matter how diligently one does it or how often one changes their clothes, it takes a long time before one can get rid of the vermin caused by the abundance of their grease. One sister spends part of each day at this" (96).

On Wabanaki women's distinctively hybrid clothing, see Bruce J. Bourque and Laureen A. LaBar, *Uncommon Threads: Wabanaki Textiles, Clothing, and Costume* (Augusta, Me.: Maine State Museum, 2009), 21–35, 100–108.

26. Nash writes, "When cultural identity is coded onto physical movements such as dancing or hunting, the experience of performing those movements creates a sense of order and continuity in the world," "Antic Deportments," 170.

27. Joseph Laurent, *New Familiar Abenakis and English Dialogues* (Québec: Leger Brousseau, 1884), 7, 55; Bunny McBride, *Women of the Dawn* (Lincoln: University of Nebraska Press, 1999), xi, 15–16. Mali, anglicized as Molly, became a popular name for Wabanaki women from the eighteenth through the twentieth centuries. The name Mali makes sense for Esther Wheelwright individually as well, because the religious name she took in the convent was Marie-Joseph de l'Enfant Jésus.

28. The famous Deerfield raid was almost singular as a wintertime attack. Thomas Wickman, in "'Winters Embittered with Hardships': Severe Cold, Wabanaki Power, and English

Adjustments," *William and Mary Quarterly* 72, no. 1 (2015), 57–98, argues that the incredibly cold winters at the turn of the eighteenth century offered the Wabanaki new opportunities for winter attacks in this period.

29. Nash, "The Abiding Frontier," 159–60. Compare Laurel Ulrich's description of women's and men's work in the Anglo-American community as symbolized by a blue and white checked cloth in *A Midwife's Tale: The Life of Martha Ballard, Based on Her Diary, 1785–1812* (New York: Knopf, 1990), 75–76.

Gyles describes his work in the corn harvest: "And when we had gathered our Corn and dried it, we put some into Indian Barns, i.e. Holes in the Ground lin'd & cover'd with Bark, and then with Dirt," and reports that the corn was boiled on the cob before it was shucked and dried. When reconstituted, it "swells as large, and tastes incomparably sweeter than other Corn," *Memoirs of Odd Adventures*, 11.

30. Nash, "The Abiding Frontier," chap. 3, quotation from 159–60; McBride, *Women of the Dawn*, 8–9; on the hunting and consumption of moose and bear, see Gyles, *Memoirs of Odd Adventures*, 9–10, 16–17, 22, 25, quotation from 31. Cf. Trudy Eden's sample menus and recipes for Anglo-American colonists ca. 1675–1740 in *Cooking in America, 1540–1840* (Westport, Conn.: Greenwood, 2006), 15–72, 131–36.

31. Nash, "The Abiding Frontier," 236–39; Eugene Vetromile, *The Abnakis and Their History; or, Historical Notices of the Aborigines of Acadia* (New York: James B. Kirker, 1866), 90–91. Theda Perdue offers a similar analysis of menstrual segregation and taboos among the Cherokee in the eighteenth and nineteenth centuries in *Cherokee Women: Gender and Culture Change, 1700–1835* (Lincoln: University of Nebraska Press, 1998), 28–40. Menstrual segregation or seclusion appears to have been a widespread and long-lasting set of beliefs and practices throughout North America. See, for example, Marla N. Powers, "Menstruation and Reproduction: An Oglala Case," *Signs* 6, no. 1 (1980): 54–65; and Amelia Rector Bell's fascinating discussion of the importance of contemporary Cherokee menstrual segregation in "Separate People: Speaking of Creek Men and Women," *American Anthropologist*, n.s. 92, no. 2 (1990): 332–45.

32. Mary Snell Wheelwright was almost constantly pregnant or nursing the whole time Esther lived at home with her, so Esther may have seen the menstrual cloths only of servant women. On English views of menstruation, see Patricia Crawford, "Attitudes to Menstruation in Seventeenth-Century England," *Past and Present* 91, no. 1 (1981): 47–73.

On colonial Anglo-American women and menstruation, see Susan E. Klepp, "Lost, Hidden, Obstructed, and Repressed: Contraceptive and Abortive Technology in the Early Delaware Valley," in *Early American Technology: Making and Doing Things from the Colonial Era to 1850,* ed. Judith A. McGaw, 68–113 (Chapel Hill: University of North Carolina Press, 1994); Rebecca J. Tannenbaum, *The Healer's Calling: Women and Medicine in Early New England* (Ithaca, N.Y.: Cornell University Press, 2002), 36–38; and Brown, *Foul Bodies,* 35–36 and 141. Tannenbaum and Klepp note the importance ascribed to menstruation as a key to assessing a woman's health and the anxieties attendant on blocked or suppressed menses. There is not a great deal of evidence or discussion about how Anglo-American women at the turn of the eighteenth century might have dealt with menstruation, but a hint from *Aristotle's Compleat Masterpiece*, 26th ed. (London, 1755) suggests that the color of menstrual blood was considered important in assessing fertility, so it may have been monitored carefully: "A third Thing that Woman ought to take Care of to further Conception is, to keep the Womb in good Order; and to that End to see that the Menses come down as they ought to do: For if they are discoloured, they are out of Order" (43). This interest in menstrual blood—its absence or its presence and condition—suggest that menstruation was dealt with in a relatively straightforward and frank manner among women and girls.

33. Gyles, *Memoirs of Odd Adventures*, 31. At other points in his narrative, Gyles says that he was asked to plant and tend corn and to "dress leather," traditionally women's work, so it may be the case that male captives were treated as people of indeterminate sex, like postmenopausal women (11, 13). It is unclear that these work assignments were either punishments or insults—other Anglo-American captives describe being asked by their Native captors to do work that they would have performed in New England villages, as Mary Rowlandson was asked to work with her needle in captivity. Gyles was also a boy of only nine when he was taken, so it may be that preadolescent male Wabanaki children were expected to assist their mothers' work.

34. "First Church of Christ, Congregational, Wells, Maine," coll. 1249, Maine Historical Society, Portland. On the first page, it says that on November 9, 1701, "Samuel, Hannah, Esther, Jeremiah, Elizabeth," all "children of Mr. John Wheelwright received baptism."

35. Nash, "The Abiding Frontier," 76–77, 83–84, 156–57; Vetromile, *The Abnakis and Their History*, 88–90. Nash suggests that the modesty between the sexes may be related to their strong incest taboo.

36. Gyles, *Memoirs of Odd Adventures*, 20.

37. Day, "The Identity of the Saint Francis Indians"; Shea, *History of the Catholic Missions*, chaps. 2–3; David L. Ghere, "Myths and Methods in Abenaki Demography: Abenaki Population Recovery, 1725–1750," *Ethnohistory* 44, no. 3 (1997), 511–34, especially the map of Wabanaki villages and missions across northern New England and Quebec, 513.

38. Letter of Father Jacques Bigot, June 24, 1681, *Jesuit Relations*, 62: 24–53. Kenneth M. Morrison argues that the "Kennebec" (Norridgewock) Wabanaki were especially receptive to Catholicism because "Wabanaki Catholicism represents a syncretic intensification of their ancient religious life"; *The Solidarity of Kin*, chap. 4, quotation from 81.

39. Letter of Father Jacques Bigot, June 24, 1681, *Jesuit Relations*, 62: 27–33.

40. Day, "The Identity of the Saint Francis Indians"; Shea, *History of the Catholic Missions*, chap. 3; *Jesuit Relations*, 62: 27.

41. *Jesuit Relations*, 62: 44–49.

42. Ibid., 62: 33–37.

43. Little, *Abraham in Arms*, chaps. 1 and 5.

44. Bigot, *Jesuit Relations*, 62: 45. See also discussions of the use of iron girdles by French and Native people alike in New France in *Jesuit Relations*, 62: 175–79 (among Mohawk women, ca. 1682), 35: 125 (by Father Charles Garnier in the mid-seventeenth century), and

49: 94–101 (by an Algonquian woman as reported by the Ursulines of Québec, ca. 1663–64). Greer writes about the nunlike community of three women, of whom Catherine Tekakwitha appeared to be the leader, in *Mohawk Saint*, 125–46, and of their propensity to engage in severe mortifications of the flesh, 132–34. See also Greer's discussion of what he calls "Iroquois flagellant Christianity," 118–24.

45. Jacques Bigot, *Relation de la Mission Abnaquise de St. François de Sales, l'année 1702* (New York: Presse Cramoisy de Jean Marie Shea, 1865), hereafter *Relation de 1702*, 12.

46. Allan Greer, "Colonial Saints: Gender, Race, and Hagiography in New France," *William and Mary Quarterly*, 3rd ser., 57, no. 2 (2000): 323–48.

47. *Jesuit Relations*, 49: 97. For other references to iron girdles used by both Native women and Jesuits in the *Jesuit Relations*, see, for example, *Jesuit Relations*, 34: 181, 35: 123, and 62: 173, 177.

José António Brandão and Michael Shakir Nassaney analyze a cilice discovered in an archaeological dig at Fort St. Joseph in southwestern Michigan in "Suffering for Jesus: Penitential Practices at Fort St. Joseph (Niles, Michigan) During the French Regime," *Catholic Historical Review* 94, no. 3 (2008): 476–99. The provenance of these devices is unknown, although presumably they were made in Europe. However, Father Jacques Gravier included a list of supplies required for the missions among the Illinois in a 1702 letter in which he requested "3 dozen Spools of fine iron wire, or Else a roll of fine wire," which could have been used to make these appliances (*Jesuit Relations*, 66: 29).

48. Lafitau, *Customs of the American Indians*, 2: 155–62; Daniel K. Richter, "War and Culture: The Iroquois Experience," *William and Mary Quarterly*, 3rd. ser., 40 (1983): 528–59; quotation from Gyles, *Memoirs of Odd Adventures*, 20.

49. See, for example, Sleeper-Smith on Jacques Gravier's portrait of Marie Rouensa, *Indian Women and French Men*, chap. 2, and Greer's description of Claude Chauchetière's portrait of Catherine Tekakwitha in *Mohawk Saint*, 18–22, 198. On the generic conventions of European representations of dying Native people, see Erik R. Seeman, "Reading Indians' Deathbed Scenes: Ethnohistorical and Representational Approaches," *Journal of American History* 88, no. 1 (2001): 17–47.

50. *Jesuit Relations*, 65: 89–91; *Relation de 1701*, 21–29, quotation from 21.

51. *Relation de 1702*, 13; *Jesuit Relations*, 63: 48–49.

52. Lafitau, *Customs of the American Indians*, 1: 218.

53. Ibid., 1: 218–19.

54. *Jesuit Relations*, 62, 48–51.

55. Ibid., 63: 26–27, 30–31. See also the letter Jacques Bigot wrote to the Reverend Mother of the Visitation Sisters of Annecy to accompany the "collier pourcelaine" on November 9, 1684, *Copie d'une Lettre Escrite Par Le Père Jacques Bigot de la Compagnie de Jésus, l'an 1684, pur accompagner un collier de pourcelaine envoiée par les Abnaquis de la Mission de Sainct François de Sales dans la Nouvelle France au tombeau de leur Sainct Patron à Annecy* (Manate: De La Presse Cramoisy de Jean-Marie Shea, 1858); William Curtis Farabee, "Recent Discovery of Ancient Wampum Belts," *Museum Journal* 13, no. 1 (1922): 46–54. On the manufacture of both wampum

and Wabanaki women's devotional "colliers de porcelain" (wampum belts), see Jonathan C. Lainey, *La "Monnaie des Sauvages": Les Colliers de Wampum d'Hier à Aujourd'hui* (Québec: Septentrion, 2004), esp. 11–86.

56. *Jesuit Relations,* 62: 28–43; 63: 70–73; *Répertoire des Actes de Baptême, Mariage, et Sépulture et des Rencensements du Québec ancien,* vol 3 (Montreal: University of Montreal Press, 1980), Mission St. Joseph de Sillery, 327.

57. *Jesuit Relations,* 62: 38–39; on Wabanaki death customs and burial traditions, see Seeman, "Reading Indians' Deathbed Scenes," 34–36, 40. See also Eric Seeman, *Death in the New World: Cross-Cultural Encounters, 1492–1800* (Philadelphia: University of Pennsylvania Press, 2010), chap. 4.

Algonquian peoples appear to have buried meaningful objects with the dead from prehistoric times to the colonial period. See, for example, Charles C. Willoughby, *Prehistoric Burial Places in Maine* (Cambridge, Mass.: Peabody Museum of American Archaeology and Ethnology, 1898); Kathleen Bragdon, *Native Peoples of Southern New England, 1500–1650* (Norman: University of Oklahoma Press, 1996), 233–41; Patricia E. Rubertone, *Grave Undertakings: An Archaeology of Roger Williams and the Narragansett Indians* (Washington, D.C.: Smithsonian Institution Press, 2001), chap. 7.

58. *Jesuit Relations,* 65: 90–93. See also Ann M. Little, "'Keep me with you, so that I might not be damned': Age and Captivity in Colonial Borderlands Warfare," in *Age in America: The Colonial Era to the Present,* ed. Corinne Field and Nicholas L. Syrett (New York: New York University Press, 2015), 23–46.

59. *Jesuit Relations,* 65: 92–93; *Relation de 1702,* 24–25.

60. *Jesuit Relations,* 66: 209–11; Registre des Entrees et Sortie des Petites Filles Francaises et Sauvages de 1641, Pensionnat 1/E.3.4.1.1.1, tome 1, Archives du Monastère des Ursulines de Québec, Québec, P.Q., hereafter AMUQ, entries for May 26 and July 27, 1683, and January 1 and 19, 1687/88. For more on the brothers Bigot, see *Jesuit Relations,* 62: 271, notes 1 and 2, and Thomas Charland, "Bigot, Jacques," in *DCB* 2: 63–64; or University of Toronto/Université Laval, 2003–, http://www.biographi.ca/en/bio/bigot_jacques_2E.html, accessed May 8, 2015; Thomas Charland, "Bigot, Vincent," in *DCB* 2: 64–65; or University of Toronto/Université Laval, 2003–, http://www.biographi.ca/en/bio/bigot_vincent_2E .html, accessed May 8, 2015.

61. Coleman, *New England Captives Carried to Canada,* 1: 121–23; see *Collection de manuscrits contenant lettres, mémoires, et autres documents historiques relatifs à la Nouvelle-France* (Québec: A. Coté et Cie, 1883), 2: 309, 327; quotation from 327.

62. Coleman, *New England Captives Carried to Canada,* 1: 410–13; Julie Wheelwright, *Esther: The Remarkable True Story of Esther Wheelwright: Puritan Child, Native Daughter, Mother Superior* (Toronto: HarperCollins, 2011), 79–81.

63. For example, "Les Annales des Ursulines de Quebec, vol. I, 1639–1822," 1/E, 12, 1, 0, 0, 1 (AMUQ) says that she was six when abducted from "the tower of Boston" by the Wabanaki, 1: 147. In "Registre des Entrées, Vetures et Professions des Religieuses Ursulines de Québec, 1647–1783," 1/G7.1.1.1 (AMUQ), the entry for October 2, 1712, records her age

incorrectly as fifteen and a half; in fact, she was sixteen and a half (b. March 31, 1696). The plaque commemorating her life and superiorship in the halls of the Ursuline monastery today records her as two years younger.

3. Esther *Anglaise*

1. The *Dictionary of Canadian Biography* entries for Louise-Élisabeth de Joybert de Soulanges et de Marson (1673–1740) and Philippe de Rigaud, Marquis de Vaudreuil (1643–1725), suggest that the marquise was thirty years her husband's junior. See Yves F. Zoltvany, "Rigaud de Vaudreuil, Philippe de, Marquis de Vaudreuil," in *Dictionary of Canadian Biography* (University of Toronto/Université Laval, 1966), hereafter *DCB*, 2: 565–74; or University of Toronto/Université Laval, 2003–, http://www.biographi.ca/en/bio/rigaud_de_vaudreuil _philippe_de_2E.html, accessed May 8, 2015; and Yves F. Zoltvany, "Joybert de Soulanges et de Marson, Louise-Élisabeth de," in *DCB* 2: 301–2; or University of Toronto/Université Laval, 2003–, http://www.biographi.ca/en/bio/joybert_de_soulanges_et_de_marson_louise _elisabeth_de_2E.html, accessed May 8, 2015. On French Canadian childhood in ancien régime New France, see Peter N. Moogk, "*Les Petits Sauvages:* The Children of Eighteenth-Century New France," in *Histories of Canadian Children and Youth,* ed. Nancy Janovicek and Joy Parr (Toronto: Oxford University Press Canada, 2003), 36–56.

2. Natalie Zemon Davis, *Women on the Margins: Three Seventeenth-Century Lives* (Cambridge: Harvard University Press, 1995), 63–139. Wendat (Huron) and Iroquois were the most common Native students in Marie de l'Incarnation's lifetime (1599–1672), while Wabanaki students became more common only toward the end of the seventeenth century. This is perhaps due to the near-constant warfare between England (and New England) and France (and New France) from the 1680s to 1713 described in chap. 2.

3. Registre des Entrees et Sortie des Petites Filles Francaises et Sauvages de 1641, Pensionnat 1/E.3.4.1.1.1, tome 1, hereafter Pensionnat 1, Archives du Monastère des Ursulines de Québec, Québec, P.Q., hereafter AMUQ, entries for May 26 and July 27, 1683, and January 1 and 19, 1687/88; Les Annales des Ursulines de Québec, vol. 1, 1639–1822, 1/E, 12, 1, 0, 0, 1, hereafter Annales 1, 139, 147, AMUQ.

4. Marcel Trudel, "Champlain, Samuel de," in *Dictionary of Canadian Biography* 1, University of Toronto/Université Laval, 2003–, http://www.biographi.ca/en/bio/champlain _samuel_de_1E.html, accessed July 20, 2015. For information on tours of the archaeological dig of the Château Saint-Louis, see Parks Canada's "Saint-Louis Forts and Châteaux National Historic Site," http://www.pc.gc.ca/eng/lhn-nhs/qc/saintlouisforts/index.aspx, accessed July 20, 2015. On the nobility of New France and the durability of status hierarchies, see Louise Dechêne, *Habitants and Merchants in Seventeenth Century Montreal* (Montreal: McGill-Queen's University Press, 1992), 215–36; Peter N. Moogk, *La Nouvelle France: The Making of French Canada—A Cultural History* (East Lansing: Michigan State University Press, 2000), 143–91; Jan Noel, "Caste and Clientage in an Eighteenth-Century Quebec Convent," *Canadian Historical Review* 82, no. 3 (2001), 465–90; Jan Noel, *Along a River: The First*

French Canadian Women (Toronto: University of Toronto Press, 2013), chaps. 6–7; and Sophie White, "'A Baser Commerce': Retailing, Class, and Gender in French Colonial New Orleans," *William and Mary Quarterly* 63, no. 3 (2006), 517–50.

5. *Rapport de l'Archiviste de la Province de Québec pour 1921–1922* (Québec: Ls.-A. Proulx, 1921), hereafter *Rapport, 1921–1922*, 238–61.

6. Brett Rushforth, in *Bonds of Alliance: Indigenous & Atlantic Slaveries in New France* (Chapel Hill: University of North Carolina Press, 2012), notes the presence of two enslaved Fox women in the Château Saint-Louis in 1723, 197–98; Noel, *Along a River,* 159–62; 298–99 n47.

7. 1708 "Copie de la lettre de Peter Schuyler à Vaudreuil," Série C11A. Correspondance générale; Canada [document textuel (surtout des microformes)] (R11577-4-2-F), 231–32v on microfilm, 166–67 transcription, Library and Archives of Canada, Ottawa, and available online at http://collectionscanada.gc.ca/ourl/res.php?url_ver=Z39.88-2004&url_tim =2015-07-20T21%3A49%3A36Z&url_ctx_fmt=info%3Aofi%2Ffmt%3Akev%3Amtx %3Actx&rft_dat=3064210&rfr_id=info%3Asid%2Fcollectionscanada.gc.ca%3Apam &lang=eng. For information on the Jarret de Verchères family and the French attack of Haverhill, Massachusetts, in 1708, see Céline Dupré, "Jarret de Verchères, Pierre," in *Dictionary of Canadian Biography,* vol. 2, University of Toronto/Université Laval, 2003–, http://www.biographi.ca/en/bio/jarret_de_vercheres_pierre_2E.html, accessed July 20, 2015; and Raymond Douville, "Hertel de Rouville, Jean-Baptiste," in *Dictionary of Canadian Biography,* vol. 2, University of Toronto/Université Laval, 2003–, http://www.biographi.ca/en/bio/hertel_de_rouville_jean_baptiste_2E.html, accessed July 20, 2015.

8. Davis, *Women on the Margins,* 96; Sophie White, "'To Ensure That He Would Not Give Himself Over to the Indians': Cleanliness, Frenchification, and Whiteness," *Journal of Early American History* 2, no. 2 (2012): 116.

9. On European beliefs on the dangers of bathing in the early modern era, see Kathleen M. Brown, *Foul Bodies: Cleanliness in Early America* (New Haven: Yale University Press, 2009), chap. 1; Georges Vigarello, *Concepts of Cleanliness: Changing Attitudes in France since the Middle Ages,* trans. Jean Birrell (Cambridge: Cambridge University Press, 1988), 1–77.

10. Bernard Audet, *Le Costume Paysan dans la Region de Québec au XVIIe Siècle: Île d'Orléans* (Ottawa: Éditions Leméac, 1980), chaps. 4–5; Bernard Audet, *Avoir Feu et Lieu dans l'Isle d'Orléans au XVIIe Siècle* (Québec: Université Presse de Laval, 1990), 117–40; Pat Tomczyszyn, "*Le Costume Traditionnel*: A Study of Clothing and Textiles in the Town of Québec, 1635–1760," M.S. thesis, University of Manitoba, 1999; Pat Tomczyszyn, "Sifting Through the Papers of the Past: Using Archival Documents for Costume Research in Seventeenth- and Eighteenth-Century Québec," *Material History Review* 55 (2002): 4–15. Tomczyszyn argues that the evidence suggests that the Québécois fashion appears to have been identical to French fashion before the conquest.

11. W. J. Eccles in *The Canadian Frontier, 1534–1760* (New York: Holt, Reinhart, and Winston, 1969; rpt. Albuquerque: University of New Mexico Press, 1983), 95–96, suggests that French Canadians enjoyed superior nutrition compared with the vast majority of Europeans, eating half a pound of meat and two pounds of bread daily.

12. Peter Kalm, *Peter Kalm's Travels in North America,* ed. Adolph B. Benson (New York: Dover, 1966), 2: 473–75; *Rapport, 1921–1922,* 238–61. The meals at the Château Saint-Louis were doubtless richer and more varied than the seventeenth-century habitant table described by Audet in *Avoir Feu et Lieu,* 83–104. I am indebted to Trudy Eden for the term "food security" as she describes it in *The Early American Table: Food and Society in the New World* (DeKalb: Northern Illinois University Press, 2008).

13. Marcel Trudeau, *Les Écolières des Ursulines de Québec, 1639–1686: Amerindiennes et Canadiennes* (Québec: Éditions Hurtubise, 1999), 350; Pensionnat 1: 119, AMUQ.

14. Davis, *Women on the Margins,* 81–83, 94–99; *Glimpses of the Monastery: Scenes from the History of the Ursulines of Québec during two hundred years, 1639–1839,* 2nd ed. (Québec: L. J. Demers, 1897), 5–52; Trudel, *Les Écolières des Ursulines de Québec,* 42–43.

15. Trudel, *Les Écolières des Ursulines de Québec,* 58–60; Pensionnat 1, passim, AMUQ.

16. Trudel, *Les Écolières des Ursulines de Québec,* 58–61; Pensionnat 1, passim but especially the entries for 1691–1701, 1707–8, and 1713, AMUQ.

17. Annales 1: 147, 277; "Québec Actes des Assemblées Capitul de 1686 á 1802," 1/E4, 1 1.7, 275, AMUQ.

18. Julie Wheelwright notes the privilege the Ursulines extended to Esther in calling her by the name given to her by her natal family, whereas Native girls were called only by their baptismal first names, in *Esther: The Remarkable True Story of Esther Wheelwright: Puritan Child, Native Daughter, Mother Superior* (Toronto: HarperCollins, 2011), 97.

19. Roger Magnuson, *Education in New France* (Montreal: McGill-Queen's University Press, 1992), 148–52; Dechêne, *Habitants and Merchants,* 211–36; Moogk, *La Nouvelle France,* 160–70. In her third term as mother superior, Esther Wheelwright proposed reducing the fee for boarders to 220 livres in 1771. See Conclusions des Assemblées des Discrètes de 1687 à 1865, 1/E.2.3.1.1.O 1687–1865, hereafter Discrètes, 101 (April 18, 1771), AMUQ.

20. Pensionnat 1, passim, AMUQ; *Les Ursulines de Québec, Depuis leur Établissement Jusq'a Nos Jours* (Québec: C. Darveau, 1864), 2: 200–202. See also Diane Rapley, *A Social History of the Cloister: Daily Life in the Teaching Monasteries of the Old Regime* (Montreal: McGill-Queen's University Press, 2001), 219–56.

21. Discrètes, 50 (April 21, 1710).

22. On the Ursuline orchard, see Kalm, *Peter Kalm's Travels,* 2: 470–71.

23. *Les Ursulines de Québec,* 2: 203–4. See for comparison the list of "the better part of the students found at the pensionnat from 1700 to 1739," 2: 171–76, which lists 357 students enrolled in those forty years. On the value of nutrition in disease resistance, see David S. Jones, "Virgin Soils Revisited," *William and Mary Quarterly,* 3rd. ser., 60, no. 4 (2003): 703–39. By comparison, see the high death rates reported by Carolyn C. Lougee in "'Its Frequent Visitor': Death at Boarding School in Early Modern Europe," in *Women's Education in Early Modern Europe: A History, 1500–1800,* ed. Barbara J. Whitehead, 193–224 (New York: Garland, 1999).

24. Magnuson, *Education in New France,* 76 and passim; Whitehead, *Women's Education in Early Modern Europe;* Noel, *Along a River,* 68–75.

25. Gordon Williams, *A Dictionary of Sexual Language and Imagery in Shakespearean and Stuart Literature* (London: Athlone, 1994), 2: 716. E. Jennifer Monaghan makes the point in *Learning to Read and Write in Colonial America* (Amherst: University of Massachusetts Press, 2005) that reading instruction was thought to be something that any reader could do, whereas writing instruction was considered a craft that required special skills and the use of expensive writing manuals, paper, and ink. She also notes that writing instructors commanded a higher tuition than reading teachers, 367–68.

26. Monaghan, *Learning to Read and Write in Colonial America*, 40–44; 343–44; 363–78; Caroline Winterer, *The Mirror of Antiquity: American Women and the Classical Tradition, 1750–1900* (Ithaca, N.Y.: Cornell University Press, 2007), 12–26; Whitehead, *Women's Education in Early Modern Europe*, passim; Magnuson, *Education in New France*, passim; Davis, *Women on the Margins*, 76–77.

Magnuson notes that at least one eighteenth-century elite Montreal woman, Marie-Élisabeth Bégon, knew Latin and taught it to her daughter (84). See also Céline Dupré, "Rocbert de la Morandière, Marie-Élisabeth," in *DCB* 3: 563–65, University of Toronto/Université Laval, 2003–, http://www.biographi.ca/en/bio/rocbert_de_la_morandiere_marie_elisabeth_3E.html, accessed August 25, 2014. See also Diane Rapley, *The Dévotes: Women and Church in Seventeenth-Century France* (Montreal: McGill-Queen's University Press, 1990), 142–54. Some French *religieuses* and their students were taught Latin, according to *Les Réligieux et Leurs Livres à l'Époque Moderne,* ed. Bernard Dompnier and Marie-Hélène Froeschlé-Chopard (Clermont-Ferand, France: Presses universitaires Blaise-Pascal, 2000), passim; and Heidi Keller-Lapp, "Floating Cloisters and *Femmes Fortes*: Ursuline Missionaries in Ancien Régime France and Its Colonies," Ph.D. diss., University of California-San Diego, 2005, 40–44, 362–65.

27. John Adams to Abigail Adams, April 15, 1776; John Adams to Abigail Adams Jr., April 18, 1776, both in *Adams Family Correspondence*, ed. L. H. Butterfield (Cambridge: Belknap Press of Harvard University Press, 1963), 1: 383–84; 387–88. Cheever's Latin primer was published originally in Boston in 1709 and remained in print through the eighteenth century. See Ezekiel Cheever, *A short introduction to the Latin tongue, for the use of the lower forms in the Latin School. Being the accidence* (Boston, 1709). See also Winterer's *The Mirror of Antiquity*, which details Abigail Adams's frustrations at having to supervise the teaching of Latin to their daughter and sons, and of Greek to their sons only, when she herself knew neither language, 20–21.

28. Trudel, *Les Écolières des Ursulines de Québec,* 40–43, 52, 54–55, 71–72, 78–81; Kalm, *Peter Kalm's Travels*, 2: 471. In *The Dévotes*, Rapley says that seventeenth-century French convent schools taught reading with Latin words to their primary students, and French only to more advanced students; she also says that arithmetic was considered a fairly minor subject (154–65; quotation on deportment 157–58). See also Rapley, *A Social History of the Cloister*, 219–33.

29. Registre des Entrées, Vetures et Professions des Religieuses Ursulines de Québec, 1647–1783, hereafter Entrées et Décès, 1/G7.1.1.1, Entry for Esther Anglaise/Wheelwright, AMUQ. They also record her age incorrectly as fifteen and a half; in 1712 she was sixteen and a half (b. March 31, 1696). Cf. William Foster's analysis of the surname "Anglais" in *The*

Captor's Narrative: Catholic Women and Their Puritan Men on the Early American Frontier (Ithaca, N.Y.: Cornell University Press, 2003), 101. Foster argues that use of the name for Anglo-American captive men working in Canadian convents suggests a stripping of identity akin to the social death inherent to enslavement.

30. Susan Sleeper-Smith, *Indian Women and French Men: Rethinking Cultural Encounter in the Western Great Lakes* (Amherst: University of Massachusetts Press, 2001). Emily Clark has explored the politics of the color line in New Orleans in *Masterless Mistresses: The New Orleans Ursulines and the Development of a New World Society, 1727–1834* (Chapel Hill: University of North Carolina Press, 2007), finding that the Ursulines in some ways challenged the color line in Louisiana, and in other ways supported it.

31. Esther Williams to Stephen Williams, February 28, 1710, Gratz Collection, case 8, box 28, Historical Society of Pennsylvania, Philadelphia.

32. John Demos, *The Unredeemed Captive: A Family Story from Early America* (New York: Knopf, 1994), 92; Wheelwright, *Esther,* 111–13, 183–86. See also C. Alice Baker, *True Stories of New England Captives Carried to Canada During the Old French and Indian Wars* (Greenfield, Mass.: E. A. Hall, 1897; rpt. Bowie, Md.: Heritage, 1990), 360–64, for more on the redemption of John Arms.

33. Cf. Alice Nash, "'None of the Women Were Abused': Indigenous Contexts for the Treatment of Women Captives in the Northeast," in *Sex Without Consent: Rape and Sexual Coercion in America,* ed. Merril D. Smith, 10–26 (New York: New York University Press, 2001). However, Nash agrees that European girls and women were more likely to be adopted as sisters or daughters by Wabanaki captors, and therefore sexually unavailable to their Wabanaki kin.

34. Joan Jacobs Brumberg, in *The Body Project: An Intimate History of American Girls* (New York: Vintage Books, 1997), argues that the average age at menarche has dropped nearly four full years in the past two centuries, from fifteen or sixteen around the turn of the nineteenth century, down to age twelve today (3–5).

35. Mita Choudhury, *Convents and Nuns in Eighteenth-Century French Political Culture* (Ithaca, N.Y.: Cornell University Press, 2004); Ana M. Acosta, "Hotbeds of Popery: Convents in the English Literary Imagination," *Eighteenth-Century Fiction* 15, nos. 3–4 (2003): 615–42; Ann M. Little, "Cloistered Bodies: Convents in the Anglo-American Imagination in the British Conquest of Canada," *Eighteenth Century Studies* 39, no. 2 (2006): 187–200.

36. See, for example, "1710 list of English prisoners in Canada," SC1 45X Massachusetts Archives Collection, hereafter Mass. Arch., 71: 465, Massachusetts State Archives, Boston. See also Vaudreuil to Joseph Dudley, June 16, 1711, 94–96v; William Dudley and Francis Nicholson to Vaudreuil, November 3, 1713, 266–67; and Vaudreuil to the minister, April 14, 1714, 263–65v; microfilm MG1-C11A, Library and Archives Canada, Ottawa.

37. Emma Lewis Coleman, *New England Captives Carried to Canada Between 1677 and 1760 During the French and Indian Wars* (Portland, Me.: Southworth Press, 1925; rpt. Bowie, Md.: Heritage, 1989), 1: 69–129, esp. 121–22.

38. Discrètes, 54–55, AMUQ.

39. In Entrées et Décès, Esther is listed as beginning her novitiate on October 2, 1712, at the age of fifteen, not sixteen, her actual age. Additionally, her entry in the Annales says that she was taken at age six instead of seven by the Norridgewock Wabanaki, information she presumably provided to them, so perhaps she herself was confused about her actual age, Annales 1: 147, AMUQ.

40. *Jesuit Relations,* 65: 90–93.

41. Discrètes, 55; Entrées et Décès, passim, AMUQ.

42. Livres ou Registres des Entrees des Rses Divise en Trois Parties, 1689–1778, 1/G 1.1.1.6, hereafter Livres, 70, AMUQ.

43. Annales 1: 151, 216, AMUQ.

44. Livres, 60–61, 93, AMUQ; Coleman, *New England Captives Carried to Canada,* 1: 268–69. Jordan and Davis each had a dowry that was commensurate to that of their choir nun peers. See Entrées et Décès, passim, AMUQ. In *A Social History of the Cloister,* Rapley notes that choir nuns often did the work of converse sisters if their skills and inclinations were more aligned with domestic labor (194–95).

45. Entrées et Décès, entry for "Marie Anne Dubo," November 4, 1703; Livres, 64, both at AMUQ; *Les Ursulines de Québec,* 2: 24–26, 234.

46. André Vachon, "Dubok," in *Dictionary of Canadian Biography* 1, University of Toronto/ Université Laval, 2003–, http://www.biographi.ca/en/bio/dubok_1E.html, accessed August 23, 2015; Livres, 64 AMUQ. On the importance of Native women to the fur trade, see Sylvia Van Kirk, *Many Tender Ties: Women in Fur Trade Society, 1670–1870* (Winnipeg, Man.: Watson and Dwyer, 1980; Norman: University of Oklahoma Press, 1983); Jo-Anne Fiske, Susan Sleeper-Smith, and William Wicken, eds., *New Faces of the Fur Trade: Selected Papers of the Seventh North American Fur Trade Conference, Halifax, Nova Scotia* (East Lansing: Michigan State University Press, 1998); Sleeper-Smith, *Indian Women and French Men.*

47. Cyprien Tanguay, *Dictionnaire Généalogique des Familles Canadiennes, premiere volume, depuis 1608 jusqu'à 1700* (Québec: Eusébe Senécal, 1871), 1: 202; *Jesuit Relations,* 47: 287; 55: 287–311; "Baptêmes, 1667–1679," Paroisse Notre-Dame de Québec, Marie Angelique Rabouin, September 28, 1677, Québec, P.Q. I'm indebted to researcher Tim Simmons for alerting me to this baptismal record.

48. Marcel Trudeau reports that there was a student in the Ursuline boarding school in 1650 who briefly became an Augustinian hospital nun in 1657 at the Hôtel-Dieu in Québec by the name of Geneviève-Agnès Skanudharoua, whom he calls "'the first of the Hurons to become a Christian woman," and, however briefly, the first Native nun in Canada in *Les Écolières des Ursulines de Québec,* 62, 146–47. Trudel reports that she died on November 3, 1657, two days after her clothing ceremony.

49. Sophie White, *Wild Frenchmen and Frenchified Indians: Material Culture and Race in Colonial Louisiana* (Philadelphia: University of Pennsylvania Press, 2012), chap. 4; quotations from 152, 174.

4. Sister Marie-Joseph de l'Enfant Jésus

1. The description of this clothing ceremony is taken from John England, *Substance of a Discourse . . . on the Occasion of Giving the Habit of the Ursuline Order to a Young Lady, May 19, 1835* (Charleston, S.C.: Dan. J. Dowling, 1835), 37–49. Although published more than a century after Esther's *vêture*, it was probably quite similar to the clothing ceremonies of Ursulines in Québec in the eighteenth century. See also the condescending and rabidly anti-Catholic "Account of the Ceremony of a Nun's taking the Veil," *The Moral and Entertaining Magazine* (London, June 1, 1778), 357–59; and Nancy Bradley Warren's "The Ritual for the Ordination of Nuns," describing a somewhat less elaborate late medieval Benedictine ceremony, in *Medieval Christianity in Practice*, ed. Miri Rubin, 318–23 (Princeton: Princeton University Press, 2009). The central importance of the grate, the veil, and the role of the superior (or abbess) is evident in all the ceremonies described in these sources.

2. Les Annales des Ursulines de Quebec, vol. 1, 1639–1822, hereafter Annales 1, 1/E, 12, 1, 0, 0, 1, 147, AMUQ.

3. Vaudreuil to Joseph Dudley, June 16, 1711, 94–96v, microfilm MG1-C11A, Library and Archives Canada, Ottawa, hereafter LAC. Citations to this letter and the letters in LAC in the following two notes are also available digitally at http://www.collectionscanada.gc.ca/, and are copies from the Centre des archives d'outre-mer (Aix-en-Provence, France), C11A series, vols. 32–34.

4. See Vaudreuil to Joseph Dudley, June 16, 1711, 94–96v; Joseph Dudley and Francis Nicholson to Vaudreuil, November 3, 1713, 266–67; Vaudreuil to the minister, April 14, 1714, 263–65v; microfilm MG1-C11A, LAC.

5. Vaudreuil, October 1, 1709, in *Collection de Manuscrits Relatifs a l'Histoire de la Nouvelle France* (Québec: A. Coté et Cie, 1884), 2: 506; Summary of a letter from Mme. de Vaudreuil, 1709, in *Rapport de l'Archiviste de la Province de Québec pour 1942–43* (Québec: Ls-A. Proulx, 1943), 416–17; Vaudreuil and Intendant Michel Bégon de la Picardière to the minister, November 12, 1712, 15–37; Vaudreuil to the minister, April 14, 1714, 263–65v; microfilm MG1-C11A, LAC.

6. I am indebted to Sophie White on this point.

7. "A Journall of the Travails of Major John Livingstone," *Calendar of State Papers, Colonial Series, America and West Indies, 1710–June 1711* (London, 1924), hereafter *CSP, 1710–11*, 371–86; quotations from 380–81.

8. *CSP, 1710–11*, 380–81; on Johnson Harmon, see Emma Lewis Coleman, *New England Captives Carried to Canada Between 1677 and 1760 During the French and Indian Wars* (Portland, Me.: Southworth, 1925; rpt. Bowie, Md.: Heritage, 1990), 1: 247–50.

9. *Rapport de l'Archiviste de la Province de Québec pour 1946–47* (Québec: Ls-A. Proulx, 1947), 446.

10. *Rapport de l'Archiviste de la Province de Québec pour 1947–48* (Québec: Ls-A. Proulx, 1948), 145–46, 185; Summary of a letter from Vaudreuil, August 1714, 115–16, microfilm MG1-C11A, LAC; C. Alice Baker, *True Stories of New England Captives Carried to Canada During the Old French and Indian Wars* (Greenfield, Mass.: E. A. Hall, 1897; rpt. Bowie, Md.: Heritage, 1990),

321–29; Hélène Bernier, "Silver, Mary," in *Dictionary of Canadian Biography* (Toronto: University of Toronto/Université Laval, 1966), hereafter *DCB*, 2: 606–7; or University of Toronto/Université Laval, 2003–, http://www.biographi.ca/en/bio/silver_mary_2E.html, accessed August 21, 2014.

11. See chapter 5, page 184–86.

12. Quotation from *Glimpses of the Monastery: Scenes from the History of the Ursulines of Quebec during two hundred years, 1639–1839*, 2nd ed. (Québec: L. J. Demers, 1897), 172–73. See also Alfred Hawkins, *The Quebec Guide: Comprising an historical and descriptive account of the city and every place of note in the vicinity* (Québec: W. Cowan, 1844), 14; Hubert Charbonneau, Bertrand Desjardins, André Guillaumette, Yves Landry, Jacques Légaré, and François Nault, *The First French Canadians: Pioneers in the St. Lawrence Valley* (Cranbury, N.J.: Associated University Presses, 1993), 171–78. Although the exact disease that spread in this epidemic remains unclear, its appearance in 1711 is unsurprising, given the ways in which both malnutrition and warfare mobilize disease and exacerbate its effects. See, for example, Elizabeth Fenn, *Pox Americana: The Great Smallpox Epidemic of 1775–82* (New York: Hill and Wang, 2001); David S. Jones, "Virgin Soils Revisited," *William and Mary Quarterly*, 3rd. ser., 60, no. 4 (2003): 703–39.

13. Annales 1: 142–44, AMUQ.

14. *Collection de Manuscrits* 2: 536–50; *Calendar of State Papers, Colonial Series, America and West Indies, July 1711–June 1712* (London, 1925), passim; Francis Parkman, *A Half-Century of Conflict: France and England in North America* (Boston: Little, Brown, 1922), 1: 162–82; Evan Haefeli and Kevin Sweeney, *Captors and Captives: The 1704 French and Indian Raid on Deerfield* (Amherst: University of Massachusetts Press, 2004), 196–207. In 1707, the Acts of Union between Scotland and England created Great Britain, so henceforth I'll refer to military and imperial affairs directed from London as British rather than English.

15. Hubert Charbonneau and Jacques Légaré, *Répertoire des actes de baptême mariage et sépulture et des recensements du Québec ancien* (Montreal: Les Presses de l'Université de Montréal, 1982), 13: 93. Current and former Anglo-American captives regularly witnessed the baptism of one another's children, according to Barbara E. Austen, "Captured . . . Never Came Back: Social Networks Among New England Female Captives in Canada, 1689–1763," and Alice N. Nash, "Two Stories of New England Captives: Grizel and Christine Otis of Dover, New Hampshire," both in *New England/New France, 1600–1850*, ed. Peter Benes, 28–38, 39–48, respectively (Boston: Boston University Press, 1992).

16. Baker, *True Stories of New England Captives*, 206–22, 320–21; Haefeli and Sweeney, *Captors and Captives*, 106–9; 240–42; Cyprien Tanguay, *Dictionnaire Généalogique des Familles Canadiennes* (Québec: Eusèbe Senécal, 1887), 3: 347; Céline Dupré, "Le Moyne de Longueuil, Charles, Baron de Longueuil (d. 1729)," in *DCB* 2: 401–3; or University of Toronto/Université Laval, 2003–, http://www.biographi.ca/en/bio/le_moyne_de_longueuil_charles_1729_2E.html, accessed September 17, 2013.

17. Erin L. Jordan, "Gender Concerns: Monks, Nuns, and Patronage of the Cistercian Order in Thirteenth Century Flanders and Hainault," *Speculum* 87 (2012): 62–94.

18. Registre des Entrées, Vetures et Professions des Religieuses Ursulines de Québec,

1647–1783, 1/G7.1.1.1, hereafter Entrées et Décès, passim, AMUQ; Diane Rapley, *A Social History of the Cloister: Daily Life in the Teaching Orders of the Old Regime* (Montreal: McGill-Queen's University Press, 2001), 167–73; "boot camp," 169.

19. Abigail Adams Smith, *Journal and Correspondence of Miss Adams* (New York: Wiley and Putnam, 1841), 23–24, 27. On Martha Jefferson Randolph's time at the Abbaye Royale de Penthemont, see Cynthia A. Kierner, *Martha Jefferson Randolph, Daughter of Monticello: Her Life and Times* (Chapel Hill: University of North Carolina Press, 2012), chap. 2, esp. 51–59.

20. England, *Substance of a Discourse*, 37–38; Christine Turgeon, *Le Musée des Ursulines de Québec: Art, Faith, and Culture* (Québec: Le Monastère des Ursulines de Québec, 2004), 14–15, 26–28, 36–41.

21. *Les Ursulines de Québec, Depuis leur Établissement Jusq'a Nos Jours* (Québec: C. Darveau, 1864), 2: 80–87, 200–202; quotations from 80–81. See also Gerald M. Kelly, "Thy Hand Shall Lead Me: The Story of Esther Wheelwright," unpublished manuscript in the Gerald M. Kelly Research Materials, carton 4, Massachusetts Historical Society, Boston. Kelly's filiopietistic biography follows Bigot's analysis of Esther Wheelwright's life entirely, emphasizing her English roots as opposed to her life among the Wabanaki, and crediting Providence for her conversion and deliverance.

22. *Les Ursulines de Quebéc*, 2: 82–83.

23. Ibid., 2: 83.

24. Ibid.

25. England, *Substance of a Discourse*, 39.

26. Ibid., 39–42; *Journal and Correspondence of Miss Adams*, 24. For a detailed description and video depiction of dressing in the Ursuline habit with the robe, cincture, rosary, cap, band, wimple, and veil, see http://www.ipir.ulaval.ca/fiche.php?id=282, and click on "L'habit religieux des Ursulines de Québec" on the right side under "Vidéos"; accessed August 23, 2015.

27. England, *Substance of a Discourse*, 44.

28. Ibid., 44–48; *Journal and Correspondence of Miss Adams*, 25–26.

29. England, *Substance of a Discourse*, 45–49.

30. Entrées et Décès, passim, AMUQ.

31. See Diane Rapley, *The Dévotes: Women and Church in Seventeenth-Century France* (Montreal: McGill-Queen's University Press, 1990), on the development of the teaching apostolate and the ways in which teaching orders both upheld and challenged status and gender hierarchies. See also Rapley, *A Social History of the Cloister*, passim.

32. Jan Noel, "Besieged but Connected: Survival Strategies at a Quebec Convent," *Historical Studies: Canadian Catholic Historical Association* 67 (2001): 27–41; Jan Noel, "Caste and Clientage in an Eighteenth Century Québec Convent," *Canadian Historical Review* 82 (2001): 465–90; Colleen Gray, *The Congrégation de Notre-Dame, Superiors, and the Paradox of Power, 1693–1796* (Montreal: McGill-Queen's University Press, 2007); Jan Noel, *Along a River: The First French Canadian Women* (Toronto: University of Toronto Press, 2013), chap. 7.

33. Noel, *Along a River*, chaps. 6–7; *Glimpses of the Monastery*, 165–66; Livres ou Registres des

Entrées des R[eligieu]ses Divise en Trois Parties, 1689–1778, 1/G 1.1.1.6, hereafter Livres, passim, AMUQ.

34. Boucher's Ursuline granddaughters were Anne Marguerite Gaultier de Varenne (Mother of the Presentation, 1684–1726), by a daughter of his first wife as well as the daughter of René Gaultier de Varenne, himself a governor of Trois Rivières; Marie Anne de Boucherville (Mother St. Ignace, 1694–1772), his granddaughter by his son Pierre and Charlotte Denys; and Charlotte Daneau DeMuy (Mother St. Helen, 1695–1759), by his daughter Marguerite and Nicolas Daneau DuMuy, who was nominated as the governor of Louisiana but never took the post. See Livres, 57–58, AMUQ; Raymond Douville, "Boucher, Pierre," in *DCB* 2: 82–87; or University of Toronto/Université Laval, 2003–, http://www.biographi .ca/en/bio/boucher_pierre_2E.html, accessed September 12, 2013; Albert Tessier, "Gaultier de Varennes, René," in *DCB*, 1: 326–27; or University of Toronto/Université Laval, 2003–, http://www.biographi.ca/en/bio/gaultier_de_varennes_rene_1E.html, accessed September 12, 2013; in collaboration, "Boucher de Boucherville, Pierre," in *DCB* 3: 80–81; or University of Toronto/Université Laval, 2003–, http://www.biographi.ca/en/bio/boucher _de_boucherville_pierre_3E.html, accessed September 13, 2013; Gabrielle Lapointe, "Daneau de Muy, Charlotte, de Sainte-Hélène," in *DCB* 3: 161; or University of Toronto/ Université Laval, 2003–, http://www.biographi.ca/en/bio/daneau_de_muy_charlotte_3E .html, accessed September 13, 2013; George F. G. Stanley, "Daneau de Muy, Nicolas," in *DCB* 2: 168–69; or University of Toronto/Université Laval, 2003–, http://www.biographi .ca/en/bio/daneau_de_muy_nicolas_2E.html, accessed September 13, 2013.

35. Livres 57 AMUQ; Raymond Douville, "Hertel de la Fresnière, Joseph-François," in *DCB* 2: 282–84; or University of Toronto/Université Laval, 2003–, http://www.bio graphi.ca/en/bio/hertel_de_la_fresniere_joseph_francois_2E.html, accessed September 12, 2013; Robert La Roque de Roquebrune, "Thavenet, Marguerite de," in *DCB* 2: 628–29; or University of Toronto/Université Laval, 2003–, http://www.biographi.ca/en/bio/thavenet _marguerite_de_2E.html, accessed September 12, 2013; Leslie Tuttle, *Conceiving the Old Regime: Pronatalism and the Politics of Reproduction in Early Modern France* (New York: Oxford University Press, 2010), 96–104; Noel, *Along a River*, 75–83. On the *filles du roi*, see Yves Landry, *Orphelines en France, pionnières au Canada: Les Filles du Roi au XVIIe Siècle* (Montreal: Leméac, 1992; Québec: Bibliothèque Québécoise, 2013).

36. Livres, 122–23, AMUQ; C. J. Russ, "Adhémar de Lantagnac, Gaspard," in *DCB* 3: 5; or University of Toronto/Université Laval, 2003–, http://www.biographi.ca/en/bio /adhemar_de_lantagnac_gaspard_3E.html, accessed September 15, 2013.

37. Noel, *Along a River*, 185–92; *Glimpses of the Monastery*, 297–300; *Les Ursulines de Québec*, 2: 19–24, 272–73; Jean-Jacques Lefebvre, "Migeon de Branssat, Jean-Baptiste," in *DCB* 1: 508; or University of Toronto/Université Laval, 2003–, http://www.biographi.ca/en/bio /migeon_de_branssat_jean_baptiste_1E.html, accessed September 12, 2013.

38. Rapley, *A Social History of the Cloister*, 118–22; Livres, passim, AMUQ.

39. Jean-Guy Pelletier, "Renaud d'Avène de Desmeloizes, François-Marie," in *DCB* 1: 572–73; or University of Toronto/Université Laval, 2003–, http://www.biographi.ca/en

/bio/renaud_d_avene_de_desmeloizes_francois_marie, accessed September 16, 2013; Lucien Campeau, "Dupont de Neuville, Nicolas," in *DCB* 2: 204–5; or University of Toronto/ Université Laval, 2003–, http://www.biographi.ca/en/bio/dupont_de_neuville_nicolas_2E .html, accessed September 16, 2013.

40. Livres, 90–91, AMUQ; Tanguay, *Dictionnaire Généalogique,* 1: 514; *Les Ursulines de Québec,* 2: 217–21. See also the note at the back of the volume on the des Méloizes family, iv–vi.

41. *Rules and Constitutions for the Ursuline Religious, of the Presentation of Our Blessed Lady with Instructions on the Same* (New Orleans: T. Fitzwilliam, 1885), chap. 8, "On the Reception and Training of Novices," 163–72; Annales 1: 147, AMUQ.

42. Examens des Novices de 1689 à 1807, 1/G, 1, 3, 0, 0, 0, 37–38, AMUQ.

43. The specific vows of the Québec Ursulines were for "Pauvreté, chasteté, obediance; et de m'emploier a L'instruction des Petites filles françoises et Sauvages, Selon La Reigle"; Livres, 70, 93–100, AMUQ. Sophie White also dates French disillusionment with their ability to Frenchify Natives to about this period in the Illinois country as well; Sophie White, "'To Ensure That He Would Not Give Himself Over to the Indians': Cleanliness, Frenchification, and Whiteness," *Journal of Early American History* 2, no. 2 (2012): 116.

44. Noel, *Along a River,* 146–204; *Glimpses of the Monastery,* 190–98; Entrées et Décès, passim, AMUQ.

45. Marcel Trudel, *Les Écolières des Ursulines de Québec, 1639–1686: Amerindiennes et Canadiennes* (Montreal: Éditions Hurtubise, 1999), 40–41; *Glimpses of the Monastery* and *Les Ursulines de Québec,* passim; Rapley, *A Social History of the Cloister,* 167–68.

46. Christine Turgeon, "Jeanne Leber, Recluse and Embroideress (1662–1714)," *Journal of Canadian Art History* 25 (2004): 6–47; Turgeon, *Le Musée des Ursulines de Québec,* 14–15, 26–28, 36–41.

47. See Marius Barbeau's comprehensive review of the artistic skills and creations of early Canadian nuns, in which the Ursulines play a starring role, in *Saintes Artisanes,* 1, *Les Brodeuses* (Montreal: Fides, 1944), and *Saintes Artisanes,* 2, *Milles Pétites Addresses* (Montreal: Fides, 1946).

48. *Glimpses of the Monastery,* 101–2.

49. Pierre de Charlevoix, *Journal of a Voyage to North-America* (London, 1761; Readex Microprint, 1966), 1: 106 (letter 3). On the fires of 1650 and 1686 and efforts to reconstruct the convent, see *Glimpses of the Monastery,* 52–77, 122–35. On the expansion of the 1710s, see 185–88.

50. *Glimpses of the Monastery,* 187–88; *Reminiscences of Fifty Years in the Cloister, 1839–1889* (Quebec: L. J. Demers, 1897), 26; *Les Ursulines de Québec,* 2: 160.

51. Charlevoix, *Journal of a Voyage,* 1: 106 (letter 3); Peter Kalm, *Travels in North America by Peter Kalm,* ed. Adolph Benson (New York: Dover, 1967), 2: 470–71.

52. *An Historical Journal of the Campaigns in North America for the years 1757, 1758, 1759, and 1760, by Captain John Knox,* ed. Arthur G. Doughty, 3 vols. (Toronto: Champlain Society, 1914–16), hereafter *Knox's Journal,* 2: 205, 223–24, 240.

53. *Knox's Journal,* 2: 292. Scotsmen were predominant among the conquering officers, which may explain the gift of a St. Andrew's cross in particular. For other descriptions of

the Ursuline chapel, see, for example, Nathaniel Wheelwright diary, 1753–54, January 26, 1754, Massachusetts Historical Society, Boston.

54. See *Glimpses of the Monastery*, 279–80, which lists the forty-five sisters living in the convent in 1759 upon the British Conquest (thirteen lay sisters and thirty-two choir nuns), and *Les Ursulines de Québec*, 171–76, which lists the hundreds of boarding students in residence between 1700 and 1739. At any given time in the eighteenth century, the convent might house sixty to eighty individuals, in addition to the day students.

55. Most of this discussion and what follows is derived from Rapley, *A Social History of the Cloister*, 182–97.

56. Rapley, *A Social History of the Cloister*, 193–94; Trudel, *Les Écolières des Ursulines de Québec*, passim; *Les Ursulines de Québec*, 2: 171–76; *Glimpses of the Monastery*, 279–80; Registre des Entrées et Sortie des Petites Filles Françaises et Sauvages, 2: Livre des Entrées et Sorties des Pensionnaires 1719 à 1839, 1/E.3.4.1.1.1, hereafter Pensionnat 2, passim, AMUQ.

57. Rapley, *A Social History of the Cloister*, 184–86; see also the discussions of *soeurs converses* in North American convents in Emily Clark, *Masterless Mistresses: The New Orleans Ursulines and the Development of a New World Society, 1727–1834* (Chapel Hill: University of North Carolina Press, 2007), 68–72; and Sophie White, *Wild Frenchmen and Frenchified Indians: Material Culture and Race in Colonial Louisiana* (Philadelphia: University of Pennsylvania Press, 2012), 149–75. On the titles of Sister and Mother, see *Reminiscences of Fifty Years in the Cloister*, 183.

58. Diane Rapley writes perceptively of the tension between obedience to superiors and confessors and obedience to a monastic ideal that valorized excessive ascetic or penitential practices in "Her Body the Enemy: Self-Mortification in Seventeenth-Century Convents," *Proceedings of the Western Society for French History* 21 (1994): 25–35; and in *A Social History of the Cloister*: 141–47.

59. Natalie Zemon Davis, *Women on the Margins: Three Seventeenth-Century Lives* (Cambridge: Harvard University Press, 1995), 69–70.

60. Livres, passim, AMUQ.

61. *Glimpses of the Monastery*, 193–95, 233.

62. *Glimpses of the Monastery*, 338; *Reminiscences of Fifty Years in the Cloister*, 145.

63. Livres, 17, AMUQ; *Glimpses of the Monastery*, 168–69.

64. Livres, 45, AMUQ.

65. Ibid., 33. On Pope Francis's foot washing, see http://abcnews.go.com/International/pope-francis-wash-feet-inmates-holy-thursday/story?id=30065575, accessed August 17, 2015.

66. Livres, 54, AMUQ. Even accounting for weekly and seasonal fast days, the Ursuline diet was varied and nutrient dense, with meat-enriched soups and/or fish plus something else served alongside, depending on the season and availability—salads, vegetables, fruit (raw or cooked), or milk. See Trudel, *Les Écolières des Ursulines de Québec*, 42.

67. Livres, 63, AMUQ.

68. Livres, 74, AMUQ. Cf. *Les Ursulines de Québec*, 2: 349, which renders this as "comme un avare cache son tresor": as a miser hides his treasure.

69. Clark, *Masterless Mistresses*, 104; Gray, *The Congrégation de Notre-Dame*, chap. 6; Allan

Greer, *Mohawk Saint: Catherine Tekakwitha and the Jesuits* (New York: Oxford University Press, 2005), chap. 6. See also Allan Greer, *The Jesuit Relations: Natives and Missionaries in Seventeenth Century North America* (Boston: Bedford/St. Martin's, 2000), 146–54.

70. *Glimpses of the Monastery,* 193–95; Livres, 90–91, AMUQ.

71. Rapley, *A Social History of the Cloister,* 13–48; Mita Choudhury, *Convents and Nuns in Eighteenth-Century French Politics and Culture* (Ithaca, N.Y.: Cornell University Press, 2004).

72. Caroline Walker Bynum, *Holy Feast, Holy Fast: The Religious Significance of Food to Medieval Women* (Berkeley: University of California Press, 1987).

73. K. L. Suyemoto and M. L. MacDonald, "Self-Cutting in Female Adolescents," *Psychotherapy: Theory, Research, Practice, Training* 32, no. 1 (1995): 162–71; J. Haines, C. L. Williams, K. L. Brain, and G. V. Wilson, "The Psychophysiology of Self-Mutilation," *Journal of Abnormal Psychology* 104, no. 3 (1995): 471–89; A. Derouin and T. Bravender, "Living on the Edge: Self-Mutilation in Adolescents," *MCN: The American Journal of Maternal Child Nursing* 29, no. 1 (2004): 12–18; Aglaja Stirn and Andreas Hinz, "Tattoos, Body Piercings, and Self-Injury: Is There a Connection? Investigations on a Core Group of Participants Practicing Body Modification," *Psychotherapy Research: Journal for the Society of Psychotherapy Research* 18, no. 3 (2008): 326–33.

74. Ramón Gutiérrez, *When Jesus Came, the Corn Mothers Went Away: Marriage, Sexuality, and Power in New Mexico, 1500–1846* (Stanford: Stanford University Press, 1991), 66–71, 127–37; Greer, *Mohawk Saint,* chap. 5; Greer, *The Jesuit Relations,* 155–71.

75. On the lack of strict claustration, see, for example, Leslie Choquette, "'Ces Amazones du Grand Dieu': Women and Mission in Seventeenth-Century Canada," *French Historical Studies* 17 (1992): 627–55; Patricia Simpson, *Marguerite Bourgeoys and Montreal, 1640–1665* (Montreal: McGill-Queen's University Press, 1997); and Ann M. Little, "Cloistered Bodies: Convents in the Anglo-American Imagination in the British Conquest of Canada," *Eighteenth Century Studies* 39, no. 2 (2006): 187–200.

76. On the politics of Canadian martyrology, see Emma Anderson, *The Death and Afterlife of the North American Martyrs* (Cambridge: Harvard University Press, 2013).

77. Suyemoto and MacDonald, "Self-Cutting in Female Adolescents," and Haines et al., "The Psychophysiology of Self-Mutilation."

78. Caroline Walker Bynum has written about the importance of Christ's blood and wounds and blood relics in late medieval theology in "The Blood of Christ in the Later Middle Ages," *Church History* 71, no. 4 (2002): 685–714; and in "Violent Imagery in Late Medieval Piety," *German Historical Institute Bulletin* 30 (2002): 3–36. Jon F. Sensbach has written about the "blood and wounds" theology of eighteenth-century Moravians in the New World in *Rebecca's Revival: Creating Black Christianity in the Atlantic World* (Cambridge: Harvard University Press, 2005), 179–83.

5. Mother Esther

1. Les Annales des Ursulines de Quebec, vol. 1, 1639–1822, 1/E, 12, 1, 0, 0, 1, hereafter Annales 1, 147, AMUQ, records Nathaniel's visit on January 14, but Nathaniel's own jour-

nal reports that the visit happened on January 26, suggesting that the nuns had not yet switched their dating from the Julian to the Gregorian calendar along with most people in New France and colonial America in 1752.

2. Nathaniel Wheelwright diary, 1753–54, ms. S-734 or P-363, reel 11.13 (microfilm), hereafter Wheelwright diary, Massachusetts Historical Society, Boston, January 26, 1754. See also Julie Wheelwright, *Esther: The Remarkable True Story of Esther Wheelwright: Puritan Child, Native Daughter, Mother Superior* (Toronto: HarperCollins, 2011), 187–92, although she incorrectly reports that Mother Esther met with Nathaniel once in 1752 and once in 1754, when both meetings reported in his diary were in 1754.

3. Fred Anderson, *Crucible of War: The Seven Years' War and the Fate of Empire in British North America, 1754–1766* (New York: Knopf, 2000), 24, 112; Geoffrey Plank, *An Unsettled Conquest: The British Campaign Against the Peoples of Acadia* (Philadelphia: University of Pennsylvania Press, 2001), esp. chaps. 3 and 5; Eric Hinderaker, *The Two Hendricks: Unraveling a Mohawk Mystery* (Cambridge: Harvard University Press, 2010), 169–92.

4. Wheelwright diary, entries for November 1753. See also Wheelwright, *Esther,* chap. 18, and Ann M. Little, "The Life of Mother Marie-Joseph de l'Enfant Jesus; or, How a Little Girl from Wells Became a Big French Politician," *Maine History* 40, no. 4 (2002): 276–308.

5. Wheelwright Diary, November–December 1753; Pierre-L. Côté, "Duquesne de Menneville, Ange, Marquis Duquesne," in *DCB* 4: 255–58; or University of Toronto/Université Laval, 2003–, http://www.biographi.ca/en/bio/duquesne_de_menneville_ange_4E.html, accessed October 14, 2013. Julie Wheelwright notes that because of Wheelwright's travels through Canada and his family connection there, by the end of the 1750s Bostonians came to suspect him of spying for the French; *Esther,* 197–99.

6. Wheelwright diary, December 1753–January 1754; Côté, "Duquesne de Menneville, Ange, Marquis Duquesne."

7. Annales 1: 151, 216, AMUQ. Emily Clark's *Masterless Mistresses: The New Orleans Ursulines and the Development of a New World Society, 1727–1834* (Chapel Hill: University of North Carolina Press, 2007) also documents nationalist strife and a struggle for convent leadership when a group of Spanish-speaking Cuban nuns joined the convent in the 1780s and 1790s after New Orleans fell under Spanish rule (129–39).

8. Heidi Keller-Lapp describes the first century of the Ursulines and the debate among scholars as to the effects of increasing claustration after Trent in "Floating Cloisters and *Femmes Fortes:* Ursuline Missionaries in Ancien Régime France and Its Colonies," Ph.D. diss., University of California–San Diego, 2005, introduction and chaps. 1–2. Keller-Lapp also argues that their missionary work was central rather than marginal to Ursuline identity. See also Leslie Choquette, " 'Ces Amazones du Grand Dieu': Women and Mission in Seventeenth-Century Canada," *French Historical Studies* 17 (1992): 627–55; Natalie Zemon Davis, *Women on the Margins: Three Seventeenth-Century Lives* (Cambridge: Harvard University Press, 1995), 62–139; Patricia Simpson, *Marguerite Bourgeoys and Montreal, 1640–1665* (Montreal: McGill-Queen's University Press, 1997); Elizabeth Makowski, *Canon Law and Cloistered Women: Periculoso and Its Commentators, 1298–1545* (Washington, D.C.: Catholic University of America Press, 1997).

9. On the Ursulines and their efforts (along with those of other women's orders) to escape strict claustration in the sixteenth and seventeenth centuries, see Jo Ann Kay MacNamara, *Sisters in Arms: Catholic Nuns Through Two Millennia* (Cambridge: Harvard University Press, 1996), 452–88; P. Renée Baernstein, *A Convent Tale: A Century of Sisterhood in Spanish Milan* (New York: Routledge, 2002), 40–41, 53–54, 72–73; and Keller-Lapp, "Floating Cloisters and *Femmes Fortes*," chap. 2.

On Catholic religious women as educators in North America, see Clark Robenstine, "French Colonial Policy and the Education of Women and Minorities: Louisiana in the Early Eighteenth Century," *History of Education Quarterly* 32, no. 2 (1992): 193–211; Vincent Grégoire, "L'Éducation des Filles au Couvent des Ursulines de Québec à l'Époque de Marie de l'Incarnation (1639–1672)," *Seventeenth-Century French Studies* 17, no. 1 (1995): 87–98; Davis, *Women on the Margins*, 62–139; Colleen Gray, *The Congrégation of Notre-Dame, Superiors, and the Paradox of Power, 1693–1796* (Montreal: McGill-Queen's University Press, 2007); Clark, *Masterless Mistresses.*

10. Letter of 1711 and two letters dated 8 October 1757 to the Ursulines of La Rochelle and of Paris, Box: Affaires du Canada, folders: 1/N2, 1; 1/N2, 2; 1/N2, 4, AMUQ. On the supplies stocked and treatments offered by early-modern French convent infirmaries, see Diane Rapley, *A Social History of the Cloister: Daily Life in the Teaching Monasteries of the Old Regime* (Montreal: McGill-Queen's University Press, 2001), 206–10.

11. On supplementary servants, including male laborers, in early modern French convents, see Rapley, *A Social History of the Cloister*, 195. On the use of Anglo-American captive men in Canadian convents as servants and laborers, see William Foster, *The Captor's Narrative: Catholic Women and Their Puritan Men on the Early American Frontier* (Ithaca, N.Y.: Cornell University Press, 2003), chaps. 1 and 3. The Ursulines never used captive Anglo-American men, but Foster describes the work men did in other convents in New France.

12. On the connections between warfare and the circulation of disease epidemics, see Elizabeth Fenn, *Pox Americana: The Great Smallpox Epidemic of 1775–82* (New York: Hill and Wang, 2001). Queen Anne's War was also a time of epidemics in Québec, including a smallpox outbreak that killed a quarter of the city's population; *Glimpses of the Monastery: Scenes from the History of the Ursulines of Quebec during two hundred years, 1639–1839*, 2nd ed. (Québec: L. J. Demers, 1897), 170–73.

13. Annales 1: 206. See also Livres ou Registres des Entrées des R[eligieu]ses Divise en Trois Parties, 1689–1778, 1/G 1.1.1.6, hereafter Livres, for the obituaries of the choir nuns who died, 73, 98, 110, both at AMUQ.

14. Rapley, *A Social History of the Cloister*, 118–29.

15. See, for example, Lynn Botelho and Pat Thane, *Women and Ageing in British Society Since 1500* (New York: Longman, 2001); Lynn A. Botelho, *Old Age and the English Poor Law, 1500–1700* (Rochester, N.Y.: Boydell, 2004); Amy Froide, *Never Married: Singlewomen in Early Modern England* (New York: Oxford University Press, 2005); Amanda Vickery, "Mutton Dressed as Lamb? Fashioning Age in Georgian England," *Journal of British Studies* 52, no. 4 (2013): 858–86.

16. On old age care in colonial Anglo-America, see Ruth Wallis Herndon, *Unwelcome Americans: Living on the Margin in Early New England* (Philadelphia: University of Pennsylvania Press, 2001), 155–73. On older women, see Carol F. Karlsen, *The Devil in the Shape of a Woman: Witchcraft in Colonial New England* (New York: Norton, 1987), 64–116; Laurel Thatcher Ulrich, *A Midwife's Tale: The Life of Martha Ballard, Based on Her Diary, 1785–1812* (New York: Knopf, 1990), 262–85; Elaine Forman Crane, *Killed Strangely: The Death of Rebecca Cornell* (Ithaca, N.Y.: Cornell University Press, 2002), 71–76. See also Kenneth P. Minkema, "Old Age and Religion in the Writings and Life of Jonathan Edwards," *Church History* 70, no. 4 (2001): 674–704.

17. I am indebted to Fred Knight for the notion that old age may have enhanced rather than diminished a person's perceived holiness and spiritual power. Eighteenth-century France appears to have extended greater respect to the aged compared with colonial British America, and to women as well as men. See, for example, Sherri Klassen, "The Domestic Virtues of Old Age: Gendered Rites in the Fêtes de la Vieillesse," *Canadian Journal of History/Annales canadiennes d'histoire* 32, no. 3 (1997): 393–403; and David G. Troyansky, *Old Age in the Old Regime: Image and Experience in Eighteenth-Century France* (Ithaca, N.Y.: Cornell University Press, 1989).

18. For more on European and New World Catholic expectations of a "beautiful death," see Eric Seeman, *Death in the New World: Cross-Cultural Encounters, 1492–1800* (Philadelphia: University of Pennsylvania Press, 2010), chaps. 1 and 4; and Allan Greer, *Mohawk Saint: Catherine Tekakwitha and the Jesuits* (New York: Oxford University Press, 2005), chaps. 1–3.

19. Livres, 54, 71, 77, AMUQ.

20. Quebec Actes des Assemblées Capitul. de 1686 á 1802, 1/E, 7, 1, 1, 1, 0, hereafter Actes des Assemblées Capitul, 286 (May 27, 1766), AMUQ.

21. Livres, 71, AMUQ.

22. Ibid.

23. Ibid.

24. http://www.mainegenealogy.net/maine_wills.asp?source=probatecourtvol6&testator=JohnWheelwright#Will, accessed February 23, 2015.

25. Esther Wheelwright to Mary Snell Wheelwright, September 26, 1747; Archives Personnelles des Religieuses, Esther Wheelwright et famille, 1/G11; Soeur Esther Wheelwright Correspondance, AMUQ.

26. On the gender politics of how New England families treated their formerly captive daughters and sons, see Ann M. Little, *Abraham in Arms: War and Gender in Colonial New England* (Philadelphia: University of Pennsylvania Press, 2007), chap. 4. Sons were regularly induced to return to New England with job offers and inheritances, whereas daughters were disinherited if they refused to return to New England patriarchy and religion. John Wheelwright's will was typical rather than exceptional in this respect.

27. See, for example, the discussion of Mary Storer St. Germaine's correspondence with her brother, Ebenezer Storer, in Little, *Abraham in Arms,* 159–65.

28. http://www.mainegenealogy.net/maine_wills.asp?source=probatecourtvol9&testator=MaryWheelwright#will, accessed February 23, 2015.

29. Wheelwright diary, June 13, 1754.

30. Susanna Johnson, *A Narrative of the Captivity of Mrs. Johnson, together with a Narrative of James Johnson*, 3rd ed. (Windsor, Vt., 1814; rpt. Bowie, Md.: Heritage, 1990), 89–90.

31. Ibid., 89–90; see also Registre des Entrées et Sortie des Petites Filles Françaises et Sauvages, tome 2, Livre des Entrées et Sorties des Pensionnaires 1719 à 1839, 1/E.3.4.1.1.1, hereafter Pensionnat 2, AMUQ, for the entries of two girls who may have been the Phipps sisters, October 18, 1756, and October 15, 1757, 63 and 64 verso. This record notes that both of these girls (one of whom is unnamed, the other called just "Méthé" [Molly?]) both left the convent school on June 26, 1759, just before the bombing of Québec began.

32. Annales 1: 216, 218, 220, 221, AMUQ. See also *Glimpses of the Monastery*, 262–65, for more on the fire that destroyed the Augustinian hospital nuns' monastery. On Mother Charlotte Daneau de Muy de St. Hélène, see Gabrielle Lapointe, "Daneau de Muy, Charlotte, de Sainte-Hélène," in *DCB* 3: 161; or University of Toronto/Université Laval, 2003–5, http://www.biographi.ca/en/bio/daneau_de_muy_charlotte_3E.html, accessed November 10, 2014.

33. Annales 1: 229 and 227, AMUQ. For a full account of Braddock's defeat in the Battle of Monongahela and its effects, see Anderson, *Crucible of War*, 86–123.

34. *Glimpses of the Monastery*, 265–68; Letter from Mère Geneviève de St. Louis de Gonzague, *dépositaire*, to Père Alain-Xavier de Launay, September 18, 1757, in Fonds Administration Locale & Temporel, 1686–1814 SA 13-1-1-1, box 354, folder "1756–1760, Correspondance d'Affaires," 1/N 1.2.5.4.0, AMUQ. On the Acadian Expulsion, see Anderson, *Crucible of War*, 112–14.

35. Annales 1: 248, AMUQ. See also the correspondence of Mother Superior St. Marie de la Nativité (Marie Anne Migeon de Branssat) in Fonds Administration Locale & Temporel, 1686–1814 SA 13-1-1-1, box 354, folder "1755–58 Correspondance d'Affaires," 1/N 1.2.5.2.0, and the letters from Mother St. Geneviève de St. Louis de Gonzague in folder "1756–1760, Correspondance d'Affaires," 1/N 1.2.5.4.0, AMUQ, for more on the scarcity the Ursulines endured during the war.

36. Annales 1: 248–49, AMUQ; *Glimpses of the Monastery*, 269–72.

37. "Relation du Siège de Québec en 1759, par une Religieuse de l'Hopital Général de Québec," in *Collection de Mémoires et de Relations sur l'Histoire Ancienne du Canada* (Quebec: William Cowan, 1840; rpt 1927), 4–21, quotations from 4, 13; *Glimpses of the Monastery*, 272–80; *Les Ursulines de Québec*, 2: 321–27.

38. W. J. Eccles, "Montcalm, Louis-Joseph de, Marquis de Montcalm," in *DCB* 3: 458–69; or University of Toronto/Université Laval, 2003–, 2014, http://www.biographi.ca/en/bio/montcalm_louis_joseph_de_3E.html, accessed November 11; C. P. Stacey, "Wolfe, James," in *DCB* 3: 666–74; or University of Toronto/Université Laval, 2003–, http://www.biographi.ca/en/bio/wolfe_james_3E.html, accessed November 11, 2014; Annales 1: 250, AMUQ; *Glimpses of the Monastery*, 271–80; Livres, 81–82, 93 (recto and verso), AMUQ; "Relation du Siège de Québec en 1759, par une Religieuse de l'Hopital Général de Québec," 13; James Murray, *Journal of the Siege of Quebec, 1760* (Québec: Middleton and Dawson, 1871),

3. On the death of Wolfe and Montcalm and the occupation of Québec, see also Anderson, *Crucible of War,* 344–76.

39. Annales 1: 251–52, AMUQ; *Glimpses of the Monastery,* 281–86. On Murray, see G. P. Browne, "Murray, James," in *DCB* 4: 569–78; or University of Toronto/Université Laval, 2003–, http://www.biographi.ca/en/bio/murray_james_4E.html, accessed November 11, 2014.

40. *Glimpses of the Monastery,* 282–83; Colonel Malcolm Fraser, "Extract from a Manuscript Journal Relating to the Siege of Quebec in 1759," in *Manuscripts Relating to the Early History of Canada Recently Published Under the Auspices of the Literary and Historical Society of Quebec* (Québec: Middleton and Dawson, 1868; rpt. Québec: T. J. Moore), ser. 2, 26–27.

41. Fraser, "Extract from a Manuscript Journal Relating to the Siege of Quebec in 1759," 27, 29.

42. *Glimpses of the Monastery,* 297–300; Jean-Jacques Lefebvre, "Migeon de Branssat, Jean-Baptiste," in *DCB* 1: 508; or University of Toronto/Université Laval, 2003–, http://www.biographi.ca/en/bio/migeon_de_branssat_jean_baptiste_1E.html, accessed November 20, 2014; Gabrielle Lapointe, "Migeon de Branssat, Marie-Anne, de la Nativité," in *DCB* 4: 535–36; or University of Toronto/Université Laval, 2003–, http://www.biographi.ca/en/bio/migeon_de_branssat_marie_anne_4E.html, accessed December 8, 2014.

43. *Glimpses of the Monastery,* 229–31, 410–11; Actes des Assemblées Capitul, 275–76, AMUQ; Livre Contenant les Actes d'Elections des Supérieurs de ce Monastere de Ste Ursule de Québec, 1688–1839, 65–66, AMUQ.

44. *Les Ursulines de Québec,* 75–76; Actes des Assemblées Capitul, 196–321, AMUQ.

6. Esther Superior

1. Québec Actes des Assemblées Capitul. de 1686 á 1802, 1/E, 7, 1, 1, 1, 0, hereafter Actes des Assemblées Capitul, passim; "Maniere de Proceder Pour Les Elections," Monastère de Québec—1er août 1932," both at AMUQ.

2. William Petty, 1st Marquis of Lansdowne, 2nd Earl of Shelburne Papers, hereafter Shelburne Papers, vols. 59 (Papers relative to the Church in America and the papers of Bishop of London, Archbishop of York, House of Lords, 1734–67), 64 (Papers and memorials relative to the government of Canada and Quebec, 1753–67), and 66 (American Affairs, vol. 1, letters, documents, and newspapers, 1755–82), the Clements Library, University of Michigan, Ann Arbor, hereafter CL.

3. James Murray, "Description of Quebec," June 5, 1762; Shelburne Papers 64: 13–94, quotations from 60, 67–68, CL.

4. Ibid., esp. 63–70.

5. Shelburne Papers, 59: 19–77, *passim,* which includes several drafts of plans for the church in Québec dated 1765–67, most of which like Murray's counsel the preservation of women's religious orders but also predict their eventual demise, CL.

6. Étienne Montgolfier, letter of January 17, 1761, 1 CB, Vicaires généreaux, V: 8, Ar-

chives de l'Archdiocèse de Québec, Québec, P.Q., hereafter AAQ; *Glimpses of the Monastery: Scenes from the History of the Ursulines of Québec during two hundred years, 1639–1839*, 2nd ed. (Québec: L. J. Demers, 1897), 290.

7. As we have seen, in a 1747 letter to her mother, she wrote, "I am much obliged to you for the Favour you did me honouring me with one of your letters which I received the 23rd of this month, and which hath been faithfully interpreted unto me by a person of virtue," Esther Wheelwright de l'Enfant Jésus to Mary Snell Wheelwright, September 26, 1747; Archives Personnelles des Religieuses, Esther Wheelwright et famille, 1/G11; Soeur Esther Wheelwright Correspondance, AMUQ. While it's possible that she may have retained or regained a rudimentary knowledge of English, it's clear in this letter that she could not read English.

8. Gabrielle Lapointe, "Migeon de Branssat, Marie-Anne, de la Nativité," *DCB* 4: 535–36; or University of Toronto/Université Laval, 2003–, http://www.biographi.ca/en/bio/migeon_de_branssat_marie_anne_4E.html, accessed December 8, 2014.

9. Témoignage de Tuthill Hubbard en assermenté en Cour Supérieure de Boston, February 7, 1762, folder "Soeur Esther Wheelwright Correspondance," Archives Personnelles des Religieuses, Esther Wheelwright et famille, 1/G11 SA-9-4-1-2, AMUQ. See also Julie Wheelwright, *Esther: The Remarkable True Story of Esther Wheelwright: Puritan Child, Native Daughter, Mother Superior* (Toronto: HarperCollins, 2011), 196–99; and Edward P. Hamilton, "Robert Hewes and the Frenchmen: A Case of Treason?" *Proceedings of the American Antiquarian Society* 68, no. 2 (1958): 196–210.

10. Jan Noel, *Along a River: The First French Canadian Women* (Toronto: University of Toronto Press, 2013), 192–204. See also Jan Noel, "Besieged but Connected: Survival Strategies at a Quebec Convent," *Historical Studies: Canadian Catholic Historical Association* 67 (2001): 27–41; and Jan Noel, "Caste and Clientage in an Eighteenth Century Québec Convent," *Canadian Historical Review* 82 (2001): 465–90.

11. J. L. Bell, "A Bankruptcy in Boston, 1765," *Massachusetts Banker*, fourth quarter, 2008, 14–23; Wheelwright, *Esther*, 267–70; Vincent Brown, *The Reaper's Garden: Death and Power in the World of Atlantic Slavery* (Cambridge: Harvard University Press, 2008). Anne Apthorp Wheelwright, Nathaniel's wife, was the subject of a funeral sermon published by her brother East Apthorp, *The Character and Example of a Christian Woman* (Boston, 1764).

12. *Glimpses of the Monastery*, 134, 282–87, 290–93; Les Annales des Ursulines de Quebec, vol. 1, 1639–1822, 1/E, 12, 1, 0, 0, 1, hereafter Annales 1, 253, AMUQ.

13. Murray, "Description of Quebec," June 5, 1762; Shelburne Papers, 64: 13–94, quotations from 65, CL; Mère Esther Wheelwright de l'Enfant Jésus to Père Alain de Launay, S.J., Procureur de la Mission du Canada à Paris, 1761, box Affaires du Canada, 1/N2, 3; 1/N2, 5, VI (1761–72), folder M. Marie-d-l'Enfant-Jesus, sup., AMUQ.

14. See, for example, the Shelburne Papers, the Jeffery Amherst Papers, and other official government records of the Seven Years' War and occupation of Québec at the CL.

15. Murray, "Description of Quebec," June 5, 1762; Shelburne Papers 64: 66–71, CL.

16. "On the Subject of Religion with respect to Canada, May 1763," May 31, 1763, Shel-

burne Papers 64: 555; "Heads of a Plan for the Establishment of Ecclesiastical Affairs in the Province of Quebec," Shelburne Papers 59: 23, CL.

17. Actes des Assemblées Capitul, 277, 303; Conclusions des Assemblées des Discrètes de 1687 à 1865: 1/E.1.4.2.5.1, hereafter Discrètes, 88, 101; both at AMUQ.

18. Murray, "Description of Quebec," June 5, 1762; Shelburne Papers, 64: 64–65, CL.

19. Registre des Entrées et Sortie des Petites Filles Françaises et Sauvages, tome 2, Livre des Entrées et Sorties des Pensionnaires 1719 à 1839, 1/E.3.4.1.1.1, hereafter Pensionnat 2, passim; Discrètes, 88, both at AMUQ.

20. Pensionnat 2, passim; Discrètes, 101, both at AMUQ.

21. Pensionnat 2, passim, AMUQ.

22. Mère Esther Wheelwright de l'Enfant Jésus to Père Alain de Launay, 1761, AMUQ.

23. Marius Barbeau, "From Gold Threads to Porcupine Quills," *Magazine Antiques* 45 (1944): 24–26; Margaret Swain, "Moose-Hair Embroidery on Birch Bark," *Antiques,* April 1975, 726–69; Joyce Taylor Dawson, "In Search of Early Canadian Embroidery Abroad," *Material History Bulletin* 27 (1988): 39–42; Laurel Thatcher Ulrich, *The Age of Homespun: Objects and Stories in the Creation of an American Myth* (New York: Knopf, 2001), 259–61. Swain makes the connection between the New England–born Ursulines and the production of these birchbark objects, but she mistakenly writes that Esther Wheelwright was taken in 1704 from Deerfield, Massachusetts.

24. Elizabeth Simcoe, *The Diary of Mrs. John Graves Simcoe,* ed. J. Ross Robertson (Toronto: William Briggs, 1911), 65–66; Joyce Taylor Dawson, "A Note on Research in Progress: The Needlework of the Ursulines of Early Quebec," *Material History Bulletin* 5 (1978): 77; C. Alice Baker, *True Stories of New England Captives Carried to Canada During the Old French and Indian Wars* (Greenfield, Mass.: E. A. Hall, 1897; facsimile rpt. Bowie, Md.: Heritage, 1990), image of Wheelwright coat of arms on silk between pages 66 and 67; Livres ou Registres des Entrées des R[eligieu]ses Divise en Trois Parties, 1689–1778, 1/G 1.1.1.6, hereafter Livres, 71, 60 verso, 93, AMUQ.

25. Actes des Assemblées Capitul, 278; Annales 1: 258–59, both at AMUQ.

26. *Glimpses of the Monastery,* 290–95; Annales 1: 259, 262; and Registre des Entrées, Vetures et Professions des Religieuses Ursulines de Québec, 1647–1783, 1/G7.1.1.1, hereafter Entrées et Décès, entries for Françoise Besançon (March 18, 1764); Louise Taschereau (May 13, 1764); and Marie Josephe Blais (August 17, 1764), AMUQ.

27. Annales 1: 264–67; Entrées et Décès, passim, both at AMUQ. St. Angela Merici's feast day has since been moved to January 27, according to the *New Advent Catholic Encyclopedia,* http://www.newadvent.org/cathen/01481a.htm, accessed August 19, 2015.

28. Jean-Olivier Briand to Esther de l'Enfant Jésus, Supérieure, July 18, 1770, 81 CD, SS. Ursulines, 1: 15, AAQ. The bishop indeed requested that Mother Esther and the "Assistante et Sécrétaire" sign and return this letter, which is presumably why it's preserved in the archdiocesan archives.

29. Linda Evangelisti, *Nuns: A History of Convent Life* (Oxford: Oxford University Press, 2007), chap. 2.

30. Natalie Davis, *Women on the Margins: Three Seventeenth-Century Lives* (Cambridge: Harvard University Press, 1995), 63–139; Noel, "Besieged but Connected"; Dominique Deslandres, "In the Shadow of the Cloister: Representations of Holiness in New France," in *Colonial Saints: Discovering the Holy in the Americas, 1500–1800*, ed. Allan Greer and Jodi Bilinkoff, 129–52 (New York: Routledge, 2003); Ann M. Little, "Cloistered Bodies: Convents in the Anglo-American Imagination in the British Conquest of Canada," *Eighteenth Century Studies* 39, no. 2 (2006): 187–200; Emily Clark, *Masterless Mistresses: The New Orleans Ursulines and the Development of a New World Society, 1727–1834* (Chapel Hill: University of North Carolina Press, 2007); Colleen Gray, *The Congrégation de Notre-Dame, Superiors, and the Paradox of Power, 1693–1796* (Montreal: McGill-Queen's University Press, 2007).

31. Esther de l'Enfant Jésus, Supérieure, to Jean-Olivier Briand, July 21, 1770, 81 CD, SS. Ursulines, 1: 16, AAQ.

32. Sr. St. François to Jean-Olivier Briand, February 21, 1772, 81 CD, SS. Ursulines, 1: 17, AAQ.

33. *Rules and Constitutions for the Ursuline Religious, of the Presentation of Our Blessed Lady with Instructions on the Same* (New Orleans: T. Fitzwilliam, 1885), chap. 8, "On the Reception and Training of Novices," 163–72; Entrées et Décès, passim, AMUQ.

34. Sr. St. Augustin to Jean-Olivier Briand, March 7, 1772, 81 CD, SS. Ursulines, 1: 18, AAQ.

35. *Glimpses of the Monastery*, 279–80, 313–14; Entrées et Décès, passim, AMUQ.

36. Daniel Wheelwright's movement out of and into Boston was noted by local newspapers in 1761: *Boston Post-Boy and Advertiser*, July 13, 1761; *Boston Gazette and Country Journal*, November 23, 1761; *Boston Evening Post*, November 23, 1761. He also seems to have been involved in sharing military intelligence in a report about British military and French supply ships: *Boston Post-Boy and Advertiser*, October 24, 1763. Lieutenant Joshua Moody was stationed at Falmouth (just north of Portland, Maine) in 1761, according to an advertisement he placed in *Boston Post-Boy and Advertiser*, September 14, 1761; Baker, *True Stories of New England Captives*, 59–67; Gerald M. Kelly to Charles D. Childs, March 21, 1975, Gerald M. Kelly Research Materials, box 9, Massachusetts Historical Society, Boston, hereafter MHS.

37. Abigail Smith to Isaac Smith, Jr., March 16, 1763, http://masshist.org/publications /apde2/view?id=ADMS-04-01-02-0005#ptrAFC01d007n2, accessed September 11, 2014, in *Founding Families: Digital Editions of the Papers of the Winthrops and the Adamses*, ed. C. James Taylor (Boston: Massachusetts Historical Society, 2014), at http://www.masshist.org /apde2/; letters dated August 31, 1771, and September 20, 1772, Soeur Esther Wheelwright Correspondance, Archives Personnelles des Religieuses, Esther Wheelwright et famille, 1/ G11, AMUQ. I am indebted to Woody Holton, whose research for his book *Abigail Adams* (New York: Free Press, 2009) alerted me to Abigail Smith Adams's letter commenting on Esther Wheelwright. He argues convincingly that the letter is evidence of young Smith's budding feminism, 9–10, 48–52.

38. Marius Barbeau, *Saintes Artisanes II: Milles Pétites Addresses* (Montreal: Editions Fides, 1946), 51–56, esp. 56; personal communications with Anne E. Bentley, Curator of Art and

Artifacts at the Massachusetts Historical Society, January 4, 2001, and October 2, 2014; Kelly to Childs, March 21, 1975, Gerald M. Kelly Research Materials, box 9, MHS. Kelly mistakenly claims in this letter that there are no other oil paintings of mothers superior, citing Barbeau as his source. However, Barbeau writes very clearly (in French), "In some of the rooms of the [Ursuline] monastery, where the light is attenuated, there are some portraits of old nuns—for example, that of Mother Marie le Maire des Anges, 1717—which seems sincere and original. In the community room a Madonna painted by Mother Saint-François de Borgia Dechênes almost comes to life" (56). Portraits of former superiors still line the hallways of the Ursuline convent as of 2015.

7. Esther Zelatrix

1. Livres ou Registres des Entrées des R[eligieu]ses Divise en Trois Parties, 1689–1778, 1/G 1.1.1.6, hereafter Livres, 70–71, AMUQ.

2. Québec Actes des Assemblées Capitul. de 1686 à 1802, 1/E, 7, 1, 1, 1, 0, hereafter Actes des Assemblées Capitul, 305–13; Les Annales des Ursulines de Quebec, vol. 1, 1639–1822, 1/E, 12, 1, 0, 0, 1, hereafter Annales 1, 301, both at AMUQ.

3. Ann M. Little, *Abraham in Arms: War and Gender in Colonial New England* (Philadelphia: University of Pennsylvania Press, 2007), esp. chaps. 4–5; *All Canada in the Hands of the English: or, an Authentick Journal of the Proceedings of the Army, under General Amherst* (Boston: B. Mecom, 1760), 5.

4. Annales 1: 324, AMUQ. On the willingness of French Canadian *habitants* to join the American fight, see Michael P. Gabriel and S. Pascale Vergereau-Dewey, *Quebec During the American Invasion, 1775–1776: The Journal of François Baby, Gabriel Taschereau, and Jenkin Williams* (East Lansing: Michigan State University Press, 2005), esp. the introduction, xxix–xliv.

5. Elizabeth Fenn, *Pox Americana: The Great Smallpox Epidemic of 1775–82* (New York: Hill and Wang, 2001), 62–79; *Canada Preserved: The Journal of Captain Thomas Ainslie,* ed. Sheldon S. Cohen (New York: New York University and Copp Clark, 1968), 38, 57; "Journal of the Siege and Blockade of Quebec by the American Rebels, in Autumn 1775 and Winter 1776," in *Manuscripts Relating to the Early History of Canada,* 4th ser. (Québec: Dawson, 1875), 15. For more on the American army in sickness and in health, see "The Invasion of Canada in 1775," in *Manuscripts Relating to the Early History of Canada* (Québec: Middleton and Dawson, 1868; rpt. Québec: T. J. Moore, 1927).

6. Annales 1: 324–25, AMUQ.

7. Actes des Assemblées Capitul, 321; Livres, 71, both at AMUQ.

8. The remains of most of the eighteenth-century Ursulines were transferred to the Cimitière Notre-Dame de Belmont in 1996, according to Julie Wheelwright in *Esther: The Remarkable True Story of Esther Wheelwright: Puritan Child, Native Daughter, Mother Superior* (Toronto: HarperCollins, 2011), 245, 271–72.

9. On Canadian residential schools see Agnes Grant, *No End of Grief: Indian Residential Schools in Canada* (Winnipeg: Pemmican, 1996); J. R. Miller, *Shingwauk's Vision: A History of*

Native Residential Schools (Toronto: University of Toronto Press, 1996); John S. Milloy, *A National Crime: The Canadian Government and the Residential School System, 1879 to 1986* (Winnipeg: University of Manitoba Press, 1999); Paulette Regan, *Unsettling the Settler Within: Indian Residential Schools, Truth Telling, and Reconciliation in Canada* (Vancouver: University of British Columbia Press, 2010); Andrew Woolford, Jeff Benvenuto, and Alexander Laban Hinton, eds., *Colonial Genocide in Indigenous North America* (Durham, N.C.: Duke University Press, 2014).

10. Mother Charlotte Brassard de St. Claire, Supérieure, "au sujet de la dot due à Mère Esther Wheelwright de l'Enfant Jesus," to Dr. Penn of Salem, August 22, 1789, in Archives Personnelles des Religieuses, Esther Wheelwright et famille, 1/G11 SA-9-4-1-2, in the folder "Esther Wheelwright," as well as in folders marked "22 Août 1789," AMUQ. There are three copies of this letter preserved in the Ursuline archives—a French version, an English translation, and a typescript of the English translation.

11. Wheelwright, *Esther*, 11–12, 224–28, 267, 269.

12. C. Alice Baker, *True Stories of New England Captives Carried to Canada During the Old French and Indian Wars* (Greenfield, Mass.: E. A. Hall, 1897; rpt. Bowie, Md.: Heritage, 1990), esp. 35–68; *Glimpses of the Monastery: Scenes from the History of the Ursulines of Quebec during two hundred years, 1639–1839*, 2nd ed. (Québec: L. J. Demers, 1897), 175–84; Emma Lewis Coleman, *New England Captives Carried to Canada* (Portland, Maine: Southworth, 1925; rpt. Bowie, Md.: Heritage, 1989), 2 vols.

On Baker's life, see http://www.memorialhall.mass.edu/people_places/view.jsp?itemtype =1&id=1330, accessed December 15, 2014. On Coleman, see http://www.memorialhall .mass.edu/collection/itempage.jsp?itemid=1673, accessed December 15, 2014. Coleman left her research notes to the Massachusetts Historical Society in Boston, and Baker left notes and correspondence with the Pocumtuck Valley Memorial Association in Deerfield, Mass. On the colonial revival and its implications for women's history, see Marla Miller, *The Needle's Eye: Women and Work in the Age of Revolution* (Amherst: University of Massachusetts Press, 2006), 211–32.

13. Gerald M. Kelly research materials, Massachusetts Historical Society, Boston: http:// www.masshist.org/collection-guides/view/fa0119, accessed December 15, 2014. Quotation from Gerald R. Kelly, "Thy Hand Shall Lead Me: The Story of Esther Wheelwright," unpublished manuscript, 116, carton 4.

14. For an overview of government, commercial, and community involvement in the bicentennial celebrations, see Tammy S. Gordon, *The Spirit of 1976: Commerce, Community, and the Politics of Commemoration* (Amherst: University of Massachusetts Press, 2013). Gordon writes, "Consumerism and social history together had suddenly made the past seem closer, more individualized, more personal. And in the seventies, the person became political" (3).

15. Penny Wheelwright and Tim Southam, *Captive: The Story of Esther* (Toronto: Wheelwright Ink, 2005); see http://www.telefilm.ca/en/catalogues/production/captive-story-es ther, accessed December 15, 2014; quotation from Wheelwright, *Esther*, 6–7.

INDEX